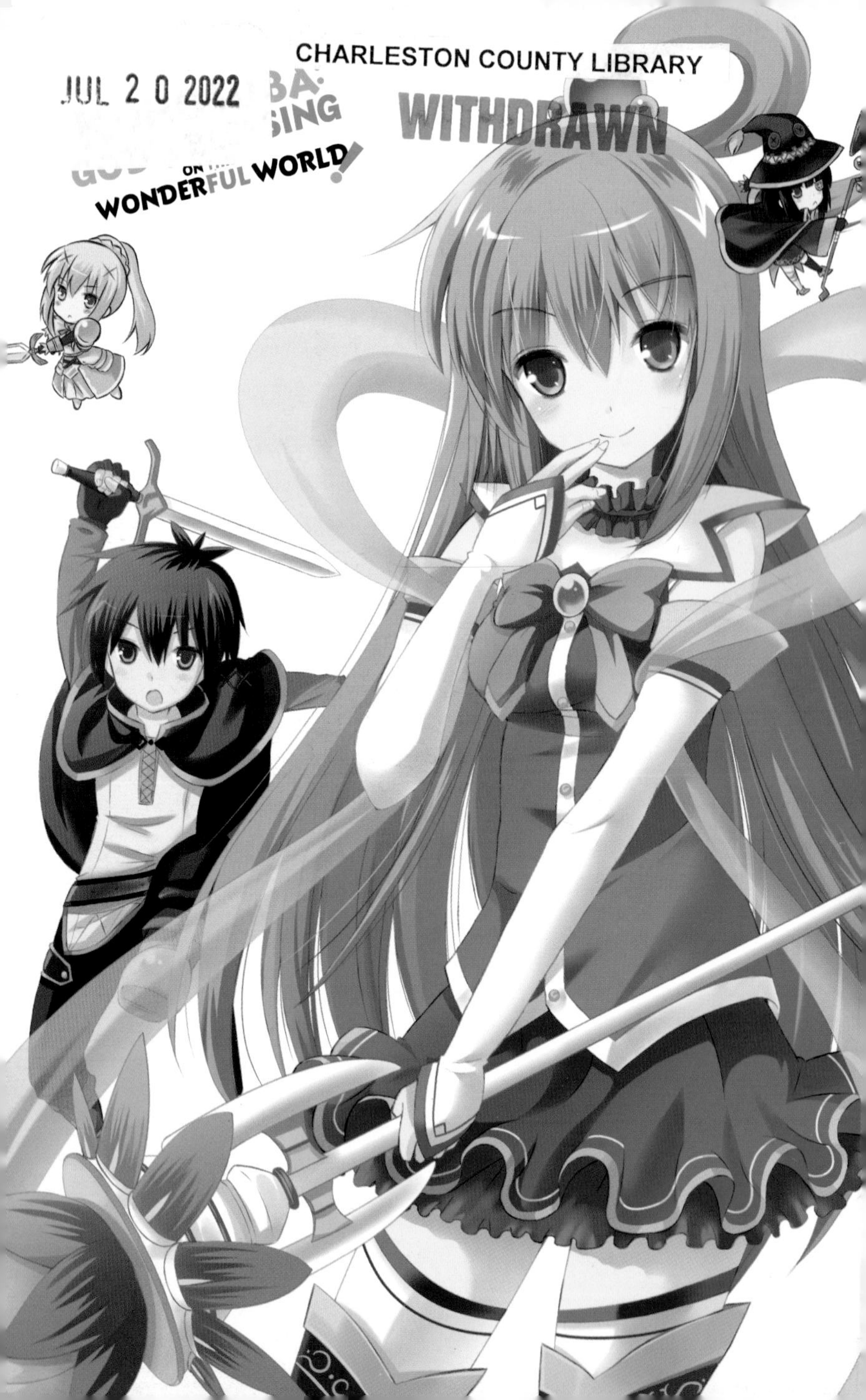
BA:
SING
ON
WONDERFUL WORLD!

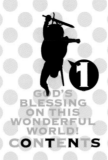

GOD'S BLESSING ON THIS WONDERFUL WORLD!

CONTENTS

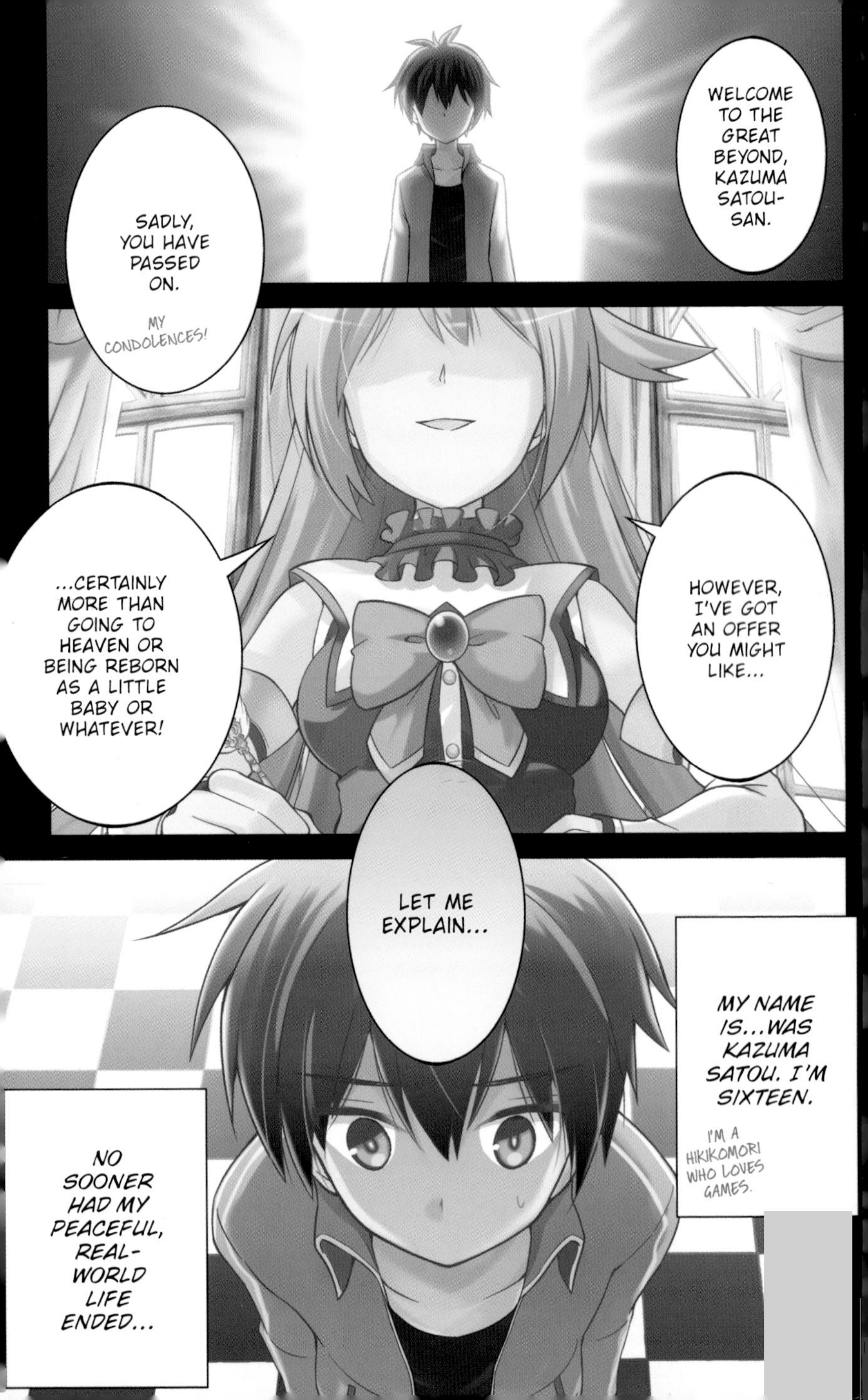
WELCOME TO THE GREAT BEYOND, KAZUMA SATOU-SAN.
SADLY, YOU HAVE PASSED ON.
MY CONDOLENCES!
HOWEVER, I'VE GOT AN OFFER YOU MIGHT LIKE...
...CERTAINLY MORE THAN GOING TO HEAVEN OR BEING REBORN AS A LITTLE BABY OR WHATEVER!
LET ME EXPLAIN...
MY NAME IS...WAS KAZUMA SATOU. I'M SIXTEEN.
I'M A HIKIKOMORI WHO LOVES GAMES.
NO SOONER HAD MY PEACEFUL, REAL-WORLD LIFE ENDED...

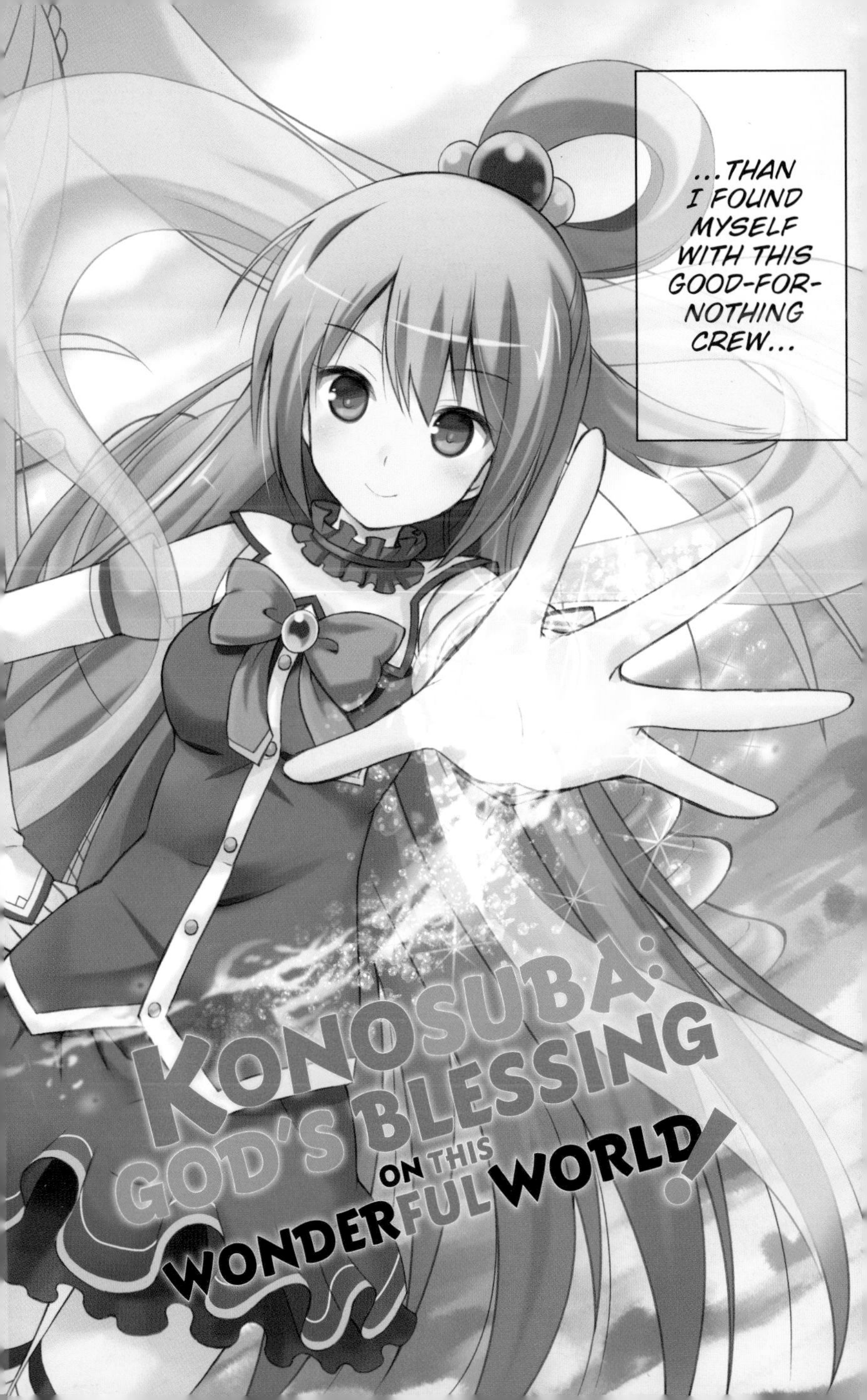
...THAN I FOUND MYSELF WITH THIS GOOD-FOR-NOTHING CREW...
KONOSUBA: GOD'S BLESSING ON THIS WONDERFUL WORLD!

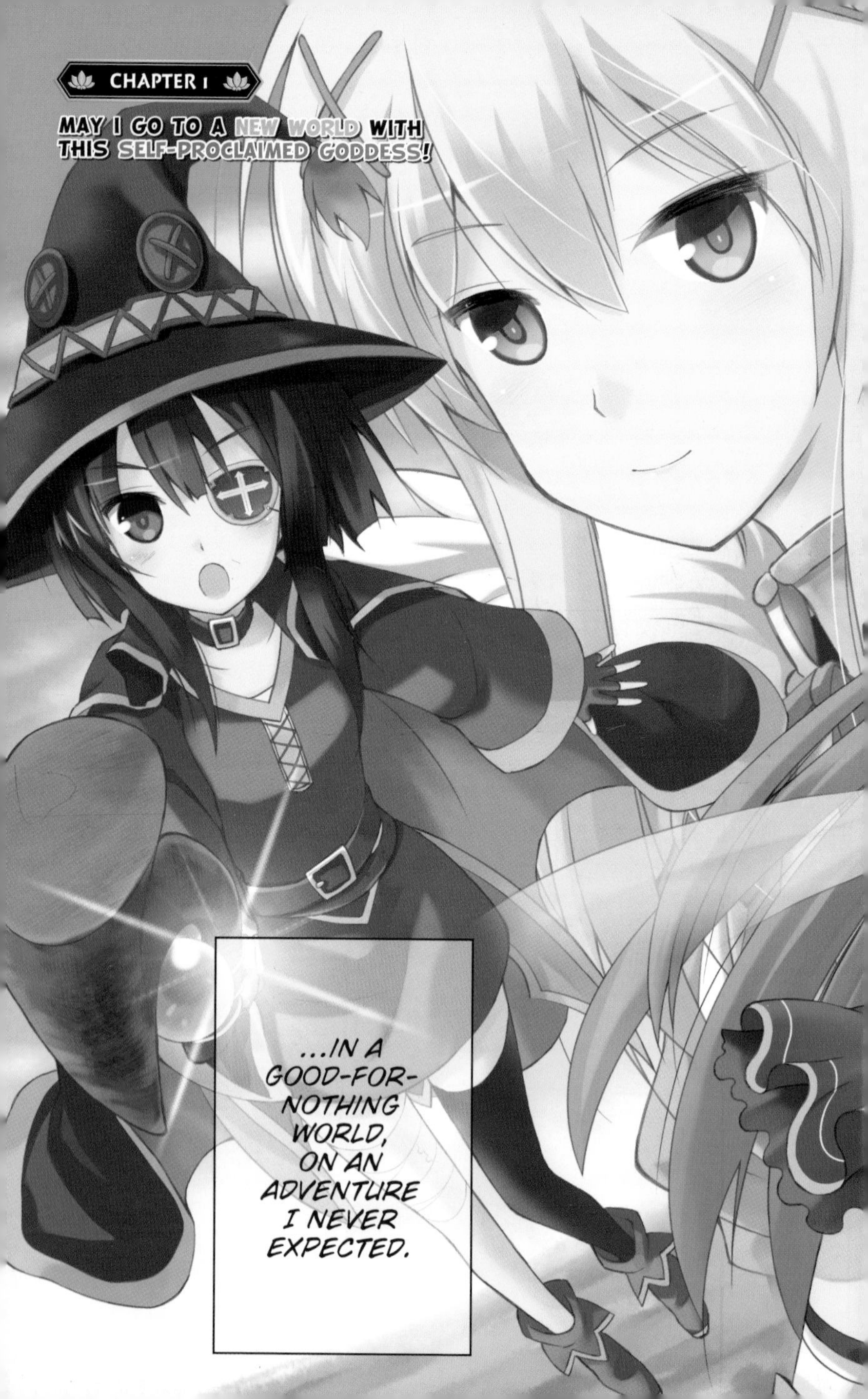
CHAPTER 1
MAY I GO TO A NEW WORLD WITH THIS SELF-PROCLAIMED GODDESS!
...IN A GOOD-FOR-NOTHING WORLD, ON AN ADVENTURE I NEVER EXPECTED.

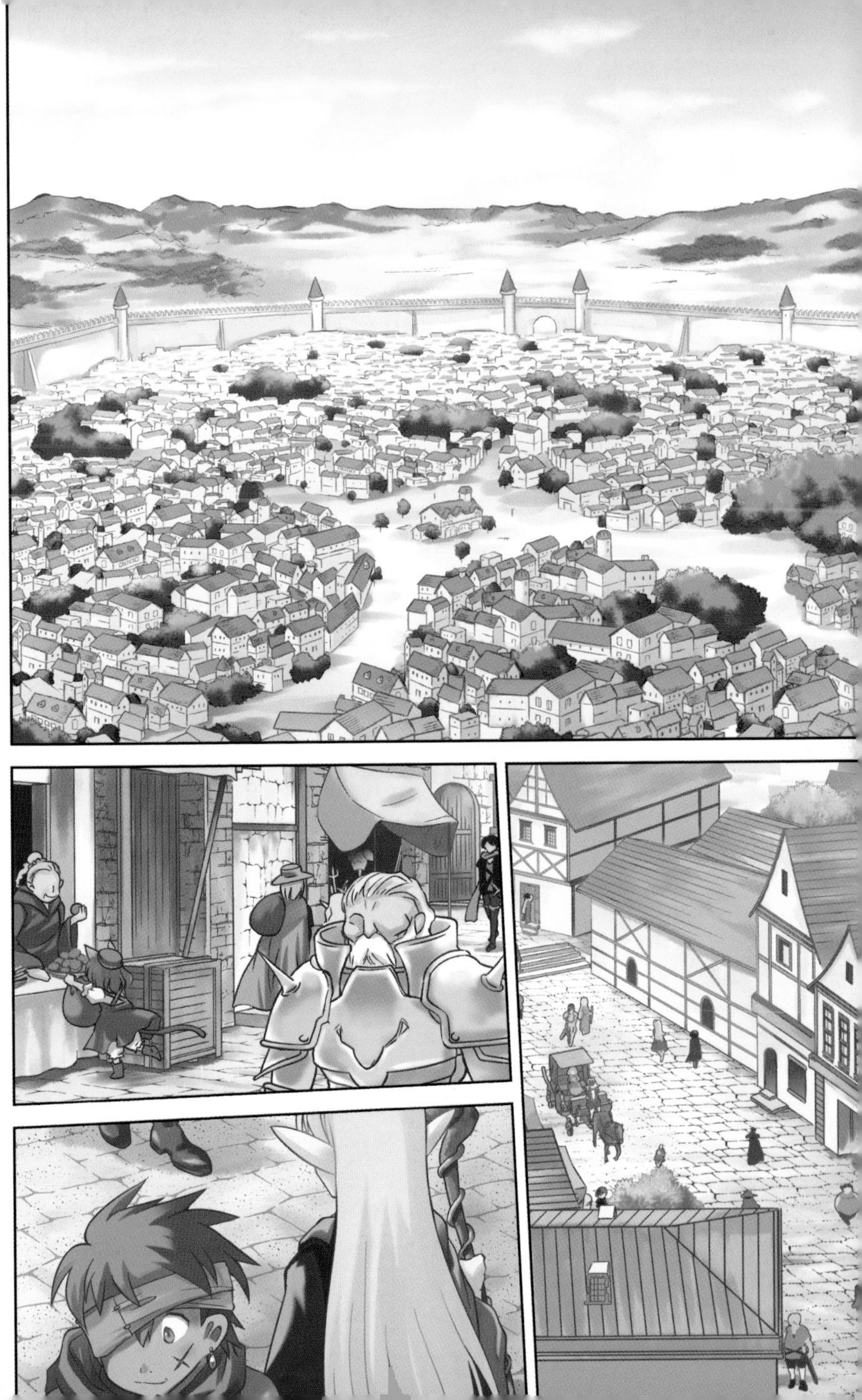

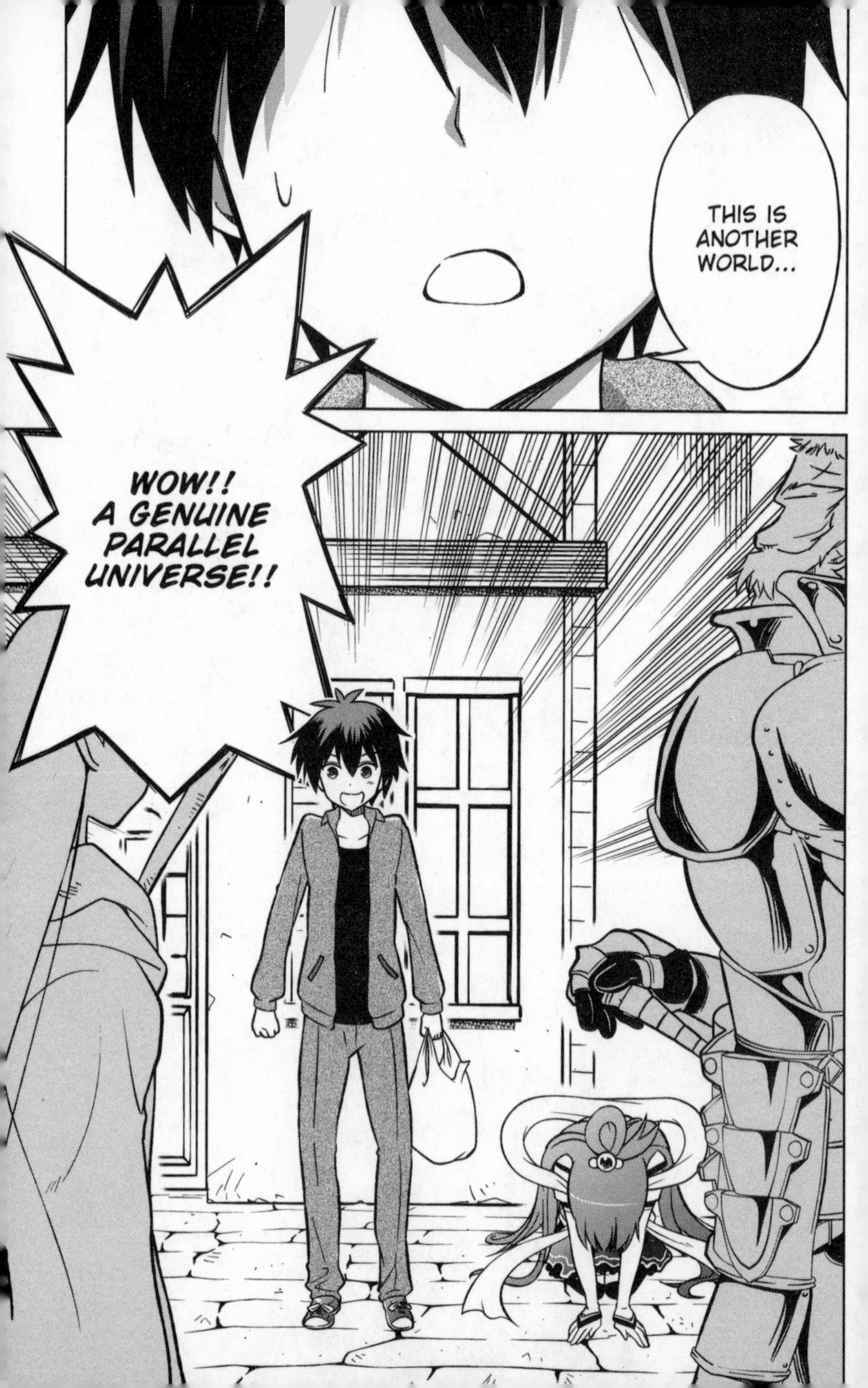
THIS IS ANOTHER WORLD...
WOW!! A GENUINE PARALLEL UNIVERSE!!

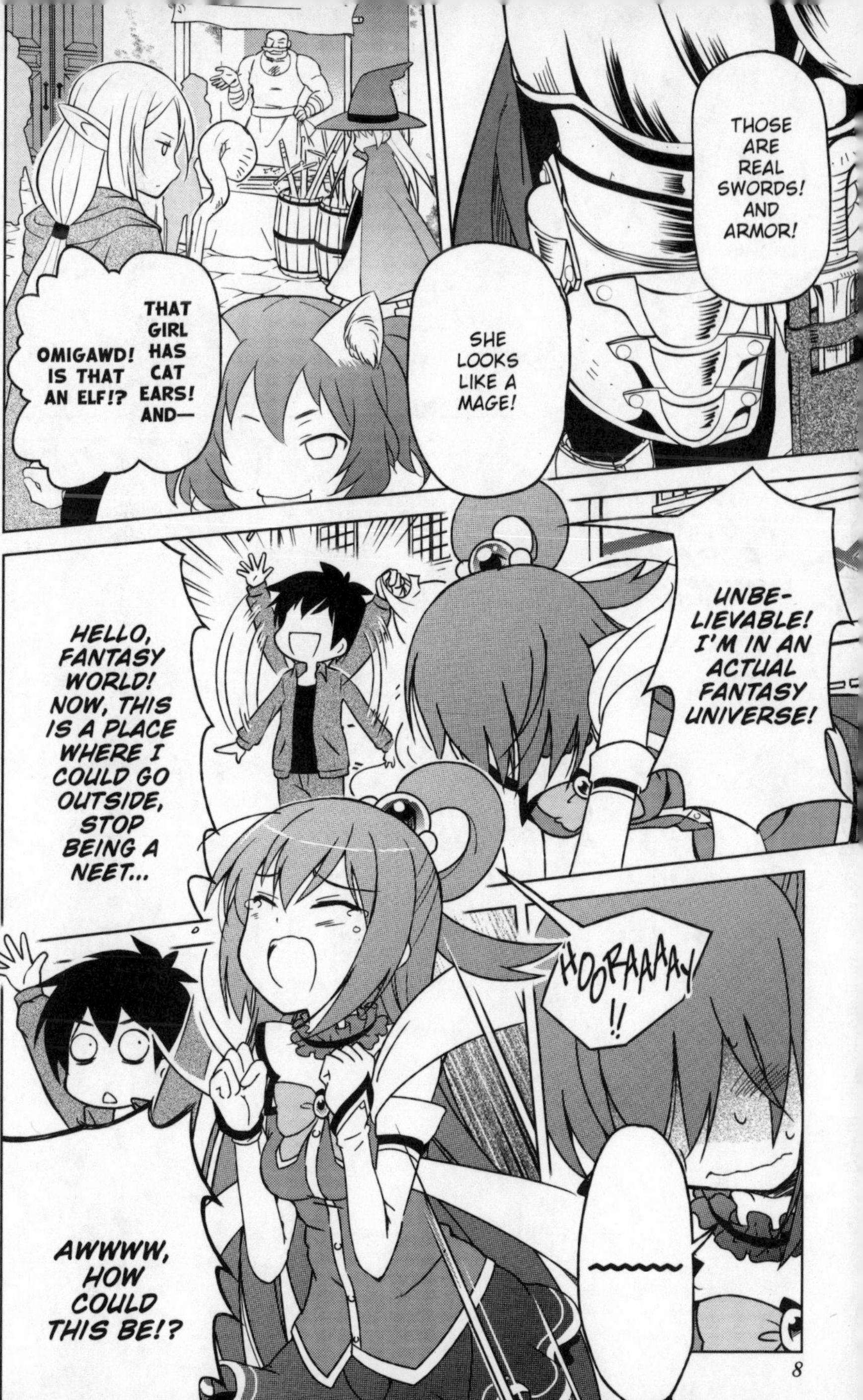
THOSE ARE REAL SWORDS! AND ARMOR!
SHE LOOKS LIKE A MAGE!
THAT GIRL HAS CAT EARS! AND—
OMIGAWD! IS THAT AN ELF!?
UNBE-LIEVABLE! I'M IN AN ACTUAL FANTASY UNIVERSE!
HELLO, FANTASY WORLD! NOW, THIS IS A PLACE WHERE I COULD GO OUTSIDE, STOP BEING A NEET...
HOORAAAAY!!
AWWWW, HOW COULD THIS BE!?

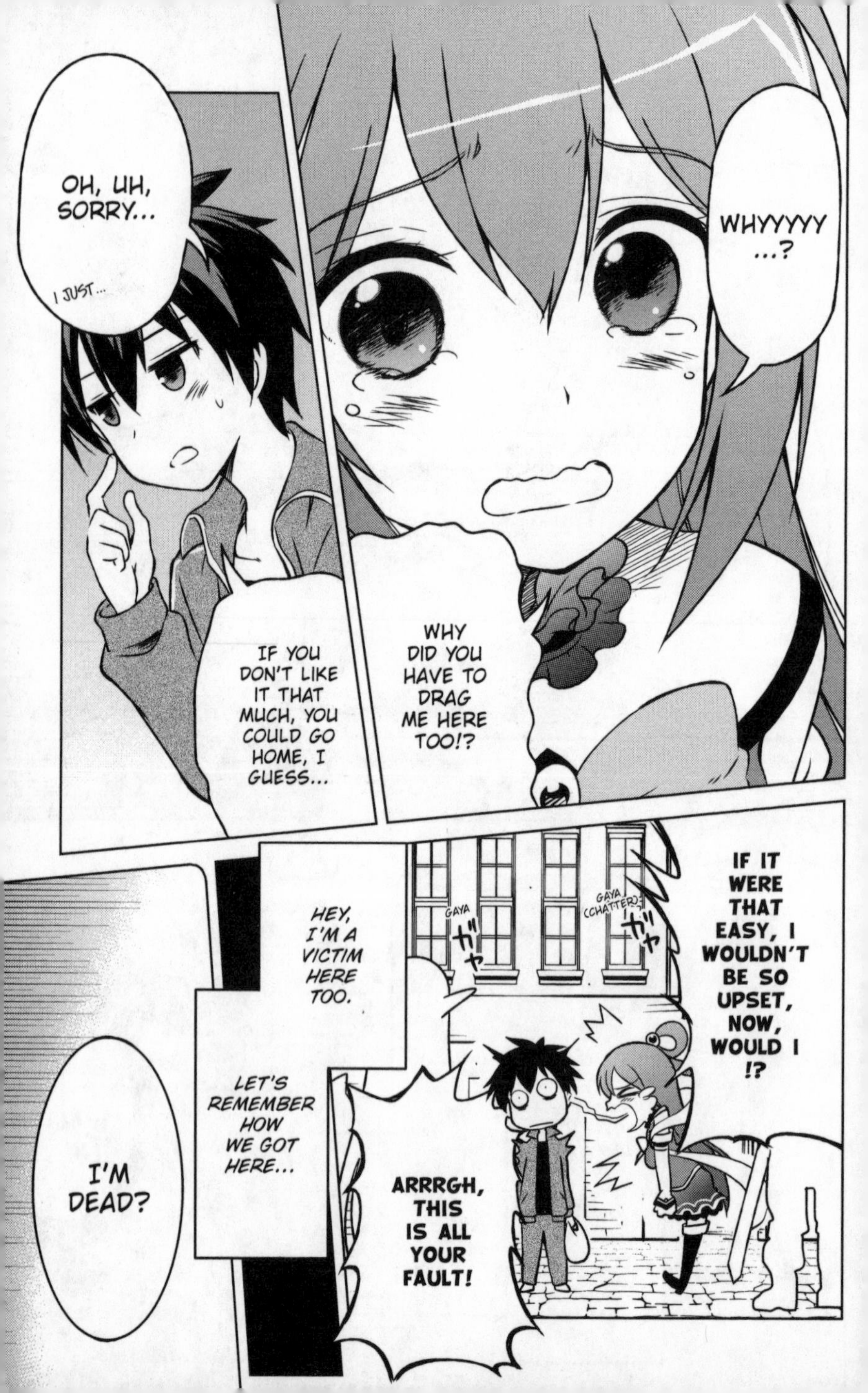
WHYYYYY ...?
WHY DID YOU HAVE TO DRAG ME HERE TOO!?
OH, UH, SORRY...
I JUST...
IF YOU DON'T LIKE IT THAT MUCH, YOU COULD GO HOME, I GUESS...
IF IT WERE THAT EASY, I WOULDN'T BE SO UPSET, NOW, WOULD I !?
GAYA (CHATTER)
ガヤ
GAYA
ガヤ
ARRRGH, THIS IS ALL YOUR FAULT!
HEY, I'M A VICTIM HERE TOO.
LET'S REMEMBER HOW WE GOT HERE...
I'M DEAD?

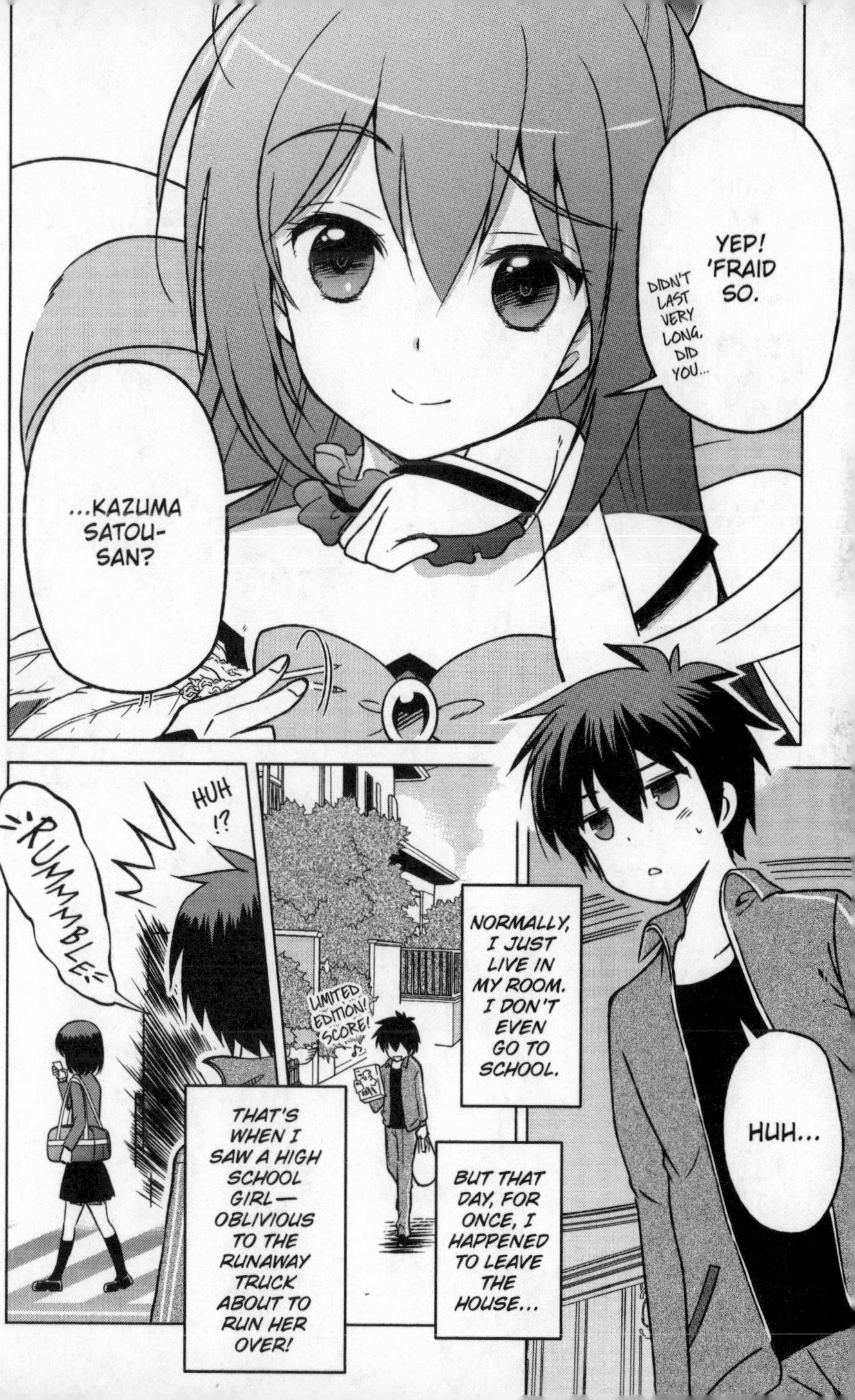
YEP! 'FRAID SO.
DIDN'T LAST VERY LONG, DID YOU...
...KAZUMA SATOU-SAN?
HUH...
NORMALLY, I JUST LIVE IN MY ROOM. I DON'T EVEN GO TO SCHOOL.
LIMITED EDITION! SCORE!
BUT THAT DAY, FOR ONCE, I HAPPENED TO LEAVE THE HOUSE...
HUH !?
RUMMMBLE
THAT'S WHEN I SAW A HIGH SCHOOL GIRL— OBLIVIOUS TO THE RUNAWAY TRUCK ABOUT TO RUN HER OVER!

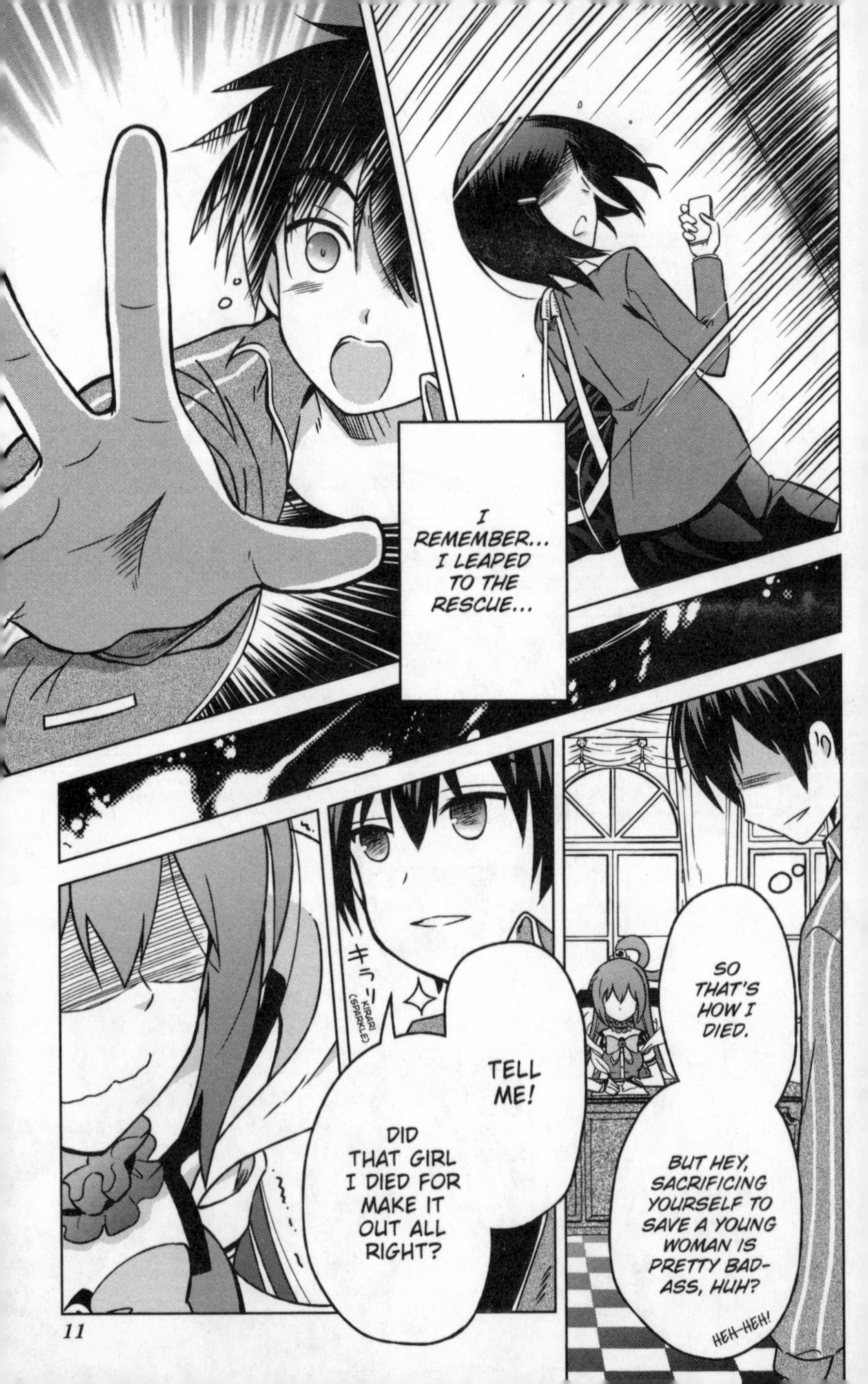
I REMEMBER... I LEAPED TO THE RESCUE...
SO THAT'S HOW I DIED.
BUT HEY, SACRIFICING YOURSELF TO SAVE A YOUNG WOMAN IS PRETTY BAD-ASS, HUH?
HEH-HEH!
TELL ME!
キラーン
KIRARI (SPARKLE)
DID THAT GIRL I DIED FOR MAKE IT OUT ALL RIGHT?

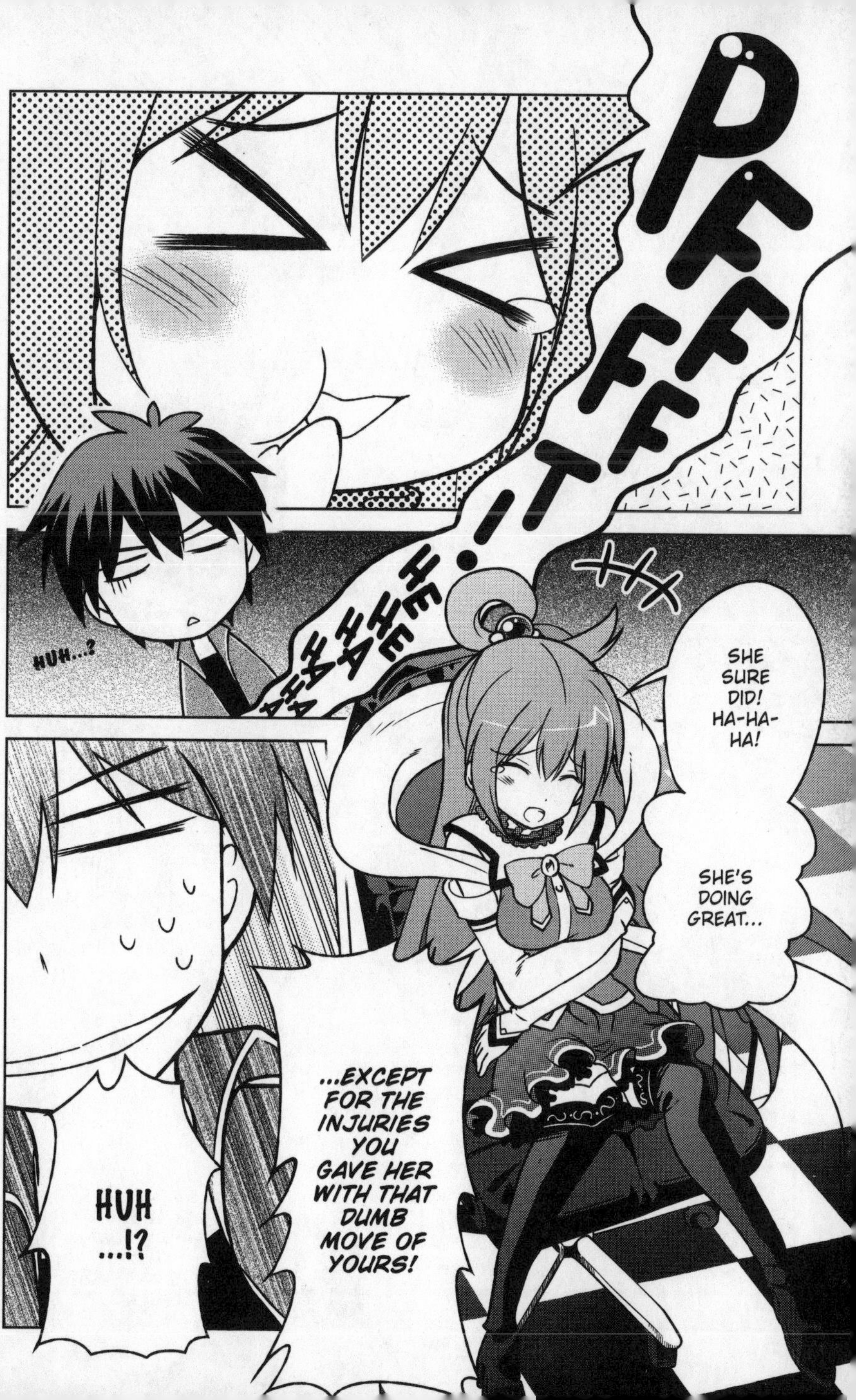
PFFFFT—!!
HEHEHAHAHA
HUH...?
SHE SURE DID! HA-HA-HA!
SHE'S DOING GREAT...
...EXCEPT FOR THE INJURIES YOU GAVE HER WITH THAT DUMB MOVE OF YOURS!
HUH...!?

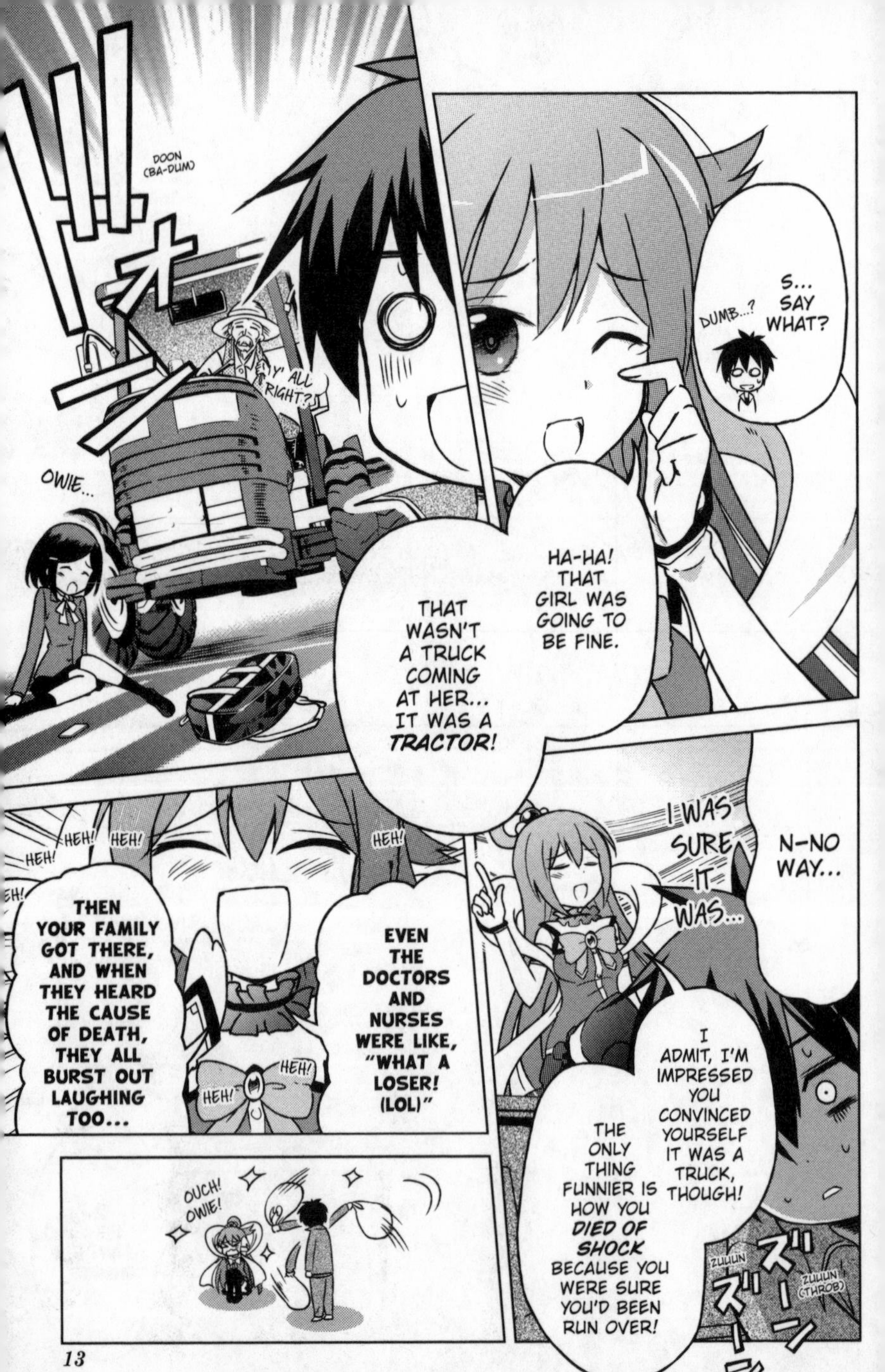
S... SAY WHAT?
DUMB...?
HA-HA! THAT GIRL WAS GOING TO BE FINE.
THAT WASN'T A TRUCK COMING AT HER... IT WAS A *TRACTOR*!
DOON (BA-DUM)
Y' ALL RIGHT?
OWIE...
N-NO WAY...
I WAS SURE IT WAS...
I ADMIT, I'M IMPRESSED YOU CONVINCED YOURSELF IT WAS A TRUCK, THOUGH!
THE ONLY THING FUNNIER IS HOW YOU *DIED OF SHOCK* BECAUSE YOU WERE SURE YOU'D BEEN RUN OVER!
ZUUUN
ZUUUN (THROB)
HEH!
EVEN THE DOCTORS AND NURSES WERE LIKE, "WHAT A LOSER! (LOL)"
THEN YOUR FAMILY GOT THERE, AND WHEN THEY HEARD THE CAUSE OF DEATH, THEY ALL BURST OUT LAUGHING TOO...
HEH! HEH! HEH!
HEH! HEH!
OUCH! OWIE!

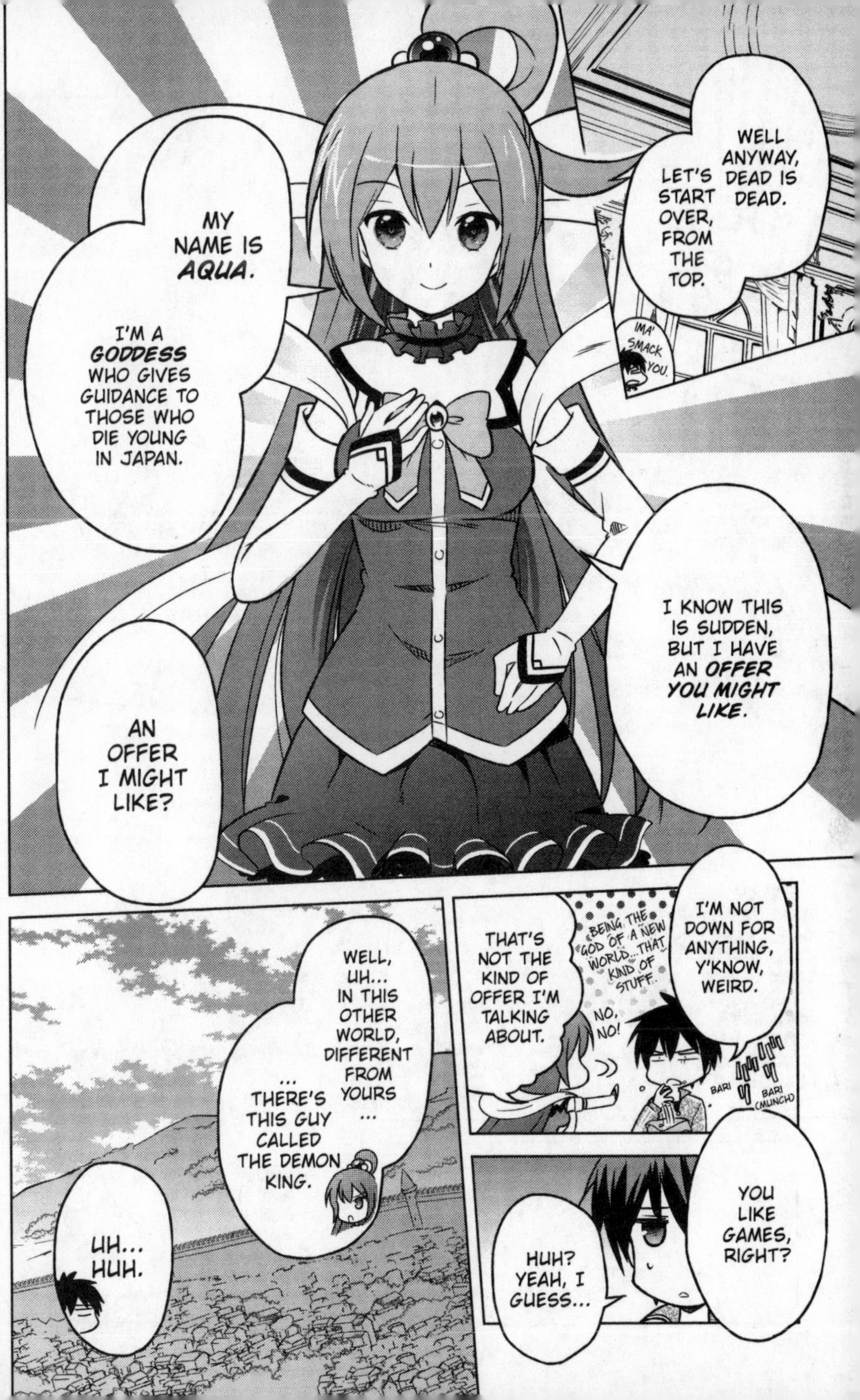
WELL ANYWAY, DEAD IS DEAD. LET'S START OVER, FROM THE TOP.
IMA' SMACK YOU.
MY NAME IS AQUA.
I'M A GODDESS WHO GIVES GUIDANCE TO THOSE WHO DIE YOUNG IN JAPAN.
I KNOW THIS IS SUDDEN, BUT I HAVE AN OFFER YOU MIGHT LIKE.
AN OFFER I MIGHT LIKE?
I'M NOT DOWN FOR ANYTHING, Y'KNOW, WEIRD.
BARI BARI (MUNCH)
BEING THE GOD OF A NEW WORLD...THAT KIND OF STUFF.
NO, NO!
THAT'S NOT THE KIND OF OFFER I'M TALKING ABOUT.
YOU LIKE GAMES, RIGHT?
HUH? YEAH, I GUESS...
WELL, UH... IN THIS OTHER WORLD, DIFFERENT FROM YOURS ...
... THERE'S THIS GUY CALLED THE DEMON KING.
UH... HUH.

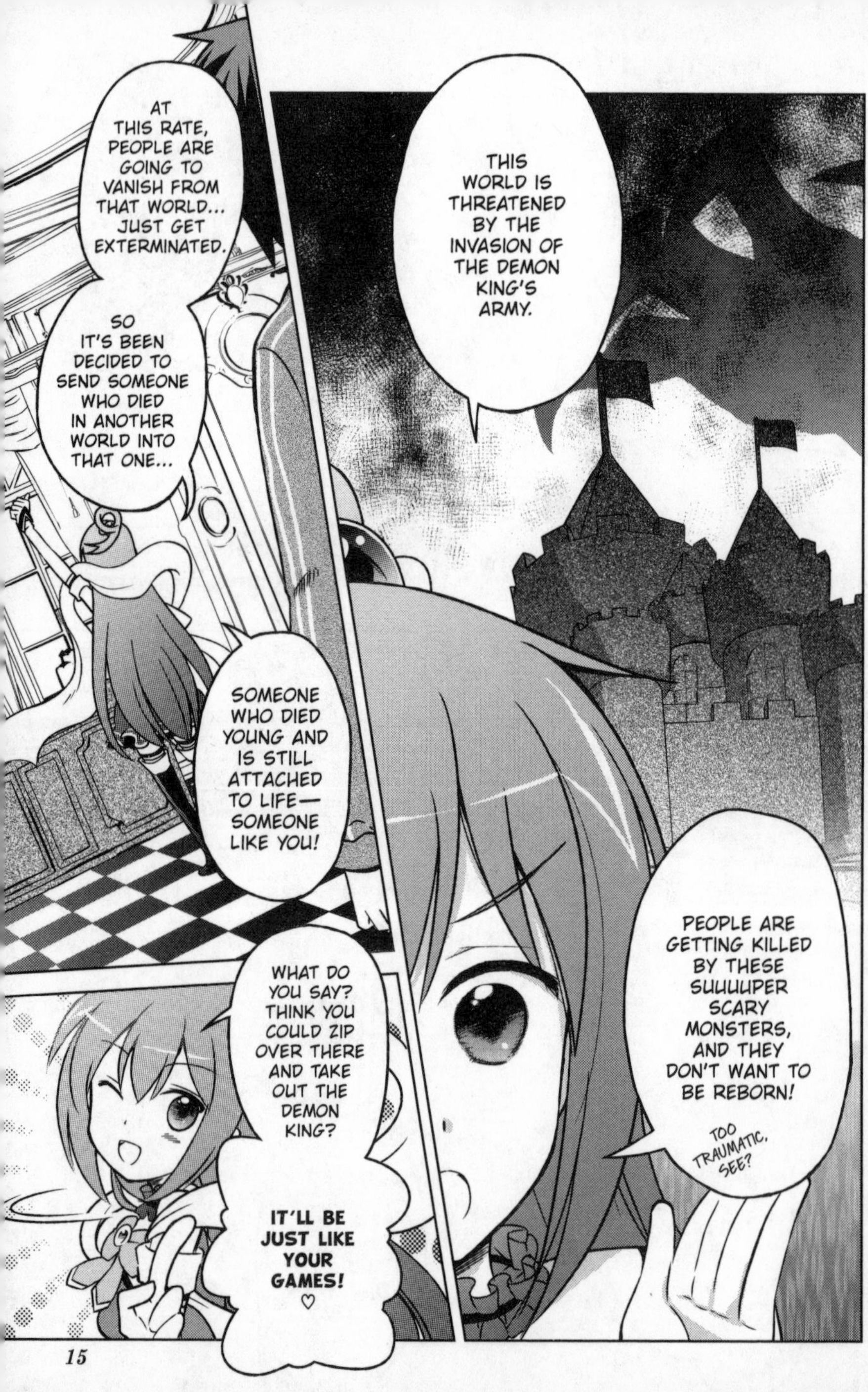
THIS WORLD IS THREATENED BY THE INVASION OF THE DEMON KING'S ARMY.
PEOPLE ARE GETTING KILLED BY THESE SUUUUPER SCARY MONSTERS, AND THEY DON'T WANT TO BE REBORN!
TOO TRAUMATIC, SEE?
AT THIS RATE, PEOPLE ARE GOING TO VANISH FROM THAT WORLD... JUST GET EXTERMINATED.
SO IT'S BEEN DECIDED TO SEND SOMEONE WHO DIED IN ANOTHER WORLD INTO THAT ONE...
SOMEONE WHO DIED YOUNG AND IS STILL ATTACHED TO LIFE—SOMEONE LIKE YOU!
WHAT DO YOU SAY? THINK YOU COULD ZIP OVER THERE AND TAKE OUT THE DEMON KING?
IT'LL BE JUST LIKE YOUR GAMES! ♡

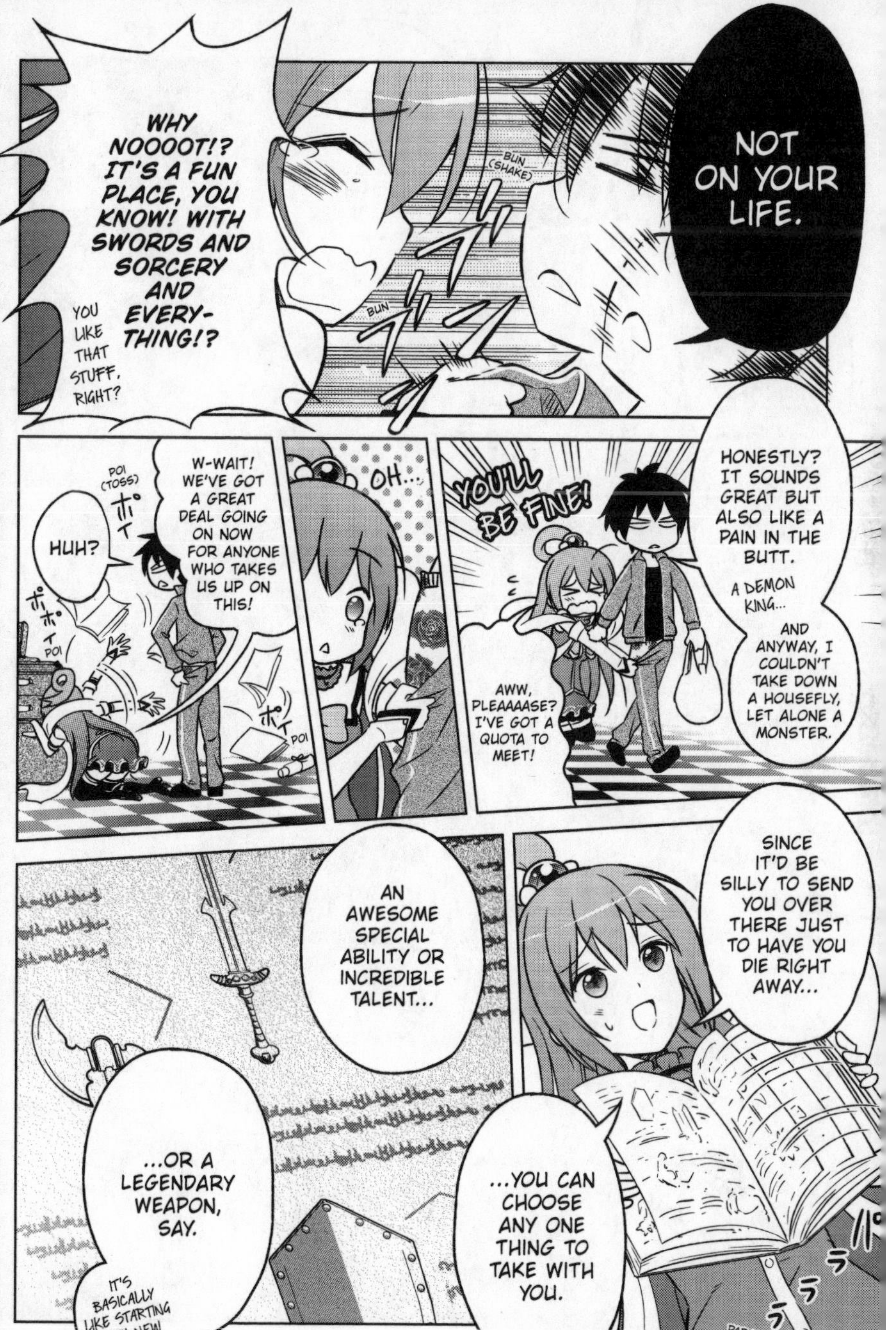
NOT ON YOUR LIFE.
BUN (SHAKE)
BUN
WHY NOOOOT!? IT'S A FUN PLACE, YOU KNOW! WITH SWORDS AND SORCERY AND EVERYTHING!?
YOU LIKE THAT STUFF, RIGHT?
HONESTLY? IT SOUNDS GREAT BUT ALSO LIKE A PAIN IN THE BUTT.
A DEMON KING...
AND ANYWAY, I COULDN'T TAKE DOWN A HOUSEFLY, LET ALONE A MONSTER.
YOU'LL BE FINE!
AWW, PLEAAAASE? I'VE GOT A QUOTA TO MEET!
OH...
W-WAIT! WE'VE GOT A GREAT DEAL GOING ON NOW FOR ANYONE WHO TAKES US UP ON THIS!
POI (TOSS)
HUH?
POI
POI
SINCE IT'D BE SILLY TO SEND YOU OVER THERE JUST TO HAVE YOU DIE RIGHT AWAY...
...YOU CAN CHOOSE ANY ONE THING TO TAKE WITH YOU.
PARARARA (FLIP)
AN AWESOME SPECIAL ABILITY OR INCREDIBLE TALENT...
...OR A LEGENDARY WEAPON, SAY.
IT'S BASICALLY LIKE STARTING WITH NEW GAME+!

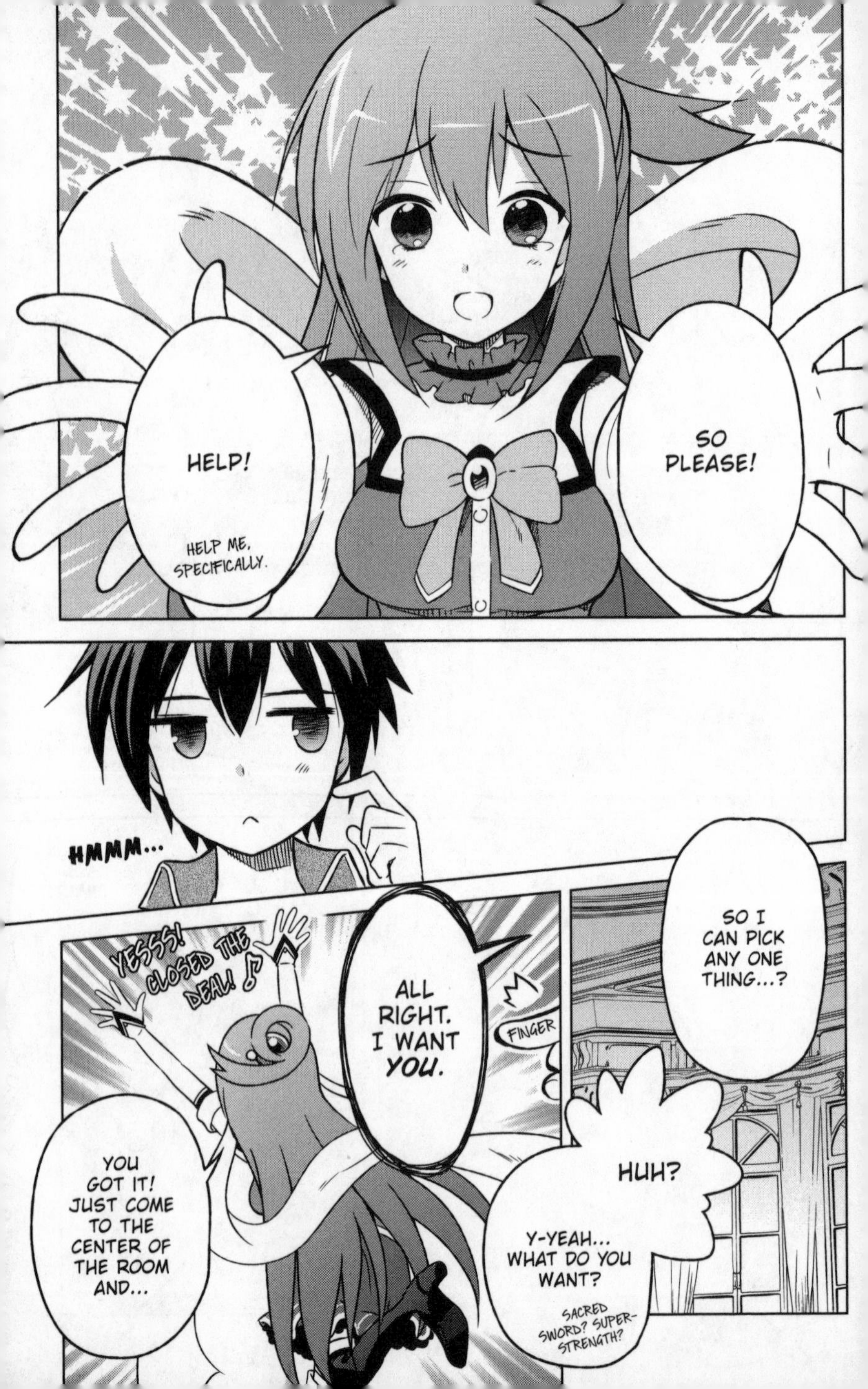
SO PLEASE!
HELP!
HELP ME, SPECIFICALLY.
HMMM...
SO I CAN PICK ANY ONE THING...?
Y-YEAH... WHAT DO YOU WANT?
SACRED SWORD? SUPER-STRENGTH?
HUH?
FINGER
ALL RIGHT. I WANT YOU.
YESSS! CLOSED THE DEAL! ♪
YOU GOT IT! JUST COME TO THE CENTER OF THE ROOM AND...

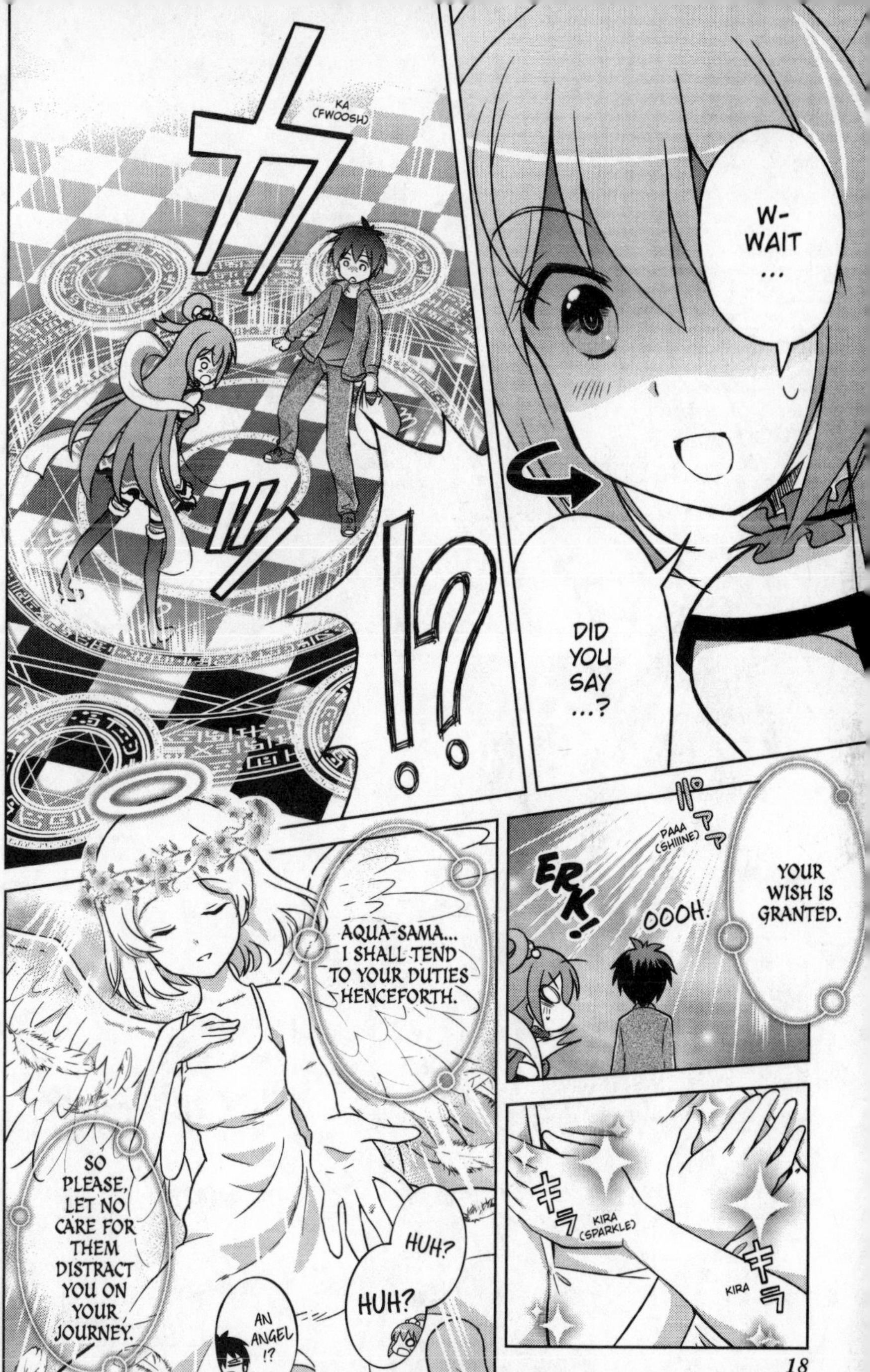
W-WAIT...
DID YOU SAY...?
KA (FWOOSH)
!?
PAAA (SHIIINE)
YOUR WISH IS GRANTED.
ERK!
OOOH.
KIRA (SPARKLE)
KIRA
AQUA-SAMA... I SHALL TEND TO YOUR DUTIES HENCEFORTH.
SO PLEASE, LET NO CARE FOR THEM DISTRACT YOU ON YOUR JOURNEY.
HUH?
HUH?
AN ANGEL!?

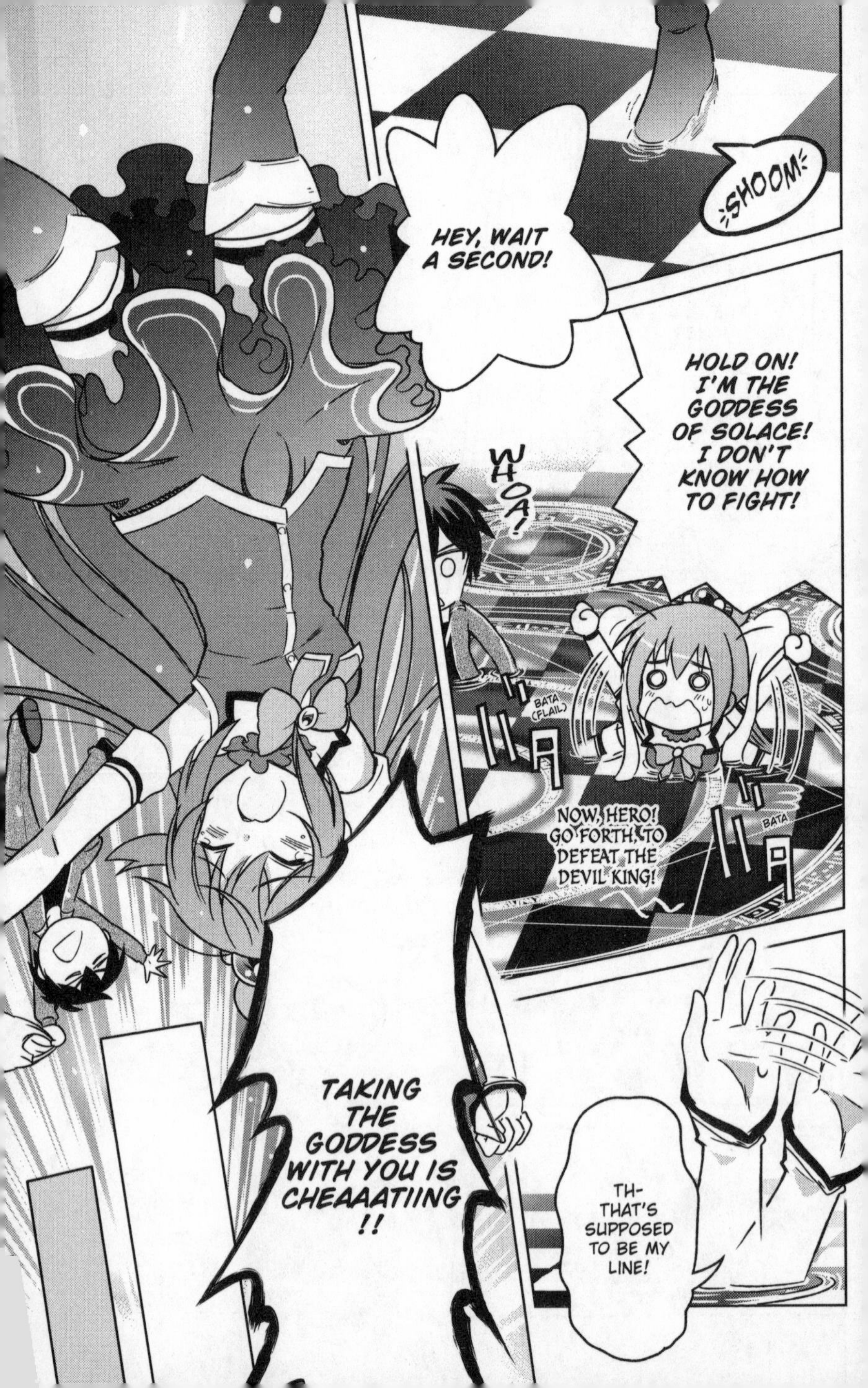
SHOOM
HOLD ON! I'M THE GODDESS OF SOLACE! I DON'T KNOW HOW TO FIGHT!
WHOA!
BATA (FLAIL)
NOW, HERO! GO FORTH, TO DEFEAT THE DEVIL KING!
BATA
TH- THAT'S SUPPOSED TO BE MY LINE!
HEY, WAIT A SECOND!
TAKING THE GODDESS WITH YOU IS CHEAAATIING !!

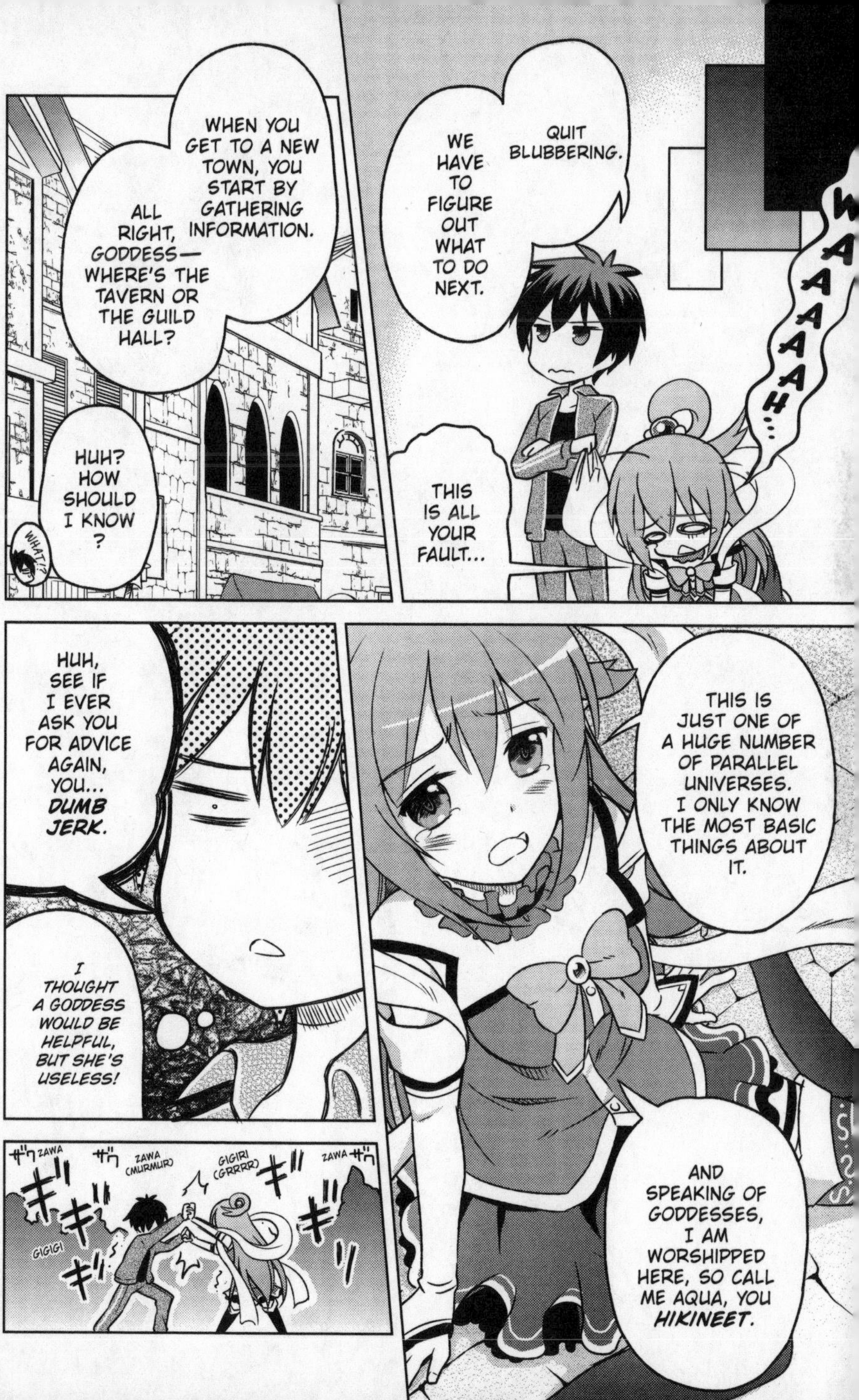
WAAAAAAAH...
QUIT BLUBBERING.
WE HAVE TO FIGURE OUT WHAT TO DO NEXT.
THIS IS ALL YOUR FAULT...
WHEN YOU GET TO A NEW TOWN, YOU START BY GATHERING INFORMATION.
ALL RIGHT, GODDESS—WHERE'S THE TAVERN OR THE GUILD HALL?
HUH? HOW SHOULD I KNOW?
WHAT!?
THIS IS JUST ONE OF A HUGE NUMBER OF PARALLEL UNIVERSES. I ONLY KNOW THE MOST BASIC THINGS ABOUT IT.
AND SPEAKING OF GODDESSES, I AM WORSHIPPED HERE, SO CALL ME AQUA, YOU ***HIKINEET***.
HUH, SEE IF I EVER ASK YOU FOR ADVICE AGAIN, YOU... ***DUMB JERK***.
I THOUGHT A GODDESS WOULD BE HELPFUL, BUT SHE'S USELESS!
ザワ ZAWA
ギギ
GIGIRI (GRRRR)
ザワ ZAWA (MURMUR)
ザワ ZAWA
GIGIGI
ギギ

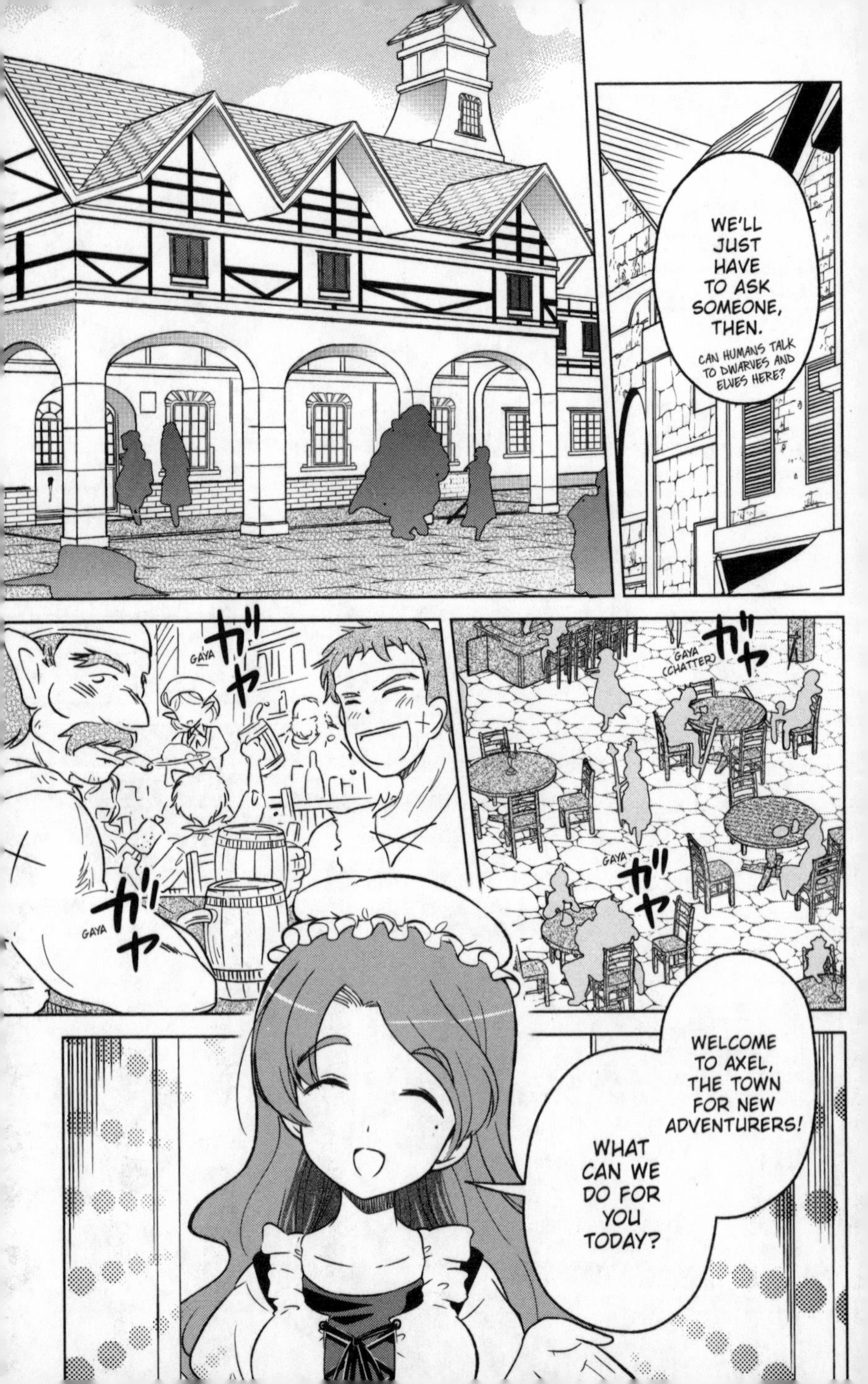
WE'LL JUST HAVE TO ASK SOMEONE, THEN.
CAN HUMANS TALK TO DWARVES AND ELVES HERE?
ガヤ
GAYA (CHATTER)
ガヤ
GAYA
ガヤ
GAYA
ガヤ
GAYA
WELCOME TO AXEL, THE TOWN FOR NEW ADVENTURERS!
WHAT CAN WE DO FOR YOU TODAY?

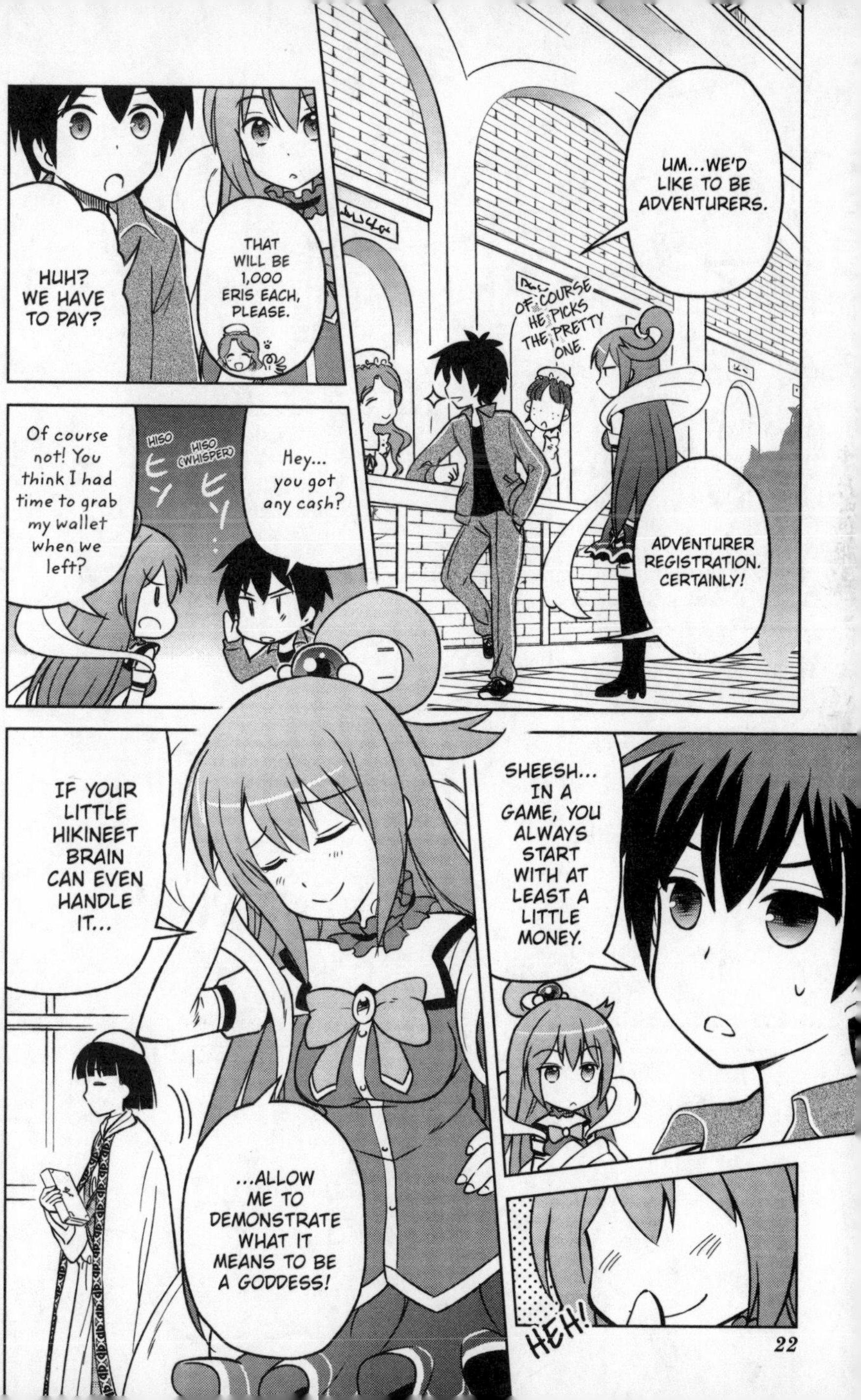
UM...WE'D LIKE TO BE ADVENTURERS.
OF COURSE HE PICKS THE PRETTY ONE.
ADVENTURER REGISTRATION. CERTAINLY!
THAT WILL BE 1,000 ERIS EACH, PLEASE.
HUH? WE HAVE TO PAY?
Hey... you got any cash?
HISO
HISO (WHISPER)
Of course not! You think I had time to grab my wallet when we left?
SHEESH... IN A GAME, YOU ALWAYS START WITH AT LEAST A LITTLE MONEY.
HEH!
IF YOUR LITTLE HIKINEET BRAIN CAN EVEN HANDLE IT...
...ALLOW ME TO DEMONSTRATE WHAT IT MEANS TO BE A GODDESS!

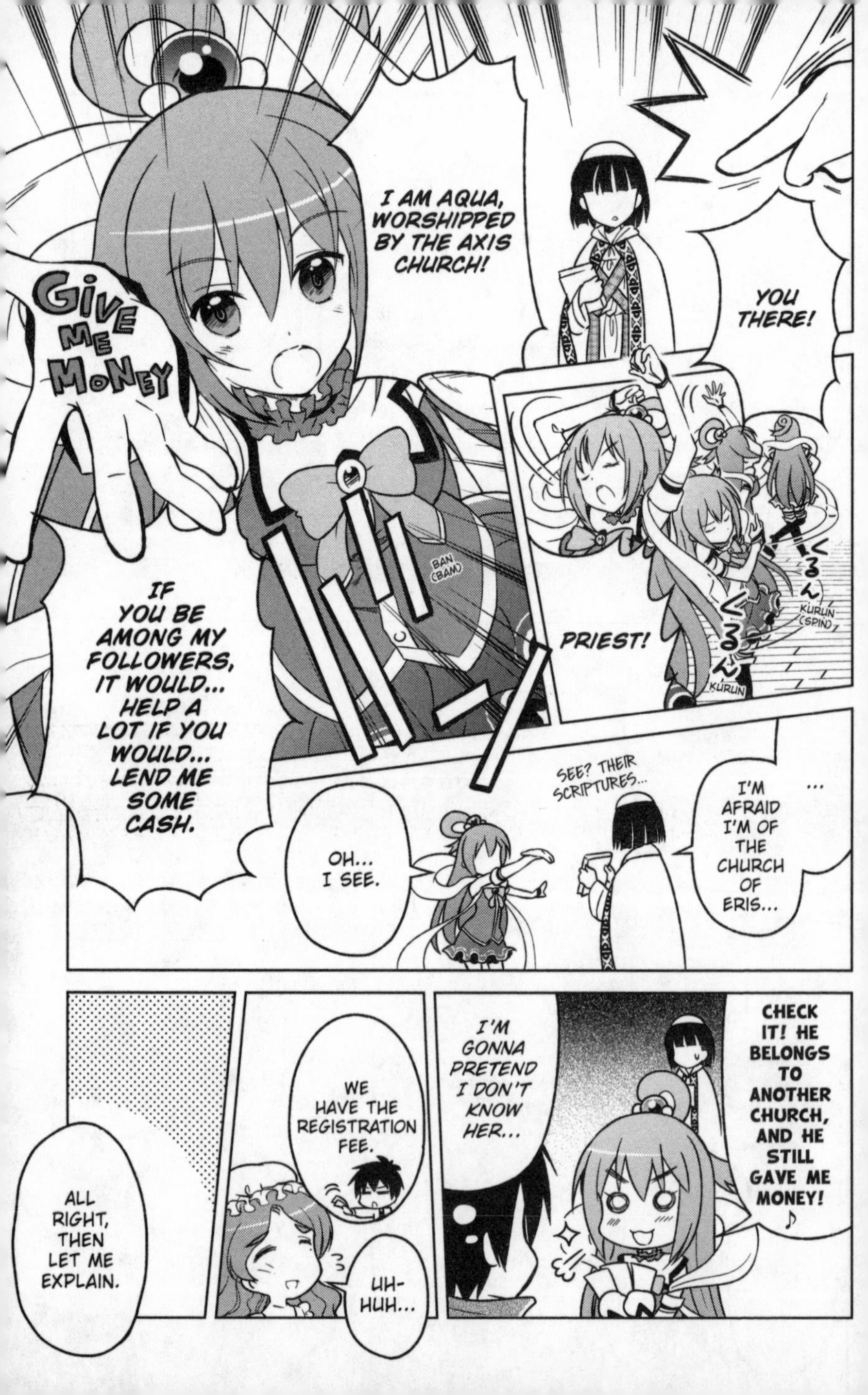

YOU THERE!
I AM AQUA, WORSHIPPED BY THE AXIS CHURCH!
PRIEST!
くるん
KURUN (SPIN)
くるん
KURUN
BAN (BAM)
GIVE ME MONEY
IF YOU BE AMONG MY FOLLOWERS, IT WOULD... HELP A LOT IF YOU WOULD... LEND ME SOME CASH.
...
I'M AFRAID I'M OF THE CHURCH OF ERIS...
SEE? THEIR SCRIPTURES...
OH... I SEE.
CHECK IT! HE BELONGS TO ANOTHER CHURCH, AND HE STILL GAVE ME MONEY! ♪
I'M GONNA PRETEND I DON'T KNOW HER...
WE HAVE THE REGISTRATION FEE.
UH-HUH...
ALL RIGHT, THEN LET ME EXPLAIN.

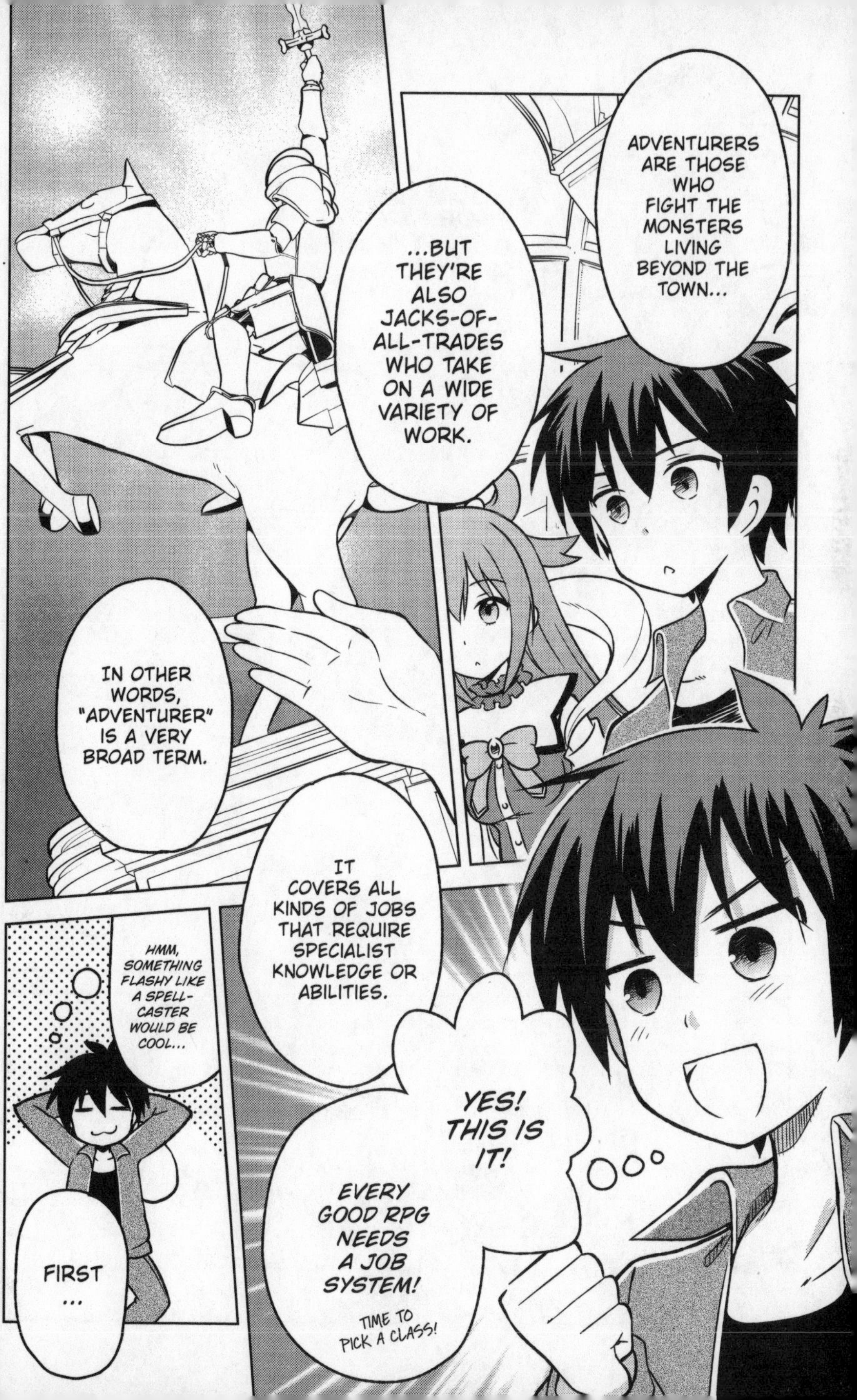
ADVENTURERS ARE THOSE WHO FIGHT THE MONSTERS LIVING BEYOND THE TOWN...
...BUT THEY'RE ALSO JACKS-OF-ALL-TRADES WHO TAKE ON A WIDE VARIETY OF WORK.
IN OTHER WORDS, "ADVENTURER" IS A VERY BROAD TERM.
IT COVERS ALL KINDS OF JOBS THAT REQUIRE SPECIALIST KNOWLEDGE OR ABILITIES.
YES! THIS IS IT!
EVERY GOOD RPG NEEDS A JOB SYSTEM!
TIME TO PICK A CLASS!
HMM, SOMETHING FLASHY LIKE A SPELL-CASTER WOULD BE COOL...
FIRST ...

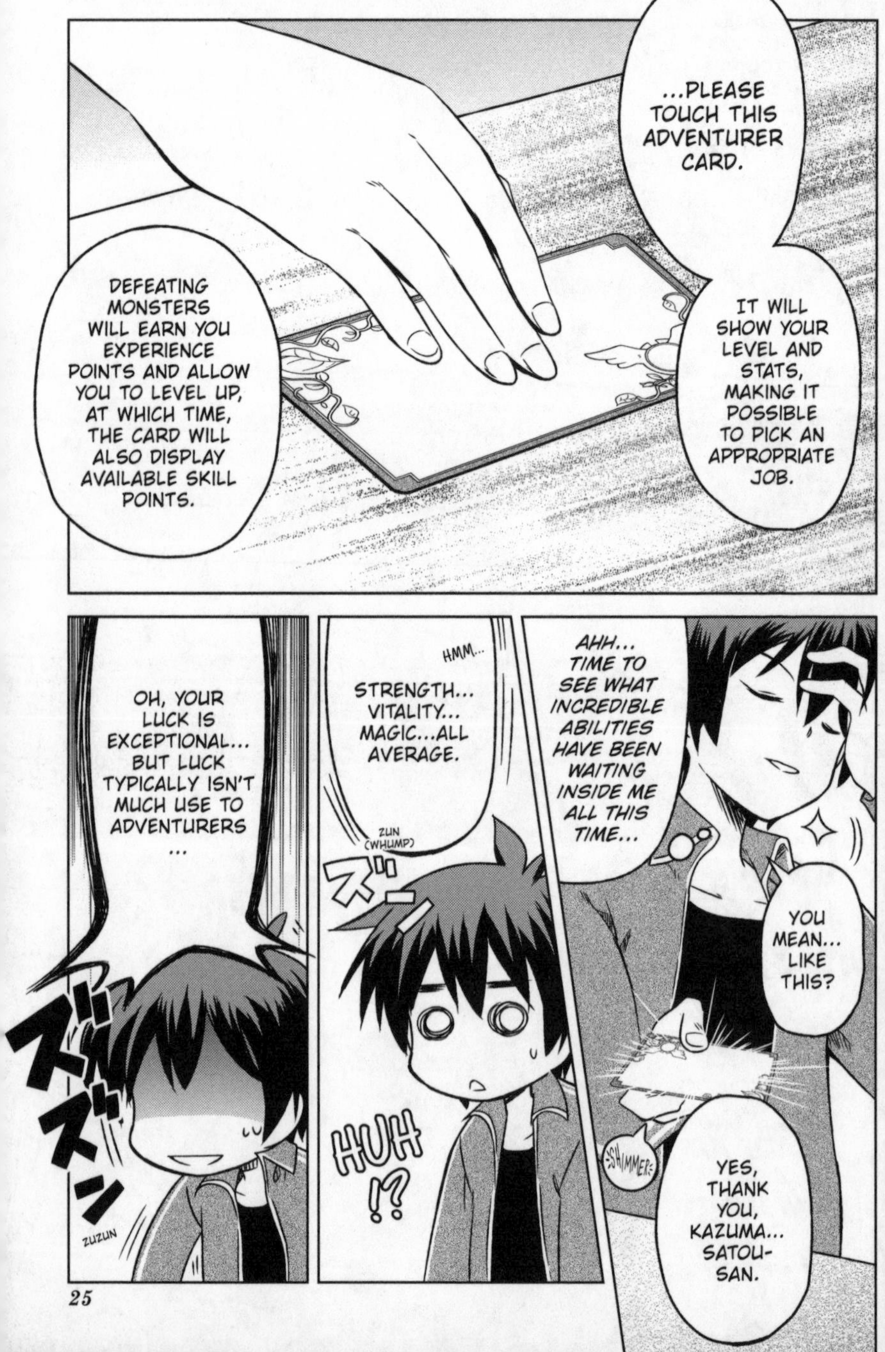
...PLEASE TOUCH THIS ADVENTURER CARD.
IT WILL SHOW YOUR LEVEL AND STATS, MAKING IT POSSIBLE TO PICK AN APPROPRIATE JOB.
DEFEATING MONSTERS WILL EARN YOU EXPERIENCE POINTS AND ALLOW YOU TO LEVEL UP, AT WHICH TIME, THE CARD WILL ALSO DISPLAY AVAILABLE SKILL POINTS.
AHH... TIME TO SEE WHAT INCREDIBLE ABILITIES HAVE BEEN WAITING INSIDE ME ALL THIS TIME...
YOU MEAN... LIKE THIS?
SHIMMER
YES, THANK YOU, KAZUMA... SATOU-SAN.
HMM...
STRENGTH... VITALITY... MAGIC...ALL AVERAGE.
ZUN (WHUMP)
HUH !?
OH, YOUR LUCK IS EXCEPTIONAL... BUT LUCK TYPICALLY ISN'T MUCH USE TO ADVENTURERS ...
ZUZUN

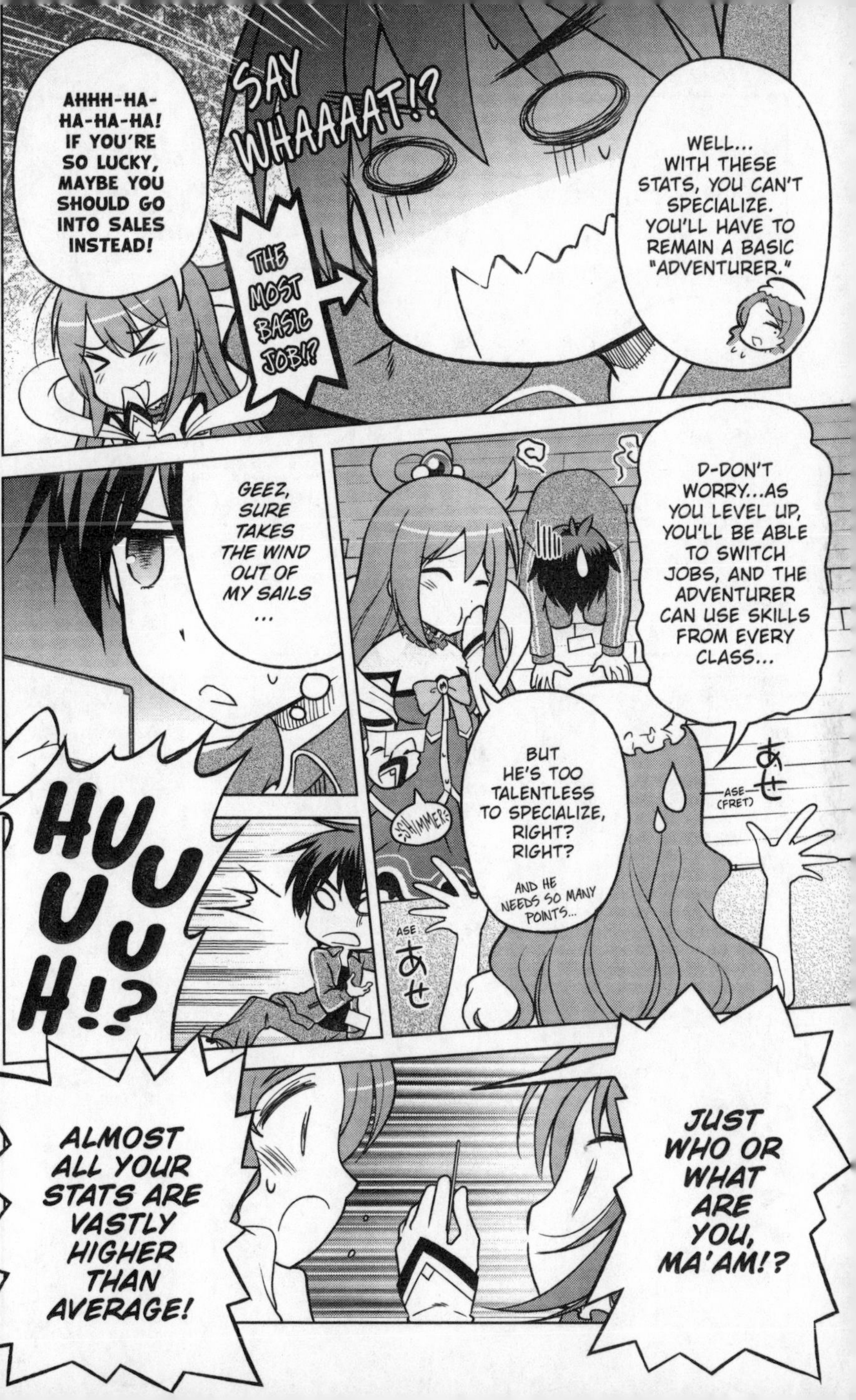
WELL... WITH THESE STATS, YOU CAN'T SPECIALIZE. YOU'LL HAVE TO REMAIN A BASIC "ADVENTURER."
SAY WHAAAAT!?
THE MOST BASIC JOB!?
AHHH-HA-HA-HA-HA-HA! IF YOU'RE SO LUCKY, MAYBE YOU SHOULD GO INTO SALES INSTEAD!
D-DON'T WORRY...AS YOU LEVEL UP, YOU'LL BE ABLE TO SWITCH JOBS, AND THE ADVENTURER CAN USE SKILLS FROM EVERY CLASS...
あせ
ASE (FRET)
BUT HE'S TOO TALENTLESS TO SPECIALIZE, RIGHT? RIGHT?
AND HE NEEDS SO MANY POINTS...
SHIMMER
ASE
あせ
GEEZ, SURE TAKES THE WIND OUT OF MY SAILS ...
HUUUUUH!?
JUST WHO OR WHAT ARE YOU, MA'AM!?
ALMOST ALL YOUR STATS ARE VASTLY HIGHER THAN AVERAGE!

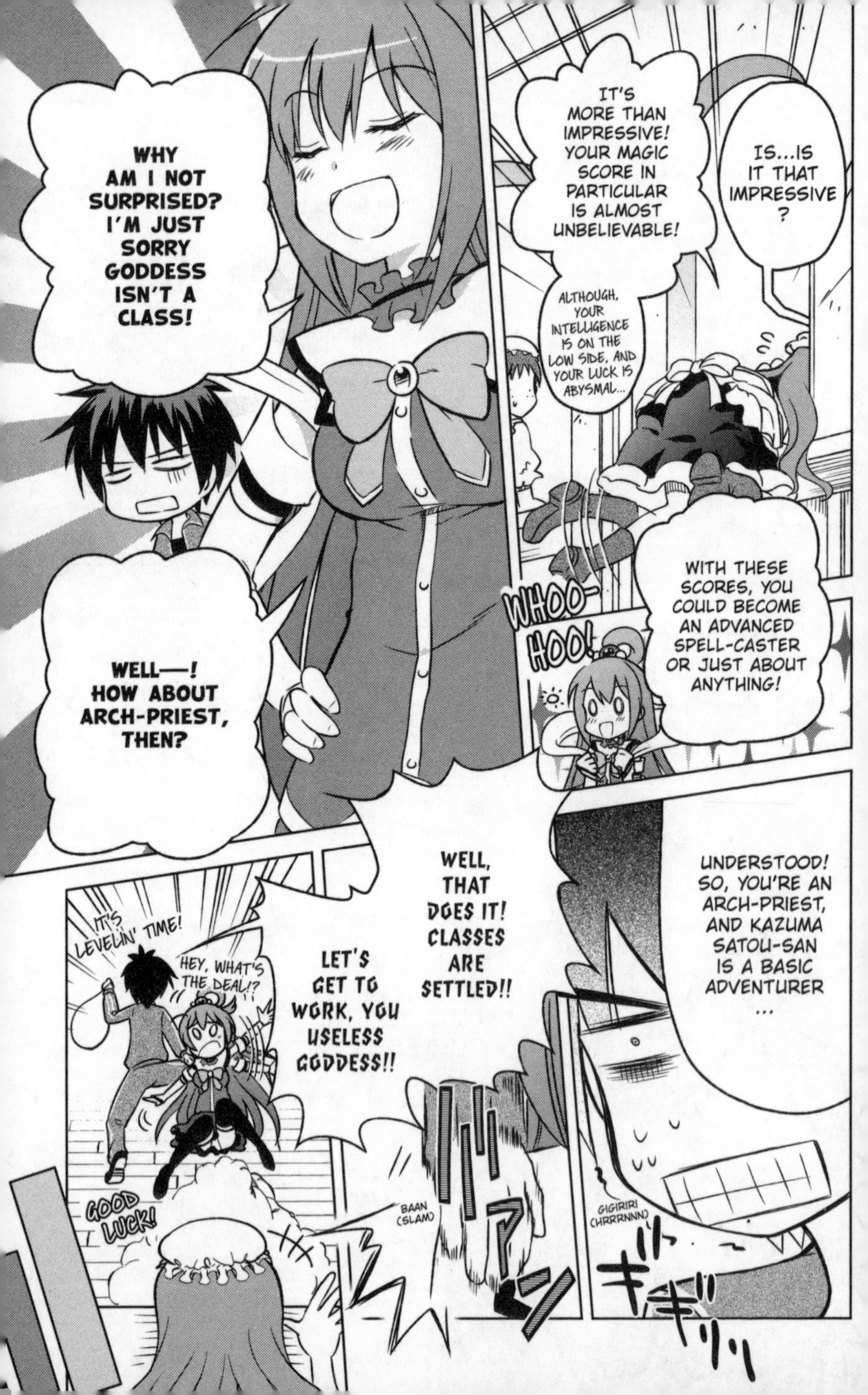

IS...IS IT THAT IMPRESSIVE?
IT'S MORE THAN IMPRESSIVE! YOUR MAGIC SCORE IN PARTICULAR IS ALMOST UNBELIEVABLE!
ALTHOUGH, YOUR INTELLIGENCE IS ON THE LOW SIDE, AND YOUR LUCK IS ABYSMAL...
WITH THESE SCORES, YOU COULD BECOME AN ADVANCED SPELL-CASTER OR JUST ABOUT ANYTHING!
WHOO-HOO!
WHY AM I NOT SURPRISED? I'M JUST SORRY GODDESS ISN'T A CLASS!
WELL—! HOW ABOUT ARCH-PRIEST, THEN?
UNDERSTOOD! SO, YOU'RE AN ARCH-PRIEST, AND KAZUMA SATOU-SAN IS A BASIC ADVENTURER...
GIGIRIRI (HRRRNNN)
WELL, THAT DOES IT! CLASSES ARE SETTLED!!
BAAN (SLAM)
LET'S GET TO WORK, YOU USELESS GODDESS!!
IT'S LEVELIN' TIME!
HEY, WHAT'S THE DEAL!?
GOOD LUCK!

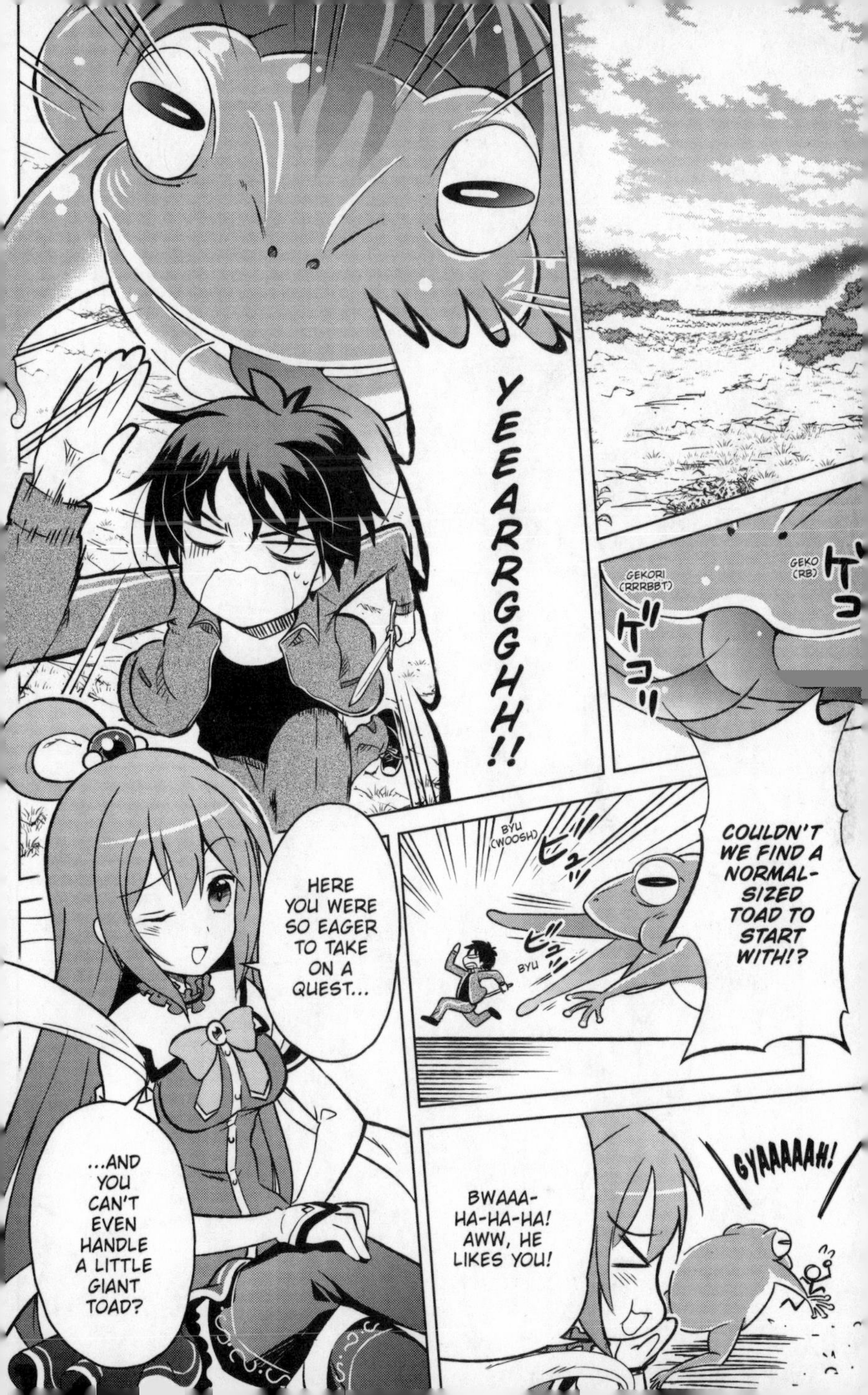
YEEARRGGHH!!
GEKO (RB)
GEKORI (RRRBBT)
COULDN'T WE FIND A NORMAL-SIZED TOAD TO START WITH!?
BYU (WOOSH)
BYU
HERE YOU WERE SO EAGER TO TAKE ON A QUEST...
...AND YOU CAN'T EVEN HANDLE A LITTLE GIANT TOAD?
GYAAAAAH!
BWAAA-HA-HA-HA! AWW, HE LIKES YOU!

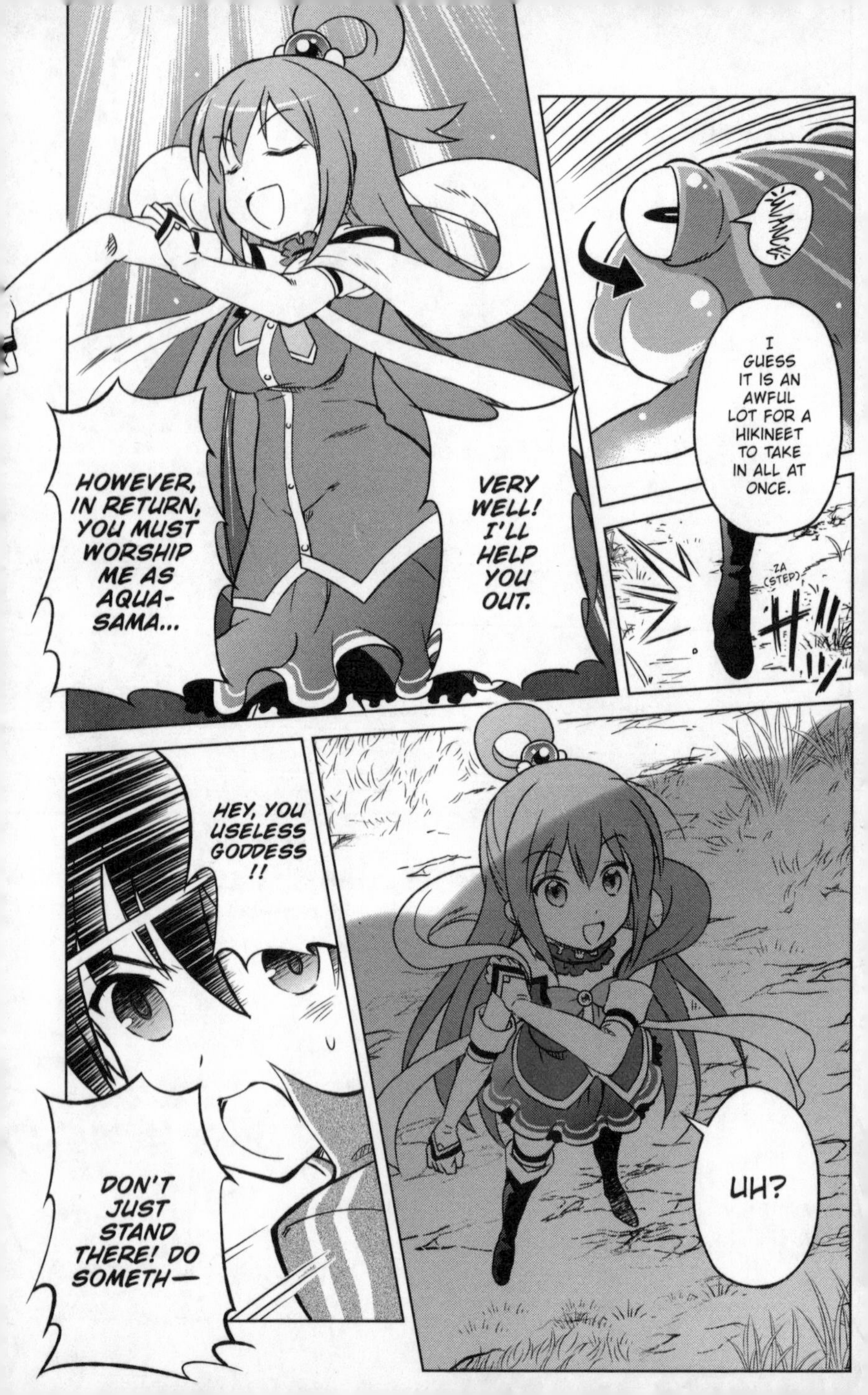
I GUESS IT IS AN AWFUL LOT FOR A HIKINEET TO TAKE IN ALL AT ONCE.
ZA (STEP)
VERY WELL! I'LL HELP YOU OUT.
HOWEVER, IN RETURN, YOU MUST WORSHIP ME AS AQUA-SAMA...
UH?
HEY, YOU USELESS GODDESS !!
DON'T JUST STAND THERE! DO SOMETH—

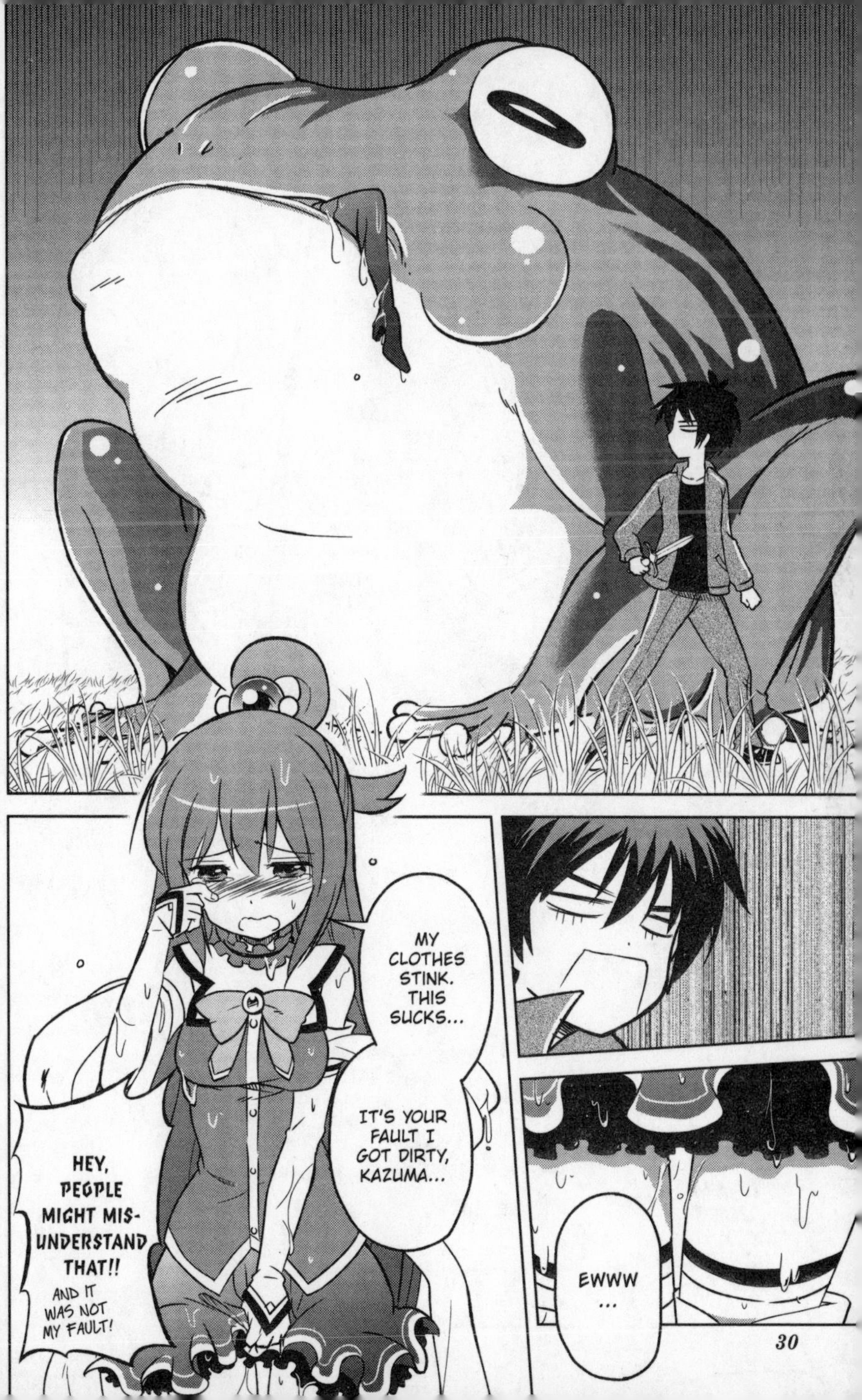
EWWW...
MY CLOTHES STINK. THIS SUCKS...
IT'S YOUR FAULT I GOT DIRTY, KAZUMA...
HEY, PEOPLE MIGHT MIS-UNDERSTAND THAT!!
AND IT WAS NOT MY FAULT!

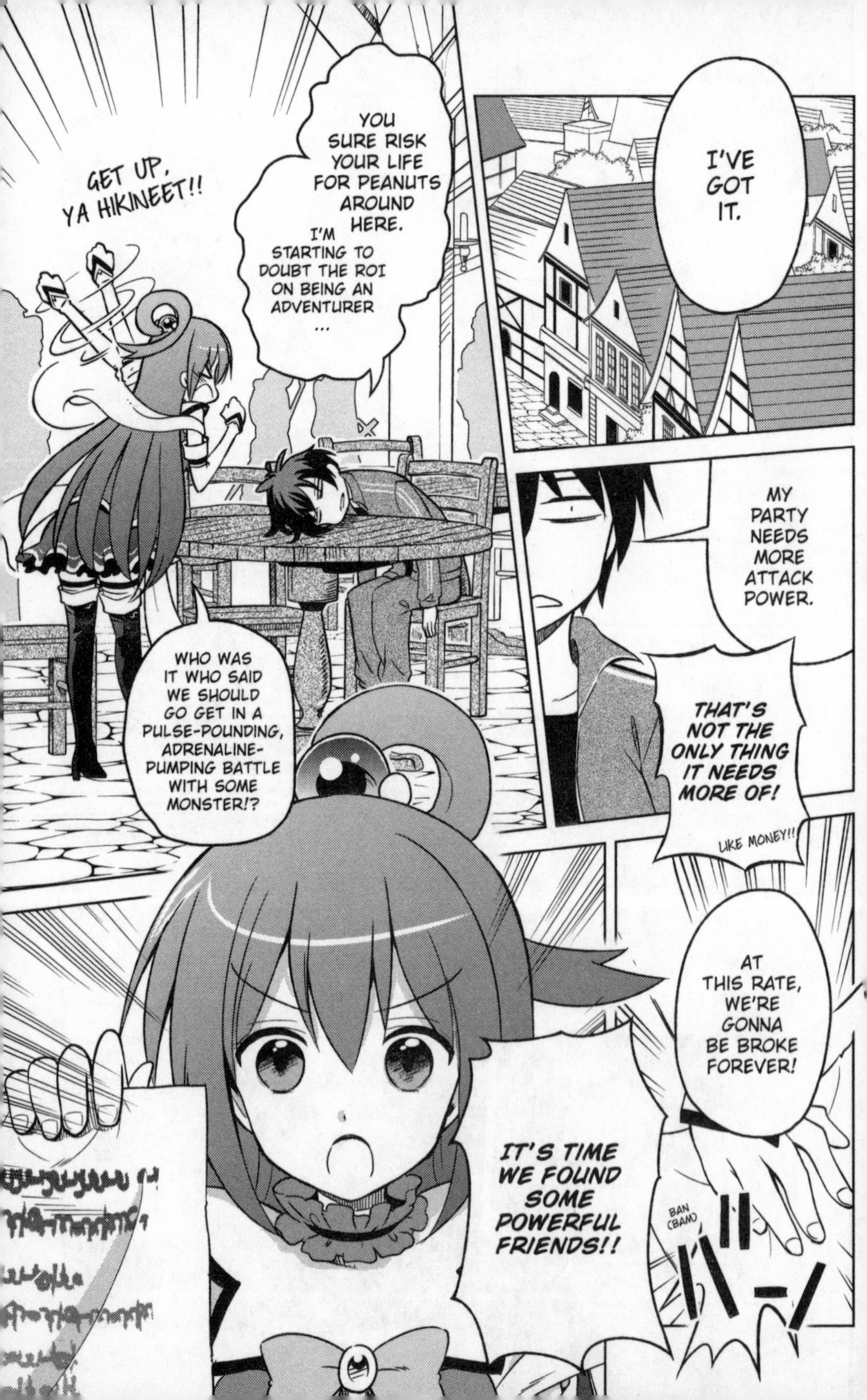
I'VE GOT IT.
MY PARTY NEEDS MORE ATTACK POWER.
THAT'S NOT THE ONLY THING IT NEEDS MORE OF!
LIKE MONEY!!
YOU SURE RISK YOUR LIFE FOR PEANUTS AROUND HERE.
I'M STARTING TO DOUBT THE ROI ON BEING AN ADVENTURER ...
GET UP, YA HIKINEET!!
WHO WAS IT WHO SAID WE SHOULD GO GET IN A PULSE-POUNDING, ADRENALINE-PUMPING BATTLE WITH SOME MONSTER!?
AT THIS RATE, WE'RE GONNA BE BROKE FOREVER!
BAN (BAM)
IT'S TIME WE FOUND SOME POWERFUL FRIENDS!!

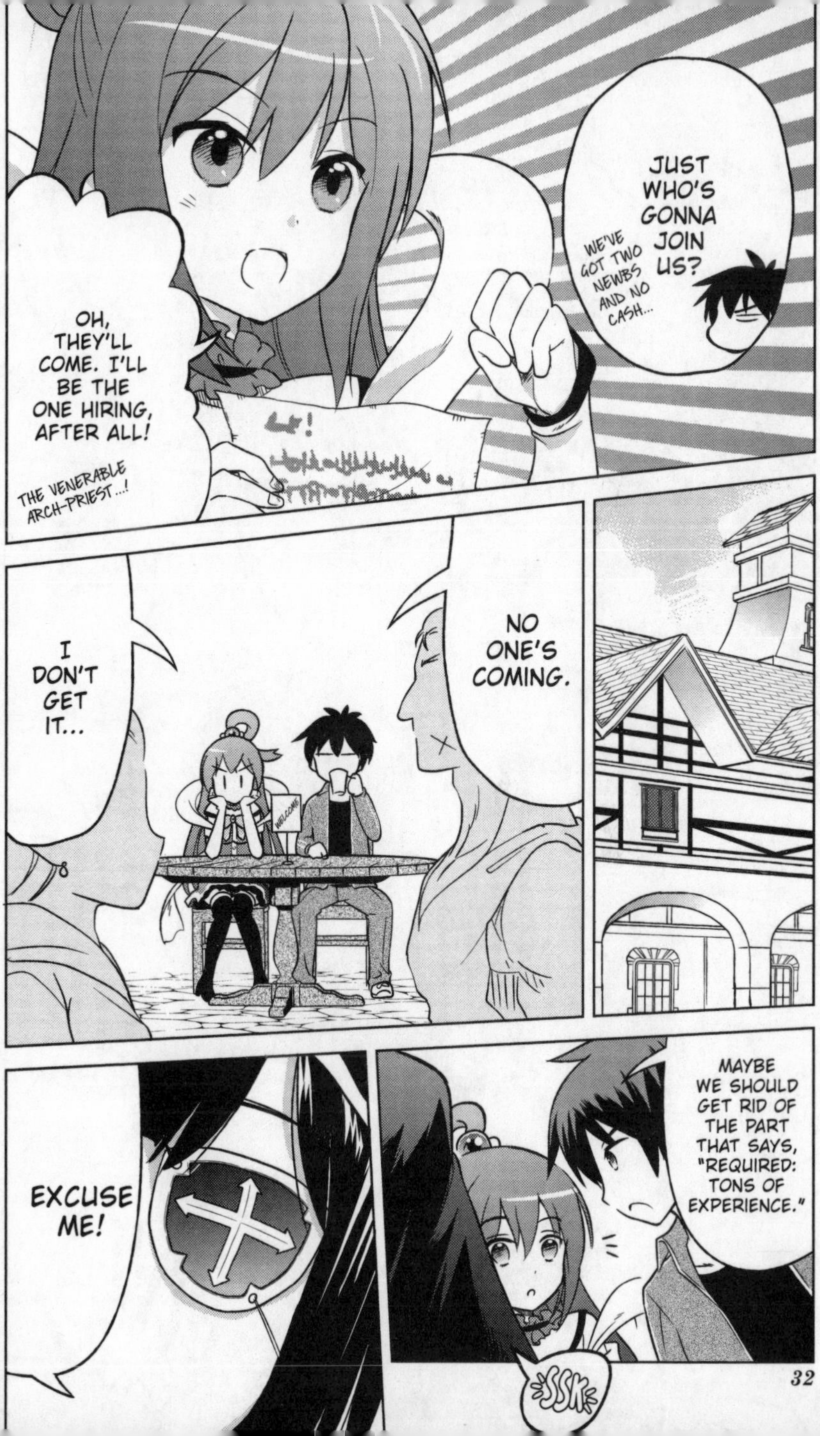
JUST WHO'S GONNA JOIN US?
WE'VE GOT TWO NEWBS AND NO CASH...
OH, THEY'LL COME. I'LL BE THE ONE HIRING, AFTER ALL!
THE VENERABLE ARCH-PRIEST...!
NO ONE'S COMING.
WELCOME
I DON'T GET IT...
MAYBE WE SHOULD GET RID OF THE PART THAT SAYS, "REQUIRED: TONS OF EXPERIENCE."
SSK
EXCUSE ME!

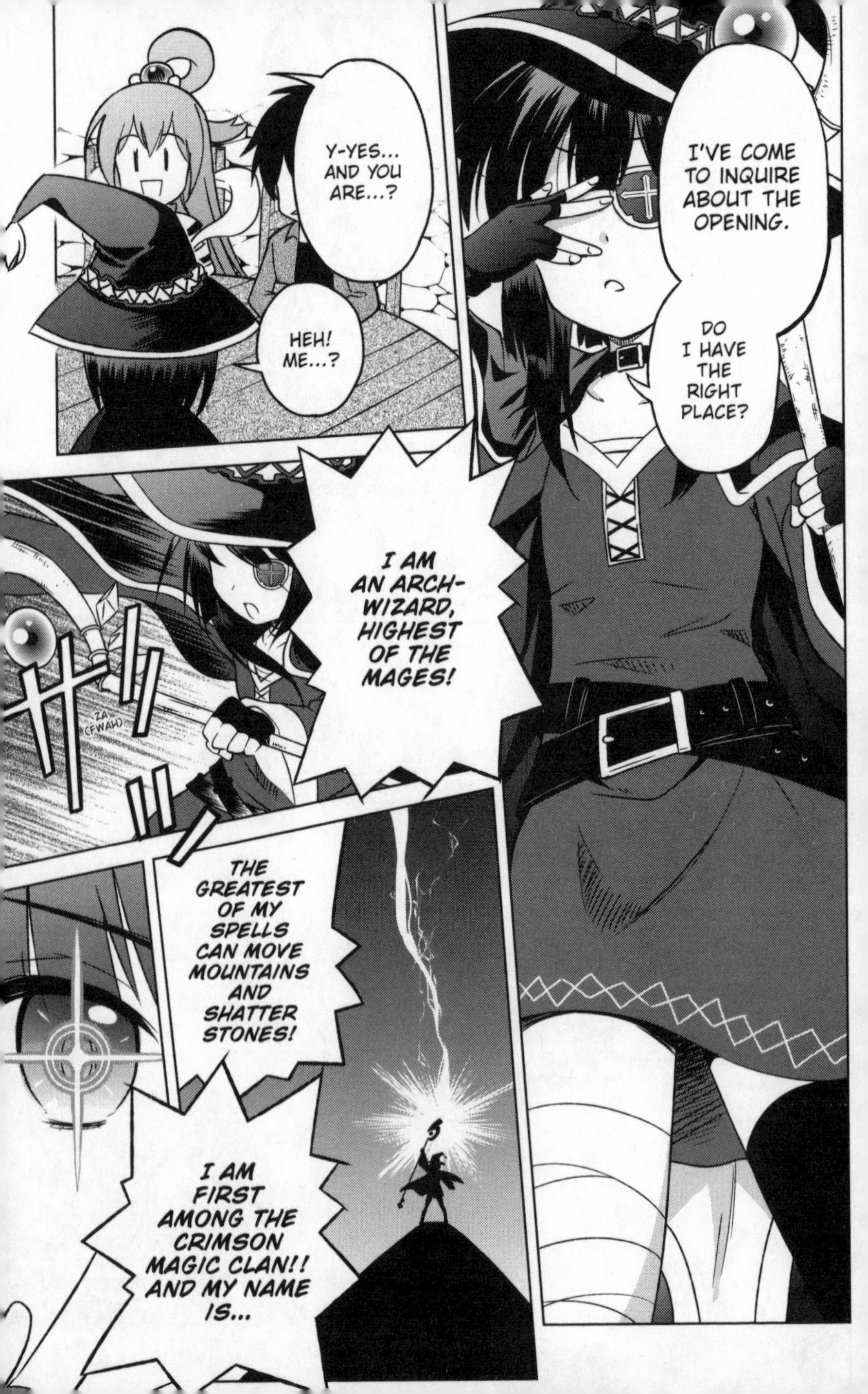
I'VE COME TO INQUIRE ABOUT THE OPENING.
DO I HAVE THE RIGHT PLACE?
Y-YES... AND YOU ARE...?
HEH! ME...?
I AM AN ARCH-WIZARD, HIGHEST OF THE MAGES!
ZA (FWAH)
THE GREATEST OF MY SPELLS CAN MOVE MOUNTAINS AND SHATTER STONES!
I AM FIRST AMONG THE CRIMSON MAGIC CLAN!! AND MY NAME IS...

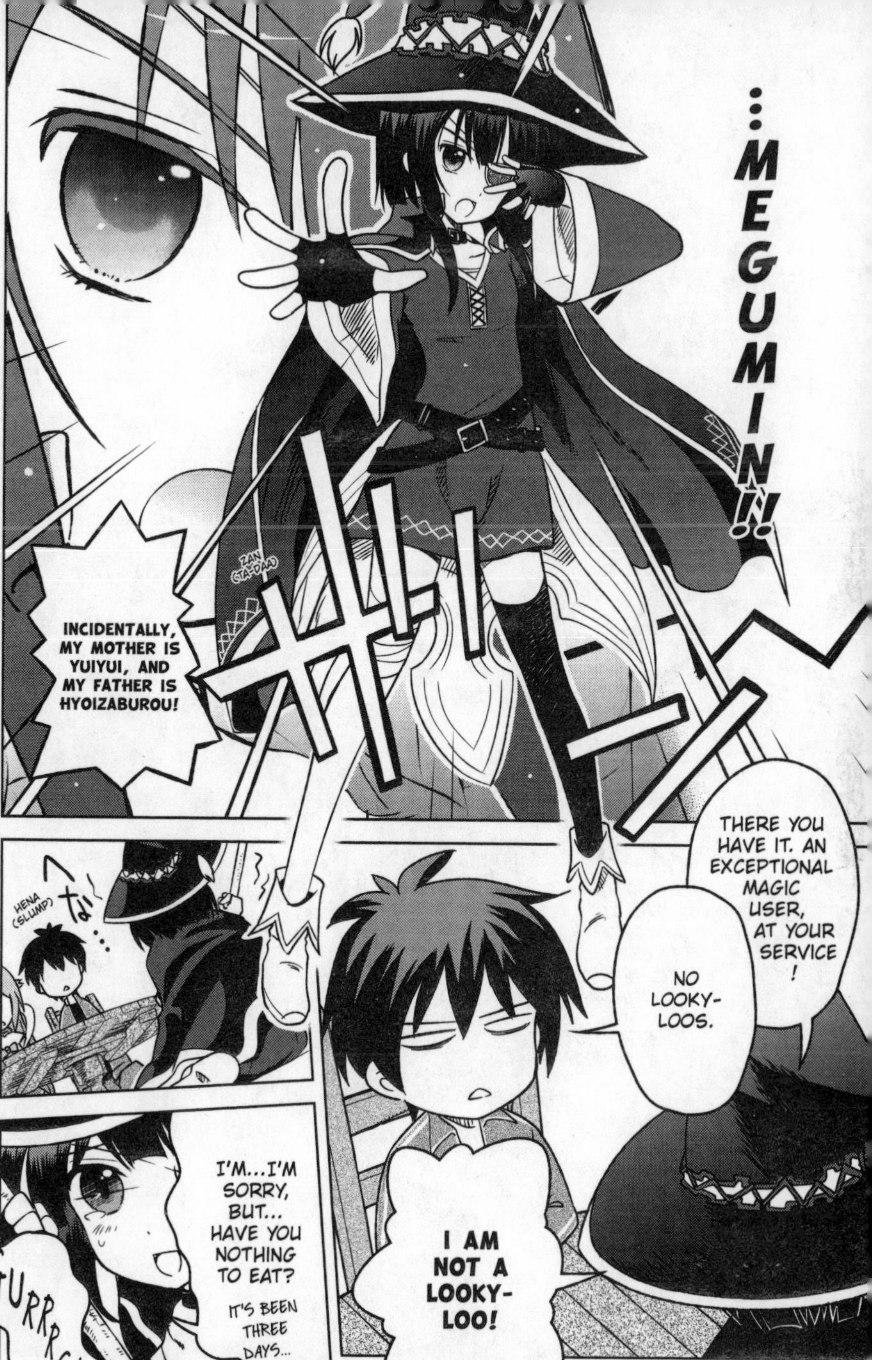
...MEGUMIN!!
ZAN (TA-DAA)
INCIDENTALLY, MY MOTHER IS YUIYUI, AND MY FATHER IS HYOIZABUROU!
THERE YOU HAVE IT. AN EXCEPTIONAL MAGIC USER, AT YOUR SERVICE!
NO LOOKY-LOOS.
I AM NOT A LOOKY-LOO!
HENA (SLUMP)
な...
I'M...I'M SORRY, BUT... HAVE YOU NOTHING TO EAT?
IT'S BEEN THREE DAYS...
GURRRGLE...

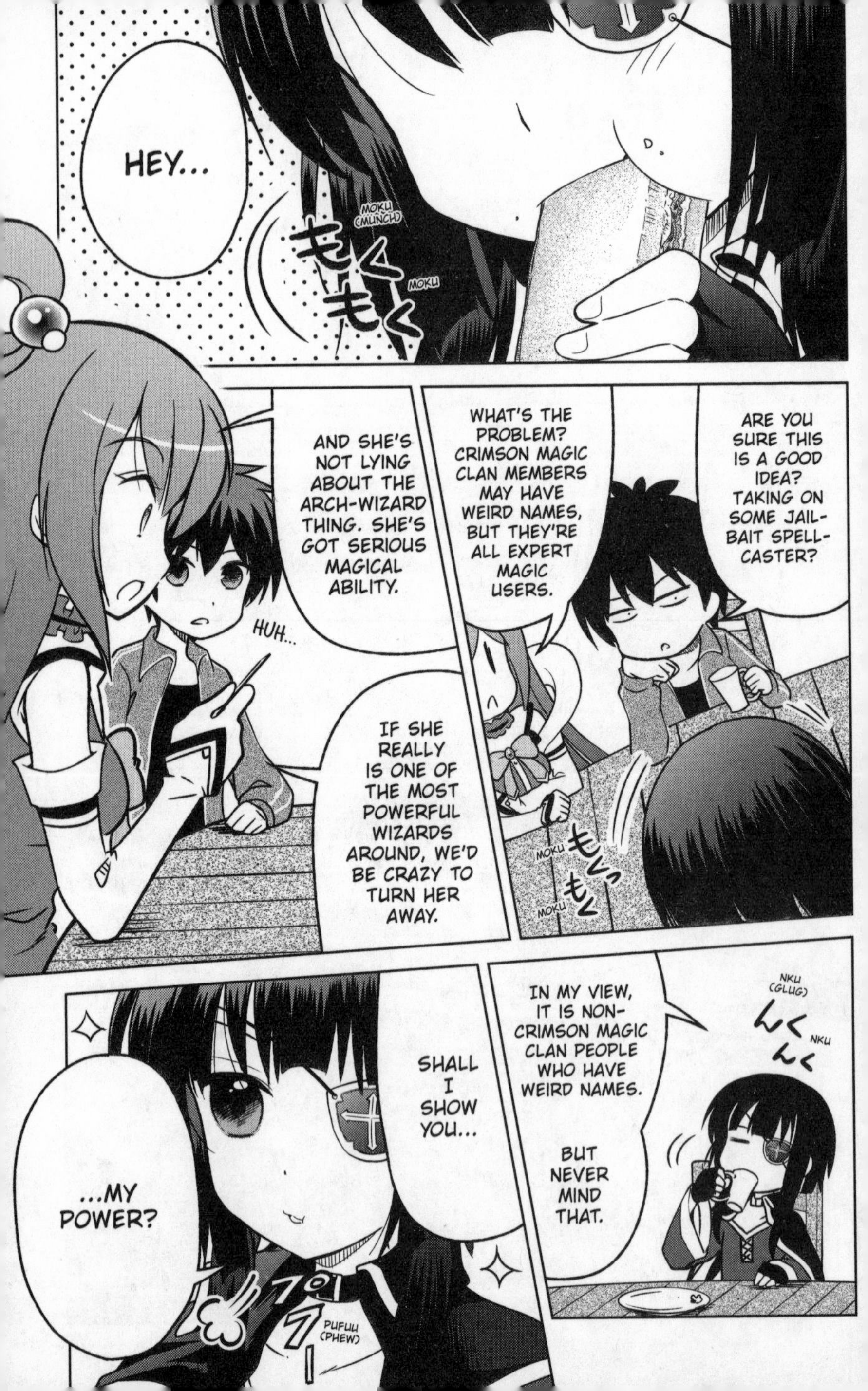
HEY...
MOKU (MUNCH)
MOKU
ARE YOU SURE THIS IS A GOOD IDEA? TAKING ON SOME JAIL-BAIT SPELL-CASTER?
WHAT'S THE PROBLEM? CRIMSON MAGIC CLAN MEMBERS MAY HAVE WEIRD NAMES, BUT THEY'RE ALL EXPERT MAGIC USERS.
MOKU
MOKU
AND SHE'S NOT LYING ABOUT THE ARCH-WIZARD THING. SHE'S GOT SERIOUS MAGICAL ABILITY.
HUH...
IF SHE REALLY IS ONE OF THE MOST POWERFUL WIZARDS AROUND, WE'D BE CRAZY TO TURN HER AWAY.
NKU (GLUG)
NKU
IN MY VIEW, IT IS NON-CRIMSON MAGIC CLAN PEOPLE WHO HAVE WEIRD NAMES.
BUT NEVER MIND THAT.
SHALL I SHOW YOU...
...MY POWER?
PUFUU (PHEW)

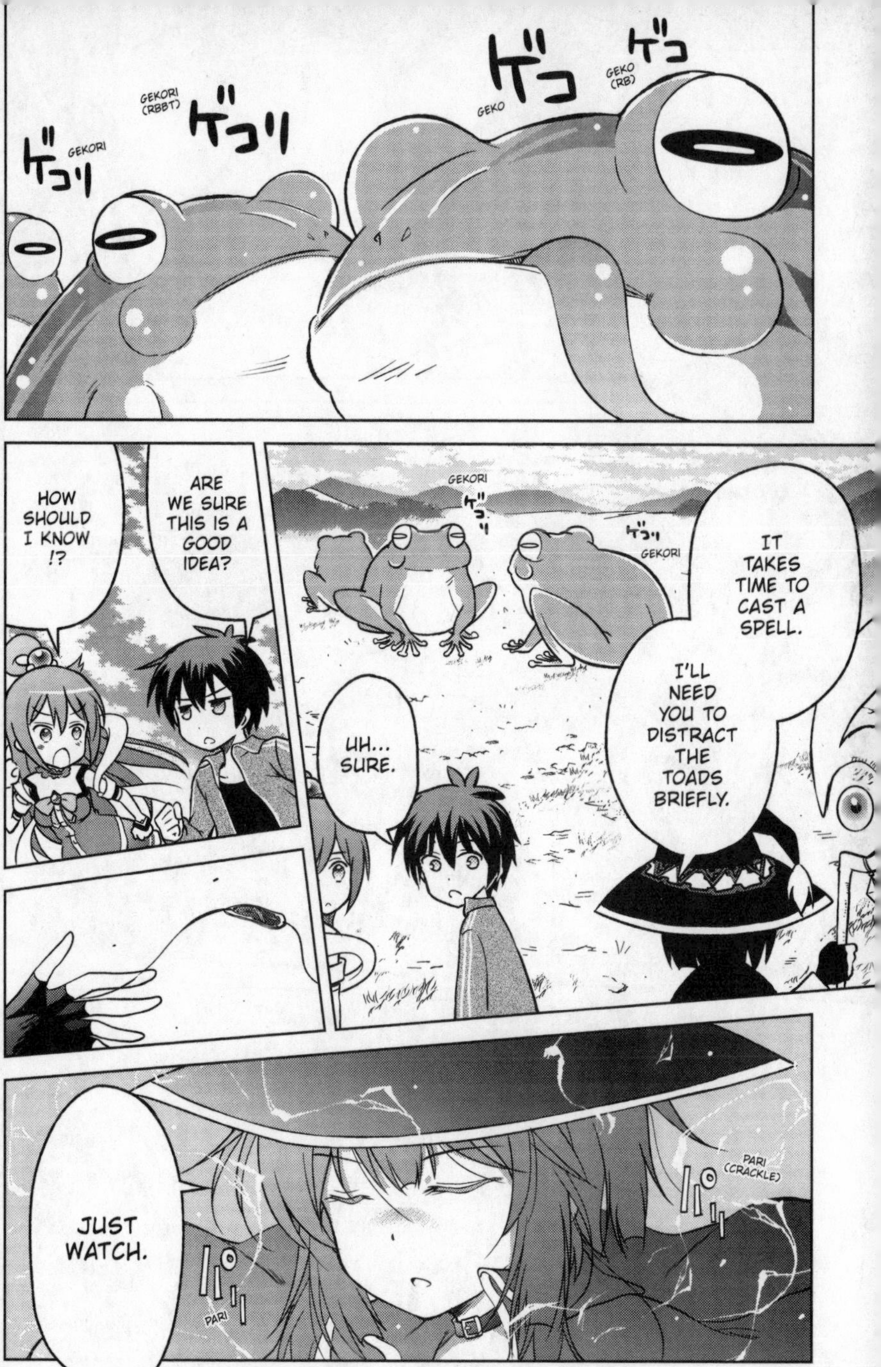
ゲコ
GEKO (RB)
ゲコ
GEKO
ゲコリ
GEKORI (RBBT)
ゲコリ
GEKORI
ゲコリ
GEKORI
ゲコリ
GEKORI
IT TAKES TIME TO CAST A SPELL.
I'LL NEED YOU TO DISTRACT THE TOADS BRIEFLY.
UH... SURE.
ARE WE SURE THIS IS A GOOD IDEA?
HOW SHOULD I KNOW !?
PARI (CRACKLE)
JUST WATCH.
PARI

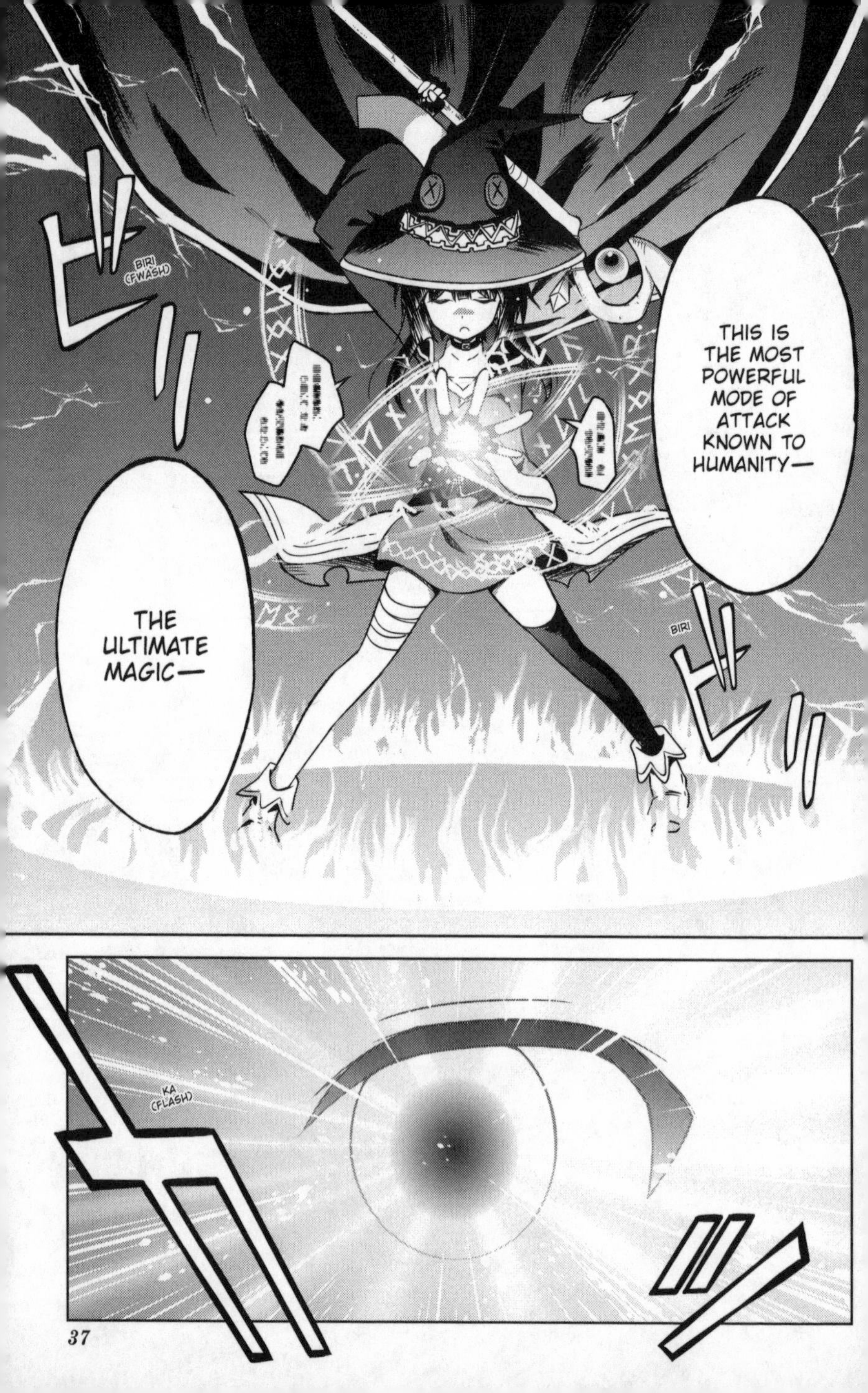
THIS IS THE MOST POWERFUL MODE OF ATTACK KNOWN TO HUMANITY—
BIRI (FWASH)
BIRI
THE ULTIMATE MAGIC—
KA (FLASH)

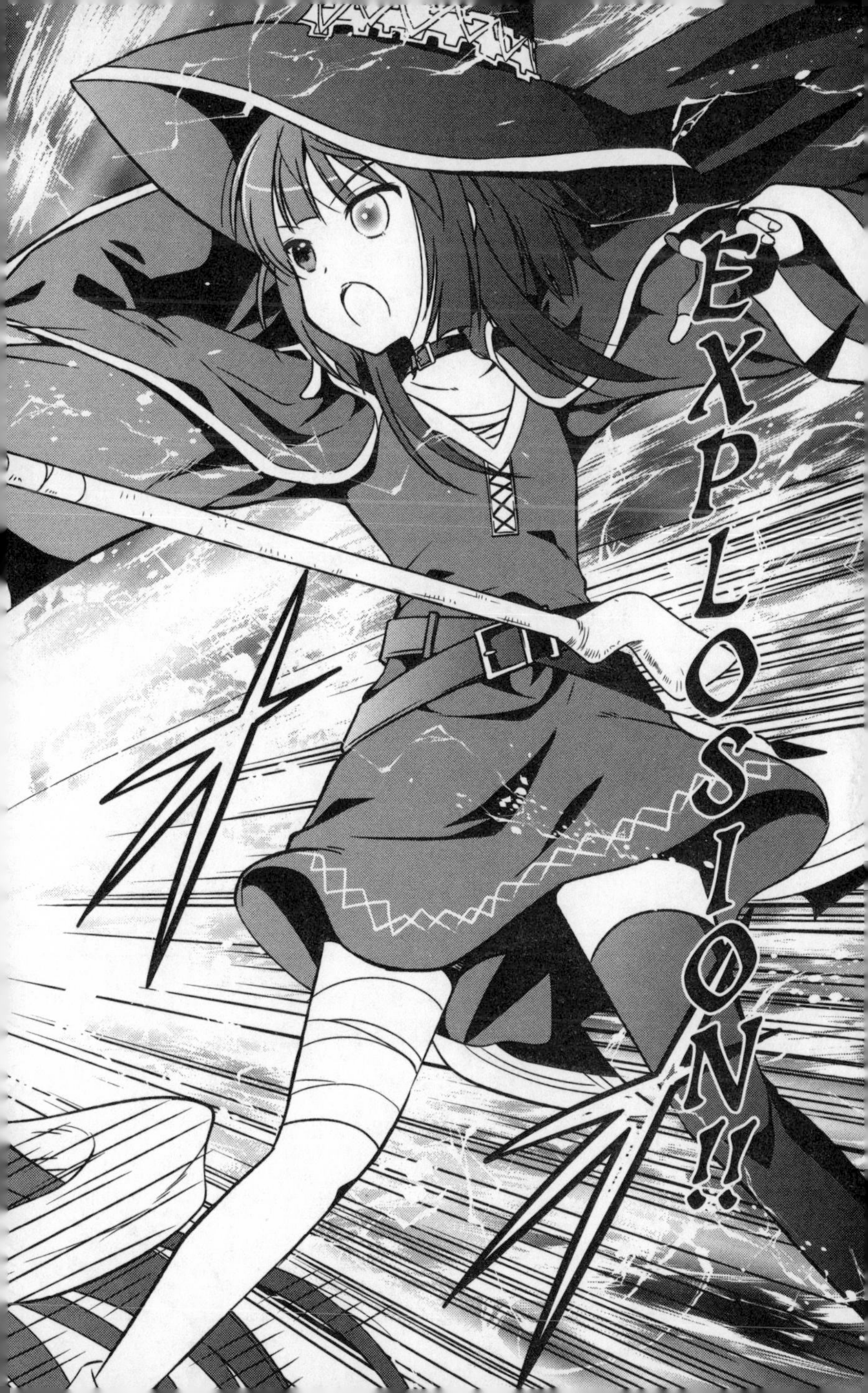
EXPLOSION!!

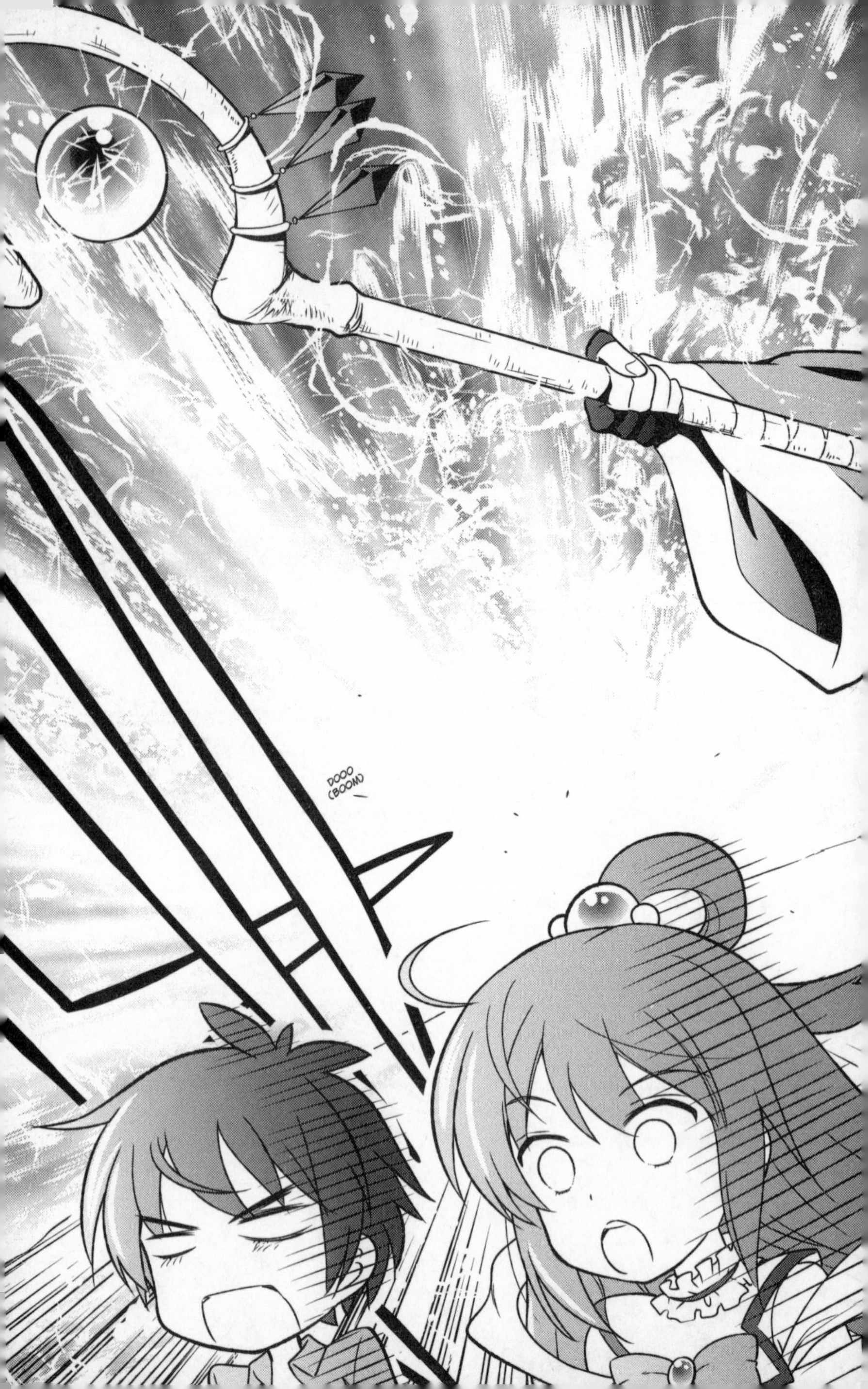
DOOO
(BOOM)

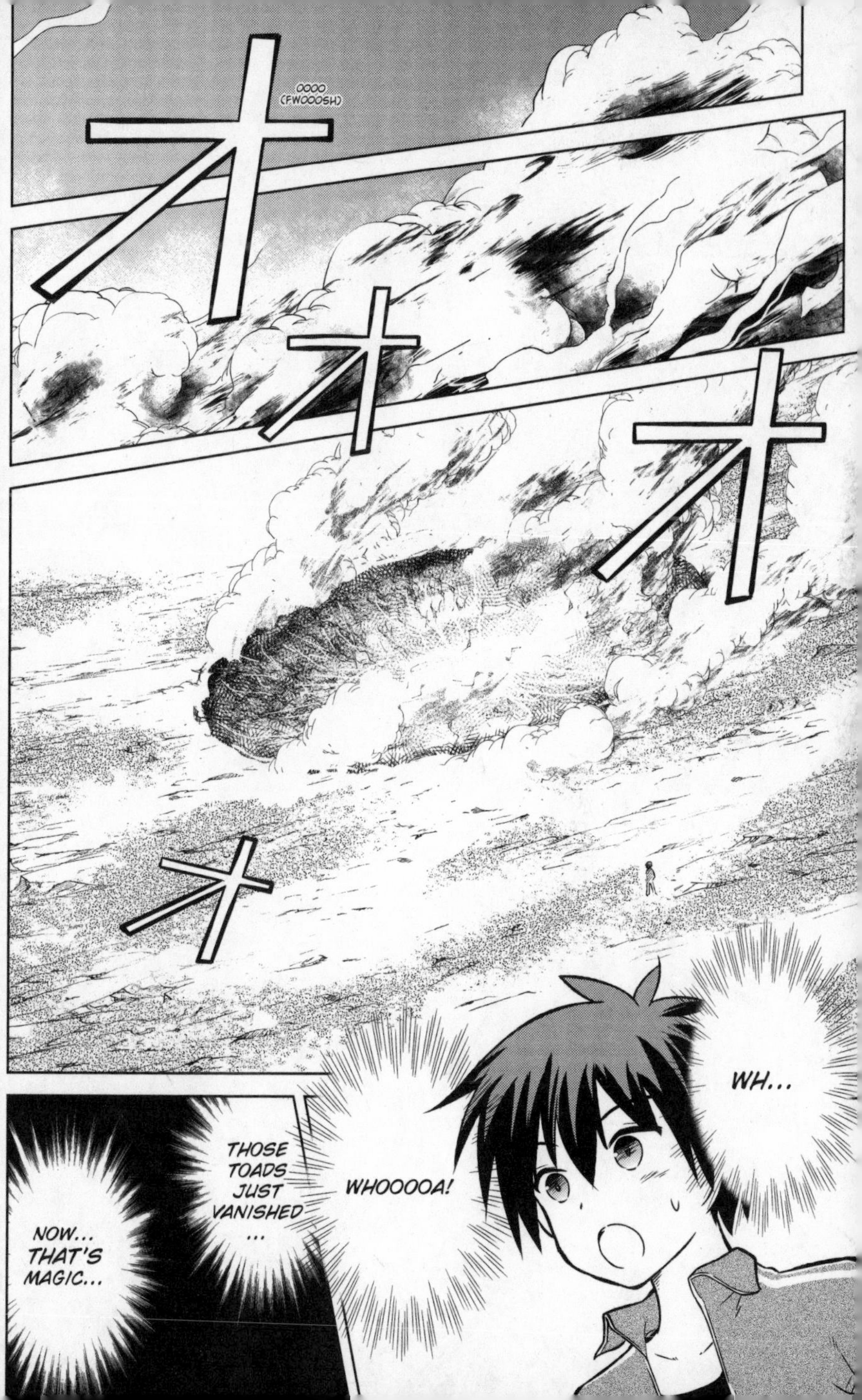
OOOO (FWOOOSH)
WH...
WHOOOOA!
THOSE TOADS JUST VANISHED...
NOW... THAT'S MAGIC...

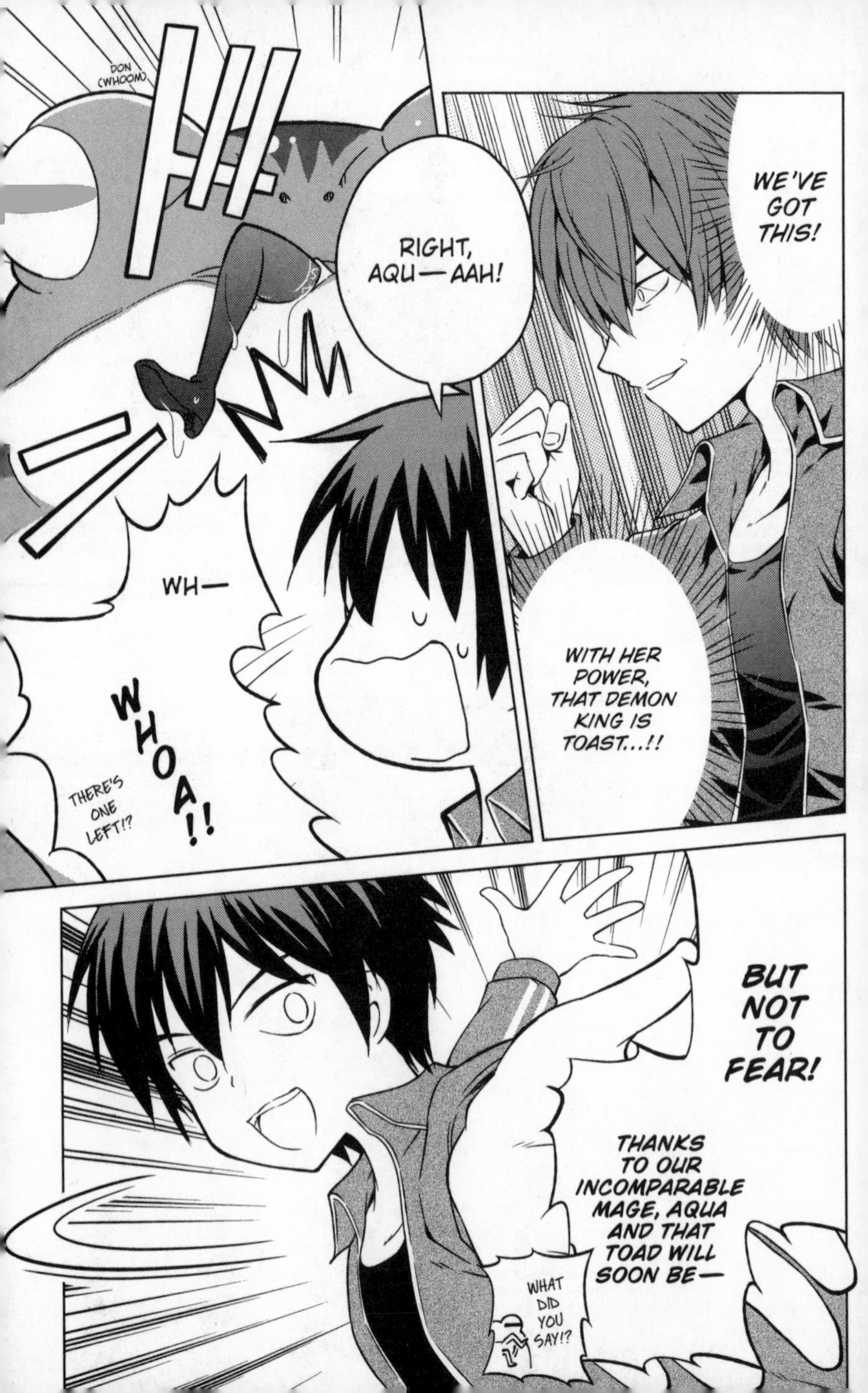
WE'VE GOT THIS!
WITH HER POWER, THAT DEMON KING IS TOAST...!!
DON (WHOOM)
RIGHT, AQU—AAH!
WH—
WHOA!!
THERE'S ONE LEFT!?
BUT NOT TO FEAR!
THANKS TO OUR INCOMPARABLE MAGE, AQUA AND THAT TOAD WILL SOON BE—
WHAT DID YOU SAY!?

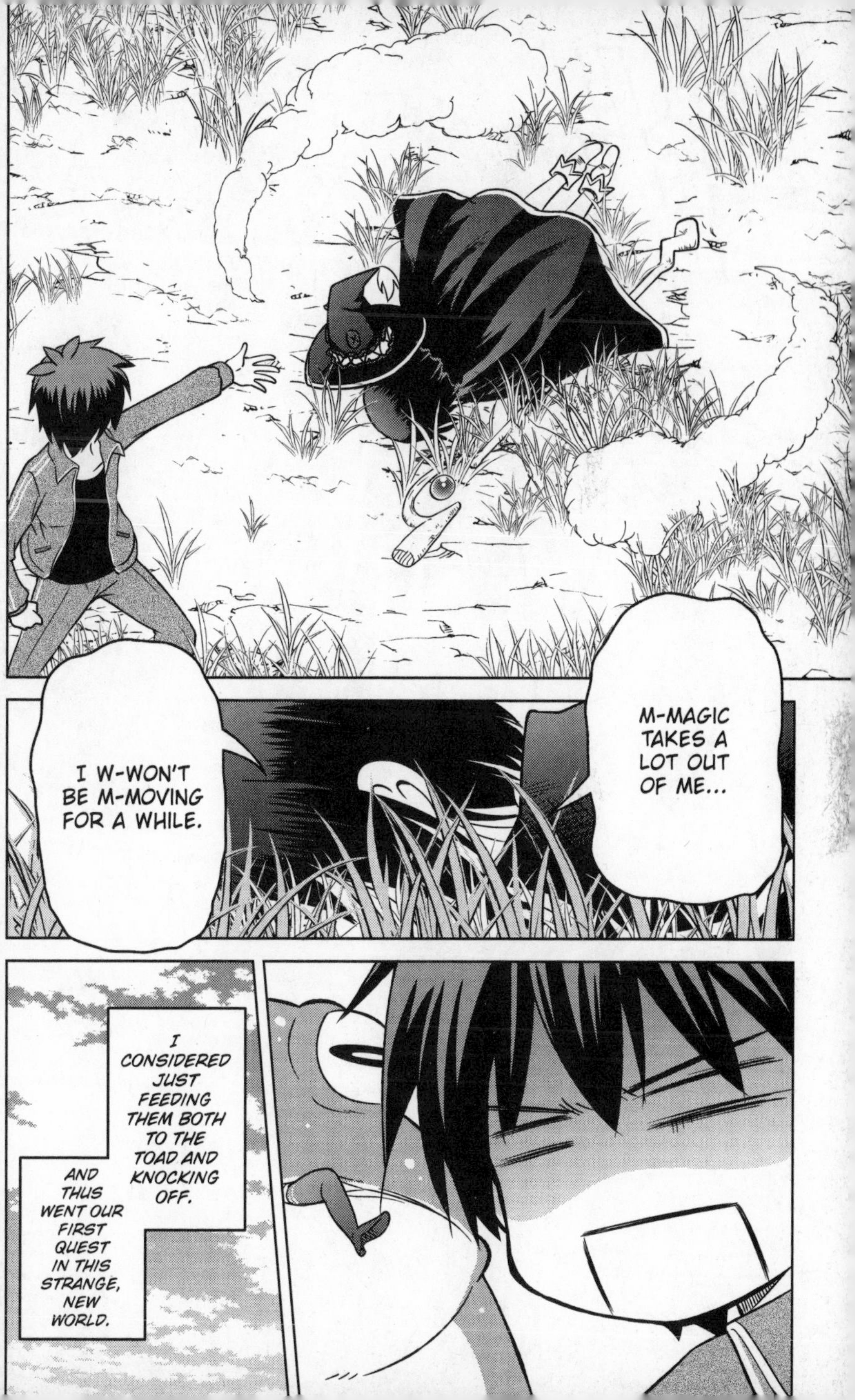
M-MAGIC TAKES A LOT OUT OF ME...
I W-WON'T BE M-MOVING FOR A WHILE.
I CONSIDERED JUST FEEDING THEM BOTH TO THE TOAD AND KNOCKING OFF.
AND THUS WENT OUR FIRST QUEST IN THIS STRANGE, NEW WORLD.

GOD'S
BLESSING
ON THIS
WONDERFUL
WORLD!
1

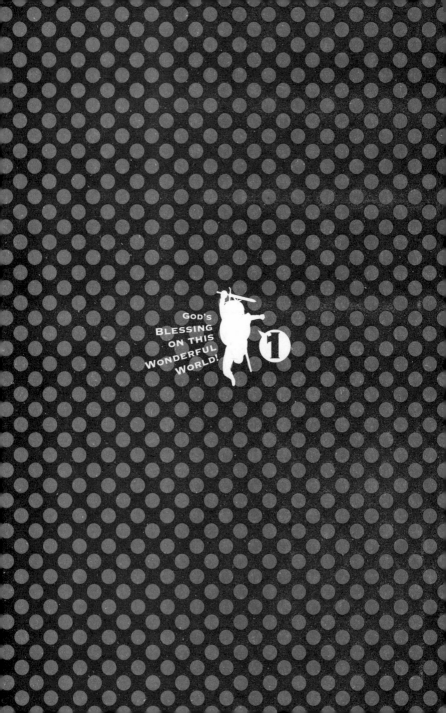

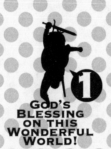

GOD'S
BLESSING
ON THIS
WONDERFUL
WORLD!

CHAPTER 2 MAY THERE BE JOY FOR THIS BEAUTIFUL EXPERT!

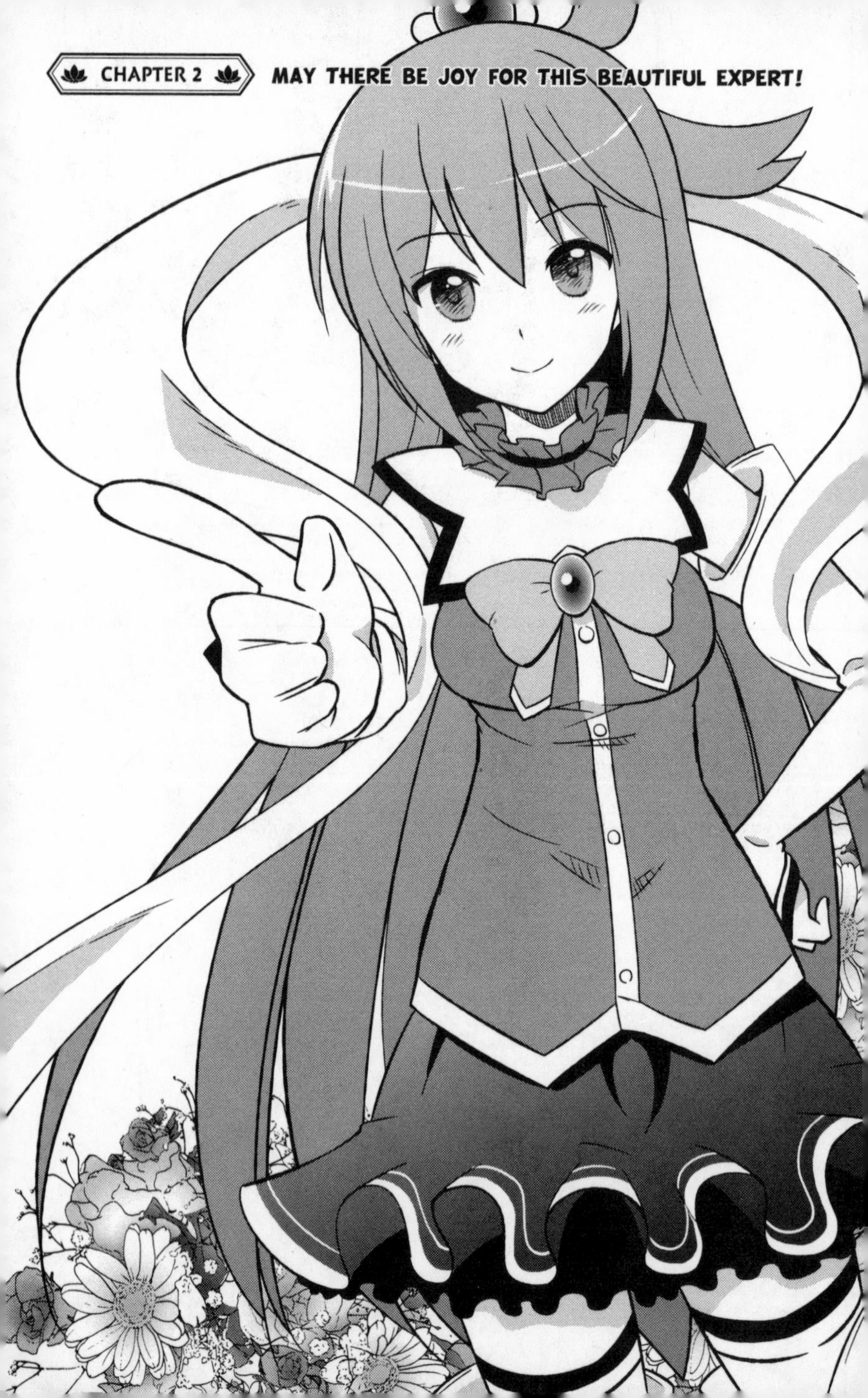

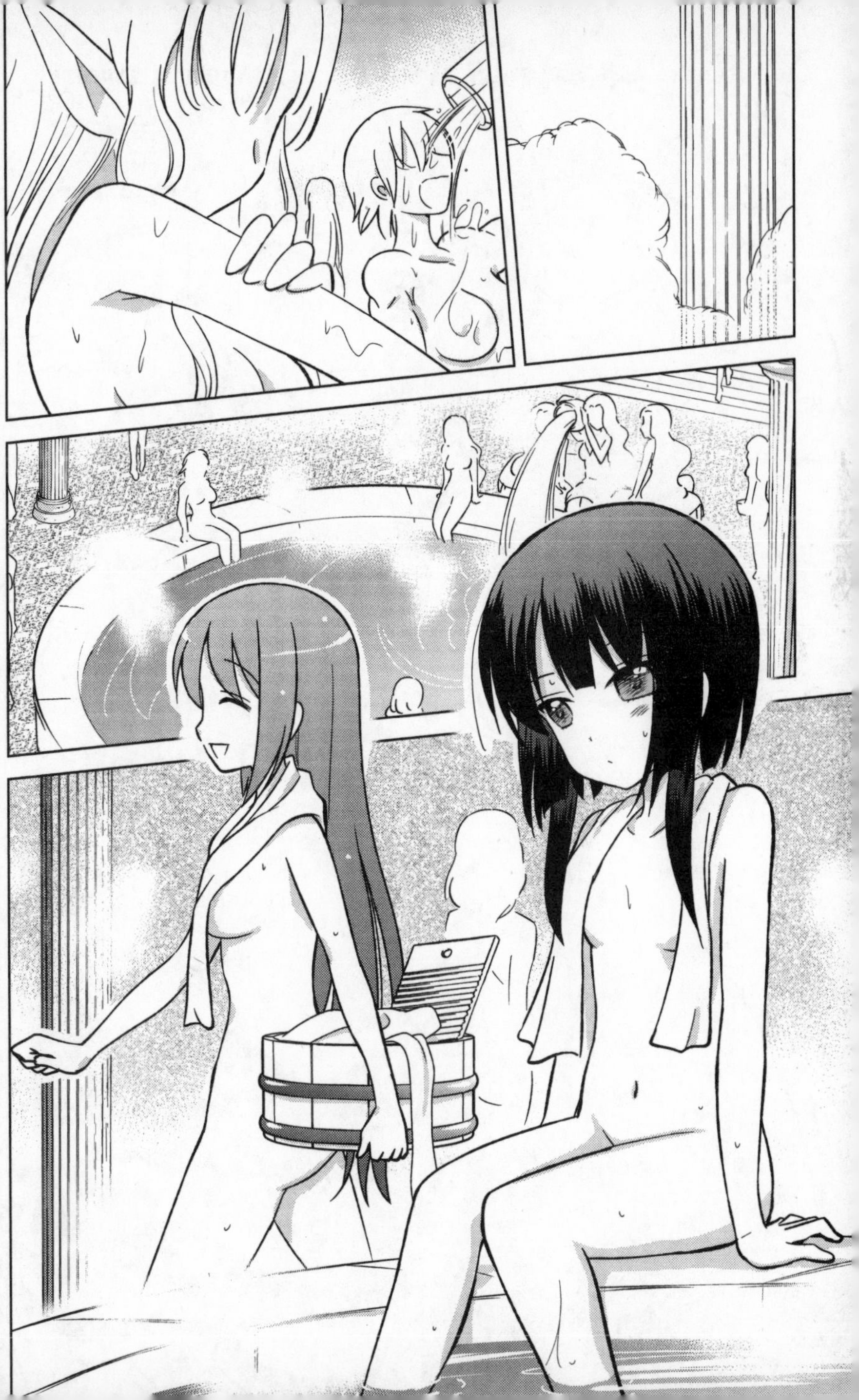

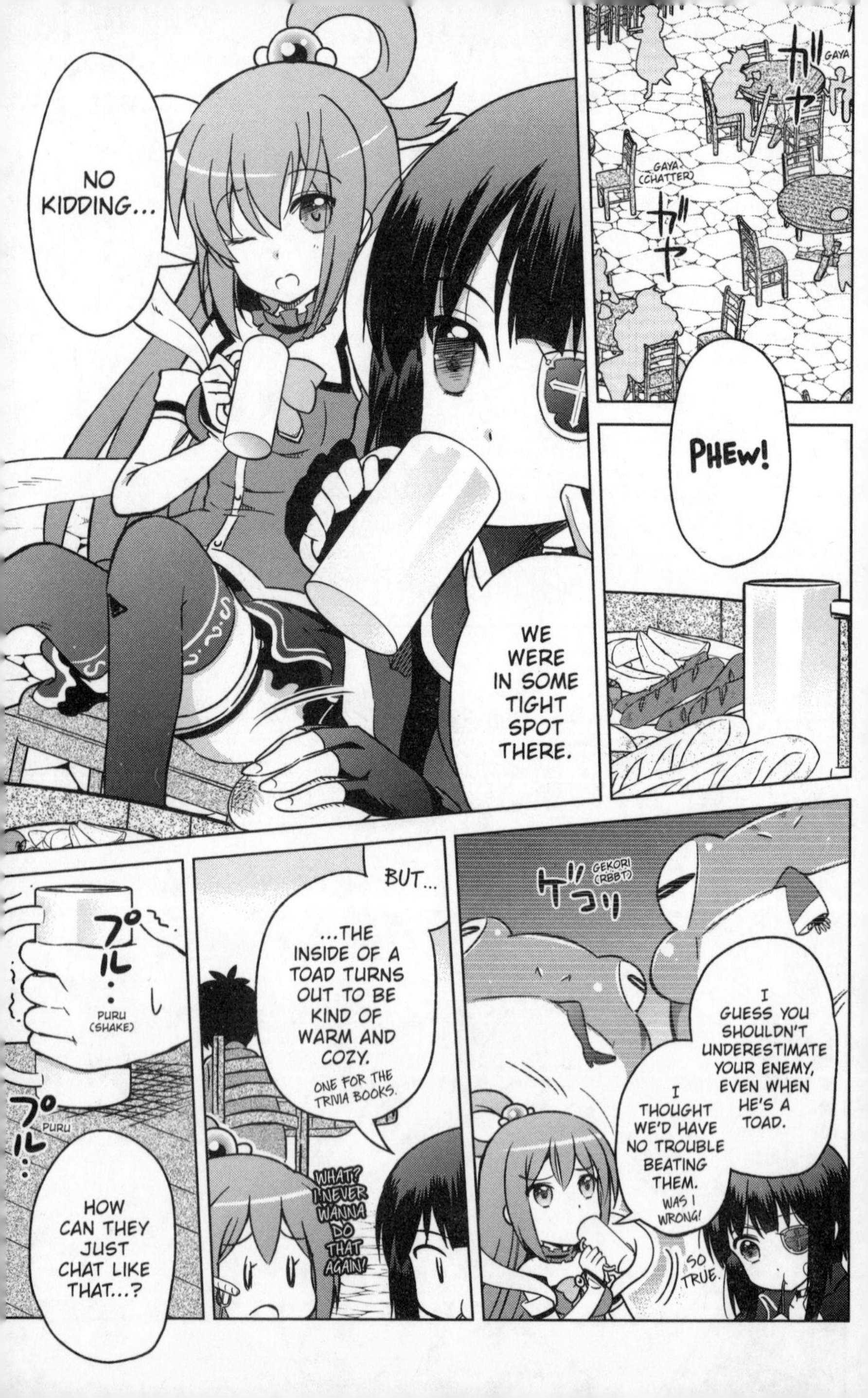
ガヤ
GAYA
ガヤ
GAYA (CHATTER)
PHEW!
WE WERE IN SOME TIGHT SPOT THERE.
NO KIDDING...
ゲコリ
GEKORI (RBBT)
I GUESS YOU SHOULDN'T UNDERESTIMATE YOUR ENEMY, EVEN WHEN HE'S A TOAD.
I THOUGHT WE'D HAVE NO TROUBLE BEATING THEM.
WAS I WRONG!
SO TRUE.
BUT...
...THE INSIDE OF A TOAD TURNS OUT TO BE KIND OF WARM AND COZY.
ONE FOR THE TRIVIA BOOKS.
WHAT? I NEVER WANNA DO THAT AGAIN!
プル
PURU (SHAKE)
プル
PURU
HOW CAN THEY JUST CHAT LIKE THAT...?

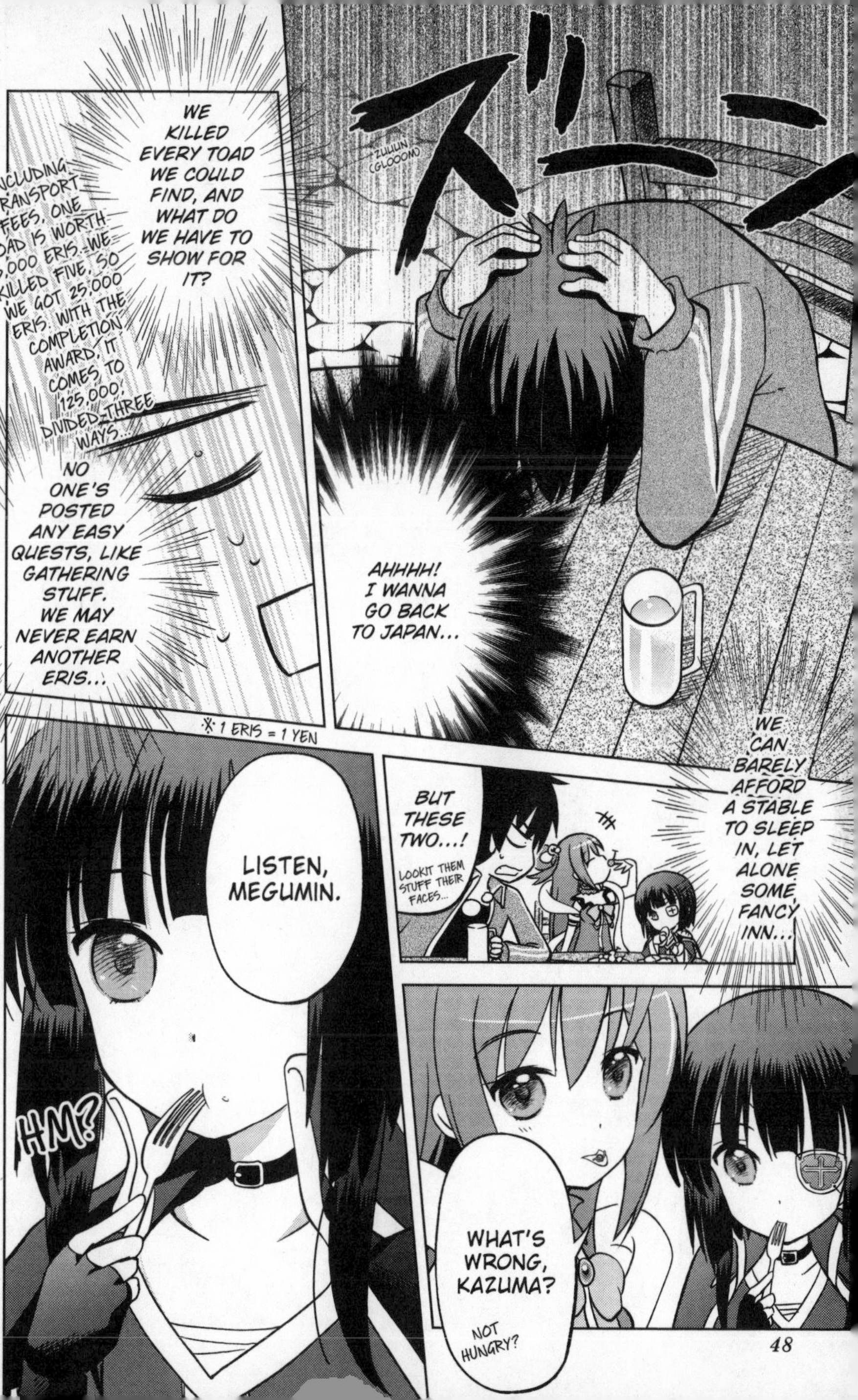
ZUUUN (GLOOOM)
AHHHH! I WANNA GO BACK TO JAPAN...
WE KILLED EVERY TOAD WE COULD FIND, AND WHAT DO WE HAVE TO SHOW FOR IT?
INCLUDING TRANSPORT FEES, ONE TOAD IS WORTH 5,000 ERIS. WE KILLED FIVE, SO WE GOT 25,000 ERIS. WITH THE COMPLETION AWARD, IT COMES TO 125,000, DIVIDED THREE WAYS...
NO ONE'S POSTED ANY EASY QUESTS, LIKE GATHERING STUFF. WE MAY NEVER EARN ANOTHER ERIS...
※1 ERIS = 1 YEN
WE CAN BARELY AFFORD A STABLE TO SLEEP IN, LET ALONE SOME FANCY INN...
BUT THESE TWO...!
LOOKIT THEM STUFF THEIR FACES...
WHAT'S WRONG, KAZUMA?
NOT HUNGRY?
LISTEN, MEGUMIN.
HM?

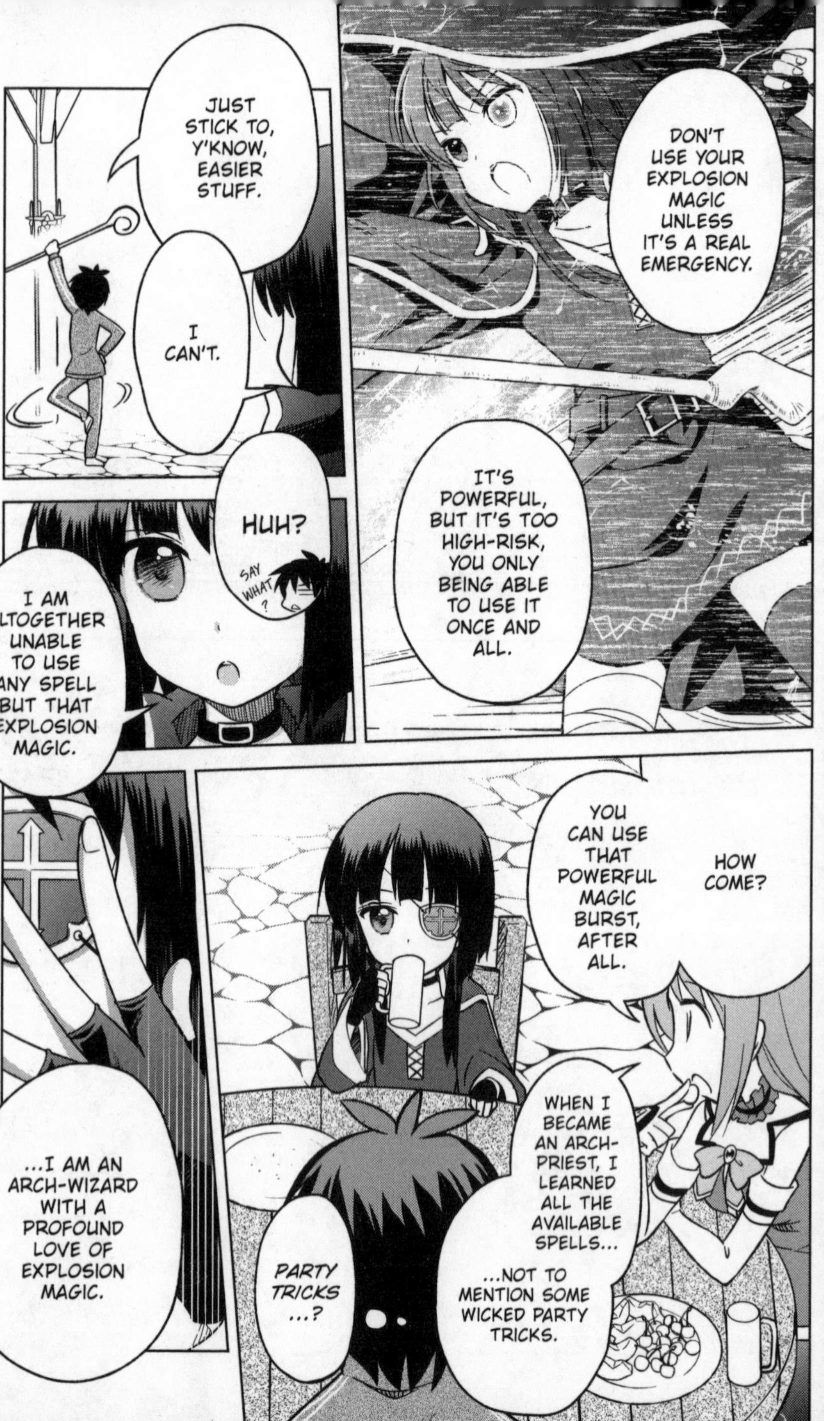
DON'T USE YOUR EXPLOSION MAGIC UNLESS IT'S A REAL EMERGENCY.
IT'S POWERFUL, BUT IT'S TOO HIGH-RISK, YOU ONLY BEING ABLE TO USE IT ONCE AND ALL.
JUST STICK TO, Y'KNOW, EASIER STUFF.
I CAN'T.
HUH?
SAY WHAT?
I AM ALTOGETHER UNABLE TO USE ANY SPELL BUT THAT EXPLOSION MAGIC.
HOW COME?
YOU CAN USE THAT POWERFUL MAGIC BURST, AFTER ALL.
WHEN I BECAME AN ARCH-PRIEST, I LEARNED ALL THE AVAILABLE SPELLS...
...NOT TO MENTION SOME WICKED PARTY TRICKS.
PARTY TRICKS ...?
...I AM AN ARCH-WIZARD WITH A PROFOUND LOVE OF EXPLOSION MAGIC.

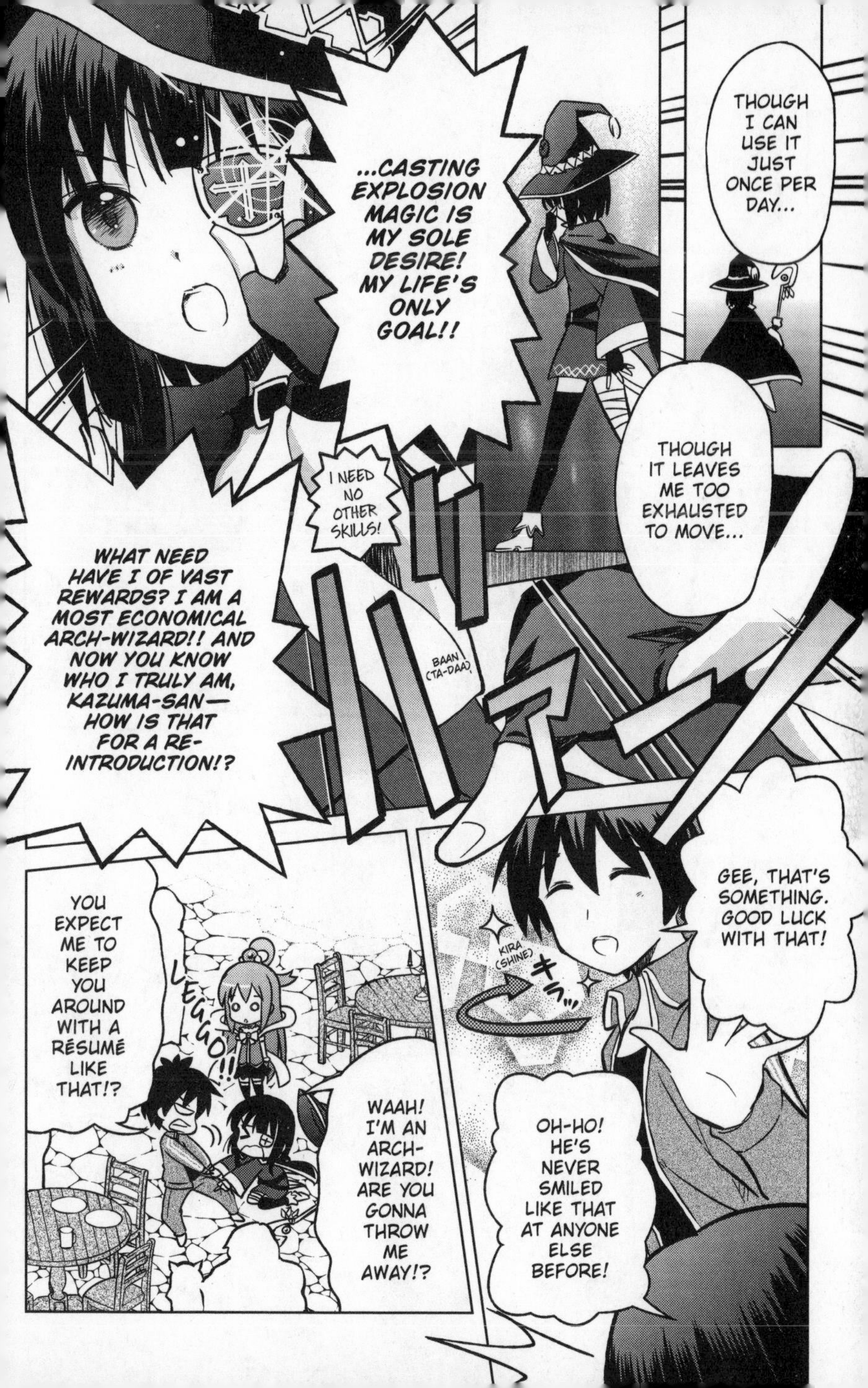
THOUGH I CAN USE IT JUST ONCE PER DAY...
THOUGH IT LEAVES ME TOO EXHAUSTED TO MOVE...
...CASTING EXPLOSION MAGIC IS MY SOLE DESIRE! MY LIFE'S ONLY GOAL!!
I NEED NO OTHER SKILLS!
WHAT NEED HAVE I OF VAST REWARDS? I AM A MOST ECONOMICAL ARCH-WIZARD!! AND NOW YOU KNOW WHO I TRULY AM, KAZUMA-SAN—HOW IS THAT FOR A RE-INTRODUCTION!?
BAAN (TA-DAA)
GEE, THAT'S SOMETHING. GOOD LUCK WITH THAT!
KIRA (SHINE)
キラッ
OH-HO! HE'S NEVER SMILED LIKE THAT AT ANYONE ELSE BEFORE!
YOU EXPECT ME TO KEEP YOU AROUND WITH A RÉSUMÉ LIKE THAT!?
LEGGO!!
WAAH! I'M AN ARCH-WIZARD! ARE YOU GONNA THROW ME AWAY!?

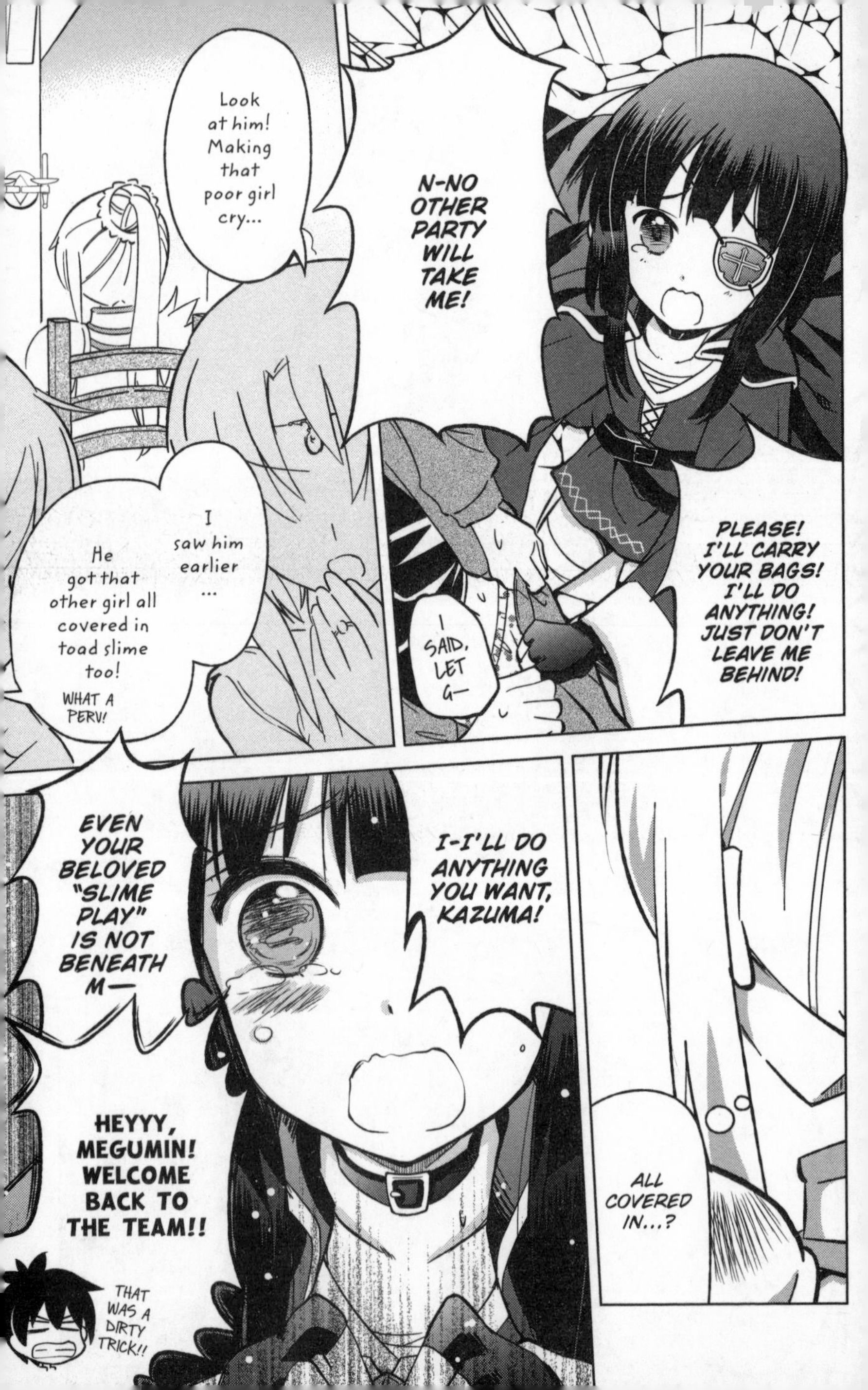
N-NO OTHER PARTY WILL TAKE ME!
PLEASE! I'LL CARRY YOUR BAGS! I'LL DO ANYTHING! JUST DON'T LEAVE ME BEHIND!
I SAID, LET G—
Look at him! Making that poor girl cry...
I saw him earlier ...
He got that other girl all covered in toad slime too!
WHAT A PERV!
ALL COVERED IN...?
I-I'LL DO ANYTHING YOU WANT, KAZUMA!
EVEN YOUR BELOVED "SLIME PLAY" IS NOT BENEATH M—
HEYYY, MEGUMIN! WELCOME BACK TO THE TEAM!!
THAT WAS A DIRTY TRICK!!

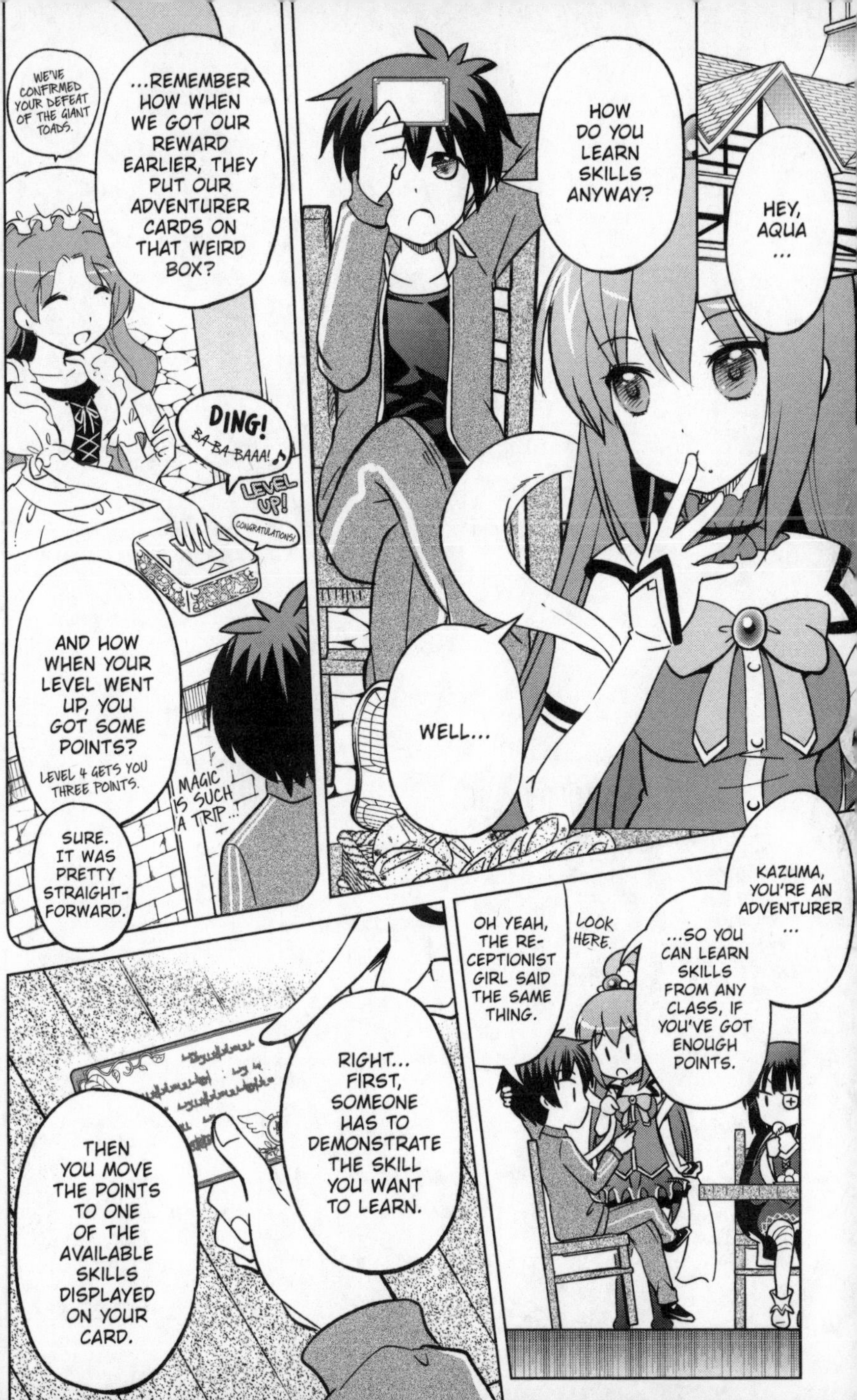
HEY, AQUA ...
HOW DO YOU LEARN SKILLS ANYWAY?
WELL...
...REMEMBER HOW WHEN WE GOT OUR REWARD EARLIER, THEY PUT OUR ADVENTURER CARDS ON THAT WEIRD BOX?
WE'VE CONFIRMED YOUR DEFEAT OF THE GIANT TOADS.
DING!
BA-BA-BAAA! ♪
LEVEL UP!
CONGRATULATIONS!
AND HOW WHEN YOUR LEVEL WENT UP, YOU GOT SOME POINTS?
LEVEL 4 GETS YOU THREE POINTS.
SURE. IT WAS PRETTY STRAIGHT-FORWARD.
MAGIC IS SUCH A TRIP...
KAZUMA, YOU'RE AN ADVENTURER ...
...SO YOU CAN LEARN SKILLS FROM ANY CLASS, IF YOU'VE GOT ENOUGH POINTS.
LOOK HERE.
OH YEAH, THE RE-CEPTIONIST GIRL SAID THE SAME THING.
RIGHT... FIRST, SOMEONE HAS TO DEMONSTRATE THE SKILL YOU WANT TO LEARN.
THEN YOU MOVE THE POINTS TO ONE OF THE AVAILABLE SKILLS DISPLAYED ON YOUR CARD.

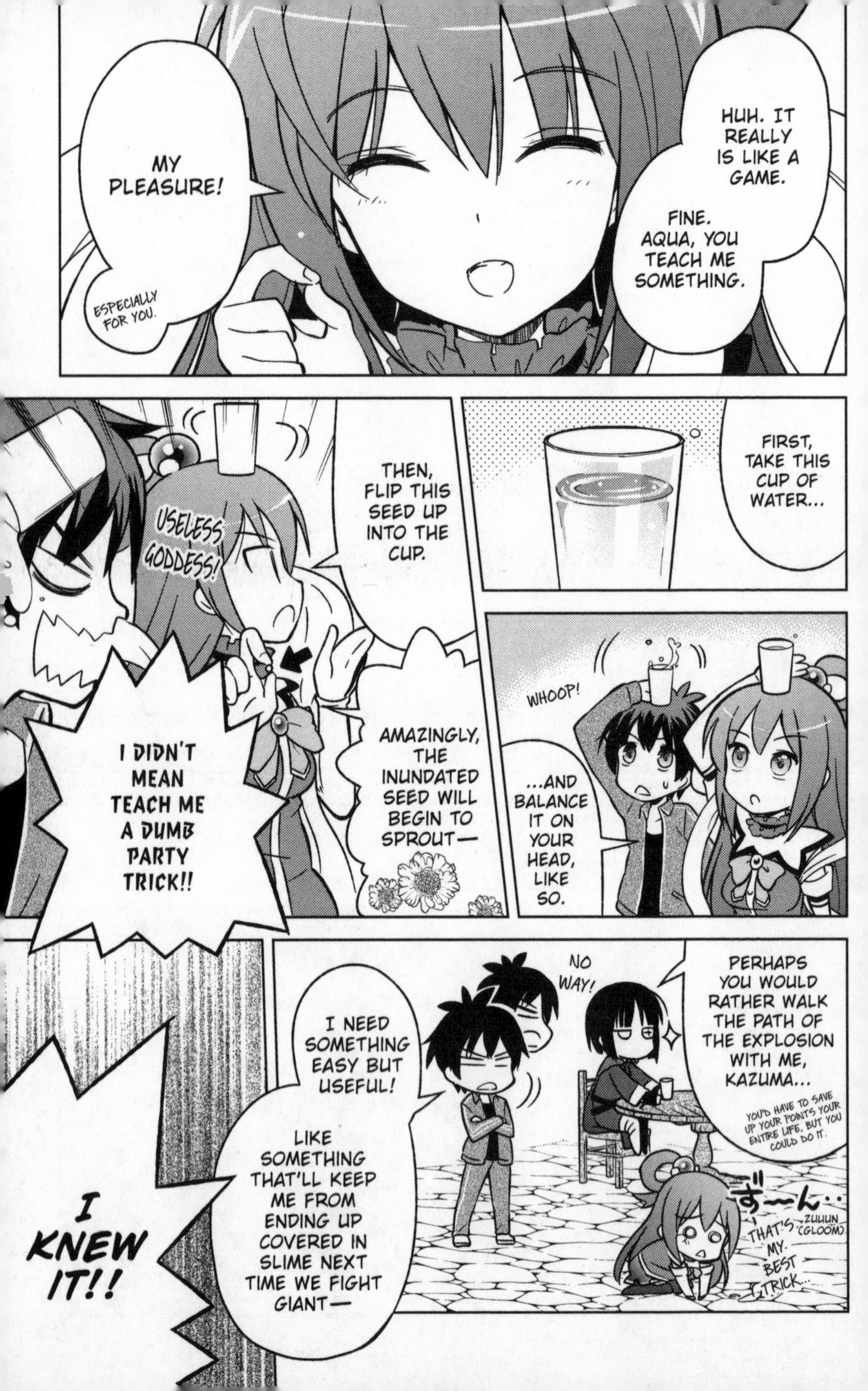
HUH. IT REALLY IS LIKE A GAME.
FINE. AQUA, YOU TEACH ME SOMETHING.
MY PLEASURE!
ESPECIALLY FOR YOU.
FIRST, TAKE THIS CUP OF WATER...
WHOOP!
...AND BALANCE IT ON YOUR HEAD, LIKE SO.
THEN, FLIP THIS SEED UP INTO THE CUP.
AMAZINGLY, THE INUNDATED SEED WILL BEGIN TO SPROUT—
USELESS GODDESS!
I DIDN'T MEAN TEACH ME A DUMB PARTY TRICK!!
I NEED SOMETHING EASY BUT USEFUL!
LIKE SOMETHING THAT'LL KEEP ME FROM ENDING UP COVERED IN SLIME NEXT TIME WE FIGHT GIANT—
PERHAPS YOU WOULD RATHER WALK THE PATH OF THE EXPLOSION WITH ME, KAZUMA...
YOU'D HAVE TO SAVE UP YOUR POINTS YOUR ENTIRE LIFE, BUT YOU COULD DO IT.
NO WAY!
ずーん‥
ZUUUN (GLOOM)
THAT'S MY BEST TRICK...
I KNEW IT!!

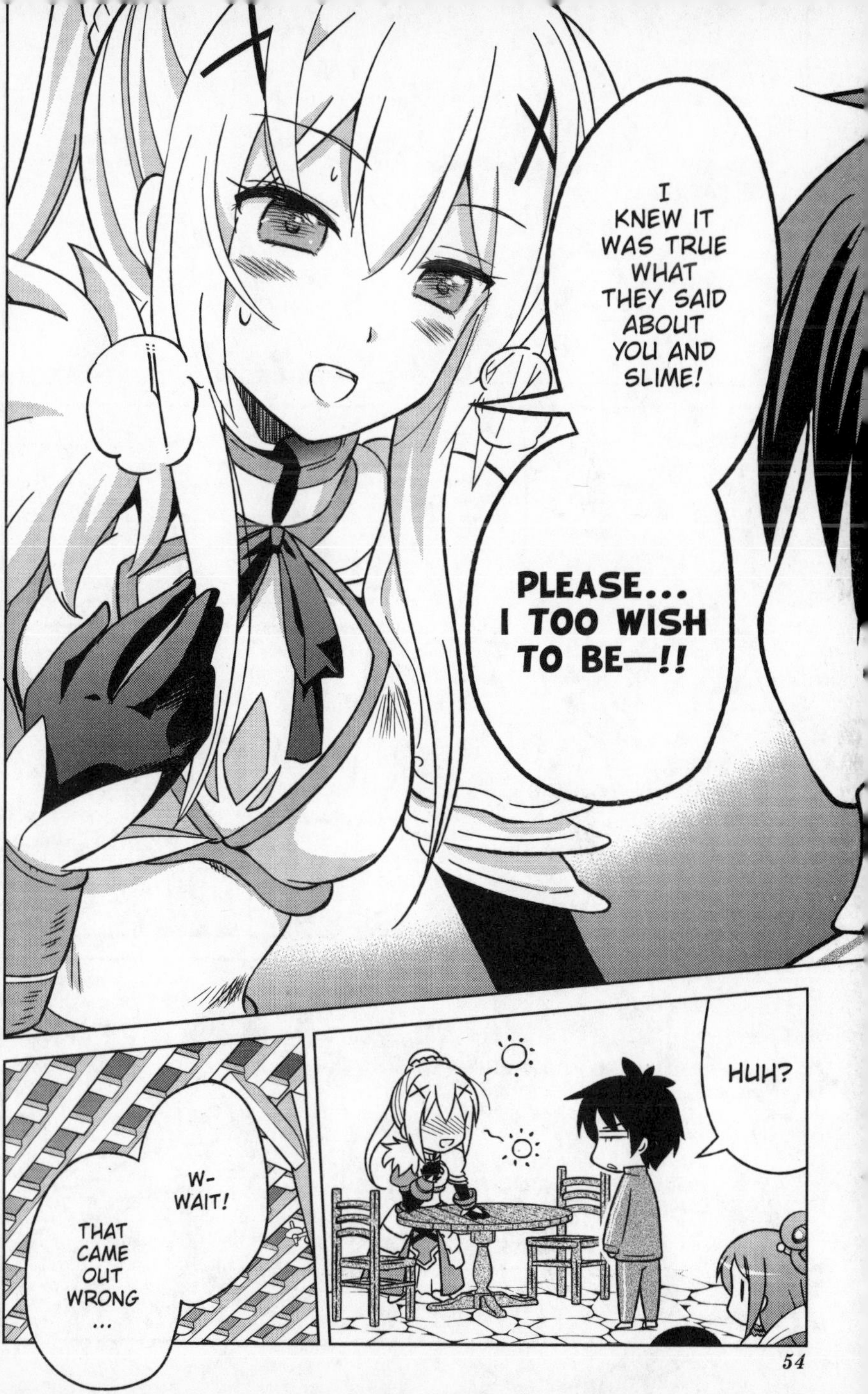

I KNEW IT WAS TRUE WHAT THEY SAID ABOUT YOU AND SLIME!
PLEASE... I TOO WISH TO BE—!!
HUH?
W-WAIT!
THAT CAME OUT WRONG ...

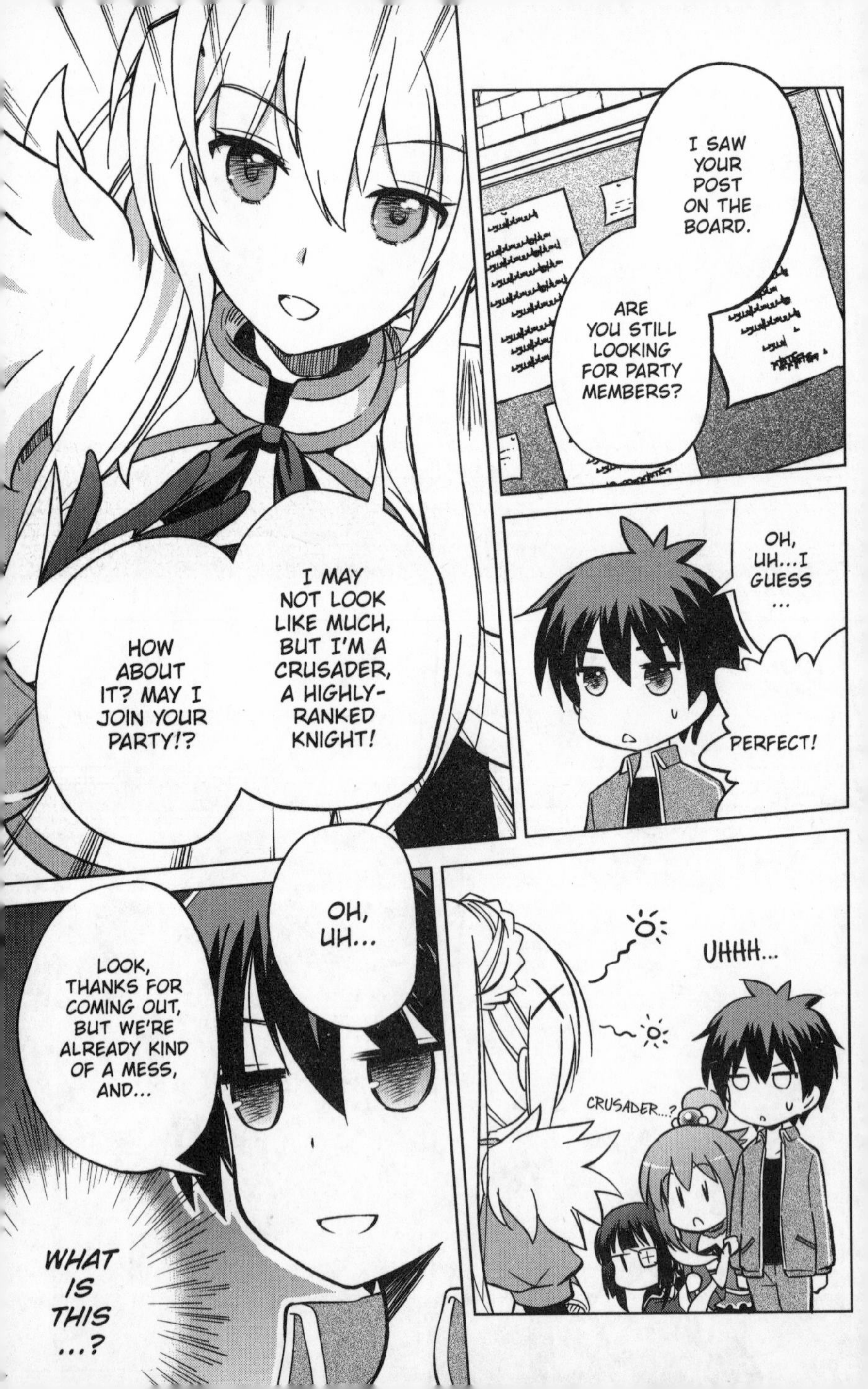
I SAW YOUR POST ON THE BOARD.
ARE YOU STILL LOOKING FOR PARTY MEMBERS?
OH, UH...I GUESS...
PERFECT!
I MAY NOT LOOK LIKE MUCH, BUT I'M A CRUSADER, A HIGHLY-RANKED KNIGHT!
HOW ABOUT IT? MAY I JOIN YOUR PARTY!?
UHHH...
CRUSADER...?
OH, UH...
LOOK, THANKS FOR COMING OUT, BUT WE'RE ALREADY KIND OF A MESS, AND...
WHAT IS THIS ...?

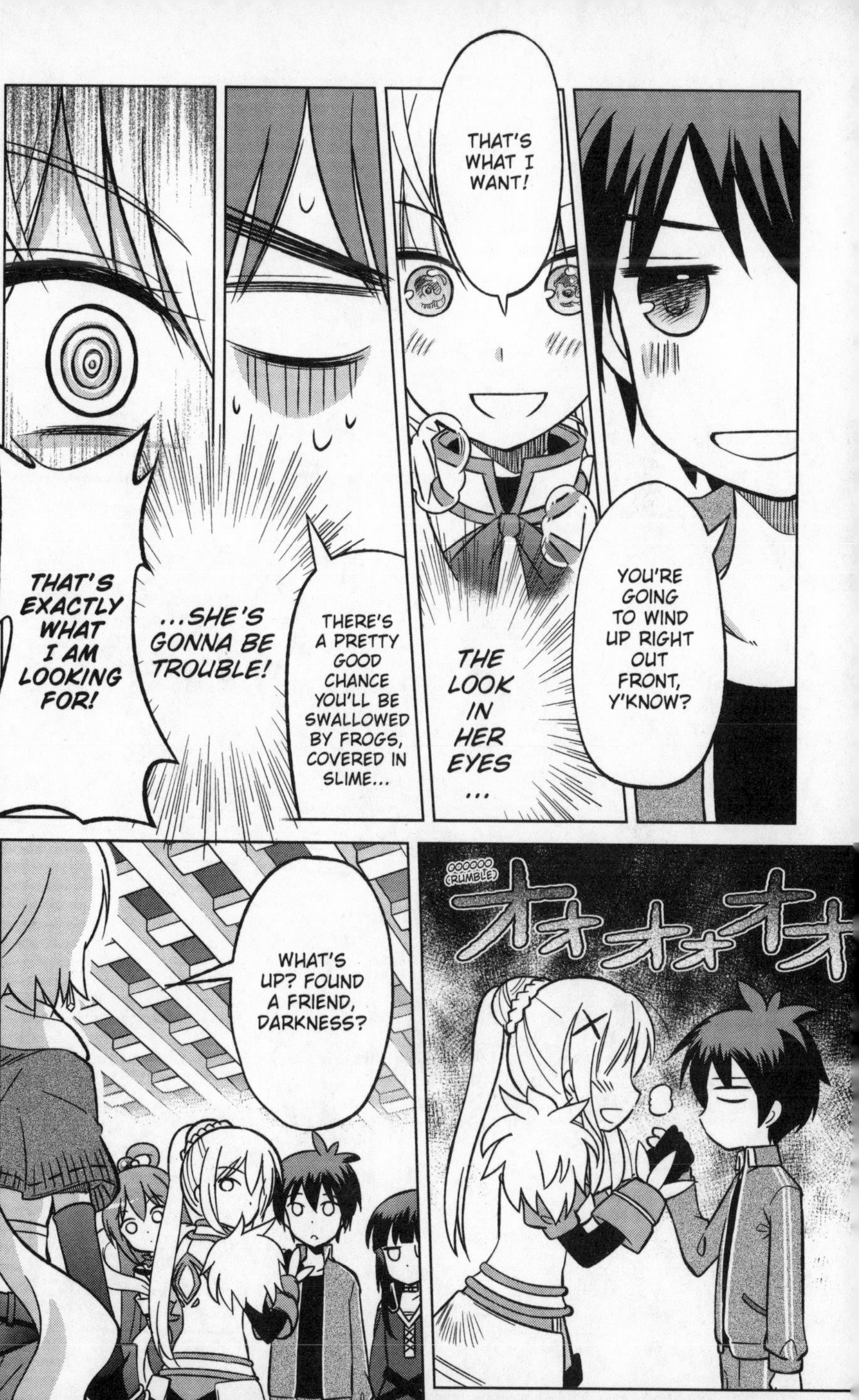
YOU'RE GOING TO WIND UP RIGHT OUT FRONT, Y'KNOW?
THAT'S WHAT I WANT!
THE LOOK IN HER EYES...
THERE'S A PRETTY GOOD CHANCE YOU'LL BE SWALLOWED BY FROGS, COVERED IN SLIME...
...SHE'S GONNA BE TROUBLE!
THAT'S EXACTLY WHAT I AM LOOKING FOR!
OOOOOO (RUMBLE)
オォオォオオ
WHAT'S UP? FOUND A FRIEND, DARKNESS?

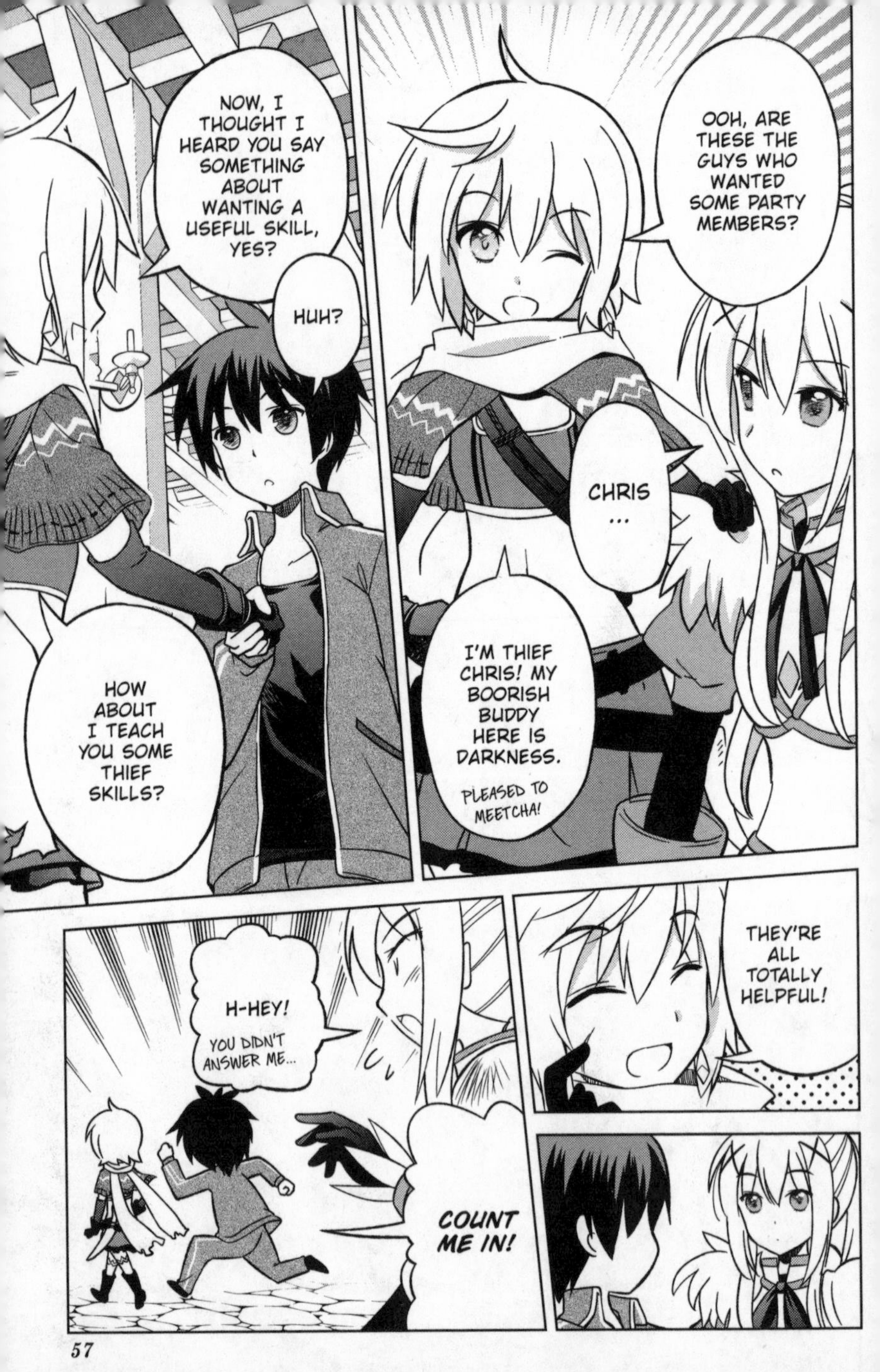

OOH, ARE THESE THE GUYS WHO WANTED SOME PARTY MEMBERS?
CHRIS...
I'M THIEF CHRIS! MY BOORISH BUDDY HERE IS DARKNESS.
PLEASED TO MEETCHA!
NOW, I THOUGHT I HEARD YOU SAY SOMETHING ABOUT WANTING A USEFUL SKILL, YES?
HUH?
HOW ABOUT I TEACH YOU SOME THIEF SKILLS?
THEY'RE ALL TOTALLY HELPFUL!
H-HEY!
YOU DIDN'T ANSWER ME...
COUNT ME IN!

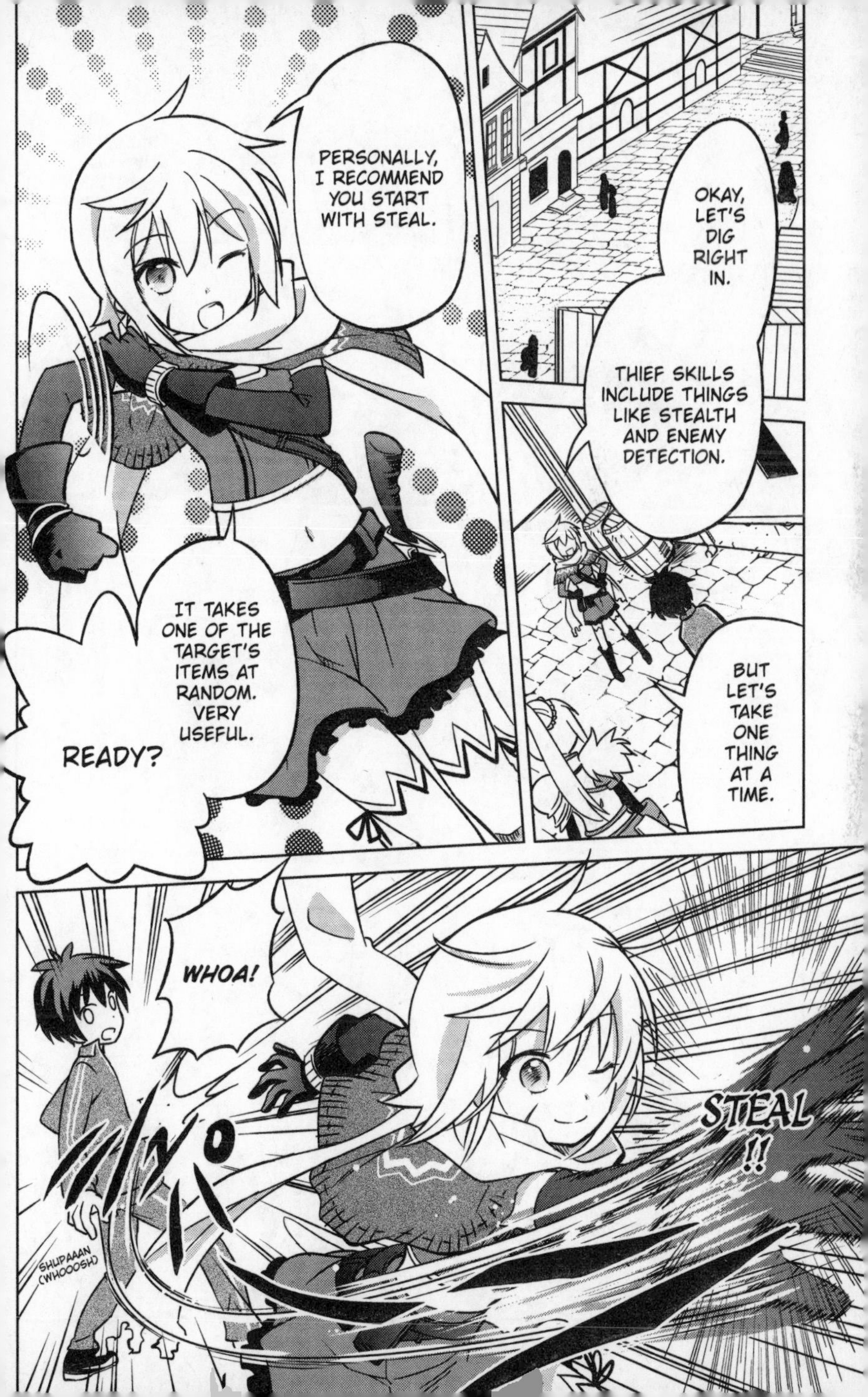
OKAY, LET'S DIG RIGHT IN.
THIEF SKILLS INCLUDE THINGS LIKE STEALTH AND ENEMY DETECTION.
BUT LET'S TAKE ONE THING AT A TIME.
PERSONALLY, I RECOMMEND YOU START WITH STEAL.
IT TAKES ONE OF THE TARGET'S ITEMS AT RANDOM. VERY USEFUL.
READY?
STEAL!!
WHOA!
SHUPAAAN (WHOOOSH)

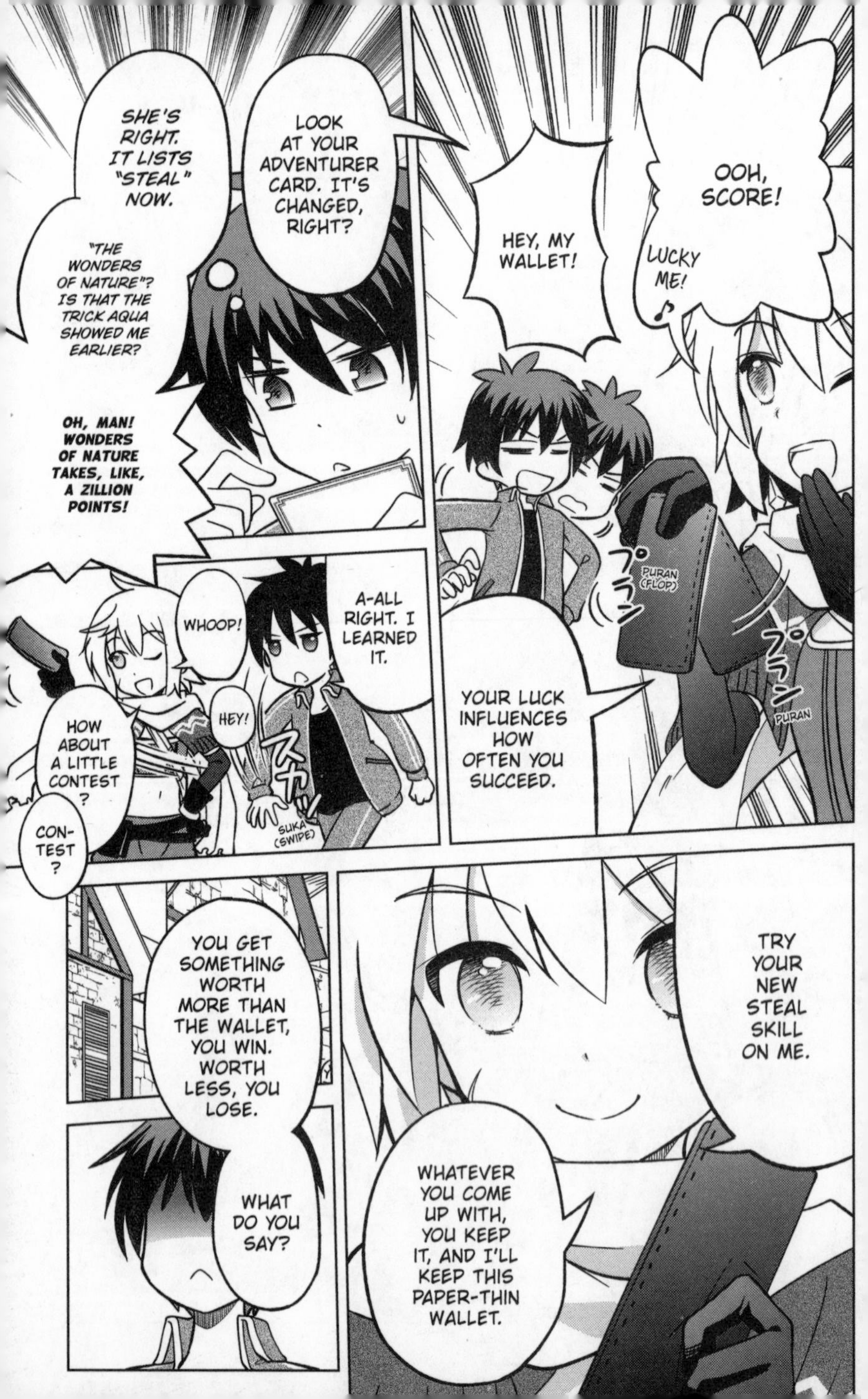
OOH, SCORE!
LUCKY ME! ♪
HEY, MY WALLET!
PURAN (FLOP)
PURAN
YOUR LUCK INFLUENCES HOW OFTEN YOU SUCCEED.
LOOK AT YOUR ADVENTURER CARD. IT'S CHANGED, RIGHT?
SHE'S RIGHT. IT LISTS "STEAL" NOW.
"THE WONDERS OF NATURE"? IS THAT THE TRICK AQUA SHOWED ME EARLIER?
OH, MAN! WONDERS OF NATURE TAKES, LIKE, A ZILLION POINTS!
A-ALL RIGHT. I LEARNED IT.
WHOOP!
HEY!
SUKA (SWIPE)
HOW ABOUT A LITTLE CONTEST?
CON-TEST?
TRY YOUR NEW STEAL SKILL ON ME.
WHATEVER YOU COME UP WITH, YOU KEEP IT, AND I'LL KEEP THIS PAPER-THIN WALLET.
YOU GET SOMETHING WORTH MORE THAN THE WALLET, YOU WIN. WORTH LESS, YOU LOSE.
WHAT DO YOU SAY?

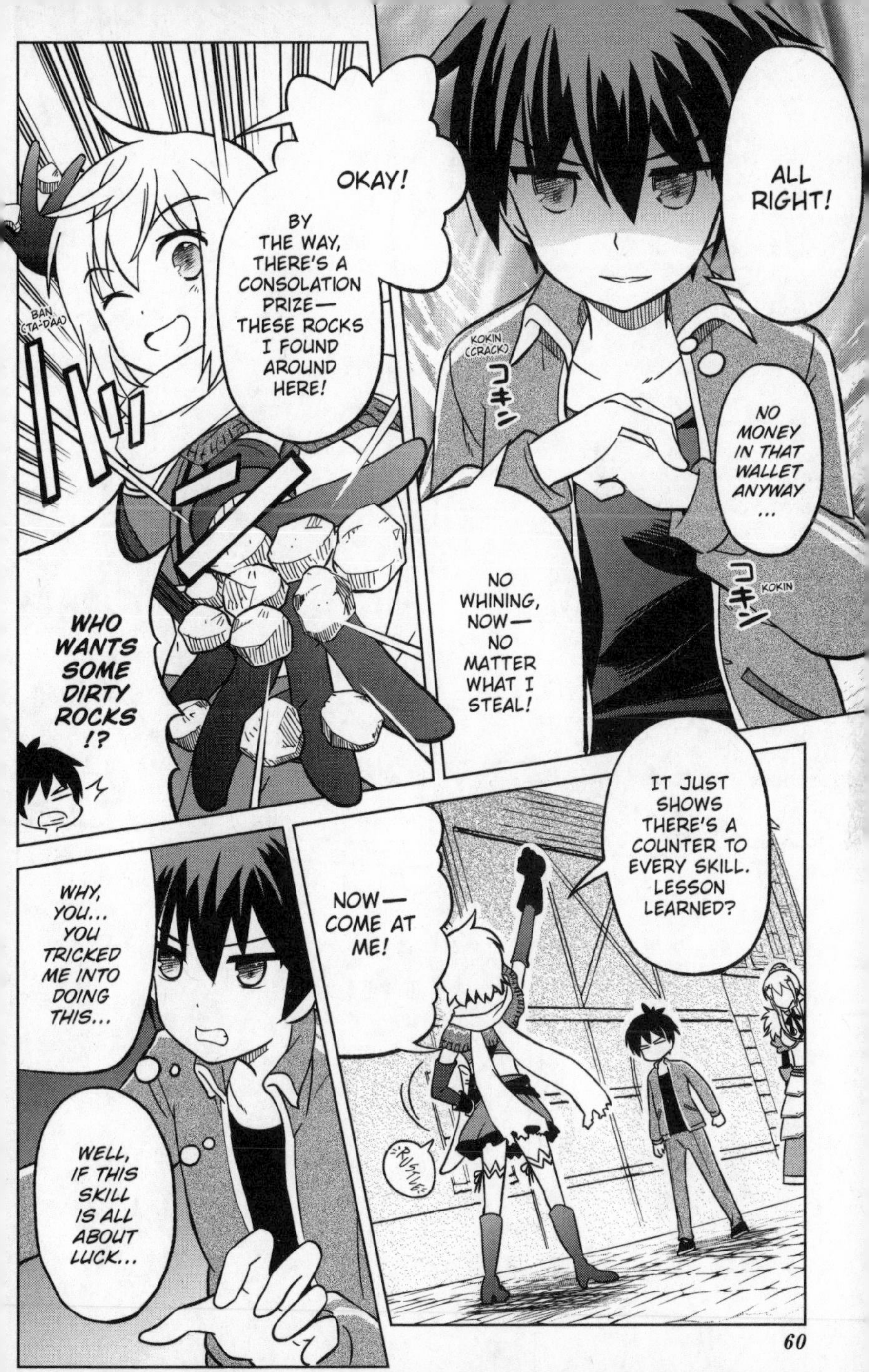
ALL RIGHT!
KOKIN (CRACK)
NO MONEY IN THAT WALLET ANYWAY...
KOKIN
NO WHINING, NOW— NO MATTER WHAT I STEAL!
OKAY!
BY THE WAY, THERE'S A CONSOLATION PRIZE— THESE ROCKS I FOUND AROUND HERE!
BAN (TA-DAA)
WHO WANTS SOME DIRTY ROCKS !?
IT JUST SHOWS THERE'S A COUNTER TO EVERY SKILL. LESSON LEARNED?
NOW— COME AT ME!
RUSTLE
WHY, YOU... YOU TRICKED ME INTO DOING THIS...
WELL, IF THIS SKILL IS ALL ABOUT LUCK...

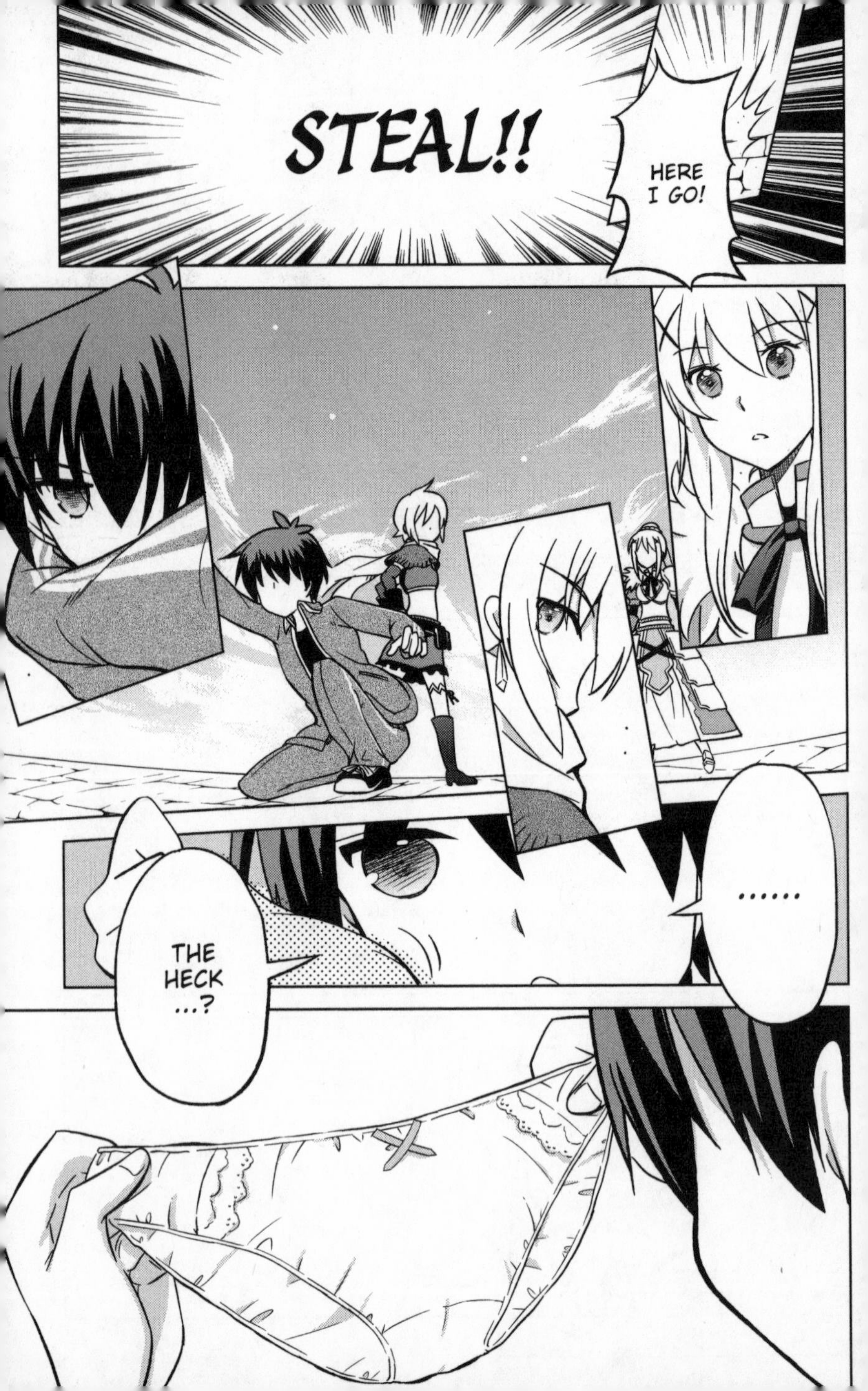
HERE I GO!
STEAL!!
......
THE HECK ...?

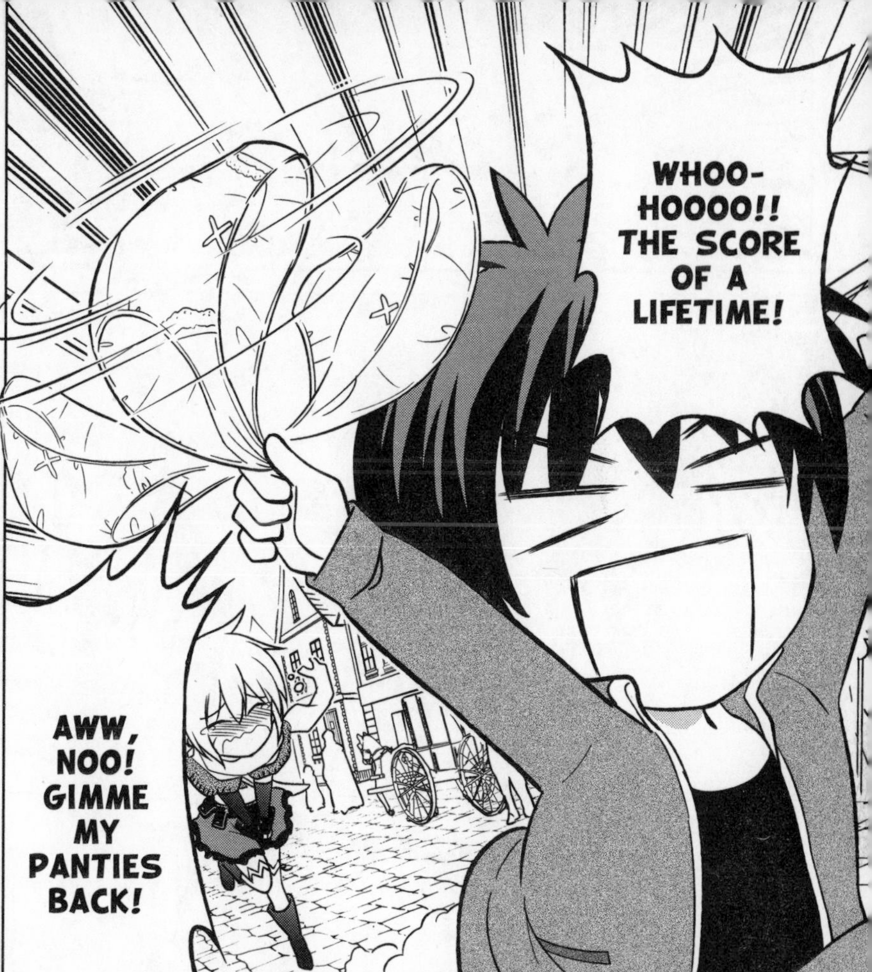
WHOO-HOOOO!! THE SCORE OF A LIFETIME!
AWW, NOO! GIMME MY PANTIES BACK!

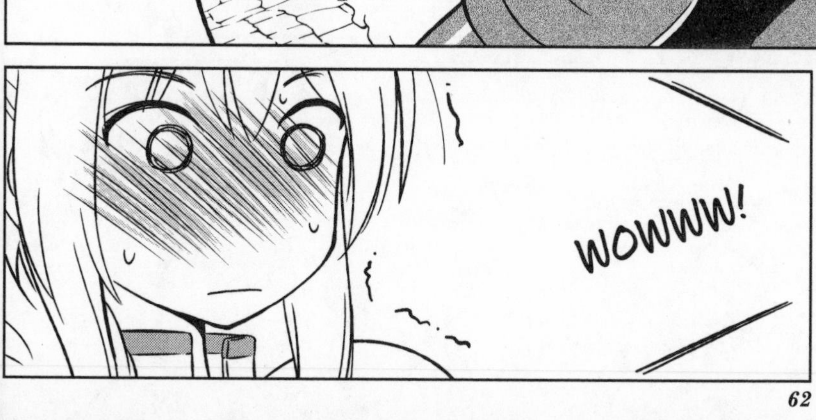
WOWWW!

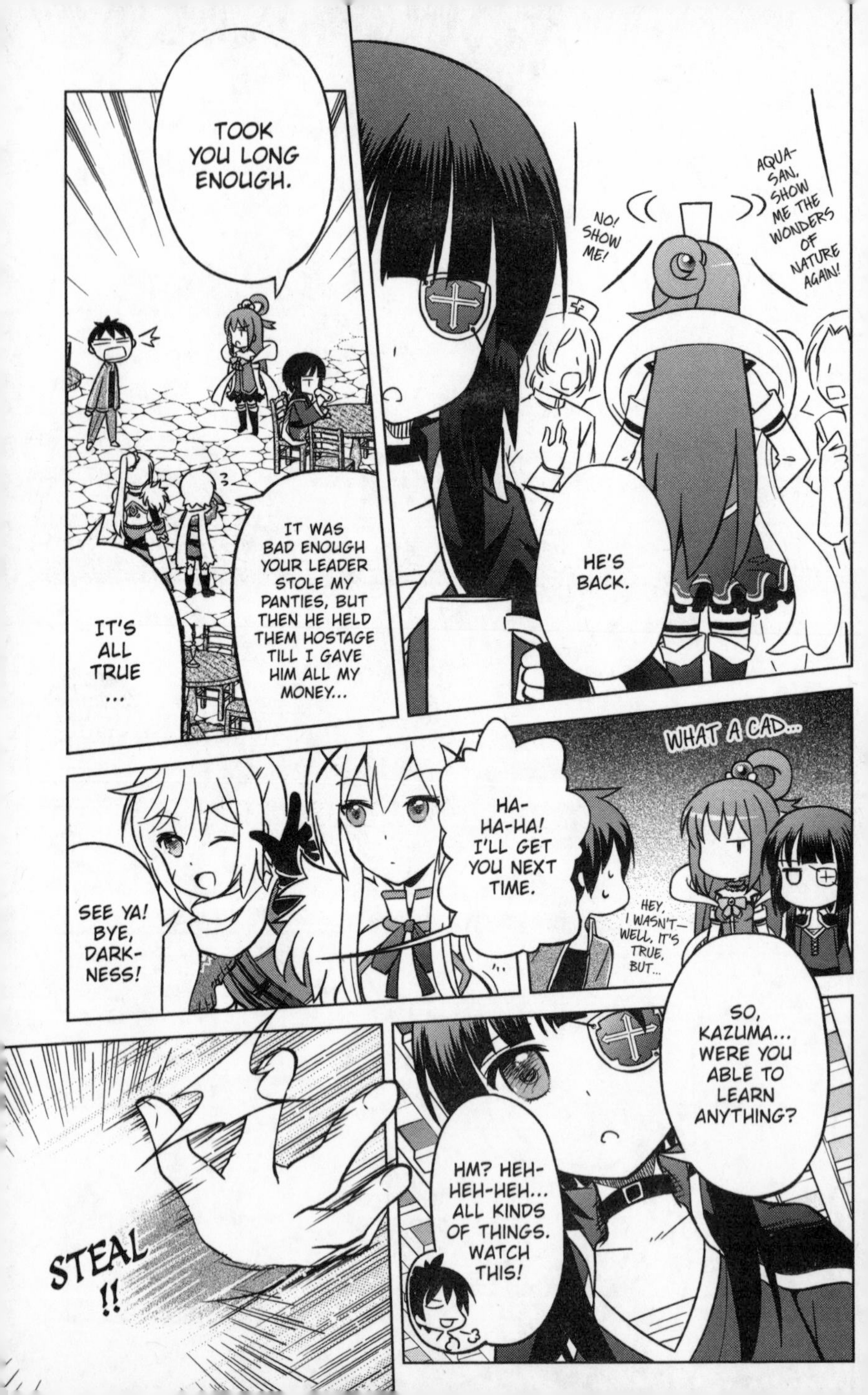
AQUA-SAN, SHOW ME THE WONDERS OF NATURE AGAIN!
NO! SHOW ME!
HE'S BACK.
TOOK YOU LONG ENOUGH.
IT WAS BAD ENOUGH YOUR LEADER STOLE MY PANTIES, BUT THEN HE HELD THEM HOSTAGE TILL I GAVE HIM ALL MY MONEY...
IT'S ALL TRUE...
WHAT A CAD...
HEY, I WASN'T— WELL, IT'S TRUE, BUT...
HA-HA-HA! I'LL GET YOU NEXT TIME.
SEE YA! BYE, DARKNESS!
SO, KAZUMA... WERE YOU ABLE TO LEARN ANYTHING?
HM? HEH-HEH-HEH... ALL KINDS OF THINGS. WATCH THIS!
STEAL!!

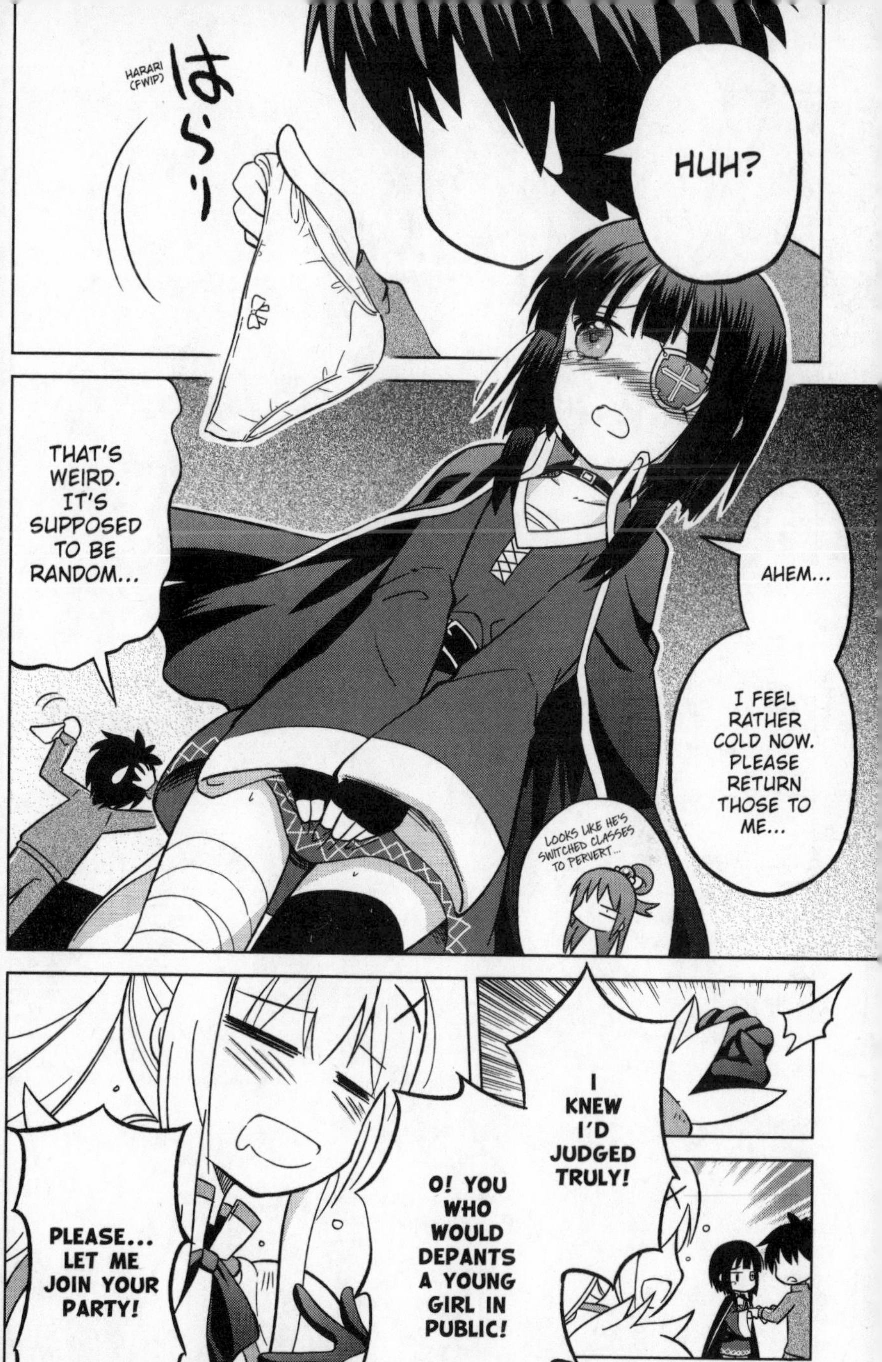
HUH?
HARARI (FWIP)
はらり
AHEM...
I FEEL RATHER COLD NOW. PLEASE RETURN THOSE TO ME...
LOOKS LIKE HE'S SWITCHED CLASSES TO PERVERT...
THAT'S WEIRD. IT'S SUPPOSED TO BE RANDOM...
I KNEW I'D JUDGED TRULY!
O! YOU WHO WOULD DEPANTS A YOUNG GIRL IN PUBLIC!
PLEASE... LET ME JOIN YOUR PARTY!

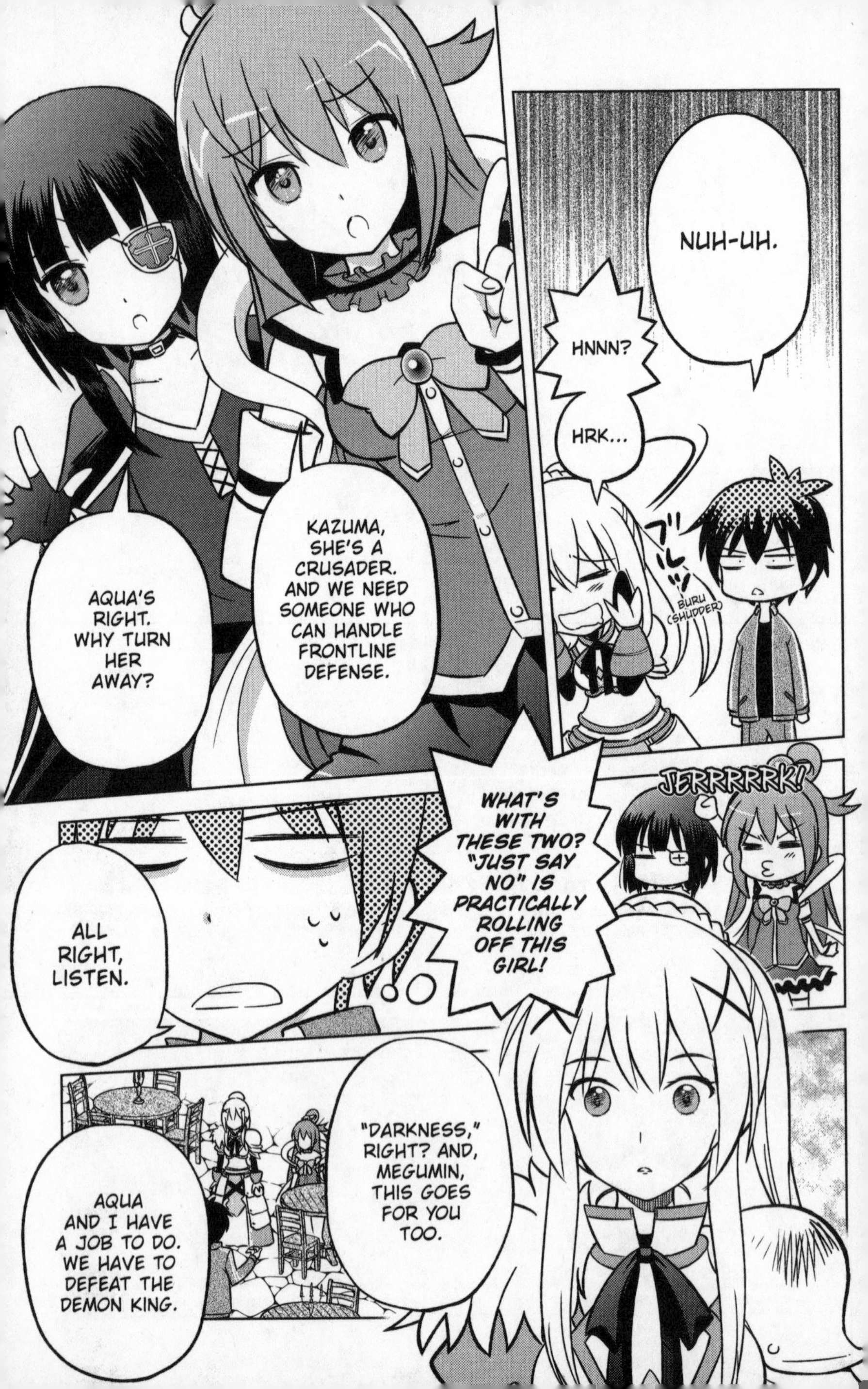
NUH-UH.
HNNN?
HRK...
ブルッ
BURU (SHUDDER)
KAZUMA, SHE'S A CRUSADER. AND WE NEED SOMEONE WHO CAN HANDLE FRONTLINE DEFENSE.
AQUA'S RIGHT. WHY TURN HER AWAY?
JERRRRRK!
WHAT'S WITH THESE TWO? "JUST SAY NO" IS PRACTICALLY ROLLING OFF THIS GIRL!
ALL RIGHT, LISTEN.
"DARKNESS," RIGHT? AND, MEGUMIN, THIS GOES FOR YOU TOO.
AQUA AND I HAVE A JOB TO DO. WE HAVE TO DEFEAT THE DEMON KING.

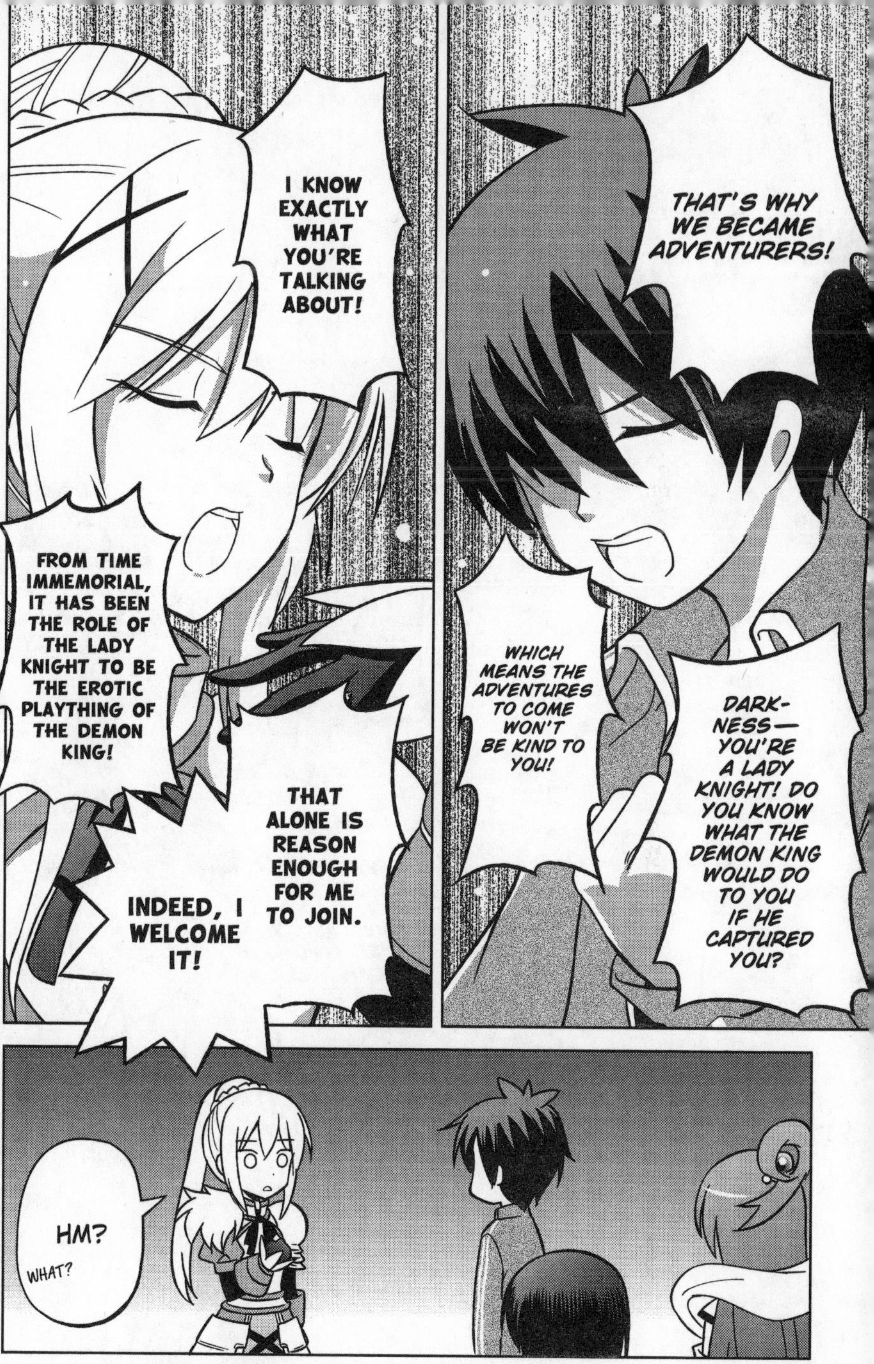
THAT'S WHY WE BECAME ADVENTURERS!
WHICH MEANS THE ADVENTURES TO COME WON'T BE KIND TO YOU!
DARK-NESS— YOU'RE A LADY KNIGHT! DO YOU KNOW WHAT THE DEMON KING WOULD DO TO YOU IF HE CAPTURED YOU?
I KNOW EXACTLY WHAT YOU'RE TALKING ABOUT!
FROM TIME IMMEMORIAL, IT HAS BEEN THE ROLE OF THE LADY KNIGHT TO BE THE EROTIC PLAYTHING OF THE DEMON KING!
THAT ALONE IS REASON ENOUGH FOR ME TO JOIN.
INDEED, I WELCOME IT!
HM?
WHAT?

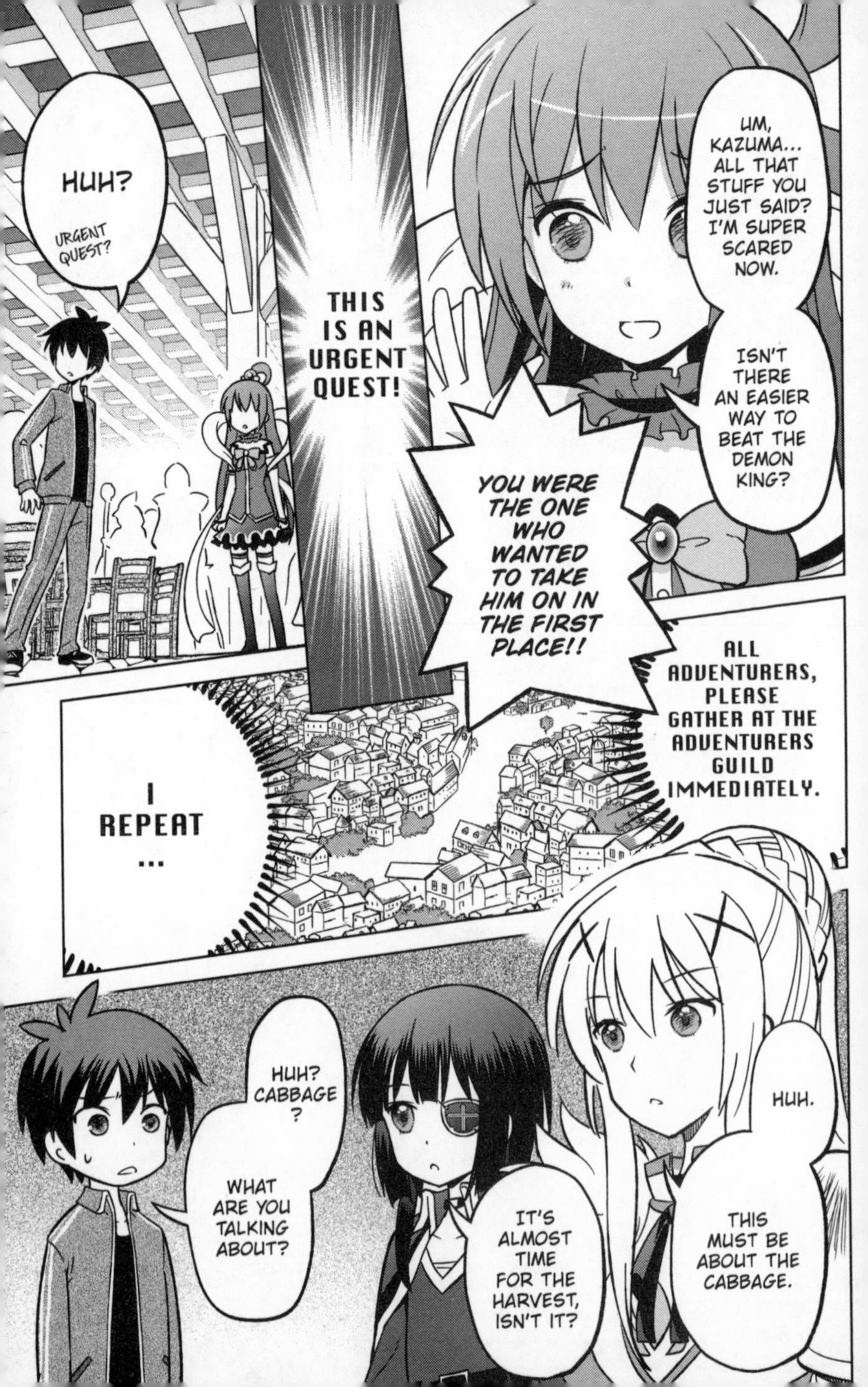
UM, KAZUMA... ALL THAT STUFF YOU JUST SAID? I'M SUPER SCARED NOW.
ISN'T THERE AN EASIER WAY TO BEAT THE DEMON KING?
YOU WERE THE ONE WHO WANTED TO TAKE HIM ON IN THE FIRST PLACE!!
THIS IS AN URGENT QUEST!
HUH?
URGENT QUEST?
ALL ADVENTURERS, PLEASE GATHER AT THE ADVENTURERS GUILD IMMEDIATELY.
I REPEAT ...
HUH.
THIS MUST BE ABOUT THE CABBAGE.
IT'S ALMOST TIME FOR THE HARVEST, ISN'T IT?
HUH? CABBAGE?
WHAT ARE YOU TALKING ABOUT?

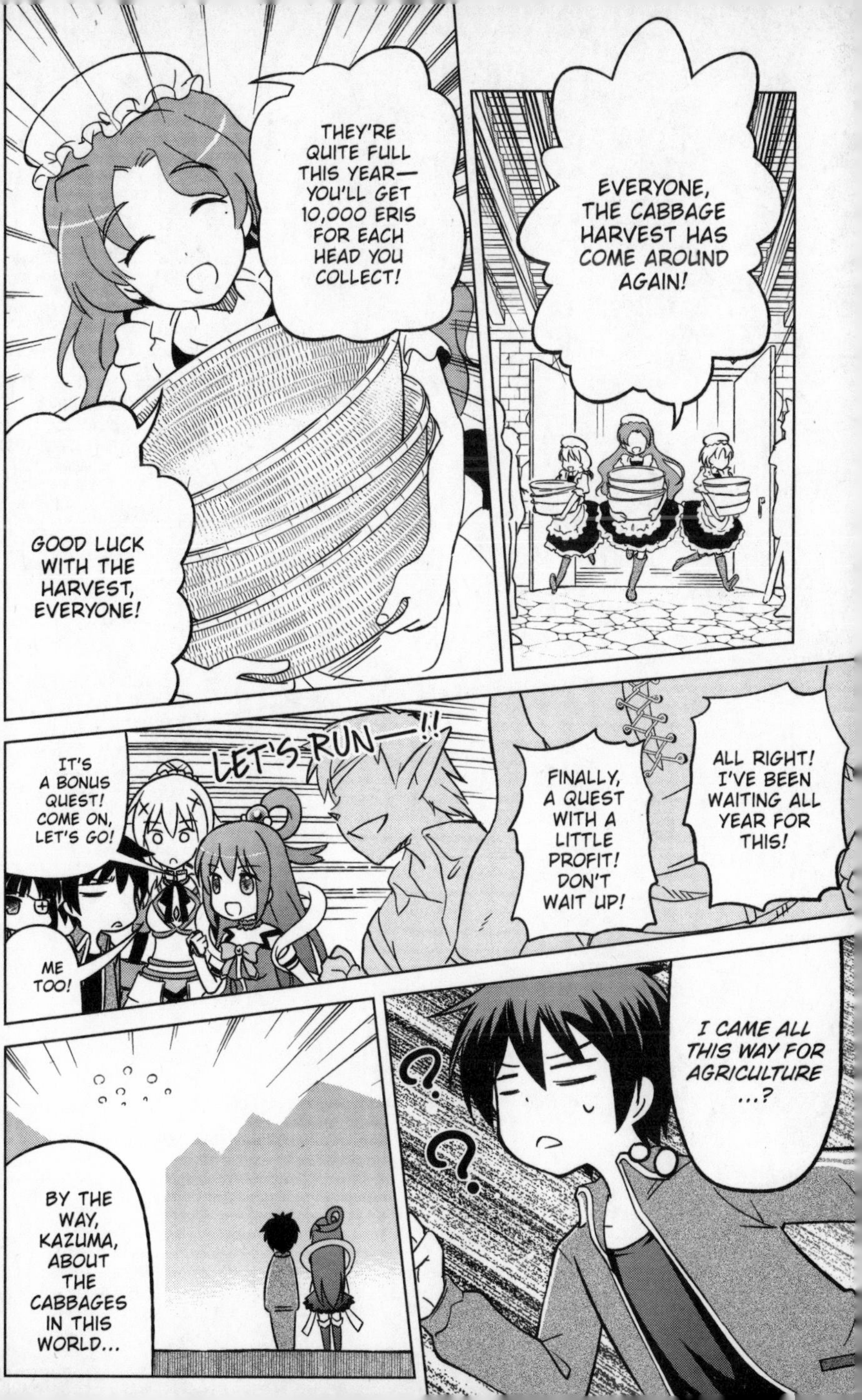
EVERYONE, THE CABBAGE HARVEST HAS COME AROUND AGAIN!
THEY'RE QUITE FULL THIS YEAR—YOU'LL GET 10,000 ERIS FOR EACH HEAD YOU COLLECT!
GOOD LUCK WITH THE HARVEST, EVERYONE!
ALL RIGHT! I'VE BEEN WAITING ALL YEAR FOR THIS!
FINALLY, A QUEST WITH A LITTLE PROFIT! DON'T WAIT UP!
LET'S RUN—!!
IT'S A BONUS QUEST! COME ON, LET'S GO!
ME TOO!
I CAME ALL THIS WAY FOR AGRICULTURE ...?
BY THE WAY, KAZUMA, ABOUT THE CABBAGES IN THIS WORLD...

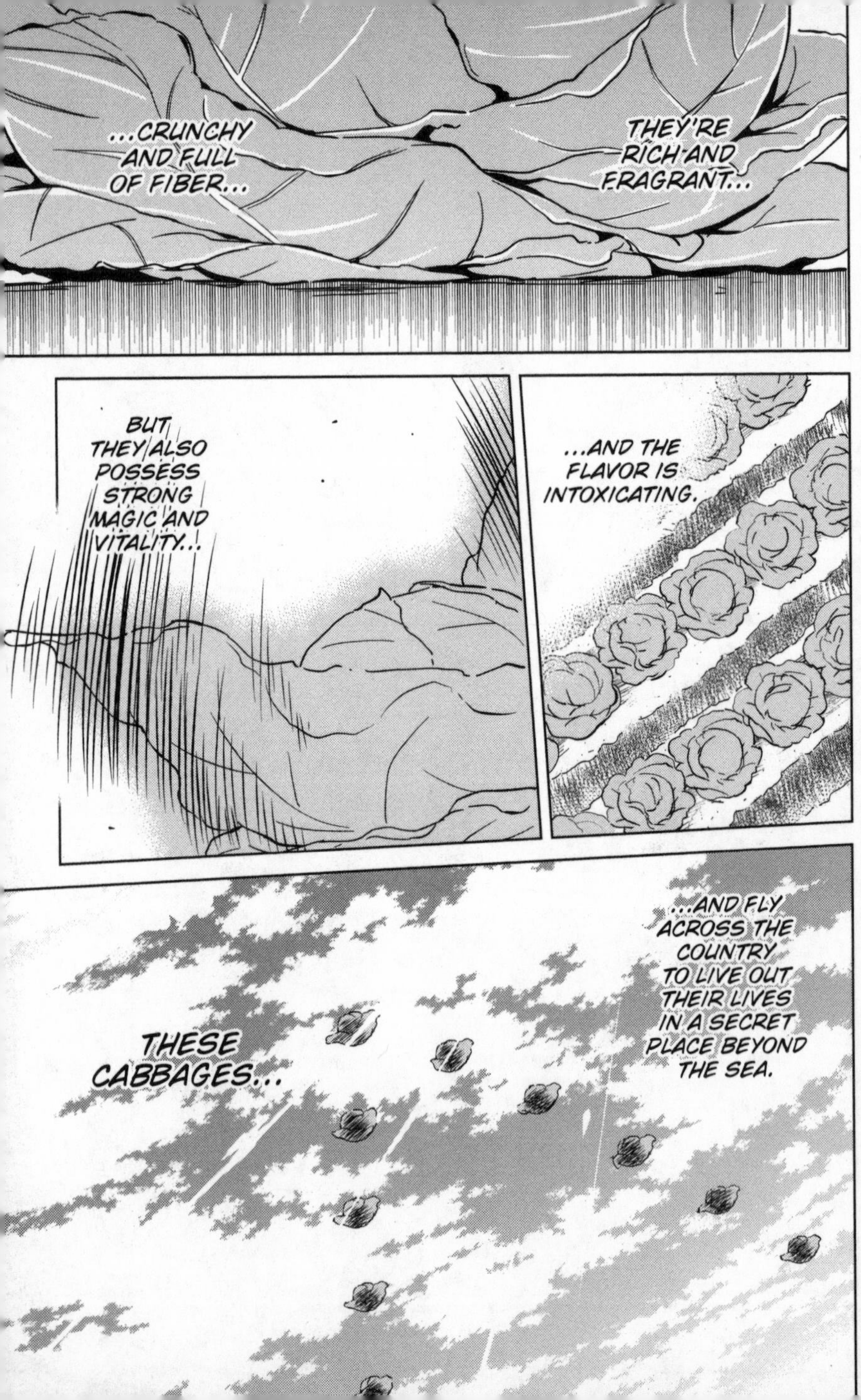
THEY'RE RICH AND FRAGRANT...
...CRUNCHY AND FULL OF FIBER...
...AND THE FLAVOR IS INTOXICATING.
BUT THEY ALSO POSSESS STRONG MAGIC AND VITALITY...
...AND FLY ACROSS THE COUNTRY TO LIVE OUT THEIR LIVES IN A SECRET PLACE BEYOND THE SEA.
THESE CABBAGES...

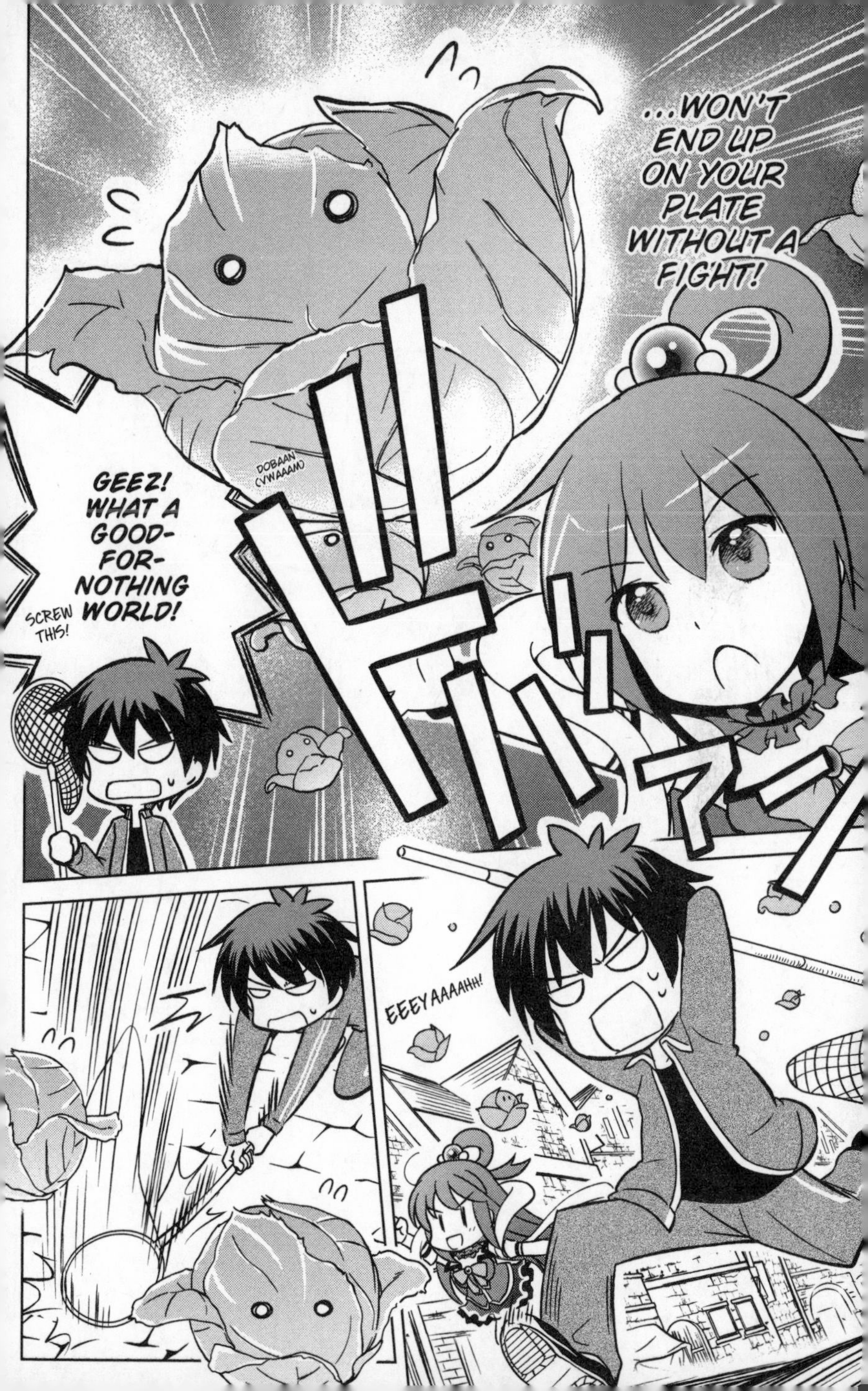
...WON'T END UP ON YOUR PLATE WITHOUT A FIGHT!
DOBAAN (VWAAAM)
GEEZ! WHAT A GOOD-FOR-NOTHING WORLD!
SCREW THIS!
EEEYAAAAHH!

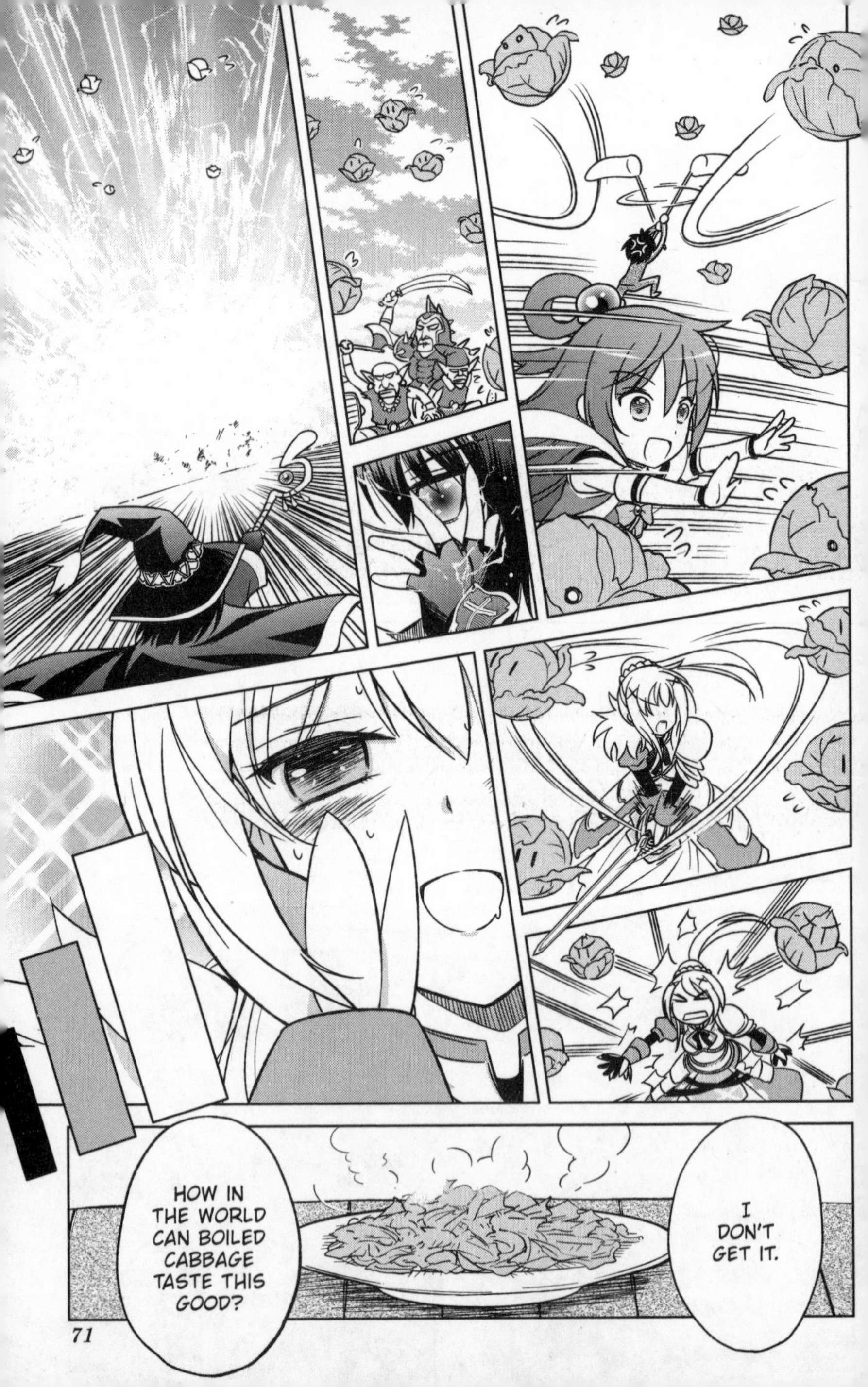
I DON'T GET IT.
HOW IN THE WORLD CAN BOILED CABBAGE TASTE THIS GOOD?

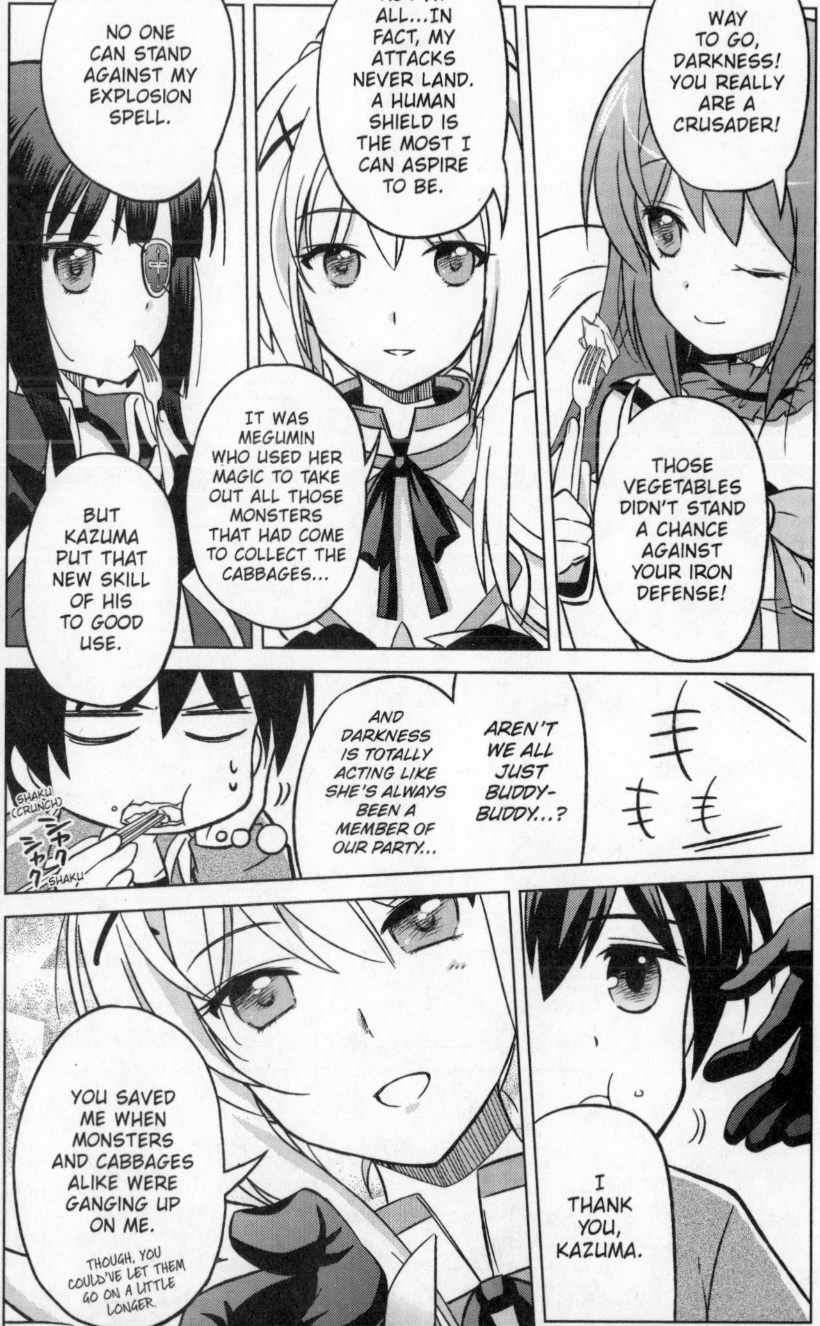
WAY TO GO, DARKNESS! YOU REALLY ARE A CRUSADER!
THOSE VEGETABLES DIDN'T STAND A CHANCE AGAINST YOUR IRON DEFENSE!
NOT AT ALL...IN FACT, MY ATTACKS NEVER LAND. A HUMAN SHIELD IS THE MOST I CAN ASPIRE TO BE.
IT WAS MEGUMIN WHO USED HER MAGIC TO TAKE OUT ALL THOSE MONSTERS THAT HAD COME TO COLLECT THE CABBAGES...
NO ONE CAN STAND AGAINST MY EXPLOSION SPELL.
BUT KAZUMA PUT THAT NEW SKILL OF HIS TO GOOD USE.
AND DARKNESS IS TOTALLY ACTING LIKE SHE'S ALWAYS BEEN A MEMBER OF OUR PARTY...
AREN'T WE ALL JUST BUDDY-BUDDY...?
SHAKU (CRUNCH)
シャク
シャク
SHAKU
I THANK YOU, KAZUMA.
YOU SAVED ME WHEN MONSTERS AND CABBAGES ALIKE WERE GANGING UP ON ME.
THOUGH, YOU COULD'VE LET THEM GO ON A LITTLE LONGER.

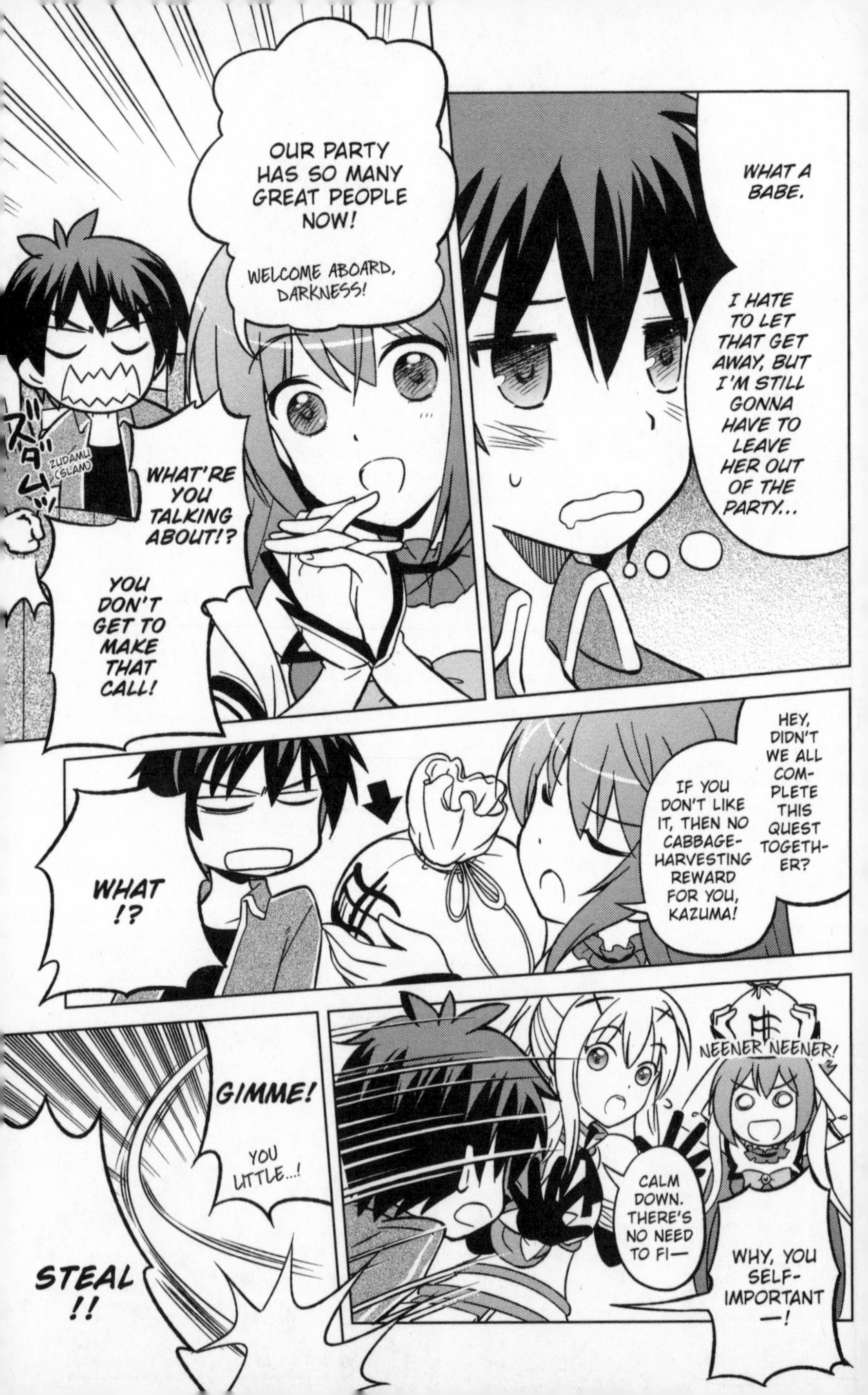
WHAT A BABE.
I HATE TO LET THAT GET AWAY, BUT I'M STILL GONNA HAVE TO LEAVE HER OUT OF THE PARTY...
OUR PARTY HAS SO MANY GREAT PEOPLE NOW!
WELCOME ABOARD, DARKNESS!
ZUDAMU (SLAM)
WHAT'RE YOU TALKING ABOUT!?
YOU DON'T GET TO MAKE THAT CALL!
HEY, DIDN'T WE ALL COMPLETE THIS QUEST TOGETHER?
IF YOU DON'T LIKE IT, THEN NO CABBAGE-HARVESTING REWARD FOR YOU, KAZUMA!
WHAT!?
NEENER NEENER!
WHY, YOU SELF-IMPORTANT—!
CALM DOWN. THERE'S NO NEED TO FI—
GIMME!
YOU LITTLE...!
STEAL!!

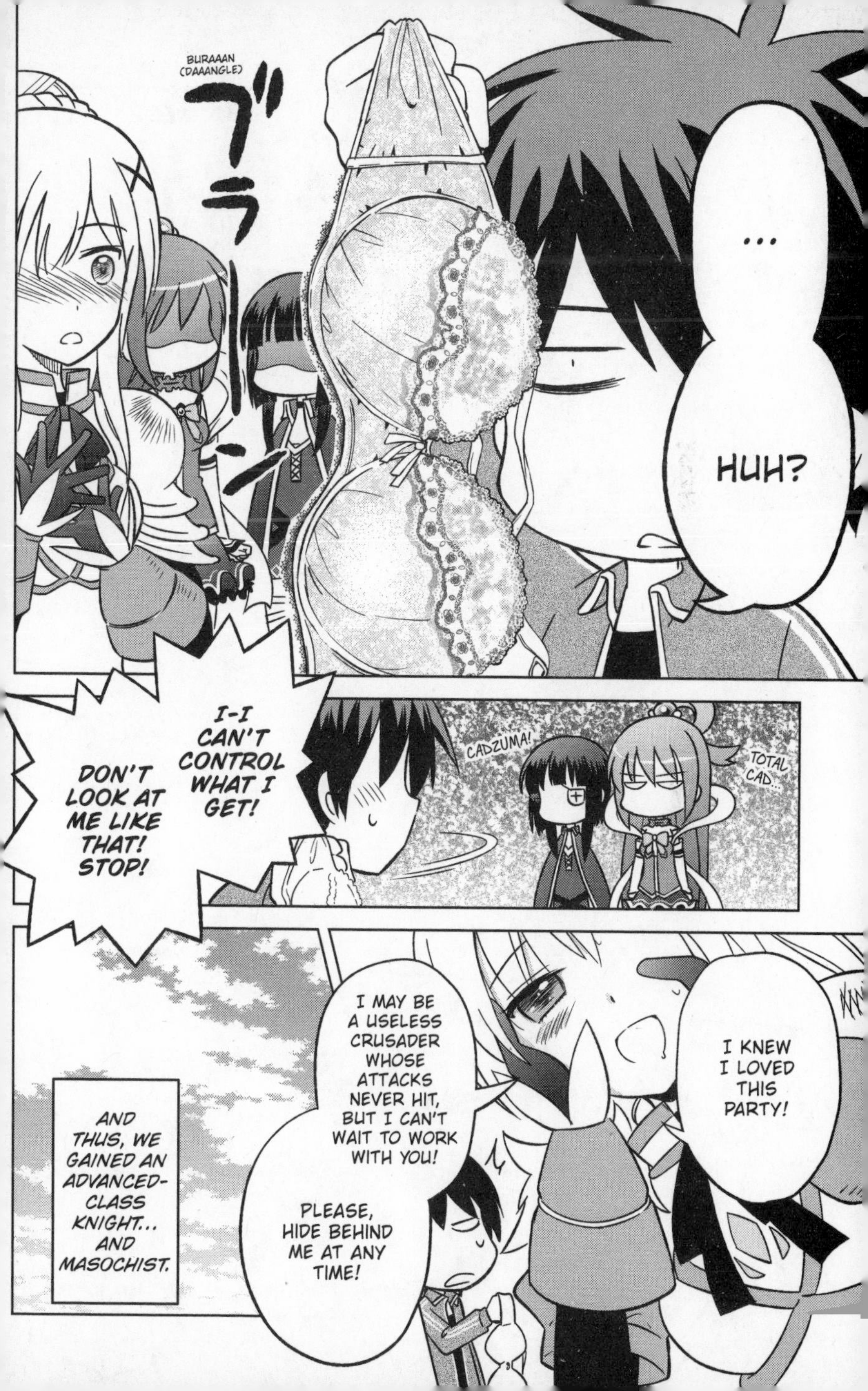
...
HUH?
BURAAAN (DAAANGLE)
TOTAL CAD...
CADZUMA!
I-I CAN'T CONTROL WHAT I GET!
DON'T LOOK AT ME LIKE THAT! STOP!
I KNEW I LOVED THIS PARTY!
I MAY BE A USELESS CRUSADER WHOSE ATTACKS NEVER HIT, BUT I CAN'T WAIT TO WORK WITH YOU!
PLEASE, HIDE BEHIND ME AT ANY TIME!
AND THUS, WE GAINED AN ADVANCED-CLASS KNIGHT... AND MASOCHIST.

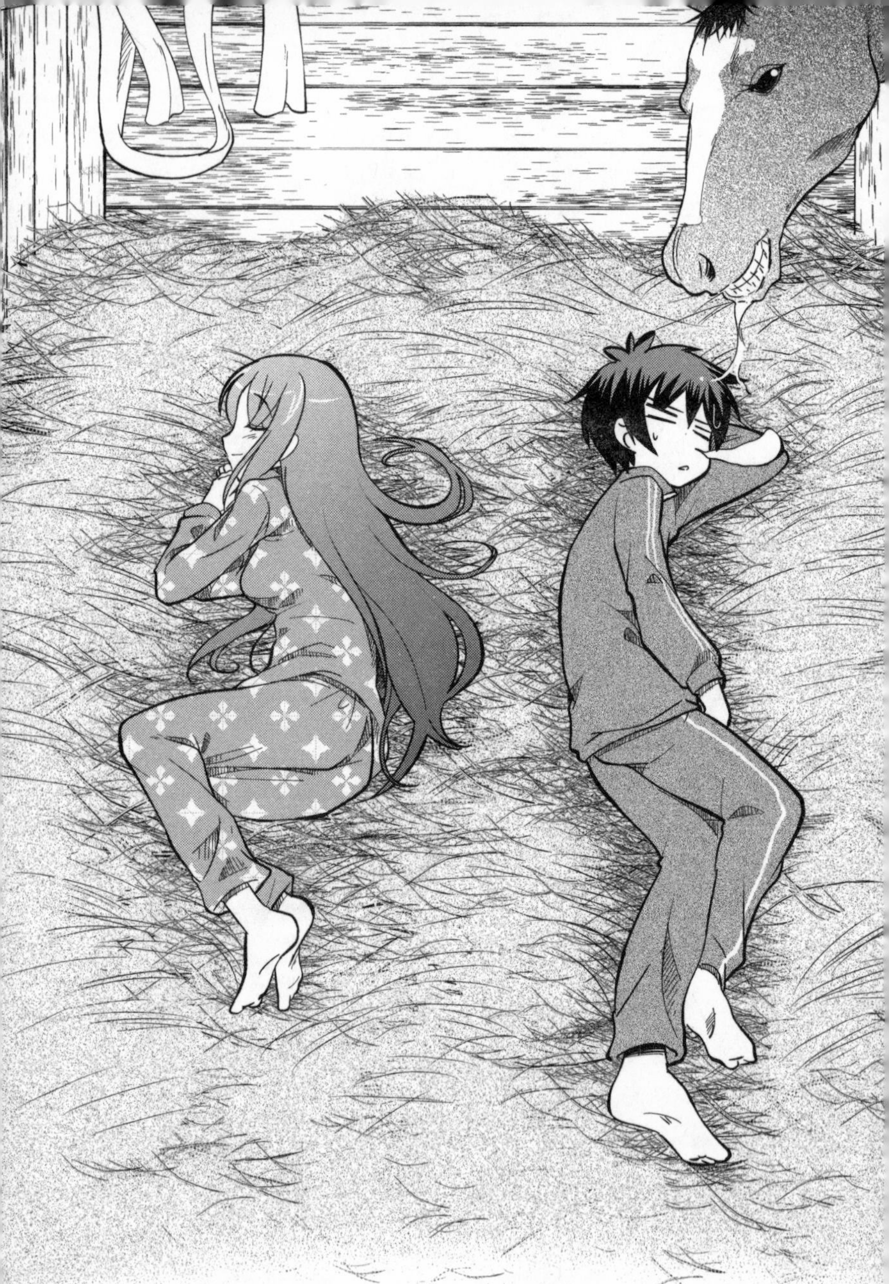

CHAPTER 3 MAY THERE BE REST TO THESE UNDEAD!

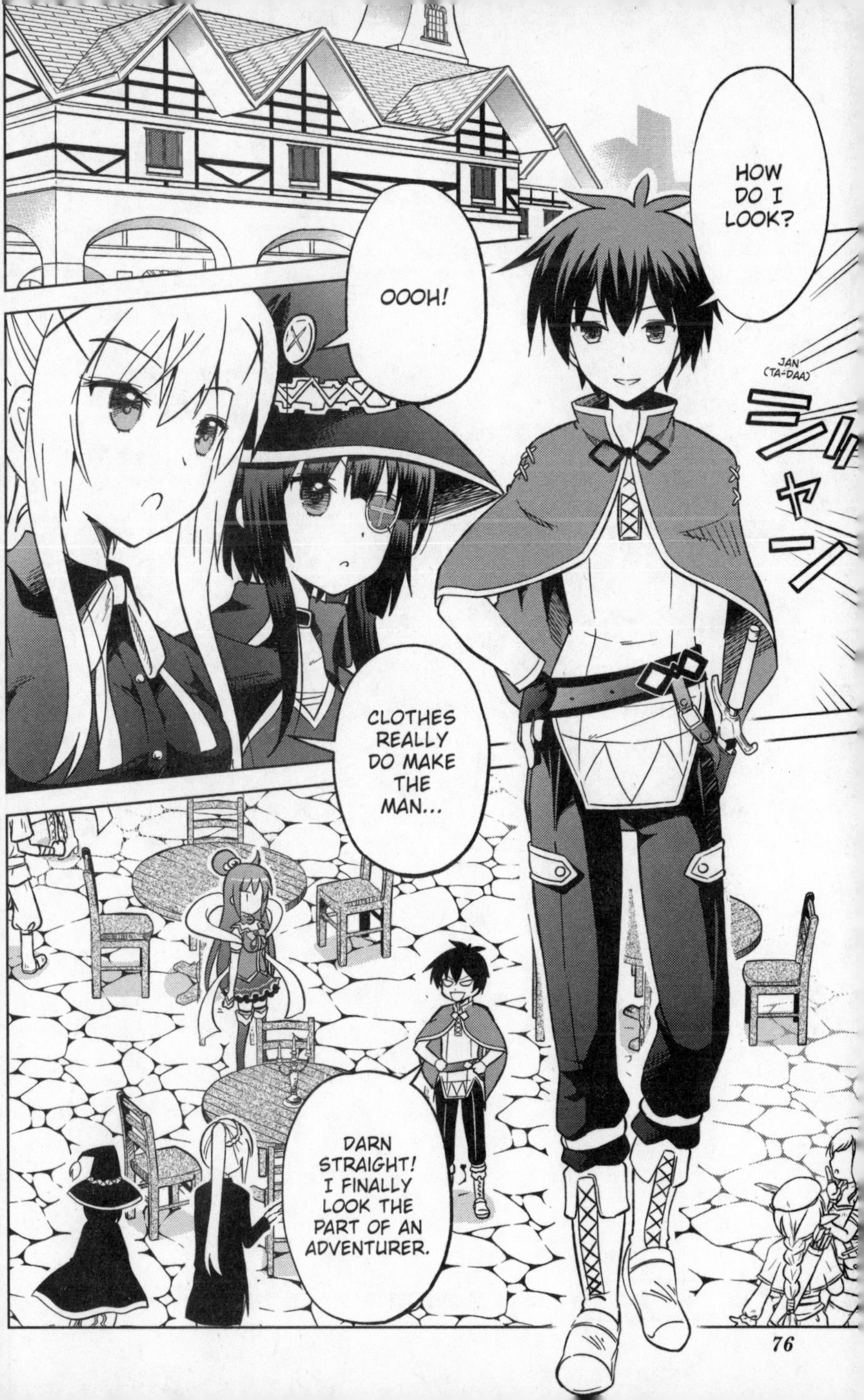
HOW DO I LOOK?
JAN (TA-DAA)
ジャーン
OOOH!
CLOTHES REALLY DO MAKE THE MAN...
DARN STRAIGHT! I FINALLY LOOK THE PART OF AN ADVENTURER.

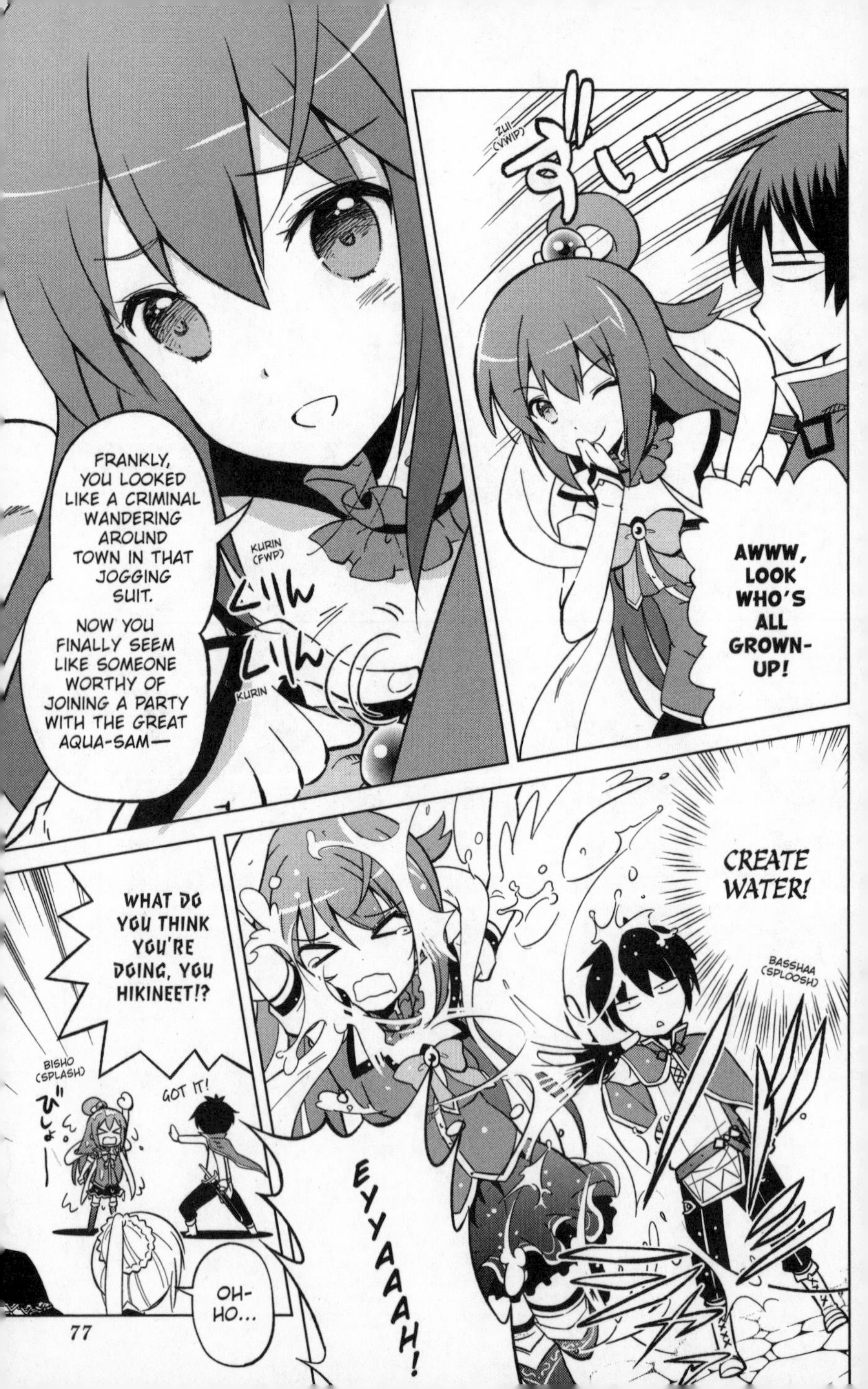
ZUI (VWIP)
AWWW, LOOK WHO'S ALL GROWN-UP!
FRANKLY, YOU LOOKED LIKE A CRIMINAL WANDERING AROUND TOWN IN THAT JOGGING SUIT.
NOW YOU FINALLY SEEM LIKE SOMEONE WORTHY OF JOINING A PARTY WITH THE GREAT AQUA-SAM—
KURIN (FWP)
KURIN
CREATE WATER!
BASSHAA (SPLOOSH)
EYYAAAH!
WHAT DO YOU THINK YOU'RE DOING, YOU HIKINEET!?
BISHO (SPLASH)
GOT IT!
OH-HO...

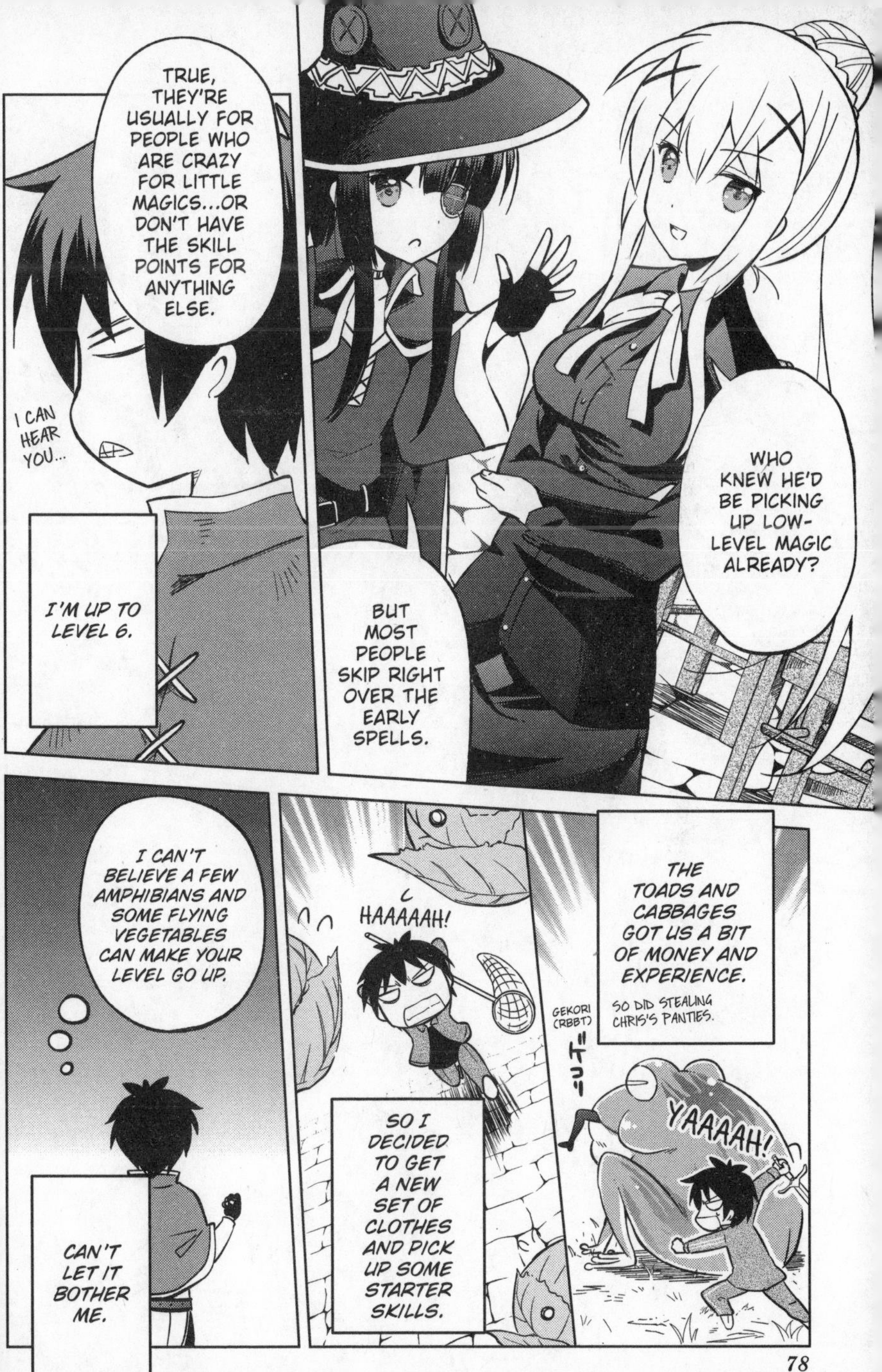
WHO KNEW HE'D BE PICKING UP LOW-LEVEL MAGIC ALREADY?
BUT MOST PEOPLE SKIP RIGHT OVER THE EARLY SPELLS.
TRUE, THEY'RE USUALLY FOR PEOPLE WHO ARE CRAZY FOR LITTLE MAGICS...OR DON'T HAVE THE SKILL POINTS FOR ANYTHING ELSE.
I CAN HEAR YOU...
I'M UP TO LEVEL 6.
THE TOADS AND CABBAGES GOT US A BIT OF MONEY AND EXPERIENCE.
SO DID STEALING CHRIS'S PANTIES.
GEKORI (RBBT)
YAAAAH!
HAAAAAH!
SO I DECIDED TO GET A NEW SET OF CLOTHES AND PICK UP SOME STARTER SKILLS.
I CAN'T BELIEVE A FEW AMPHIBIANS AND SOME FLYING VEGETABLES CAN MAKE YOUR LEVEL GO UP.
CAN'T LET IT BOTHER ME.

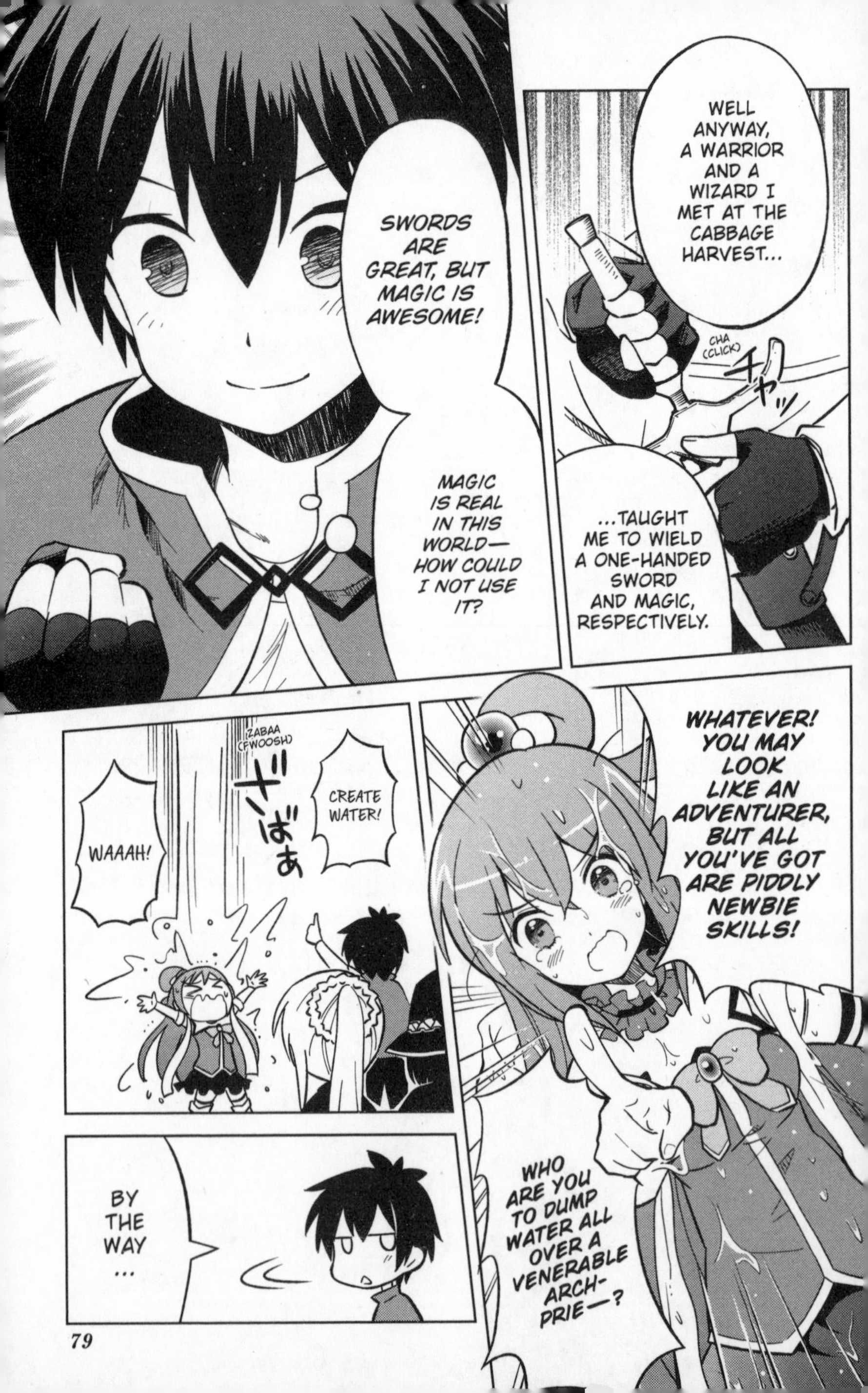
WELL ANYWAY, A WARRIOR AND A WIZARD I MET AT THE CABBAGE HARVEST...
CHA (CLICK)
チャッ
...TAUGHT ME TO WIELD A ONE-HANDED SWORD AND MAGIC, RESPECTIVELY.
SWORDS ARE GREAT, BUT MAGIC IS AWESOME!
MAGIC IS REAL IN THIS WORLD—HOW COULD I NOT USE IT?
WHATEVER! YOU MAY LOOK LIKE AN ADVENTURER, BUT ALL YOU'VE GOT ARE PIDDLY NEWBIE SKILLS!
WHO ARE YOU TO DUMP WATER ALL OVER A VENERABLE ARCH-PRIE—?
CREATE WATER!
ZABAA (FWOOSH)
ざばぁ
WAAAH!
BY THE WAY ...

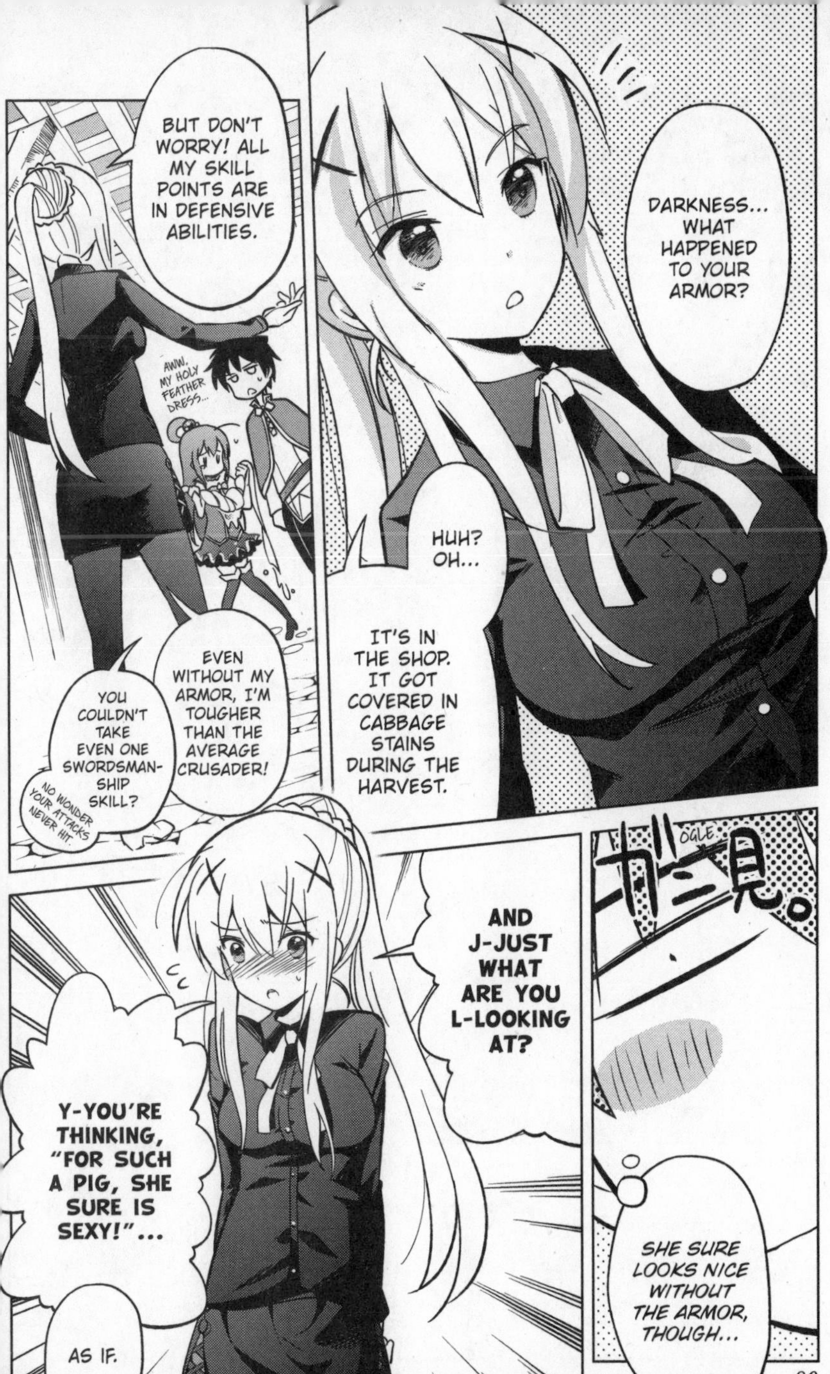
DARKNESS... WHAT HAPPENED TO YOUR ARMOR?
HUH? OH...
IT'S IN THE SHOP. IT GOT COVERED IN CABBAGE STAINS DURING THE HARVEST.
BUT DON'T WORRY! ALL MY SKILL POINTS ARE IN DEFENSIVE ABILITIES.
AWW, MY HOLY FEATHER DRESS...
EVEN WITHOUT MY ARMOR, I'M TOUGHER THAN THE AVERAGE CRUSADER!
YOU COULDN'T TAKE EVEN ONE SWORDSMAN-SHIP SKILL?
NO WONDER YOUR ATTACKS NEVER HIT.
ガン見。
OGLE
SHE SURE LOOKS NICE WITHOUT THE ARMOR, THOUGH...
AND J-JUST WHAT ARE YOU L-LOOKING AT?
Y-YOU'RE THINKING, "FOR SUCH A PIG, SHE SURE IS SEXY!"...
AS IF.

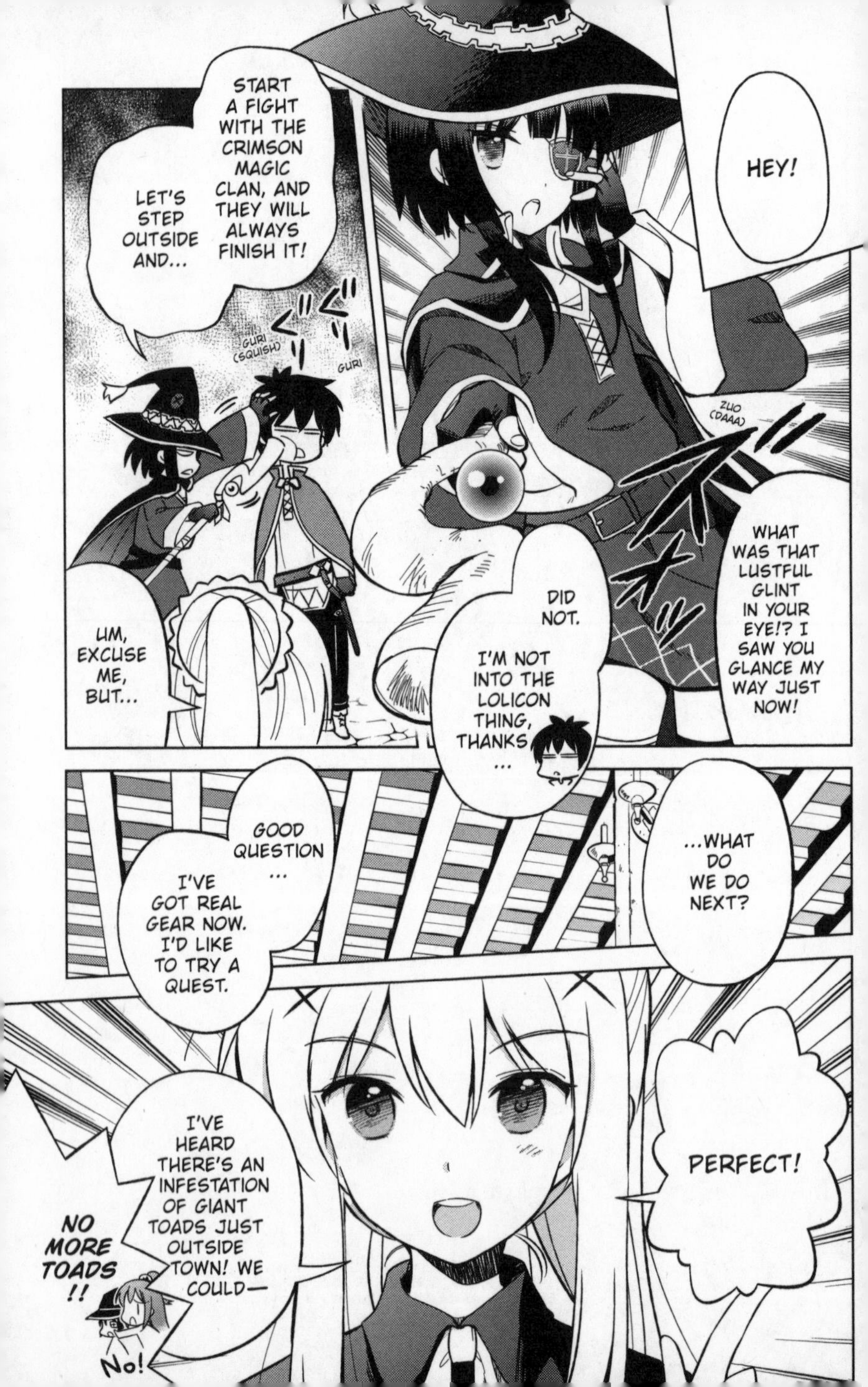
HEY!
ZUO (DAAA)
WHAT WAS THAT LUSTFUL GLINT IN YOUR EYE!? I SAW YOU GLANCE MY WAY JUST NOW!
START A FIGHT WITH THE CRIMSON MAGIC CLAN, AND THEY WILL ALWAYS FINISH IT!
LET'S STEP OUTSIDE AND...
GURI (SQUISH)
GURI
DID NOT.
I'M NOT INTO THE LOLICON THING, THANKS...
UM, EXCUSE ME, BUT...
...WHAT DO WE DO NEXT?
GOOD QUESTION...
I'VE GOT REAL GEAR NOW. I'D LIKE TO TRY A QUEST.
PERFECT!
I'VE HEARD THERE'S AN INFESTATION OF GIANT TOADS JUST OUTSIDE TOWN! WE COULD—
NO MORE TOADS!!
No!

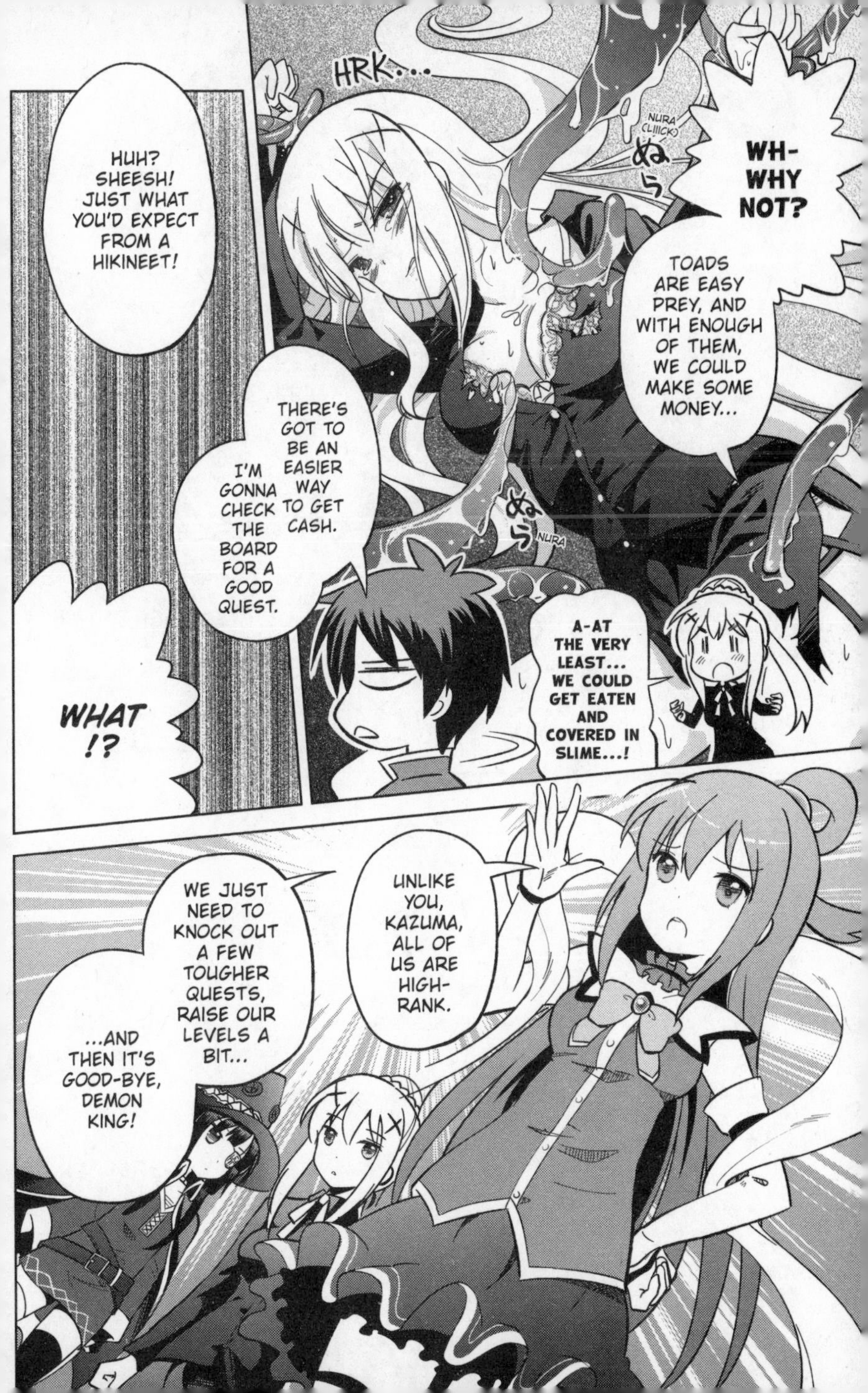
WH- WHY NOT?
NURA (LIIICK)
ぬら
HRK...
TOADS ARE EASY PREY, AND WITH ENOUGH OF THEM, WE COULD MAKE SOME MONEY...
ぬら
NURA
THERE'S GOT TO BE AN EASIER WAY TO GET CASH.
I'M GONNA CHECK THE BOARD FOR A GOOD QUEST.
A-AT THE VERY LEAST... WE COULD GET EATEN AND COVERED IN SLIME...!
HUH? SHEESH! JUST WHAT YOU'D EXPECT FROM A HIKINEET!
WHAT !?
UNLIKE YOU, KAZUMA, ALL OF US ARE HIGH-RANK.
WE JUST NEED TO KNOCK OUT A FEW TOUGHER QUESTS, RAISE OUR LEVELS A BIT...
...AND THEN IT'S GOOD-BYE, DEMON KING!

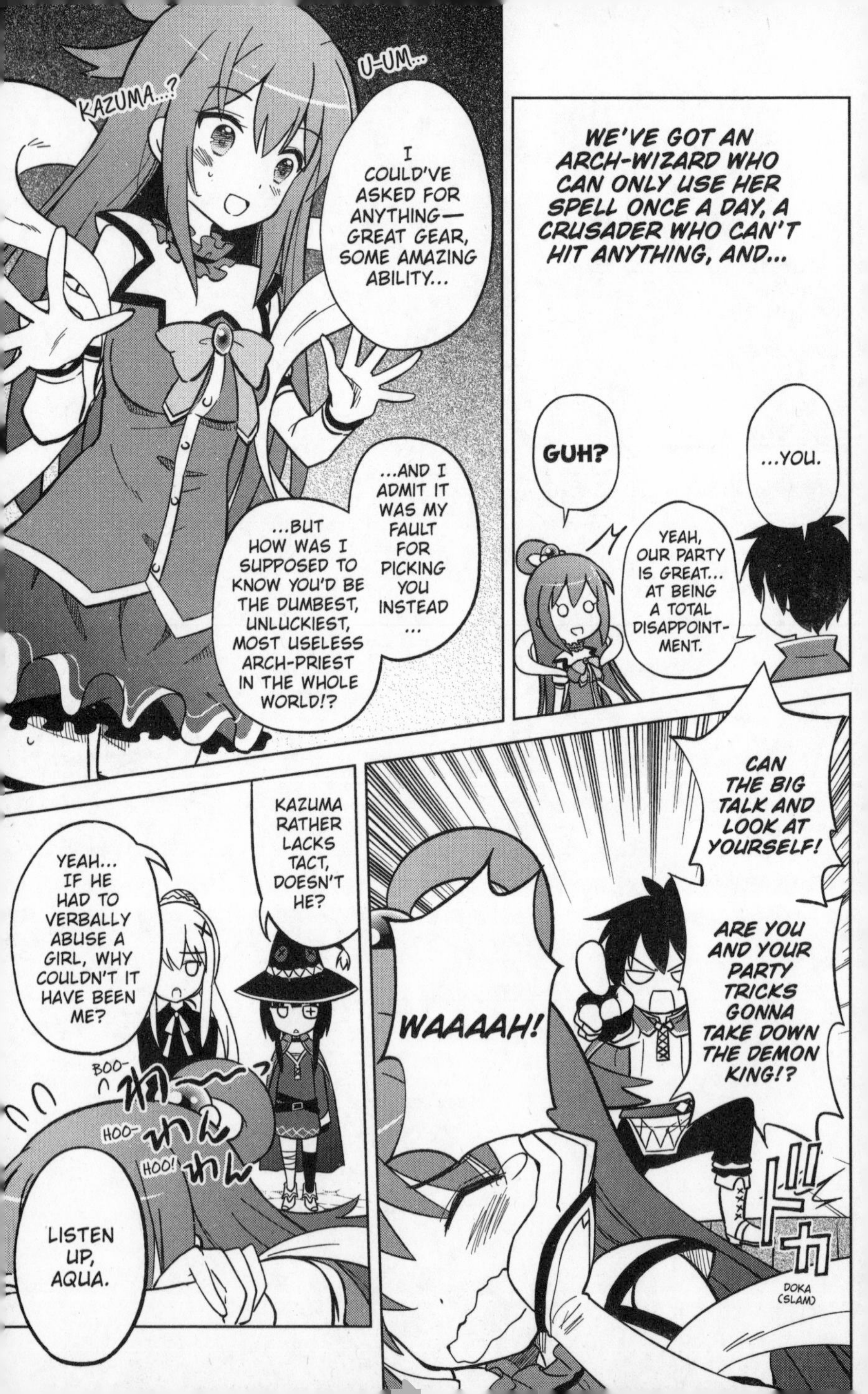
WE'VE GOT AN ARCH-WIZARD WHO CAN ONLY USE HER SPELL ONCE A DAY, A CRUSADER WHO CAN'T HIT ANYTHING, AND...
...YOU.
GUH?
YEAH, OUR PARTY IS GREAT... AT BEING A TOTAL DISAPPOINT-MENT.
U-UM...
KAZUMA...?
I COULD'VE ASKED FOR ANYTHING— GREAT GEAR, SOME AMAZING ABILITY...
...AND I ADMIT IT WAS MY FAULT FOR PICKING YOU INSTEAD...
...BUT HOW WAS I SUPPOSED TO KNOW YOU'D BE THE DUMBEST, UNLUCKIEST, MOST USELESS ARCH-PRIEST IN THE WHOLE WORLD!?
CAN THE BIG TALK AND LOOK AT YOURSELF!
ARE YOU AND YOUR PARTY TRICKS GONNA TAKE DOWN THE DEMON KING!?
WAAAAH!
DOKA (SLAM)
KAZUMA RATHER LACKS TACT, DOESN'T HE?
YEAH... IF HE HAD TO VERBALLY ABUSE A GIRL, WHY COULDN'T IT HAVE BEEN ME?
BOO-
HOO-
HOO!
LISTEN UP, AQUA.

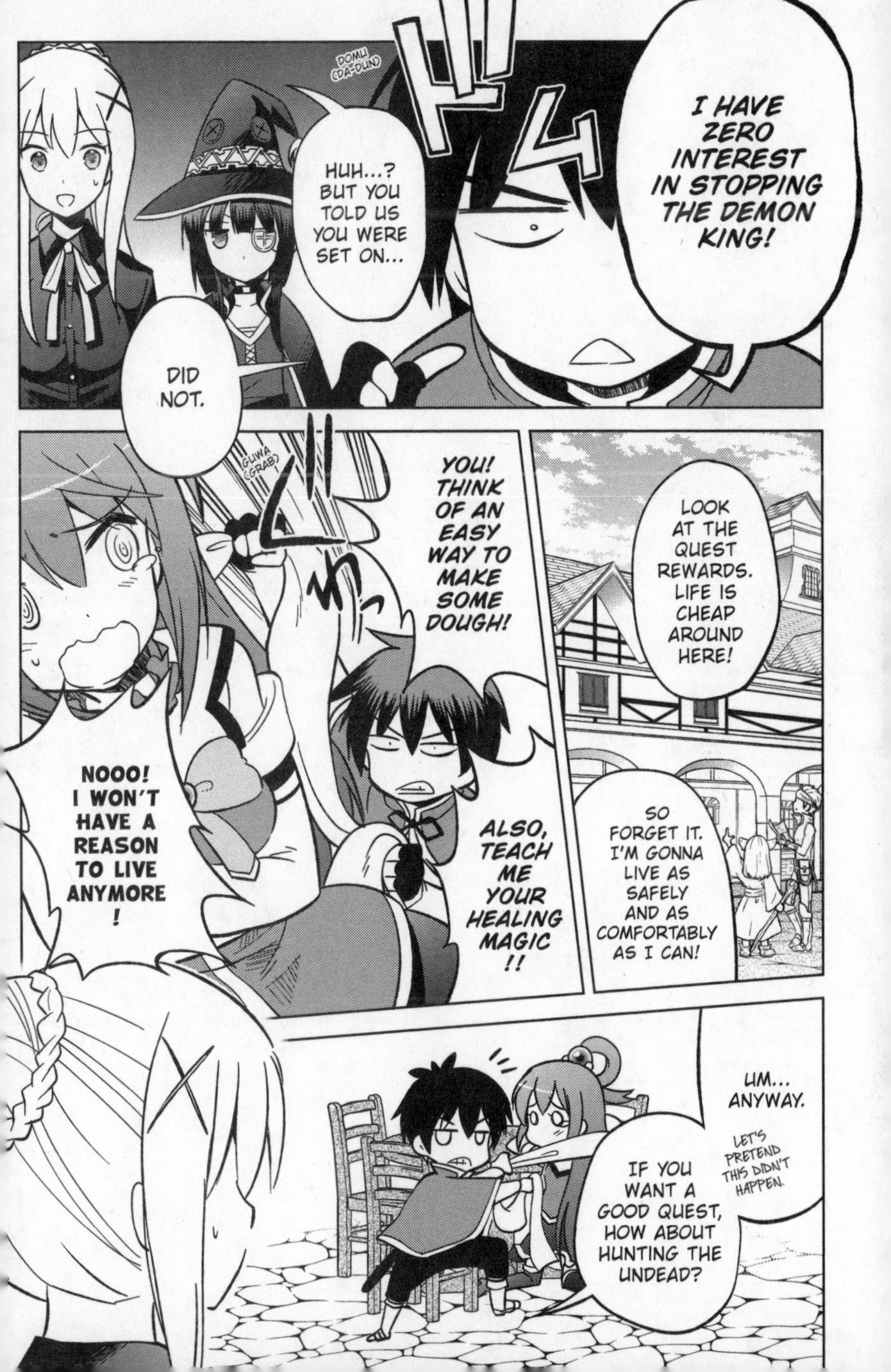
I HAVE ZERO INTEREST IN STOPPING THE DEMON KING!
DOMU (DA-DUN)
HUH...? BUT YOU TOLD US YOU WERE SET ON...
DID NOT.
LOOK AT THE QUEST REWARDS. LIFE IS CHEAP AROUND HERE!
SO FORGET IT. I'M GONNA LIVE AS SAFELY AND AS COMFORTABLY AS I CAN!
GUWA (GRAB)
YOU! THINK OF AN EASY WAY TO MAKE SOME DOUGH!
ALSO, TEACH ME YOUR HEALING MAGIC!!
NOOO! I WON'T HAVE A REASON TO LIVE ANYMORE!
UM... ANYWAY.
LET'S PRETEND THIS DIDN'T HAPPEN.
IF YOU WANT A GOOD QUEST, HOW ABOUT HUNTING THE UNDEAD?

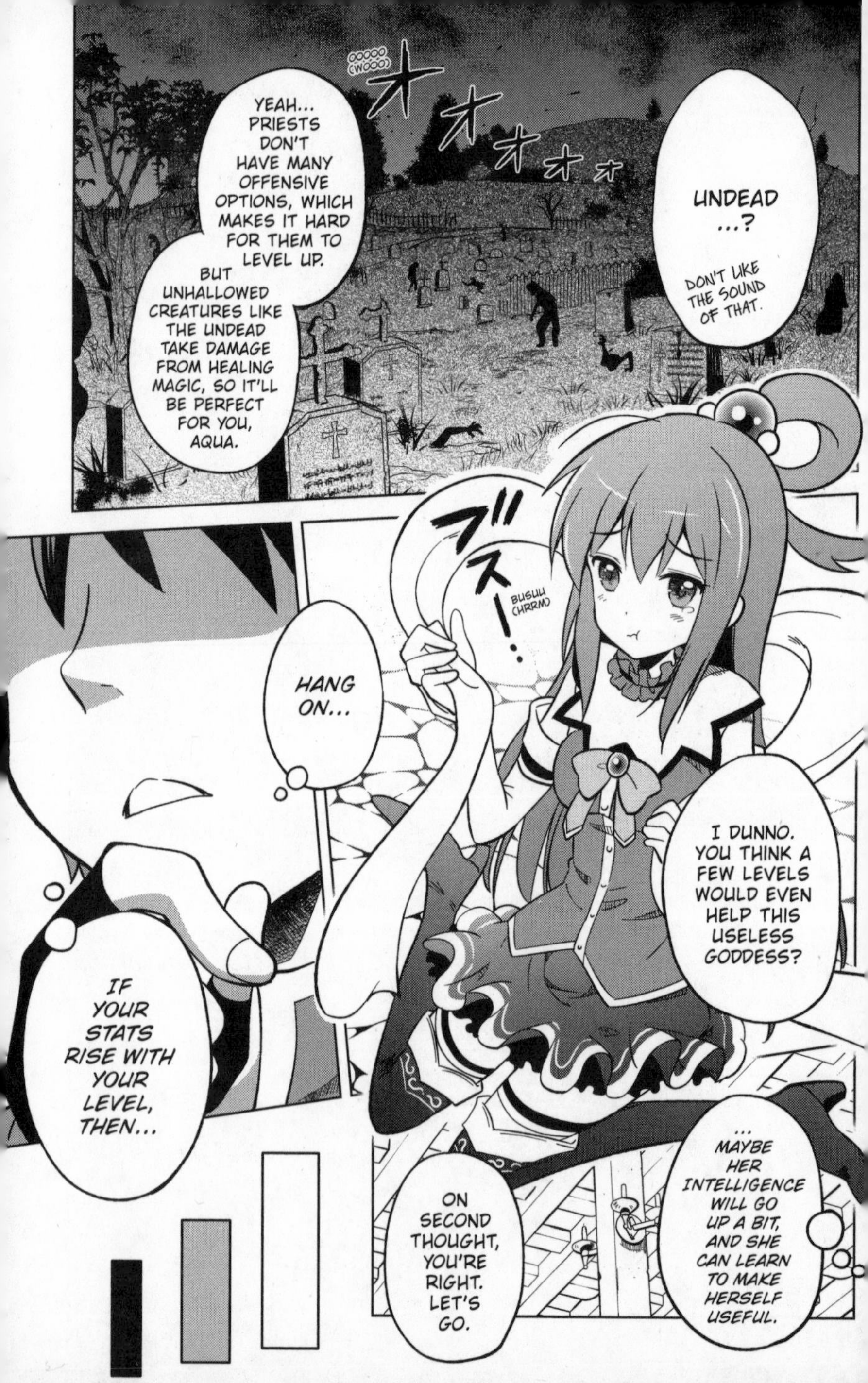

UNDEAD ...?
DON'T LIKE THE SOUND OF THAT.
OOOOO (WOOO)
YEAH... PRIESTS DON'T HAVE MANY OFFENSIVE OPTIONS, WHICH MAKES IT HARD FOR THEM TO LEVEL UP.
BUT UNHALLOWED CREATURES LIKE THE UNDEAD TAKE DAMAGE FROM HEALING MAGIC, SO IT'LL BE PERFECT FOR YOU, AQUA.
BUSUU (HRRM)
I DUNNO. YOU THINK A FEW LEVELS WOULD EVEN HELP THIS USELESS GODDESS?
HANG ON...
IF YOUR STATS RISE WITH YOUR LEVEL, THEN...
... MAYBE HER INTELLIGENCE WILL GO UP A BIT, AND SHE CAN LEARN TO MAKE HERSELF USEFUL.
ON SECOND THOUGHT, YOU'RE RIGHT. LET'S GO.

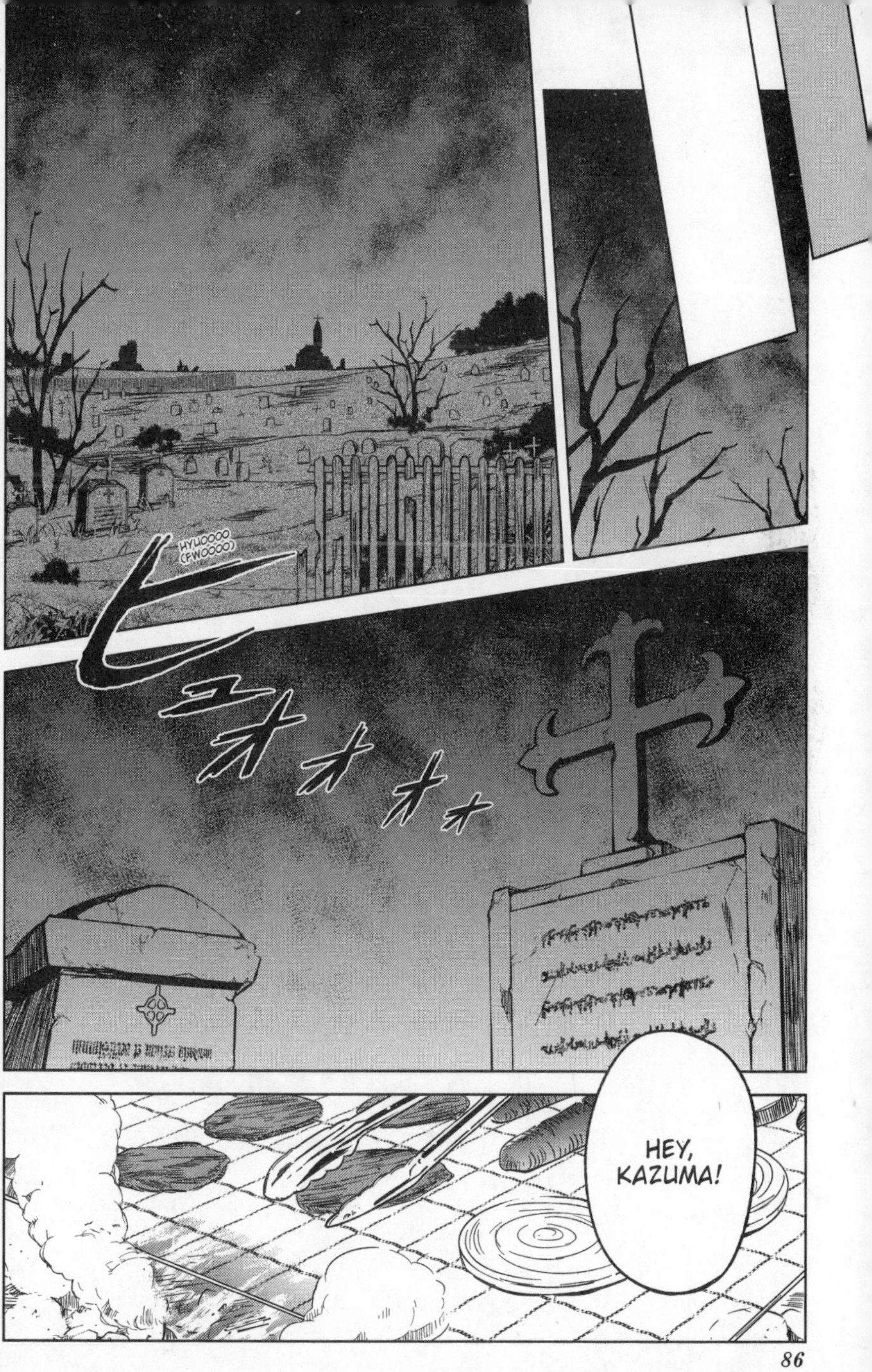
HYUOOOO
(FWOOOO)
HEY, KAZUMA!

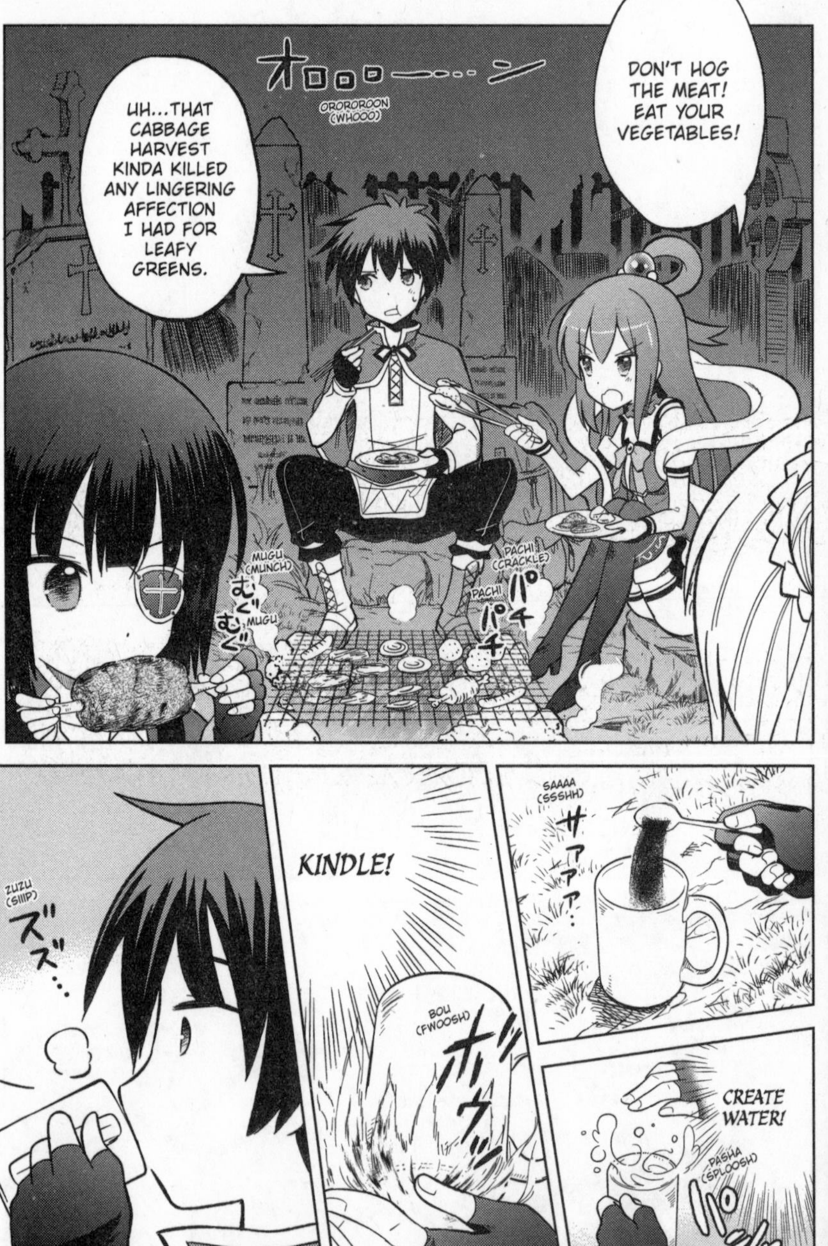
DON'T HOG THE MEAT! EAT YOUR VEGETABLES!
オロロローーン
ORORORORON (WHOOO)
UH...THAT CABBAGE HARVEST KINDA KILLED ANY LINGERING AFFECTION I HAD FOR LEAFY GREENS.
PACHI (CRACKLE) PACHI
パチパチ
MUGU (MUNCH) MUGU
むぐむぐ
SAAAA (SSSHH)
サァアア…
CREATE WATER!
PASHA (SPLOOSH)
パシャッ
KINDLE!
BOU (FWOOSH)
ボウッ
ZUZU (SIIIP)
ズズ…

※ LOW-LEVEL FIRE MAGIC

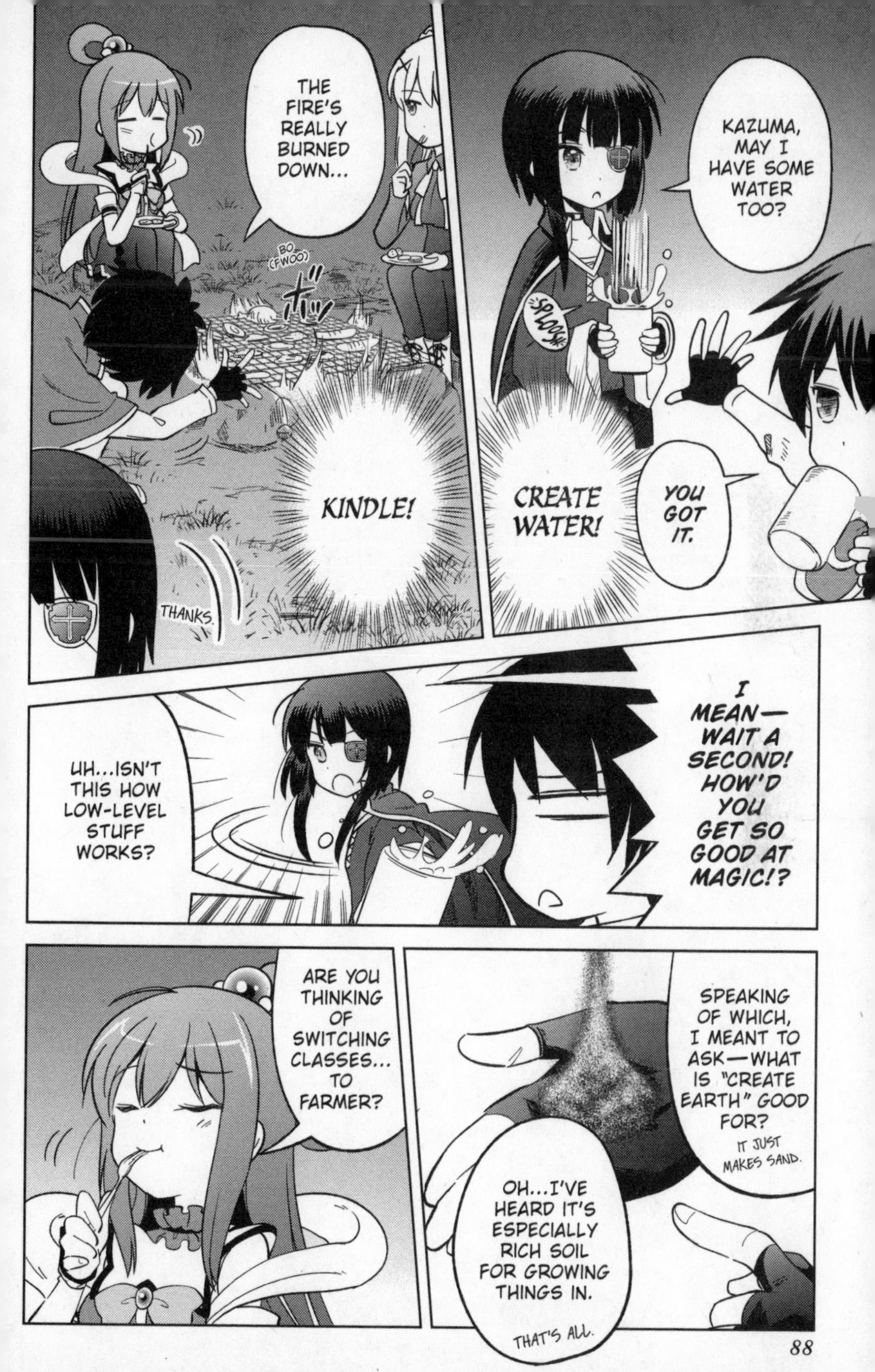

KAZUMA, MAY I HAVE SOME WATER TOO?
SPLOOSH
YOU GOT IT.
CREATE WATER!
THE FIRE'S REALLY BURNED DOWN...
BO (FWOO)
KINDLE!
THANKS.
I MEAN—WAIT A SECOND! HOW'D YOU GET SO GOOD AT MAGIC!?
UH...ISN'T THIS HOW LOW-LEVEL STUFF WORKS?
SPEAKING OF WHICH, I MEANT TO ASK—WHAT IS "CREATE EARTH" GOOD FOR?
IT JUST MAKES SAND.
OH...I'VE HEARD IT'S ESPECIALLY RICH SOIL FOR GROWING THINGS IN.
THAT'S ALL.
ARE YOU THINKING OF SWITCHING CLASSES... TO FARMER?

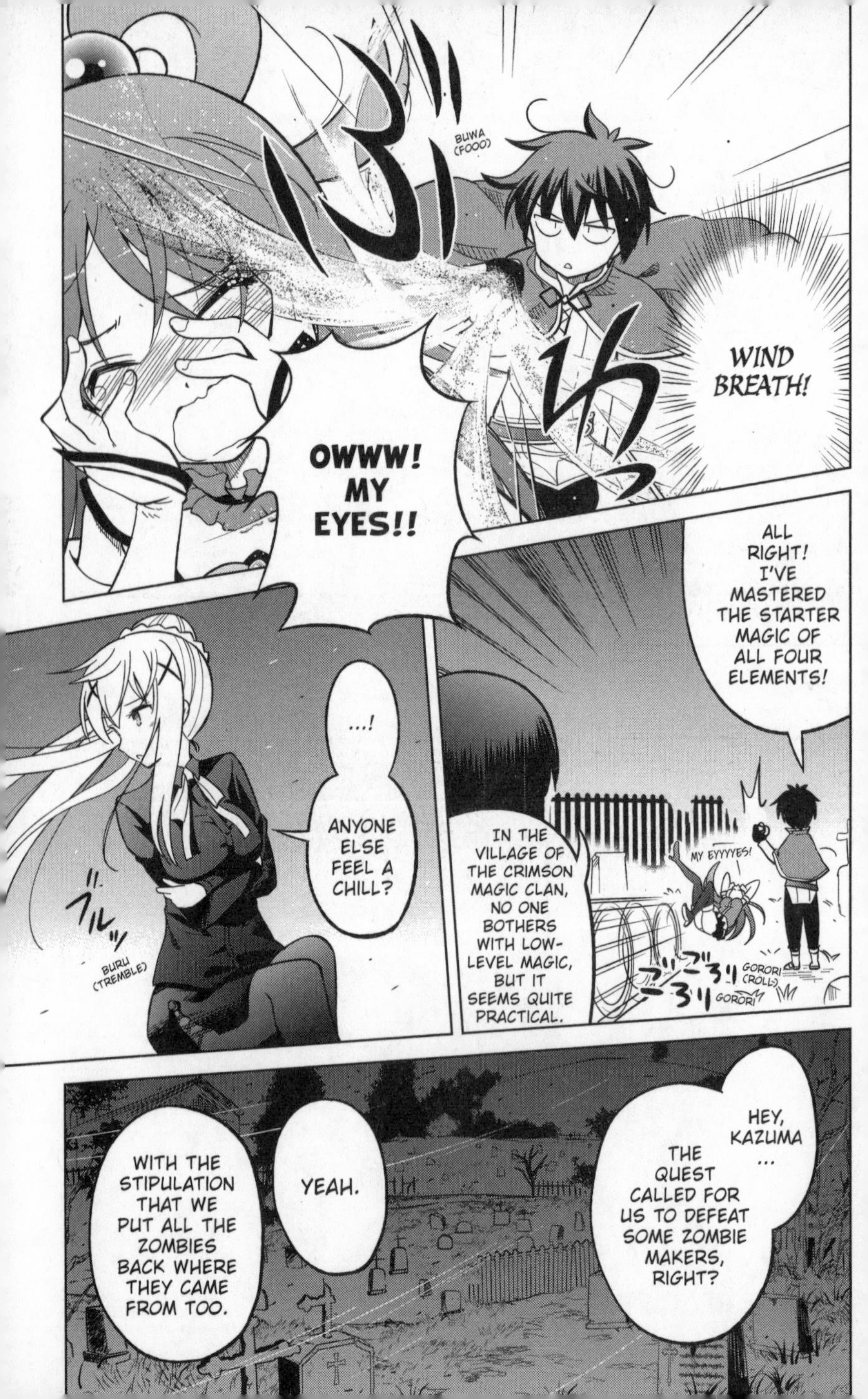
WIND BREATH!
BUWA (FOOO)
OWWW! MY EYES!!
ALL RIGHT! I'VE MASTERED THE STARTER MAGIC OF ALL FOUR ELEMENTS!
MY EYYYYES!
GORORI (ROLL) GORORI
IN THE VILLAGE OF THE CRIMSON MAGIC CLAN, NO ONE BOTHERS WITH LOW-LEVEL MAGIC, BUT IT SEEMS QUITE PRACTICAL.
...!
ANYONE ELSE FEEL A CHILL?
BURU (TREMBLE)
HEY, KAZUMA...
THE QUEST CALLED FOR US TO DEFEAT SOME ZOMBIE MAKERS, RIGHT?
YEAH.
WITH THE STIPULATION THAT WE PUT ALL THE ZOMBIES BACK WHERE THEY CAME FROM TOO.

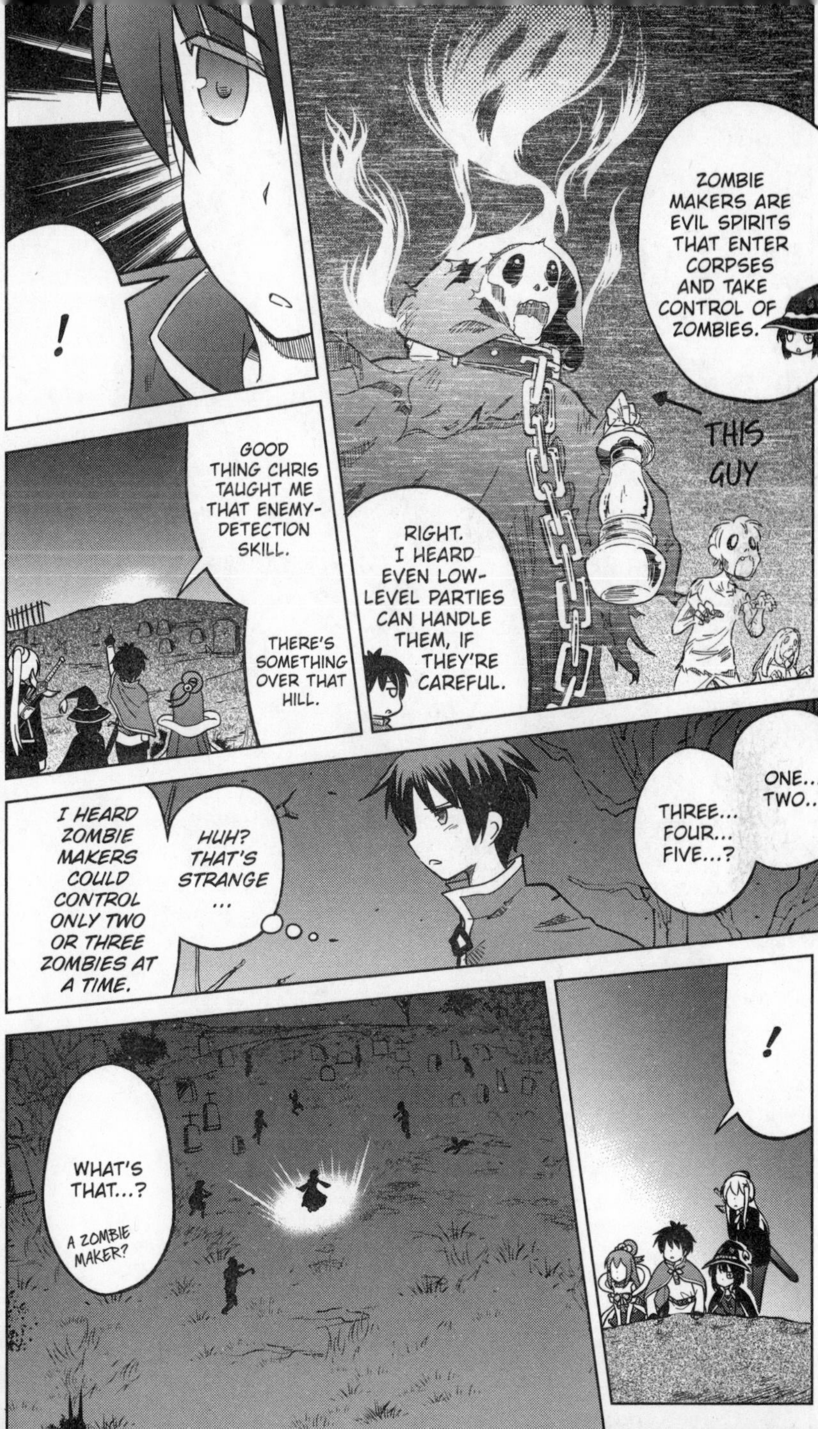
ZOMBIE MAKERS ARE EVIL SPIRITS THAT ENTER CORPSES AND TAKE CONTROL OF ZOMBIES.
THIS GUY
RIGHT. I HEARD EVEN LOW-LEVEL PARTIES CAN HANDLE THEM, IF THEY'RE CAREFUL.
!
GOOD THING CHRIS TAUGHT ME THAT ENEMY-DETECTION SKILL.
THERE'S SOMETHING OVER THAT HILL.
ONE... TWO...
THREE... FOUR... FIVE...?
HUH? THAT'S STRANGE...
I HEARD ZOMBIE MAKERS COULD CONTROL ONLY TWO OR THREE ZOMBIES AT A TIME.
!
WHAT'S THAT...?
A ZOMBIE MAKER?

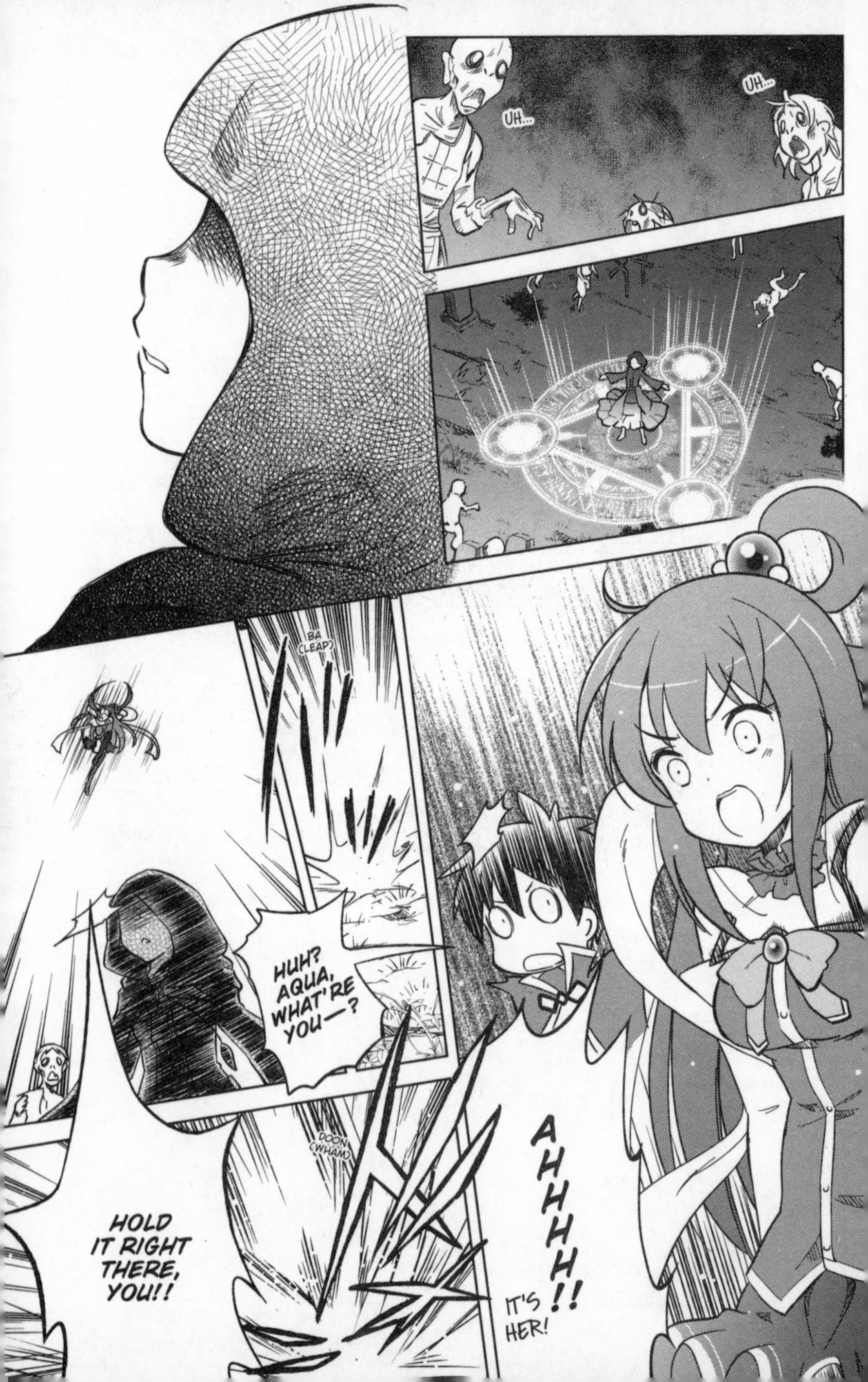
UH...
UH...
IT'S HER!
AHHHHH!!
HUH? AQUA, WHAT'RE YOU—?
BA (LEAP)
DOON (WHAM)
HOLD IT RIGHT THERE, YOU!!

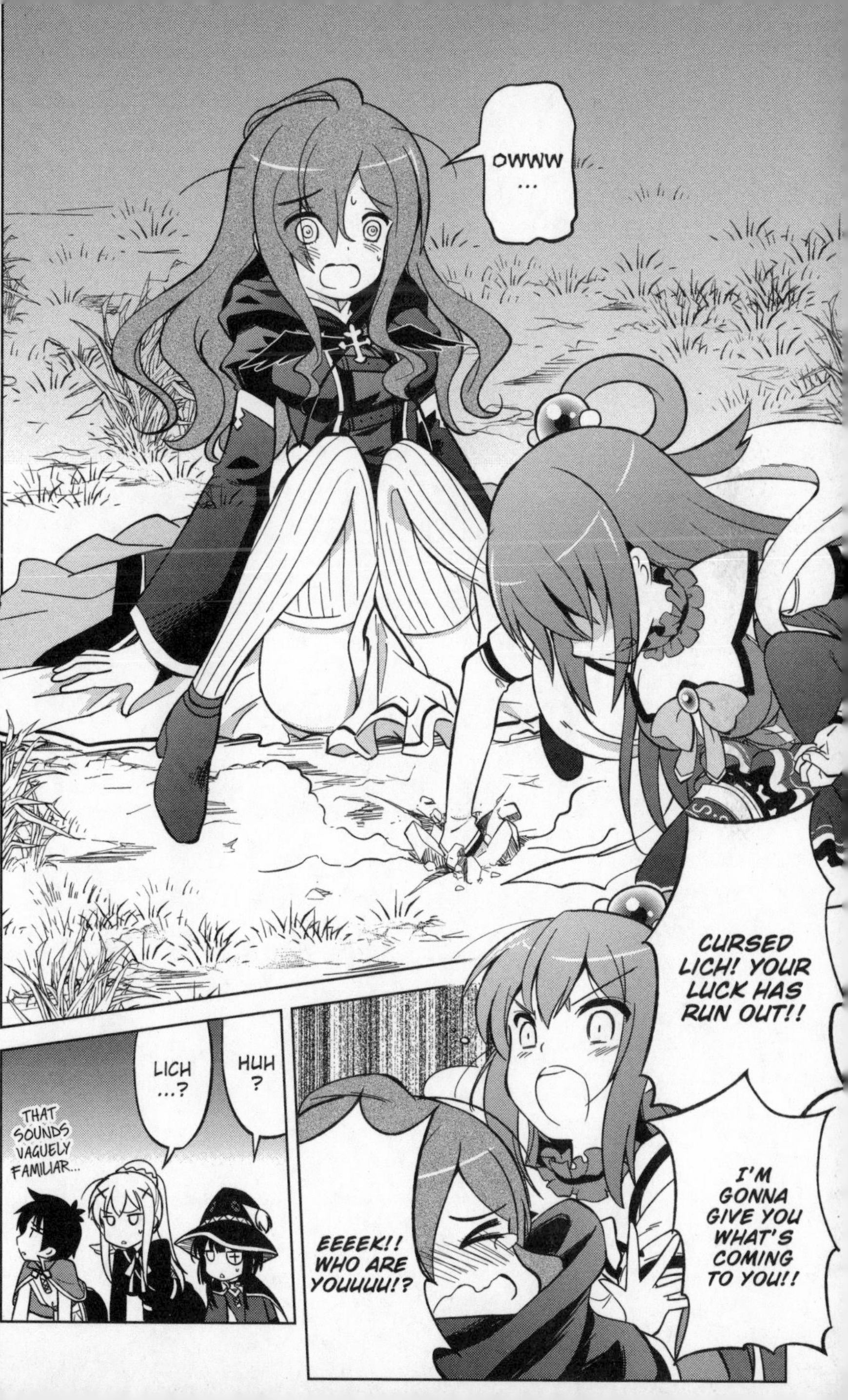
OWWW ...
CURSED LICH! YOUR LUCK HAS RUN OUT!!
I'M GONNA GIVE YOU WHAT'S COMING TO YOU!!
EEEEK!! WHO ARE YOUUUU!?
HUH?
LICH ...?
THAT SOUNDS VAGUELY FAMILIAR...

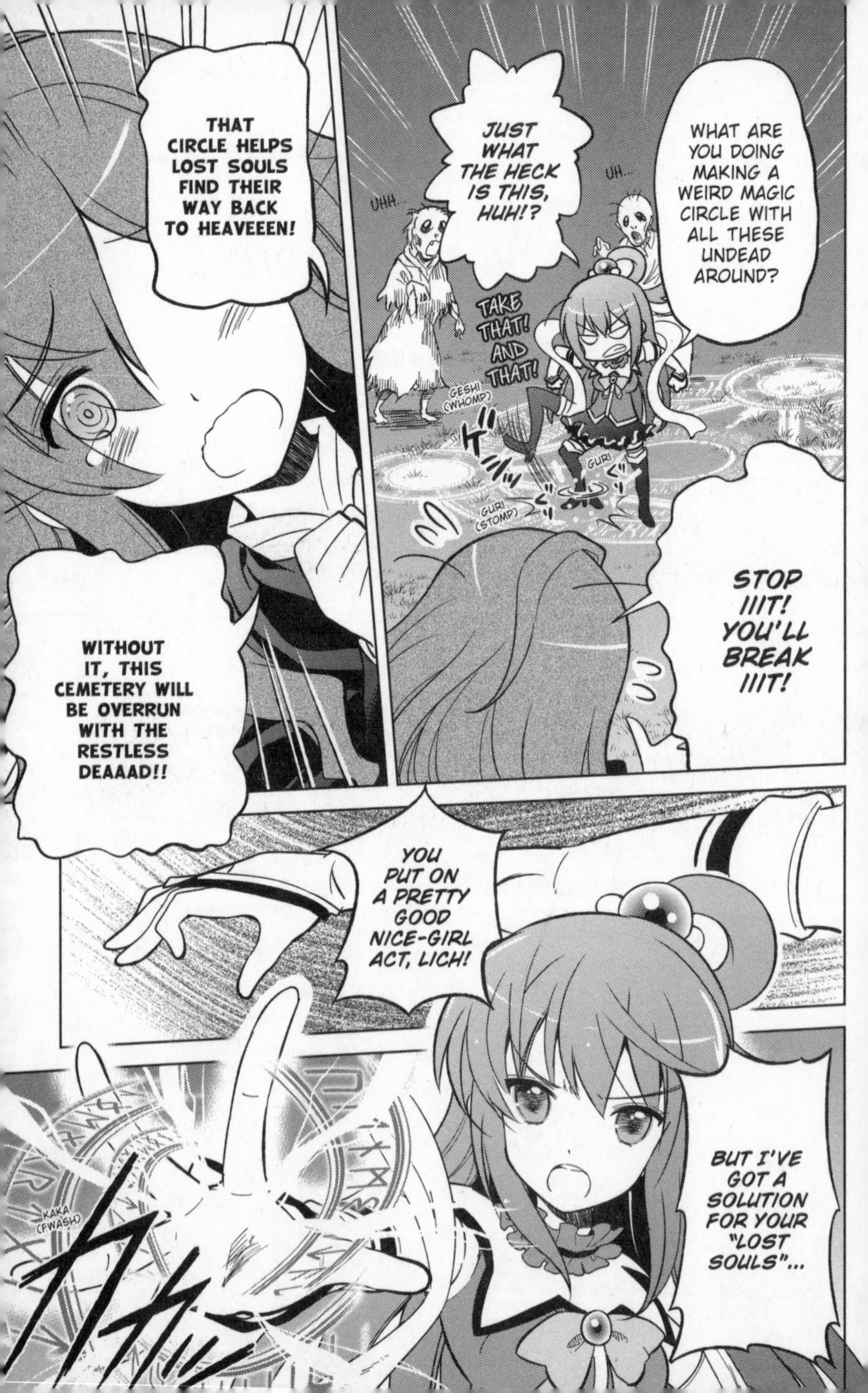
WHAT ARE YOU DOING MAKING A WEIRD MAGIC CIRCLE WITH ALL THESE UNDEAD AROUND?
UH...
JUST WHAT THE HECK IS THIS, HUH!?
UHH...
TAKE THAT! AND THAT!
GESHI (WHOMP)
GURI
GURI (STOMP)
STOP IIIT! YOU'LL BREAK IIIT!
THAT CIRCLE HELPS LOST SOULS FIND THEIR WAY BACK TO HEAVEEEN!
WITHOUT IT, THIS CEMETERY WILL BE OVERRUN WITH THE RESTLESS DEAAAD!!
YOU PUT ON A PRETTY GOOD NICE-GIRL ACT, LICH!
BUT I'VE GOT A SOLUTION FOR YOUR "LOST SOULS"...
KAKA (FWASH)

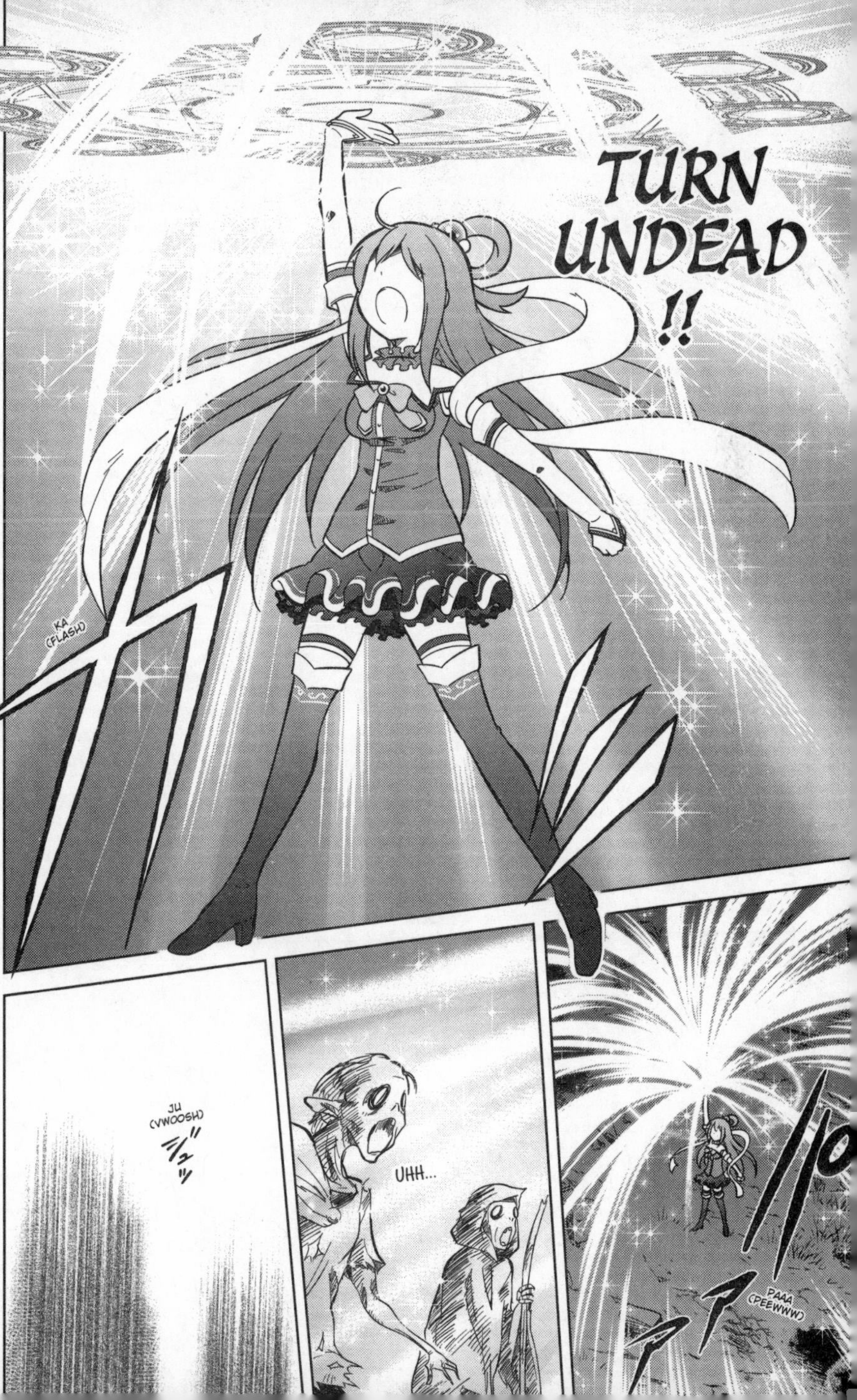
TURN UNDEAD !!
KA (FLASH)
PAAA (PEEWWW)
UHH...
JU (VWOOSH)

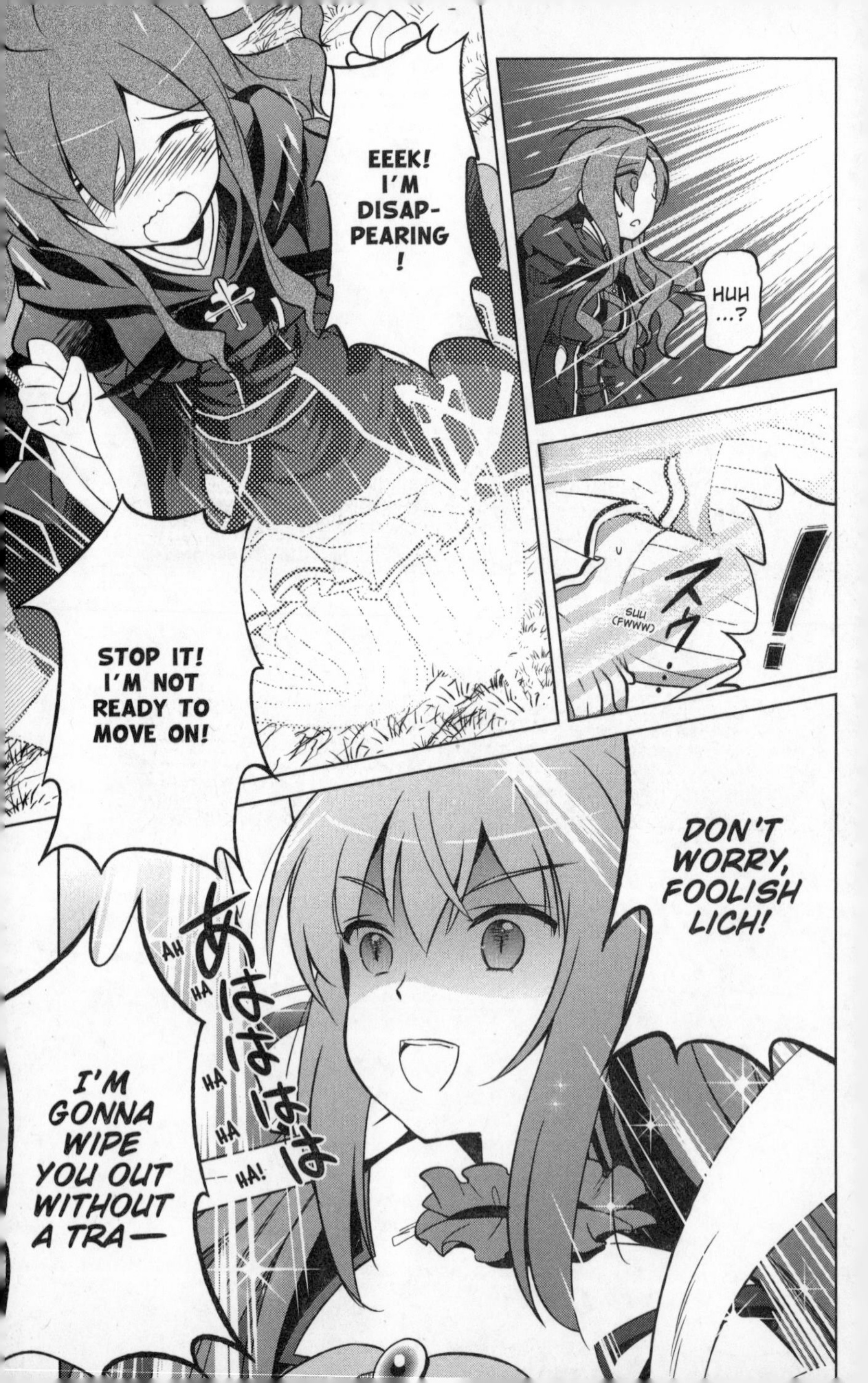
HUH ...?
!
スゥ…
SUU (FWWW)
EEEK! I'M DISAPPEARING!
STOP IT! I'M NOT READY TO MOVE ON!
DON'T WORRY, FOOLISH LICH!
あははーはは
AH HA HA HA HA!
I'M GONNA WIPE YOU OUT WITHOUT A TRA—

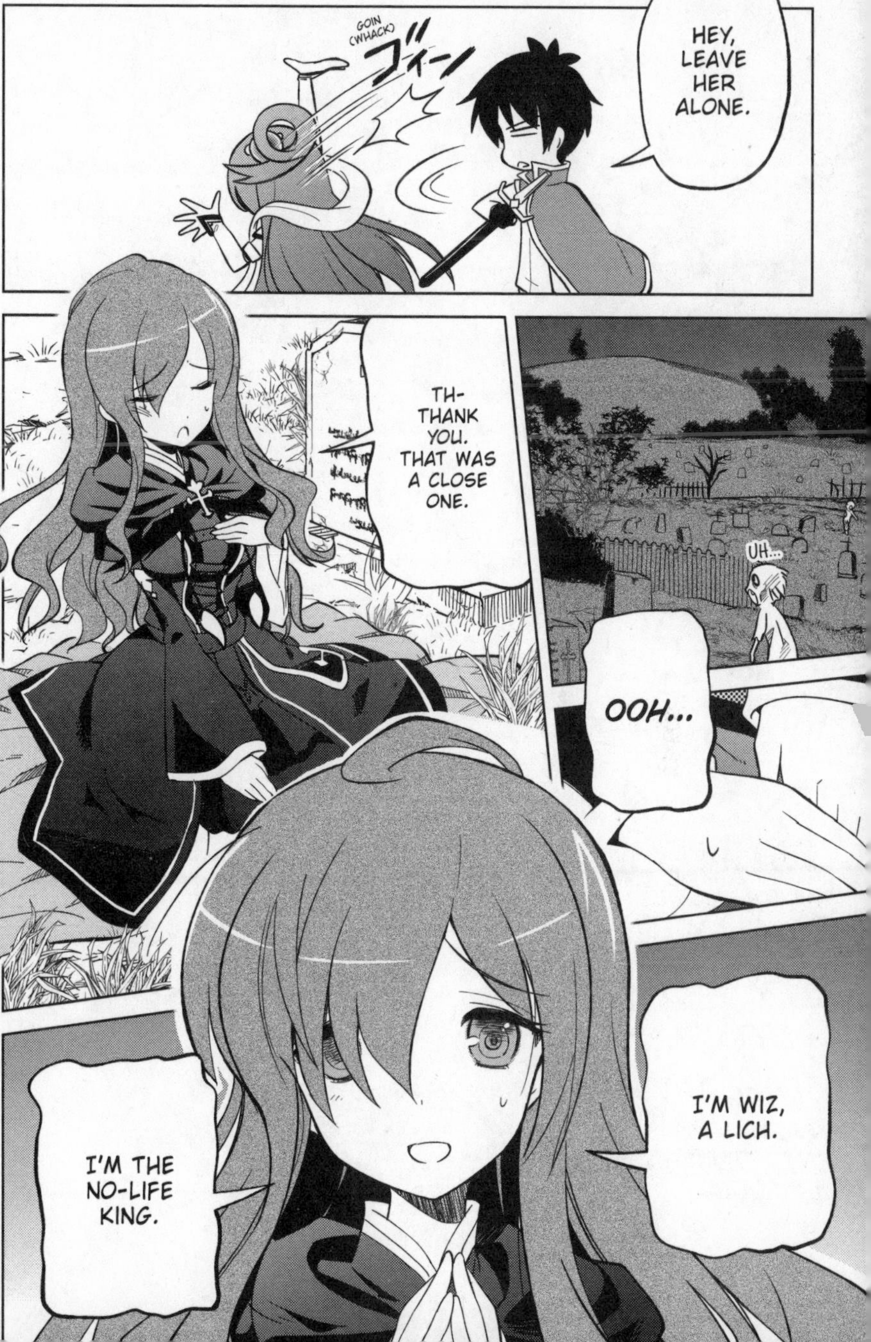
HEY, LEAVE HER ALONE.
GOIN (WHACK)
ゴィーン
UH...
OOH...
TH-THANK YOU. THAT WAS A CLOSE ONE.
I'M WIZ, A LICH.
I'M THE NO-LIFE KING.

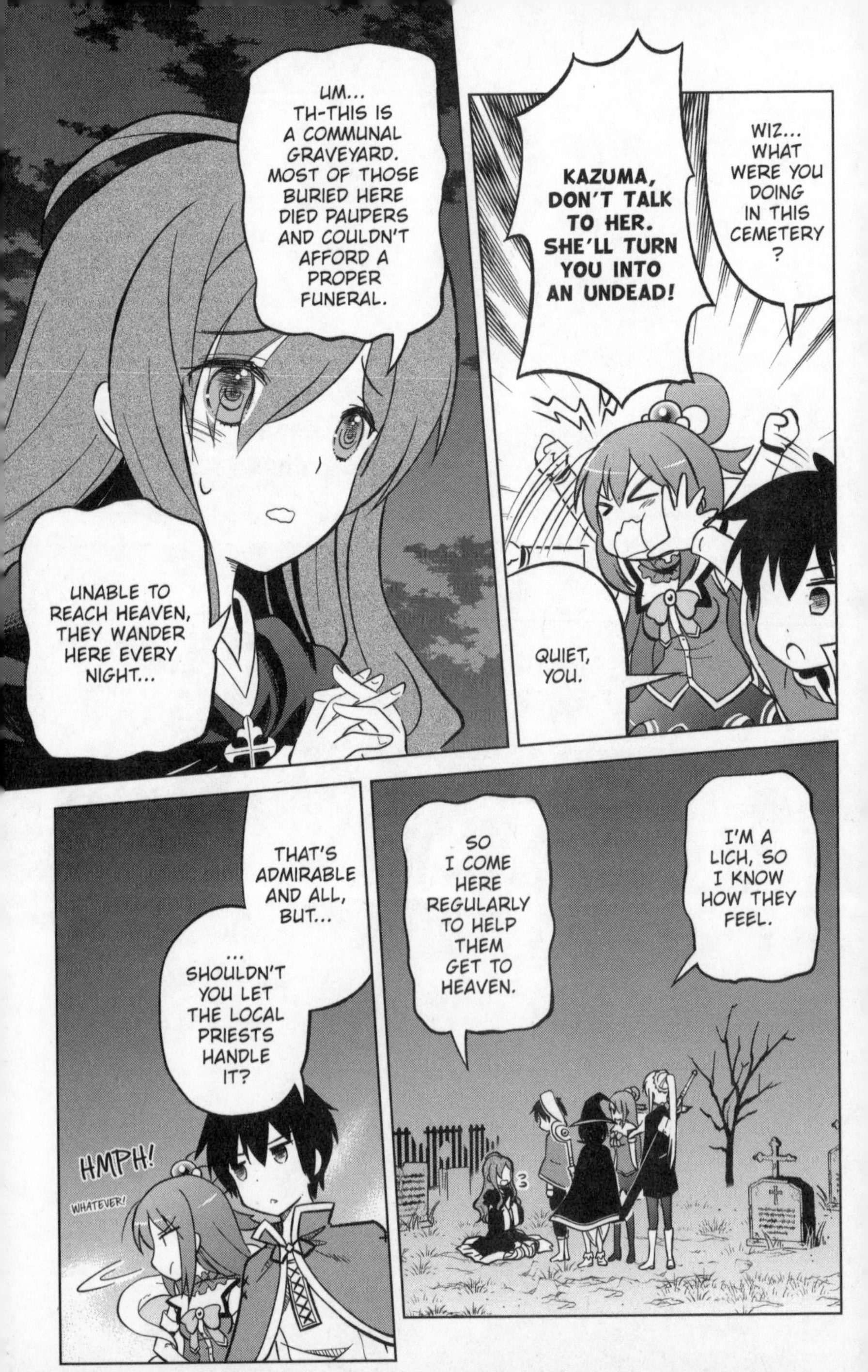
WIZ... WHAT WERE YOU DOING IN THIS CEMETERY ?
KAZUMA, DON'T TALK TO HER. SHE'LL TURN YOU INTO AN UNDEAD!
QUIET, YOU.
UM... TH-THIS IS A COMMUNAL GRAVEYARD. MOST OF THOSE BURIED HERE DIED PAUPERS AND COULDN'T AFFORD A PROPER FUNERAL.
UNABLE TO REACH HEAVEN, THEY WANDER HERE EVERY NIGHT...
I'M A LICH, SO I KNOW HOW THEY FEEL.
SO I COME HERE REGULARLY TO HELP THEM GET TO HEAVEN.
THAT'S ADMIRABLE AND ALL, BUT...
... SHOULDN'T YOU LET THE LOCAL PRIESTS HANDLE IT?
HMPH!
WHATEVER!

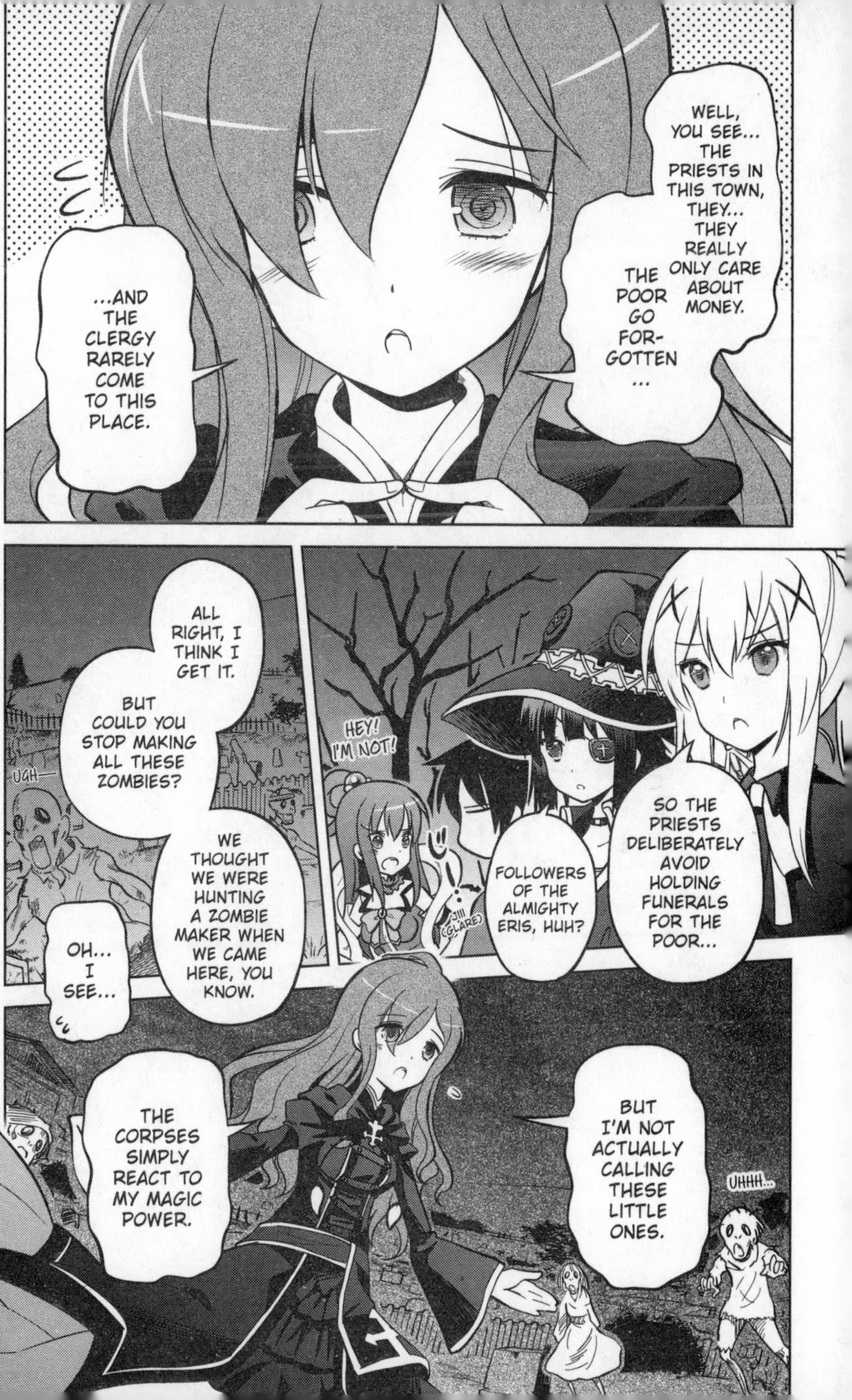
WELL, YOU SEE... THE PRIESTS IN THIS TOWN, THEY... THEY REALLY ONLY CARE ABOUT MONEY.
THE POOR GO FOR-GOTTEN ...
...AND THE CLERGY RARELY COME TO THIS PLACE.
SO THE PRIESTS DELIBERATELY AVOID HOLDING FUNERALS FOR THE POOR...
FOLLOWERS OF THE ALMIGHTY ERIS, HUH?
HEY! I'M NOT!
JIII (GLARE)
ALL RIGHT, I THINK I GET IT.
BUT COULD YOU STOP MAKING ALL THESE ZOMBIES?
UGH—
WE THOUGHT WE WERE HUNTING A ZOMBIE MAKER WHEN WE CAME HERE, YOU KNOW.
OH... I SEE...
BUT I'M NOT ACTUALLY CALLING THESE LITTLE ONES.
UHHH...
THE CORPSES SIMPLY REACT TO MY MAGIC POWER.

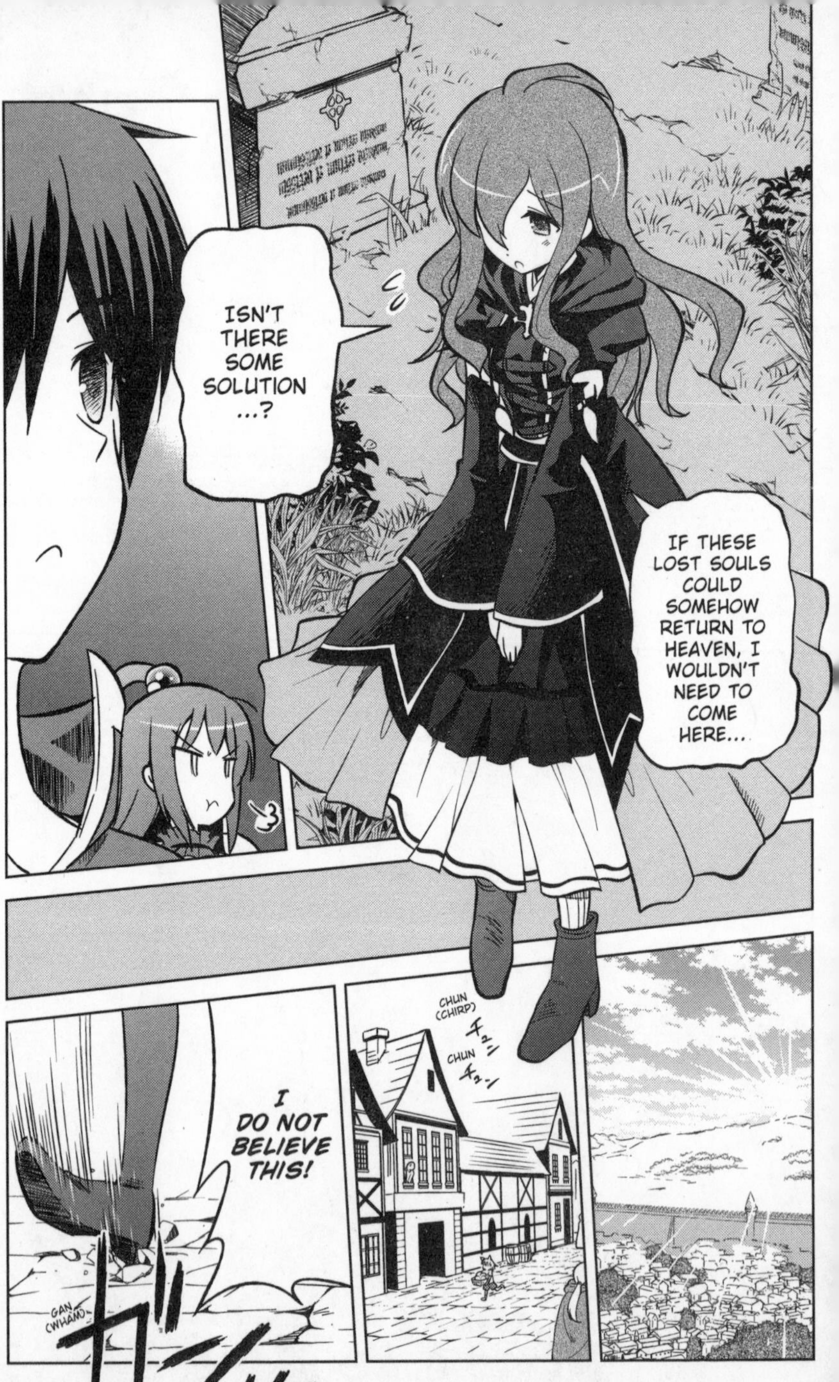
IF THESE LOST SOULS COULD SOMEHOW RETURN TO HEAVEN, I WOULDN'T NEED TO COME HERE...
ISN'T THERE SOME SOLUTION ...?
CHUN (CHIRP)
CHUN
I DO NOT BELIEVE THIS!
GAN (WHAM)

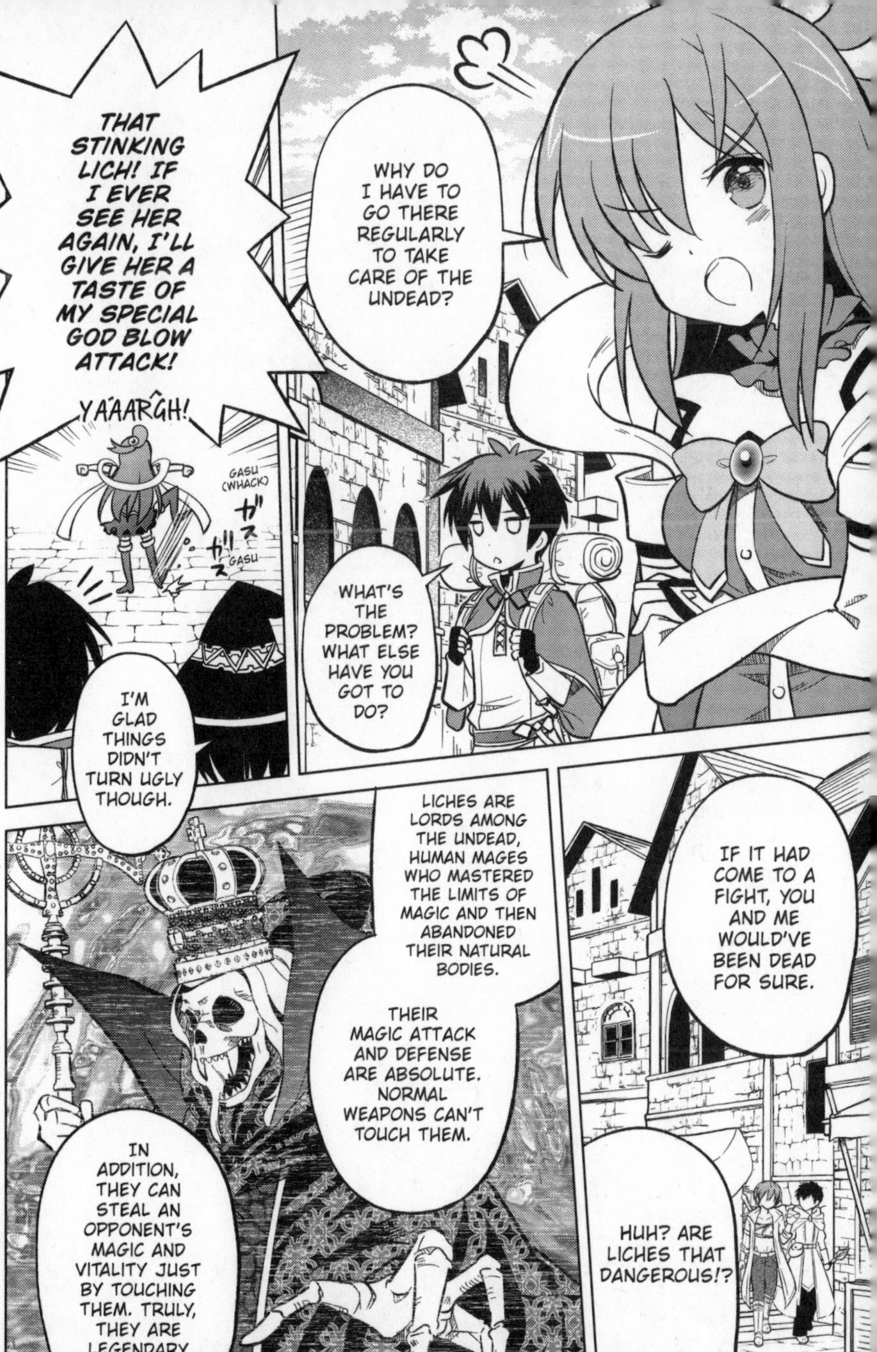
WHY DO I HAVE TO GO THERE REGULARLY TO TAKE CARE OF THE UNDEAD?
WHAT'S THE PROBLEM? WHAT ELSE HAVE YOU GOT TO DO?
THAT STINKING LICH! IF I EVER SEE HER AGAIN, I'LL GIVE HER A TASTE OF MY SPECIAL GOD BLOW ATTACK!
YAAARGH!
GASU (WHACK)
GASU
I'M GLAD THINGS DIDN'T TURN UGLY THOUGH.
IF IT HAD COME TO A FIGHT, YOU AND ME WOULD'VE BEEN DEAD FOR SURE.
HUH? ARE LICHES THAT DANGEROUS!?
LICHES ARE LORDS AMONG THE UNDEAD, HUMAN MAGES WHO MASTERED THE LIMITS OF MAGIC AND THEN ABANDONED THEIR NATURAL BODIES.
THEIR MAGIC ATTACK AND DEFENSE ARE ABSOLUTE. NORMAL WEAPONS CAN'T TOUCH THEM.
IN ADDITION, THEY CAN STEAL AN OPPONENT'S MAGIC AND VITALITY JUST BY TOUCHING THEM. TRULY, THEY ARE LEGENDARY FOES.

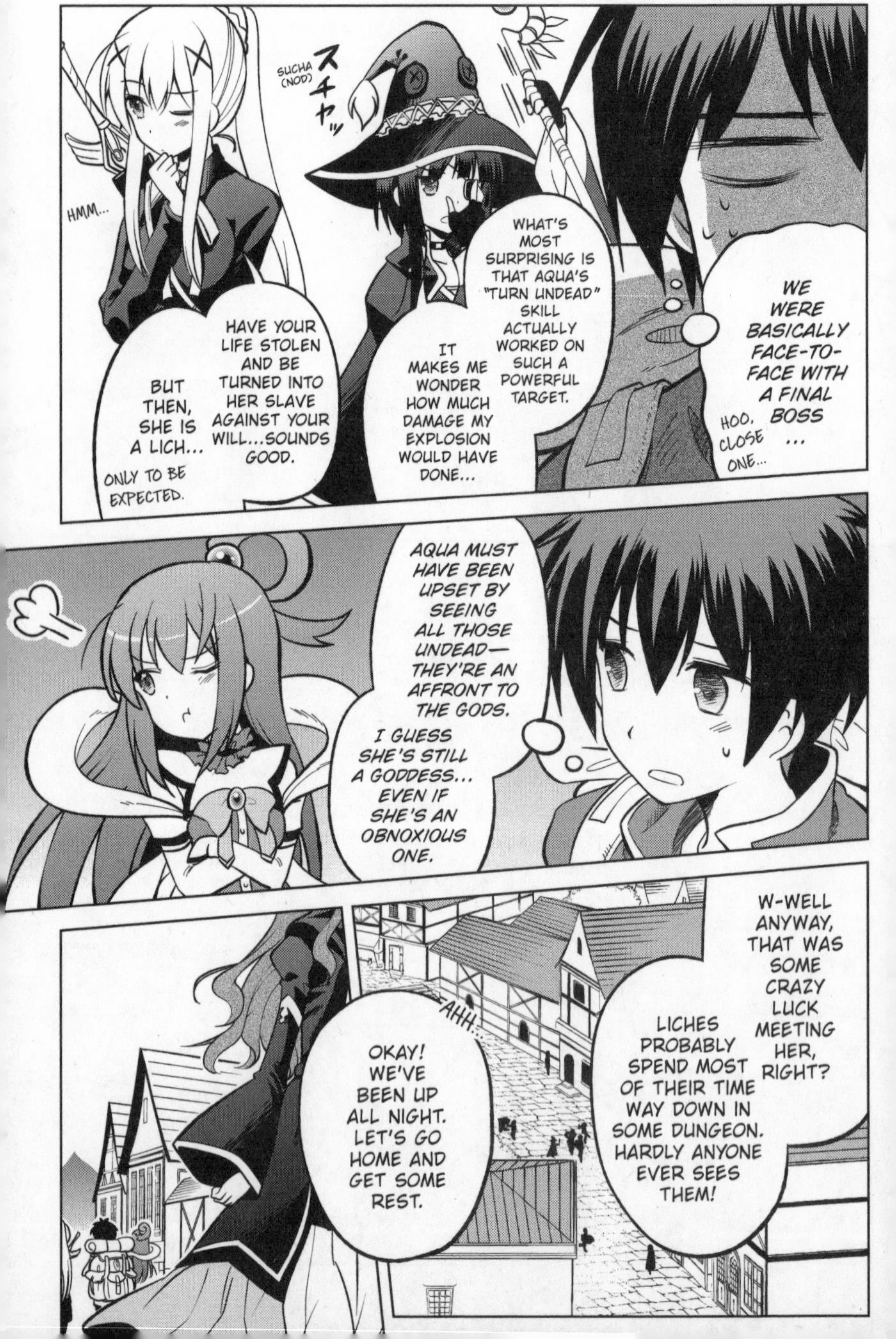
WE WERE BASICALLY FACE-TO-FACE WITH A FINAL BOSS...
HOO, CLOSE ONE...
スチャッ
SUCHA (NOD)
WHAT'S MOST SURPRISING IS THAT AQUA'S "TURN UNDEAD" SKILL ACTUALLY WORKED ON SUCH A POWERFUL TARGET.
IT MAKES ME WONDER HOW MUCH DAMAGE MY EXPLOSION WOULD HAVE DONE...
HAVE YOUR LIFE STOLEN AND BE TURNED INTO HER SLAVE AGAINST YOUR WILL...SOUNDS GOOD.
HMM...
BUT THEN, SHE IS A LICH...
ONLY TO BE EXPECTED.
AQUA MUST HAVE BEEN UPSET BY SEEING ALL THOSE UNDEAD—THEY'RE AN AFFRONT TO THE GODS.
I GUESS SHE'S STILL A GODDESS... EVEN IF SHE'S AN OBNOXIOUS ONE.
W-WELL ANYWAY, THAT WAS SOME CRAZY LUCK MEETING HER, RIGHT?
LICHES PROBABLY SPEND MOST OF THEIR TIME WAY DOWN IN SOME DUNGEON. HARDLY ANYONE EVER SEES THEM!
AHHH...
OKAY! WE'VE BEEN UP ALL NIGHT. LET'S GO HOME AND GET SOME REST.

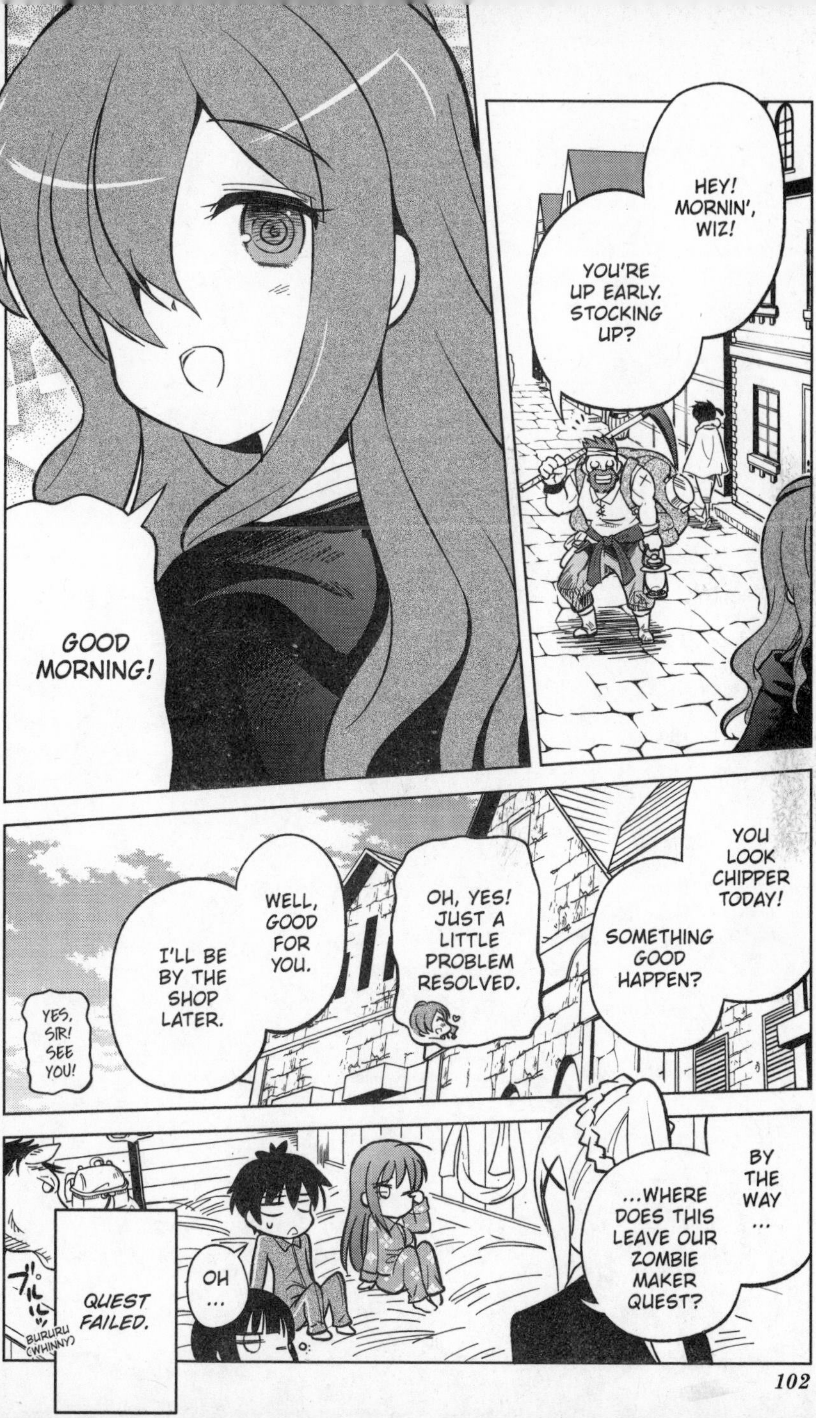
HEY! MORNIN', WIZ!
YOU'RE UP EARLY. STOCKING UP?
GOOD MORNING!
YOU LOOK CHIPPER TODAY!
SOMETHING GOOD HAPPEN?
OH, YES! JUST A LITTLE PROBLEM RESOLVED.
WELL, GOOD FOR YOU.
I'LL BE BY THE SHOP LATER.
YES, SIR! SEE YOU!
BY THE WAY...
...WHERE DOES THIS LEAVE OUR ZOMBIE MAKER QUEST?
OH...
BURURU (WHINNY)
QUEST FAILED.

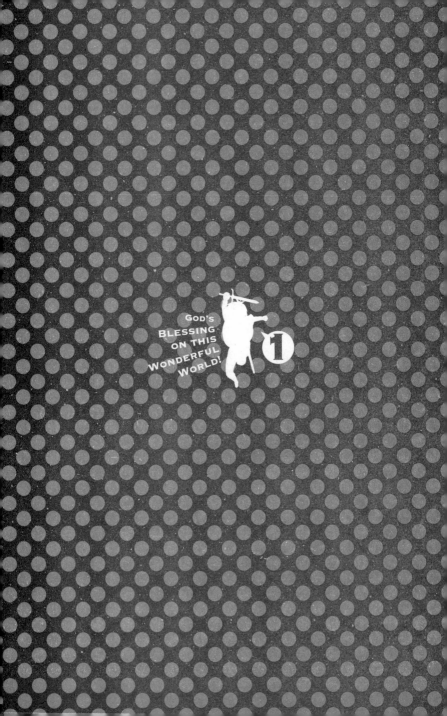

GOD'S
BLESSING
ON THIS
WONDERFUL
WORLD!

1

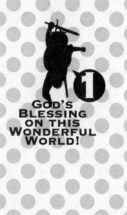

GOD'S
BLESSING
ON THIS
WONDERFUL
WORLD!

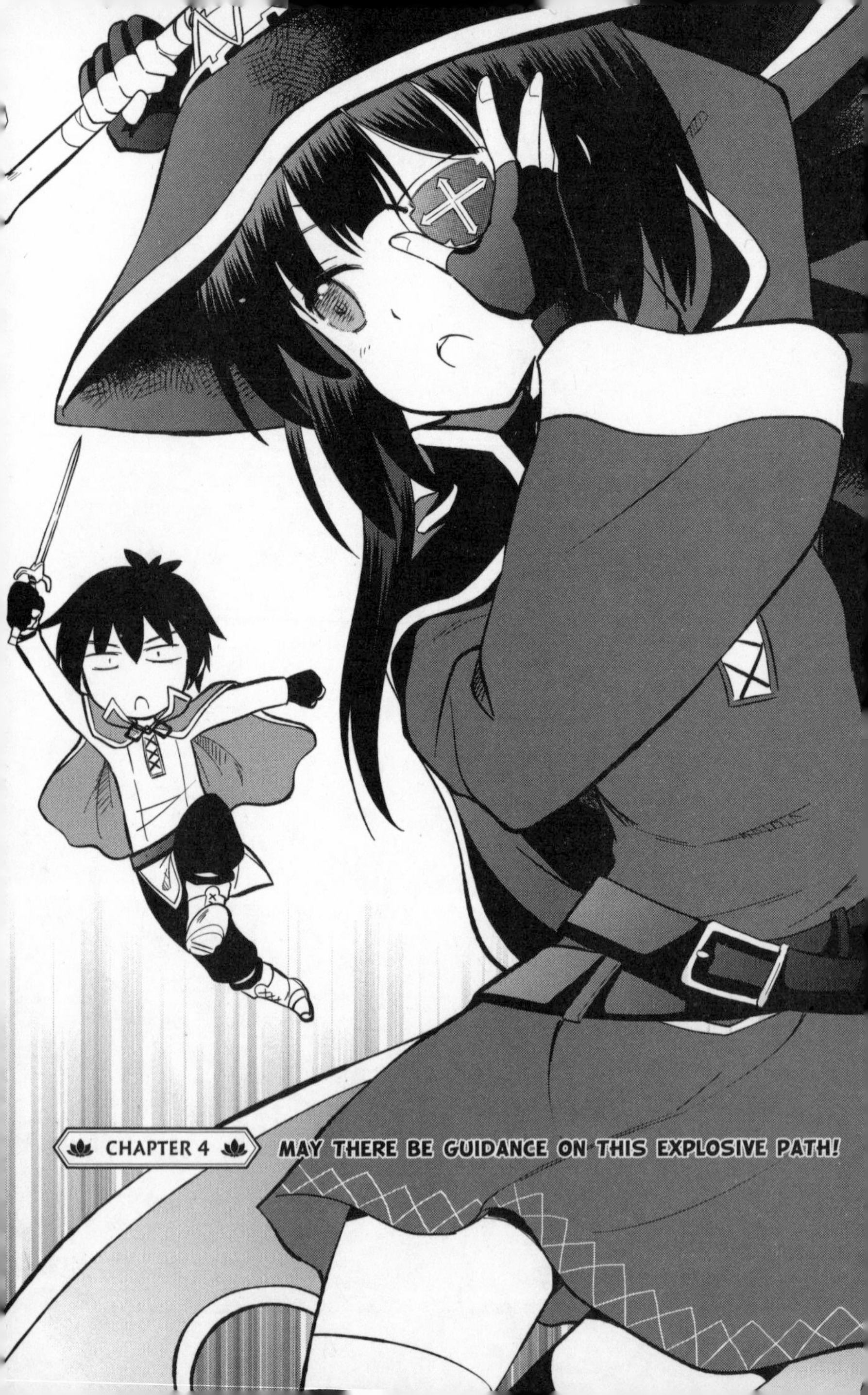
CHAPTER 4
MAY THERE BE GUIDANCE ON THIS EXPLOSIVE PATH!

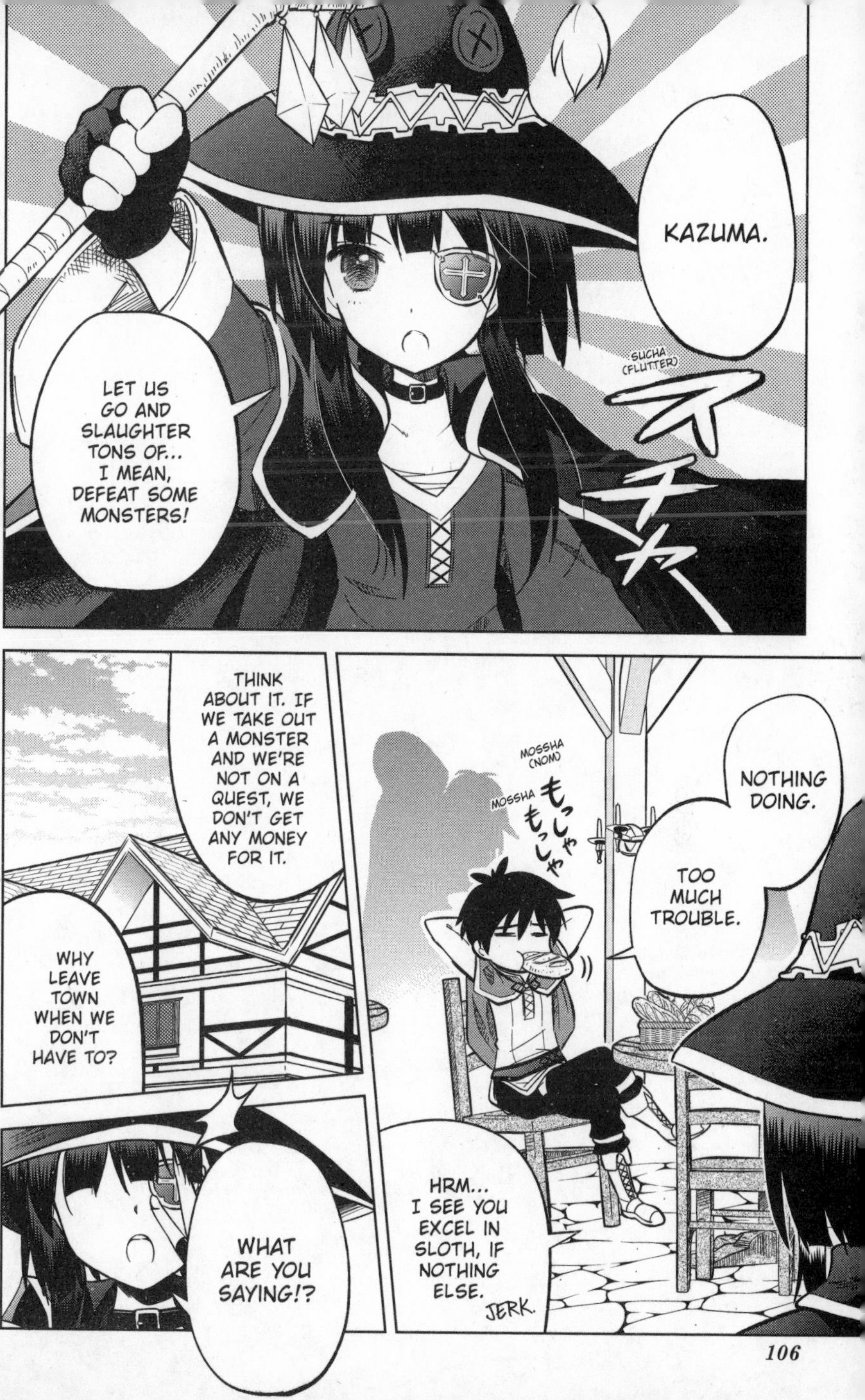
KAZUMA.
SUCHA (FLUTTER)
スチャ
LET US GO AND SLAUGHTER TONS OF... I MEAN, DEFEAT SOME MONSTERS!
NOTHING DOING.
TOO MUCH TROUBLE.
MOSSHA (NOM)
MOSSHA
もっしゃもっしゃ
HRM... I SEE YOU EXCEL IN SLOTH, IF NOTHING ELSE.
JERK.
THINK ABOUT IT. IF WE TAKE OUT A MONSTER AND WE'RE NOT ON A QUEST, WE DON'T GET ANY MONEY FOR IT.
WHY LEAVE TOWN WHEN WE DON'T HAVE TO?
WHAT ARE YOU SAYING!?

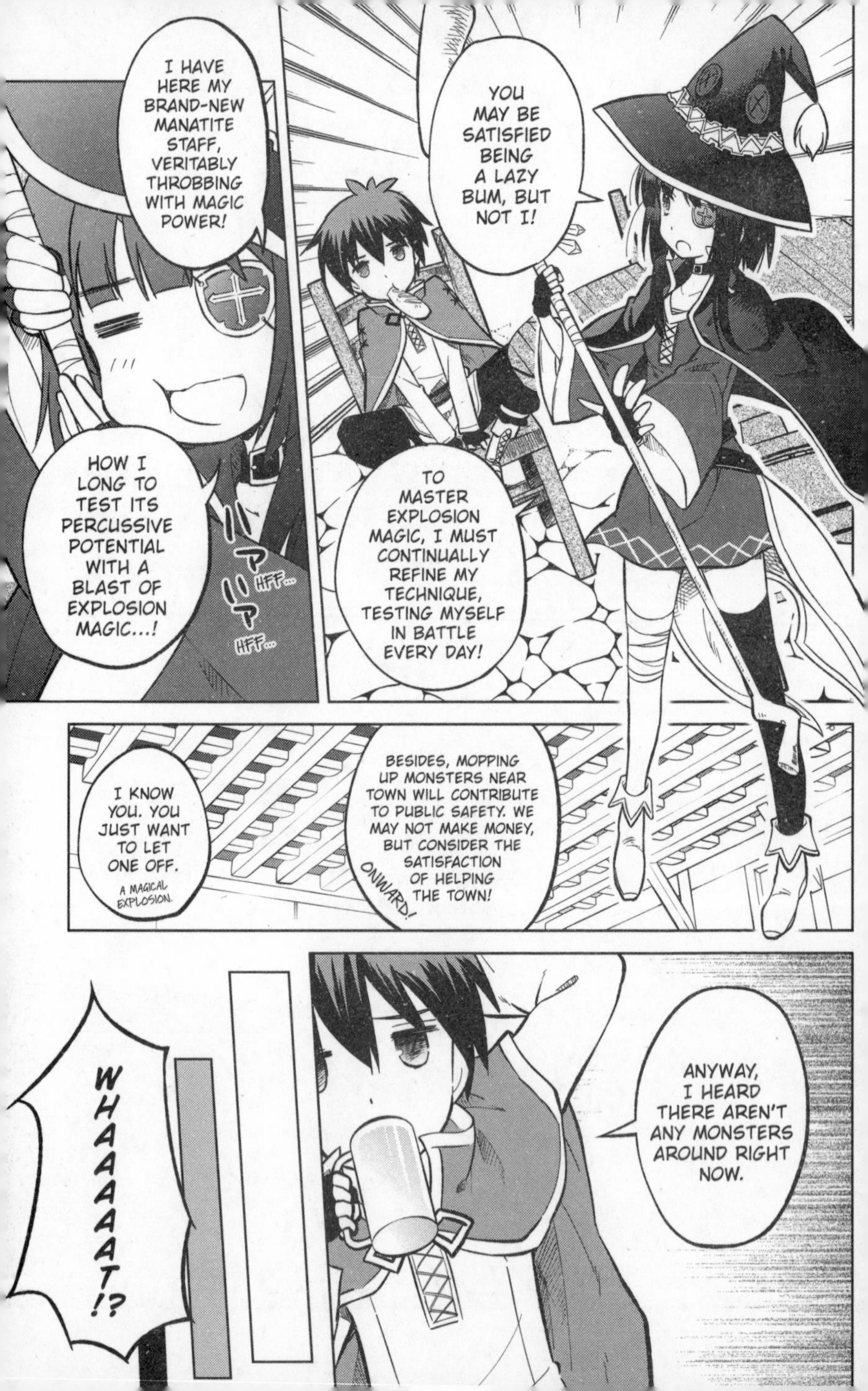
YOU MAY BE SATISFIED BEING A LAZY BUM, BUT NOT I!
TO MASTER EXPLOSION MAGIC, I MUST CONTINUALLY REFINE MY TECHNIQUE, TESTING MYSELF IN BATTLE EVERY DAY!
I HAVE HERE MY BRAND-NEW MANATITE STAFF, VERITABLY THROBBING WITH MAGIC POWER!
HOW I LONG TO TEST ITS PERCUSSIVE POTENTIAL WITH A BLAST OF EXPLOSION MAGIC...!
ハァ HFF...
ハァ HFF...
BESIDES, MOPPING UP MONSTERS NEAR TOWN WILL CONTRIBUTE TO PUBLIC SAFETY. WE MAY NOT MAKE MONEY, BUT CONSIDER THE SATISFACTION OF HELPING THE TOWN!
ONWARD!
I KNOW YOU. YOU JUST WANT TO LET ONE OFF.
A MAGICAL EXPLOSION.
ANYWAY, I HEARD THERE AREN'T ANY MONSTERS AROUND RIGHT NOW.
WHAAAAAAT!?

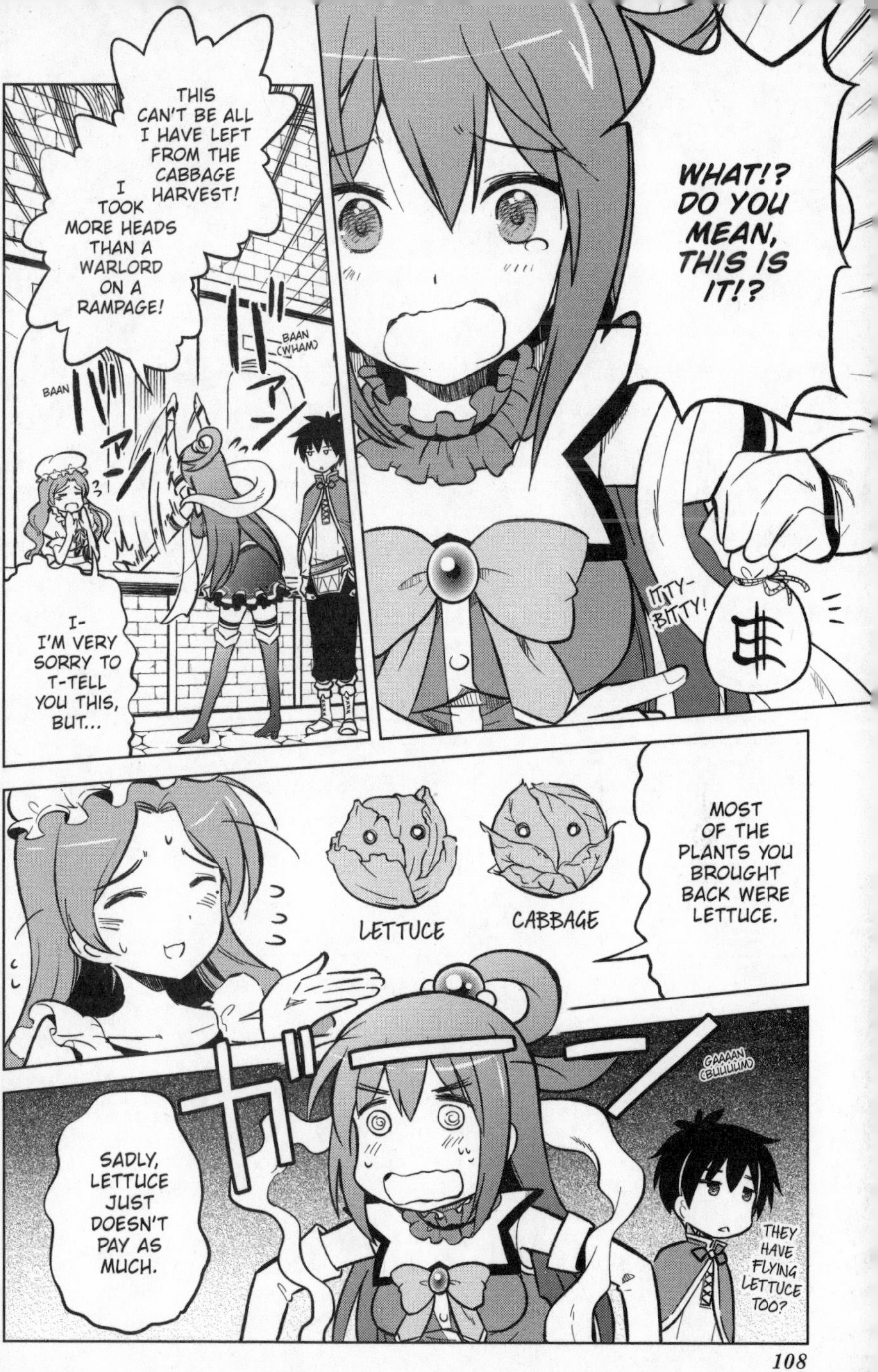
WHAT!? DO YOU MEAN, THIS IS IT!?
ITTY-BITTY!
THIS CAN'T BE ALL I HAVE LEFT FROM THE CABBAGE HARVEST!
I TOOK MORE HEADS THAN A WARLORD ON A RAMPAGE!
BAAN (WHAM)
BAAN
I- I'M VERY SORRY TO T-TELL YOU THIS, BUT...
MOST OF THE PLANTS YOU BROUGHT BACK WERE LETTUCE.
CABBAGE
LETTUCE
GAAAAN (BUUUUUM)
THEY HAVE FLYING LETTUCE TOO?
SADLY, LETTUCE JUST DOESN'T PAY AS MUCH.

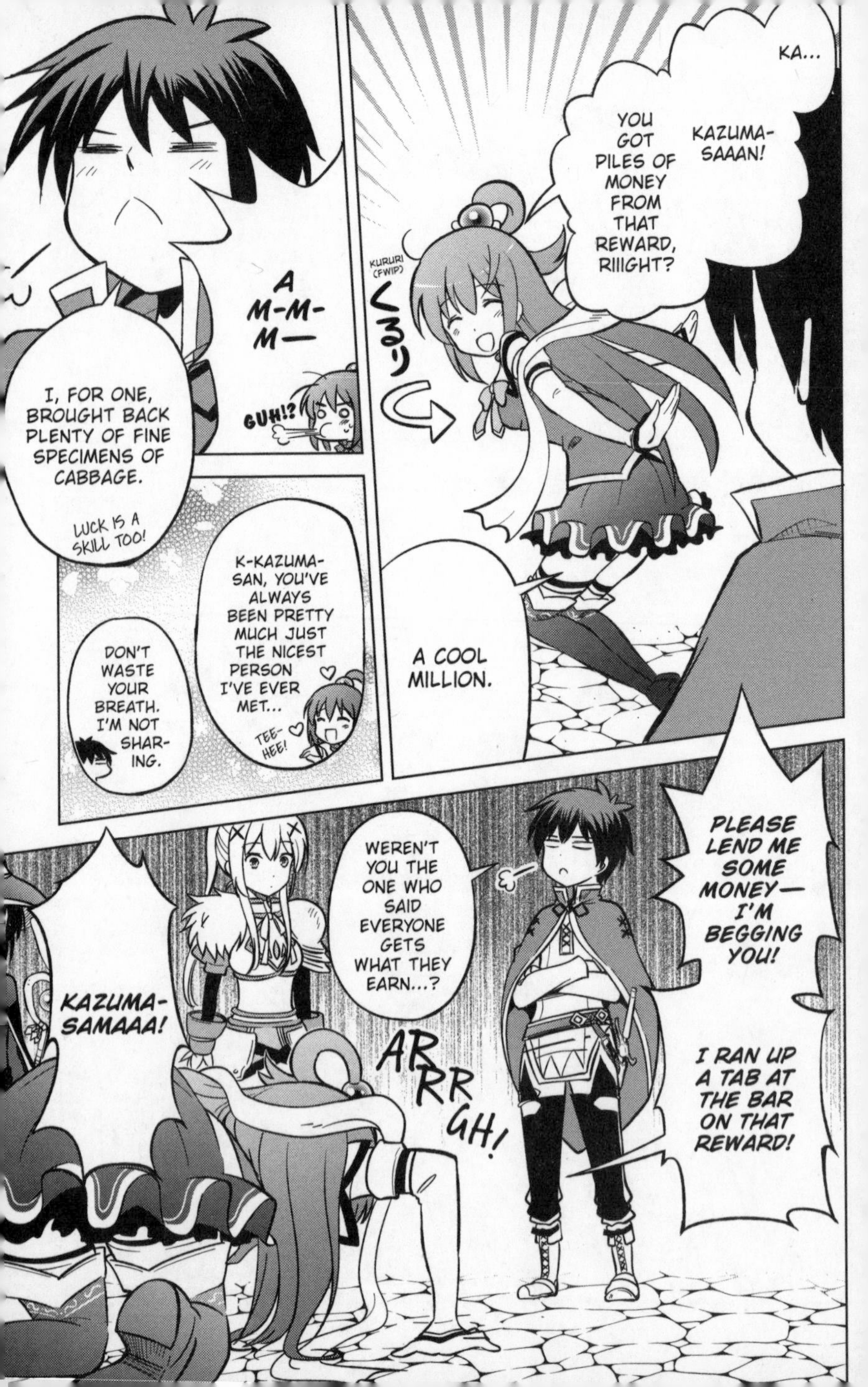
KA...
KAZUMA-SAAAN!
YOU GOT PILES OF MONEY FROM THAT REWARD, RIIIGHT?
KURURI (FWIP)
くるり
A COOL MILLION.
A M-M-M—
GUH!?
I, FOR ONE, BROUGHT BACK PLENTY OF FINE SPECIMENS OF CABBAGE.
LUCK IS A SKILL TOO!
K-KAZUMA-SAN, YOU'VE ALWAYS BEEN PRETTY MUCH JUST THE NICEST PERSON I'VE EVER MET...♡
TEE-HEE!♡
DON'T WASTE YOUR BREATH. I'M NOT SHARING.
PLEASE LEND ME SOME MONEY— I'M BEGGING YOU!
I RAN UP A TAB AT THE BAR ON THAT REWARD!
WEREN'T YOU THE ONE WHO SAID EVERYONE GETS WHAT THEY EARN...?
ARRRGH!
KAZUMA-SAMAAA!

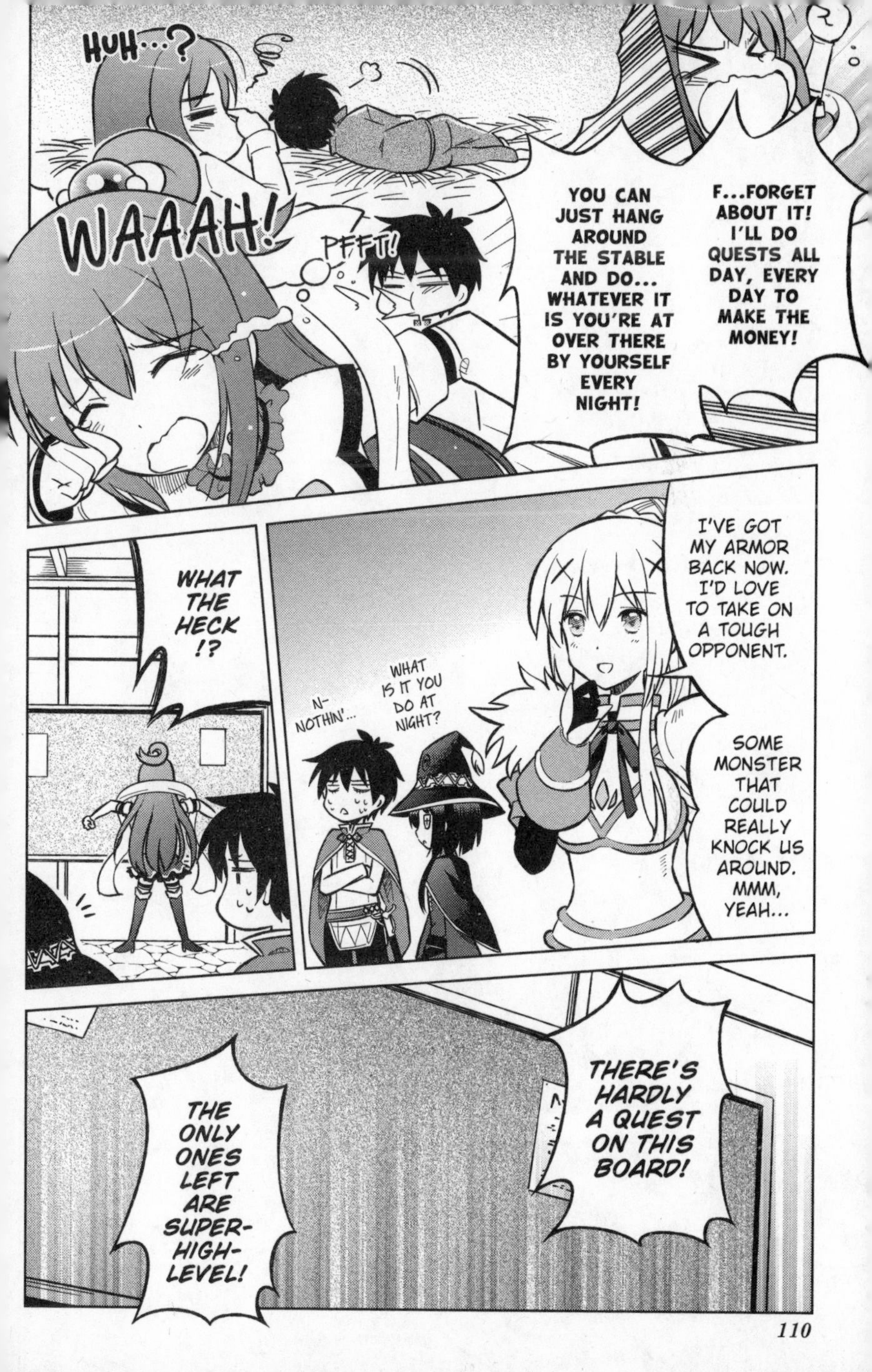
F...FORGET ABOUT IT! I'LL DO QUESTS ALL DAY, EVERY DAY TO MAKE THE MONEY!
YOU CAN JUST HANG AROUND THE STABLE AND DO... WHATEVER IT IS YOU'RE AT OVER THERE BY YOURSELF EVERY NIGHT!
HUH...?
WAAAH!
PFFT!
I'VE GOT MY ARMOR BACK NOW. I'D LOVE TO TAKE ON A TOUGH OPPONENT.
SOME MONSTER THAT COULD REALLY KNOCK US AROUND. MMM, YEAH...
WHAT IS IT YOU DO AT NIGHT?
N-NOTHIN'...
WHAT THE HECK!?
THERE'S HARDLY A QUEST ON THIS BOARD!
THE ONLY ONES LEFT ARE SUPER-HIGH-LEVEL!

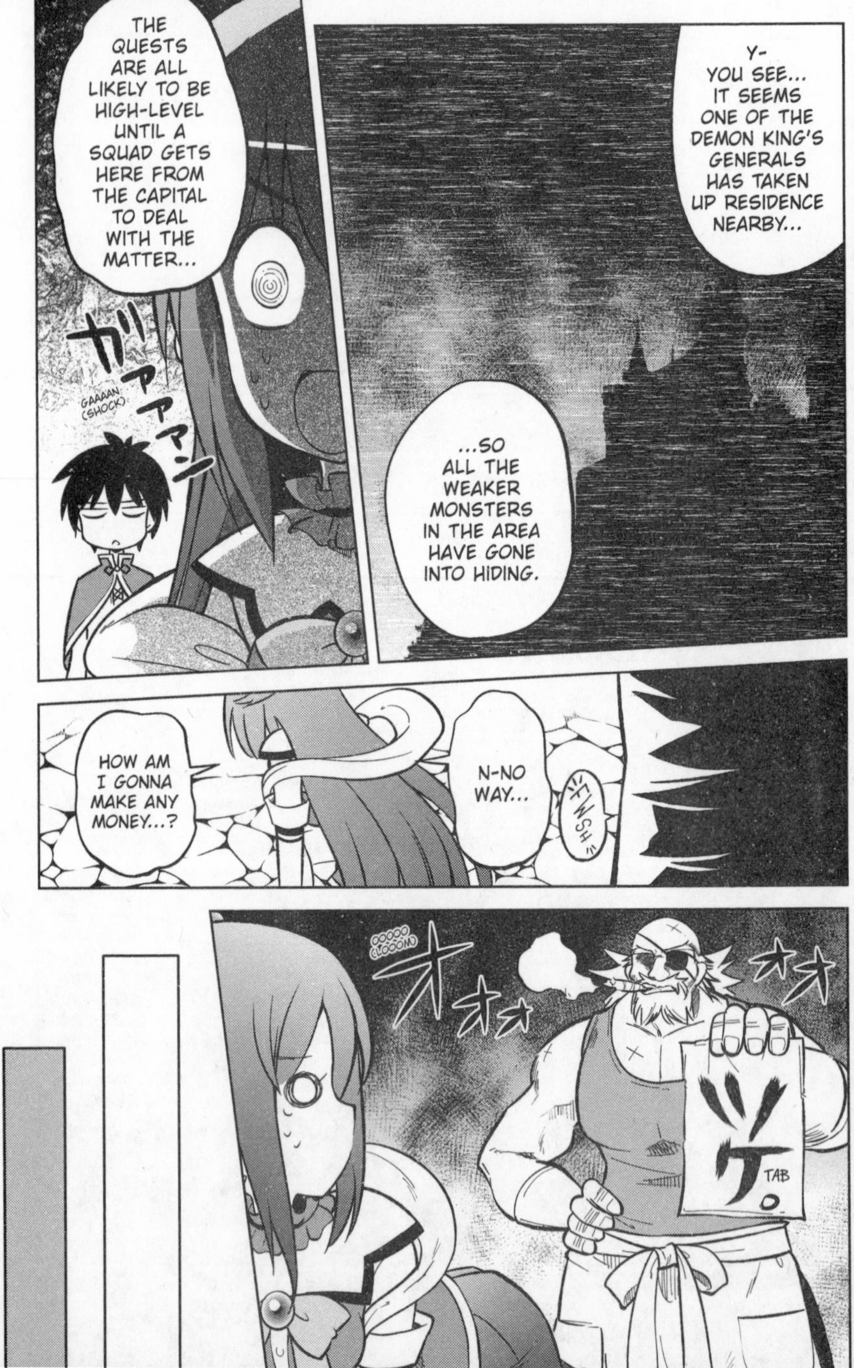
Y- YOU SEE... IT SEEMS ONE OF THE DEMON KING'S GENERALS HAS TAKEN UP RESIDENCE NEARBY...
...SO ALL THE WEAKER MONSTERS IN THE AREA HAVE GONE INTO HIDING.
THE QUESTS ARE ALL LIKELY TO BE HIGH-LEVEL UNTIL A SQUAD GETS HERE FROM THE CAPITAL TO DEAL WITH THE MATTER...
ガァァァン
GAAAAN (SHOCK)
FWSH
N-NO WAY...
HOW AM I GONNA MAKE ANY MONEY...?
オオオ
OOOOO (LOOOM)
ツケ。
TAB

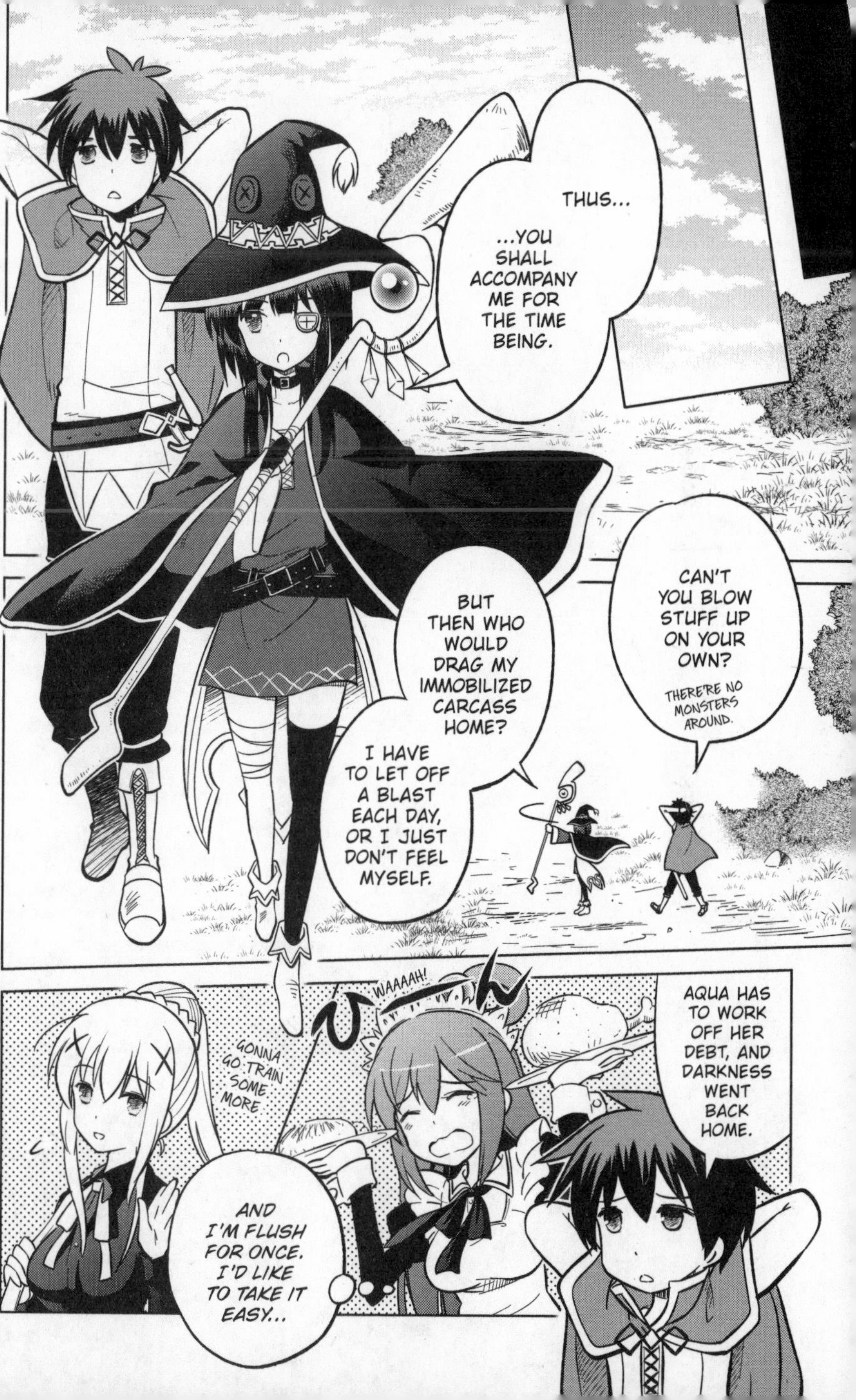
THUS...
...YOU SHALL ACCOMPANY ME FOR THE TIME BEING.
CAN'T YOU BLOW STUFF UP ON YOUR OWN?
THERE'RE NO MONSTERS AROUND.
BUT THEN WHO WOULD DRAG MY IMMOBILIZED CARCASS HOME?
I HAVE TO LET OFF A BLAST EACH DAY, OR I JUST DON'T FEEL MYSELF.
AQUA HAS TO WORK OFF HER DEBT, AND DARKNESS WENT BACK HOME.
WAAAAH!
AND I'M FLUSH FOR ONCE. I'D LIKE TO TAKE IT EASY...
GONNA GO TRAIN SOME MORE

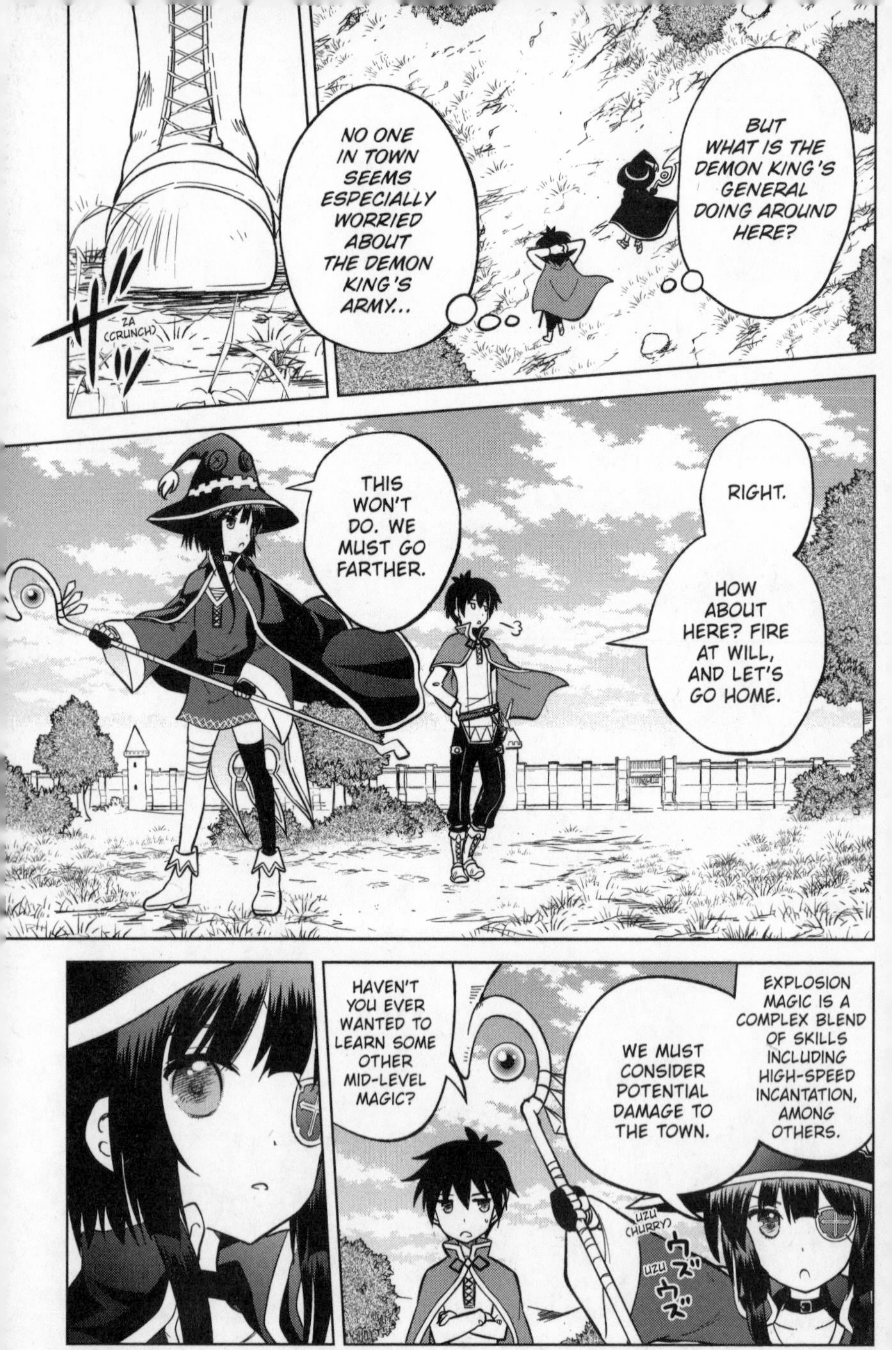
NO ONE IN TOWN SEEMS ESPECIALLY WORRIED ABOUT THE DEMON KING'S ARMY...
BUT WHAT IS THE DEMON KING'S GENERAL DOING AROUND HERE?
ZA (CRUNCH)
RIGHT.
HOW ABOUT HERE? FIRE AT WILL, AND LET'S GO HOME.
THIS WON'T DO. WE MUST GO FARTHER.
EXPLOSION MAGIC IS A COMPLEX BLEND OF SKILLS INCLUDING HIGH-SPEED INCANTATION, AMONG OTHERS.
WE MUST CONSIDER POTENTIAL DAMAGE TO THE TOWN.
HAVEN'T YOU EVER WANTED TO LEARN SOME OTHER MID-LEVEL MAGIC?
UZU (HURRY) ウズ
UZU ウズ

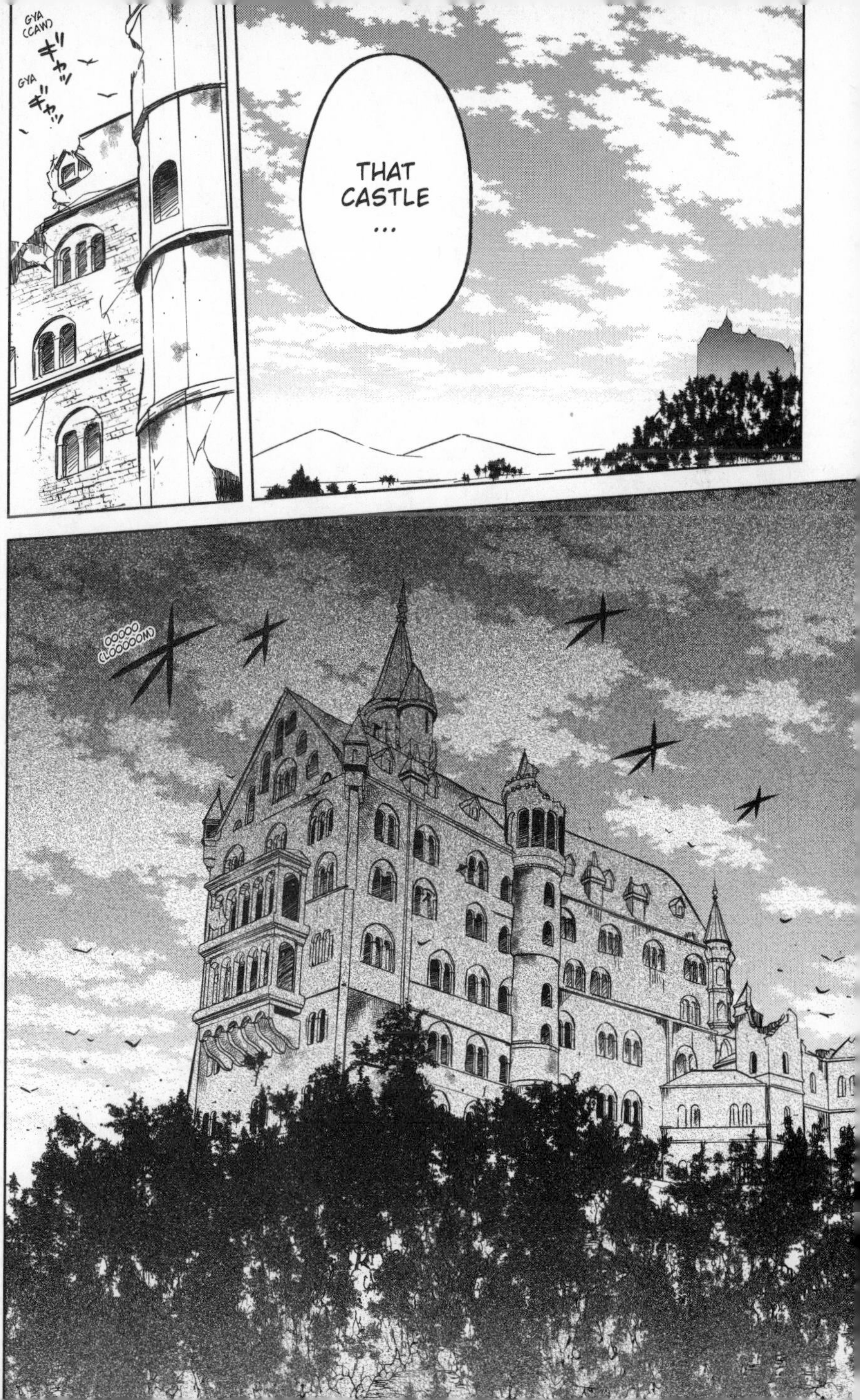
THAT CASTLE ...
GYA (CAW)
ギャッ
GYA
ギャッ
OOOOO (LOOOOOM)

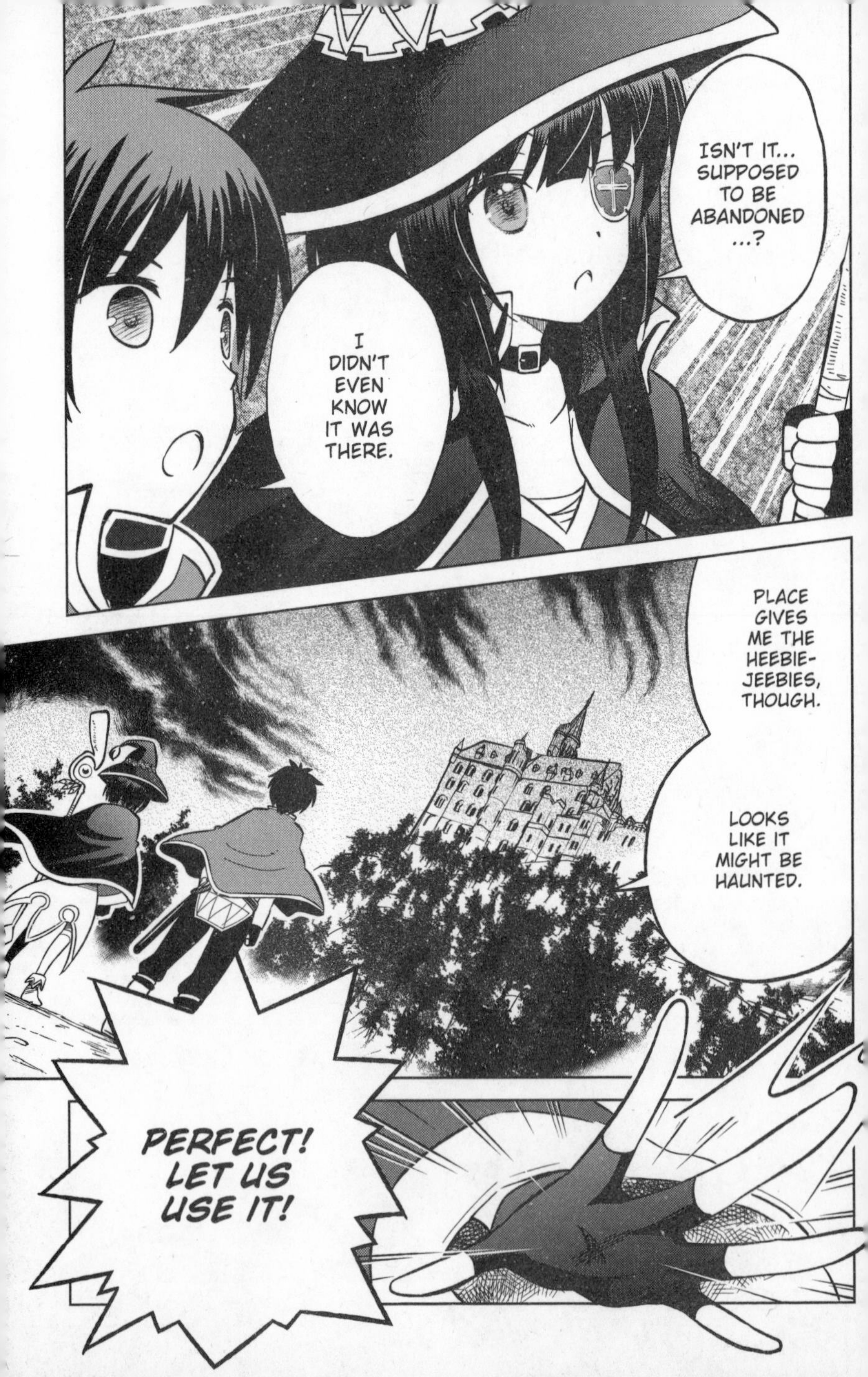
ISN'T IT... SUPPOSED TO BE ABANDONED ...?
I DIDN'T EVEN KNOW IT WAS THERE.
PLACE GIVES ME THE HEEBIE-JEEBIES, THOUGH.
LOOKS LIKE IT MIGHT BE HAUNTED.
PERFECT! LET US USE IT!

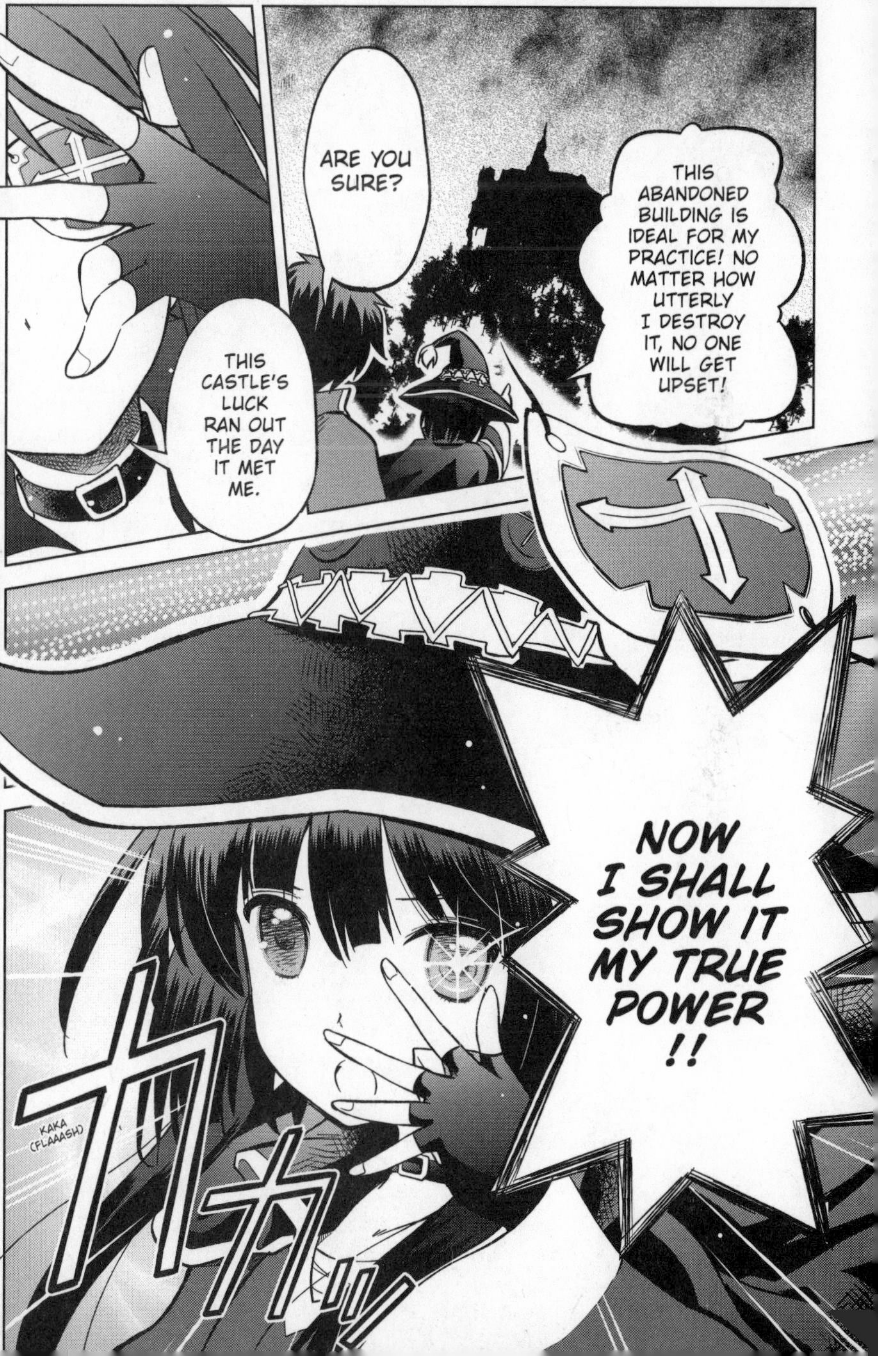
THIS ABANDONED BUILDING IS IDEAL FOR MY PRACTICE! NO MATTER HOW UTTERLY I DESTROY IT, NO ONE WILL GET UPSET!
ARE YOU SURE?
THIS CASTLE'S LUCK RAN OUT THE DAY IT MET ME.
NOW I SHALL SHOW IT MY TRUE POWER!!
KAKA (FLAAASH)

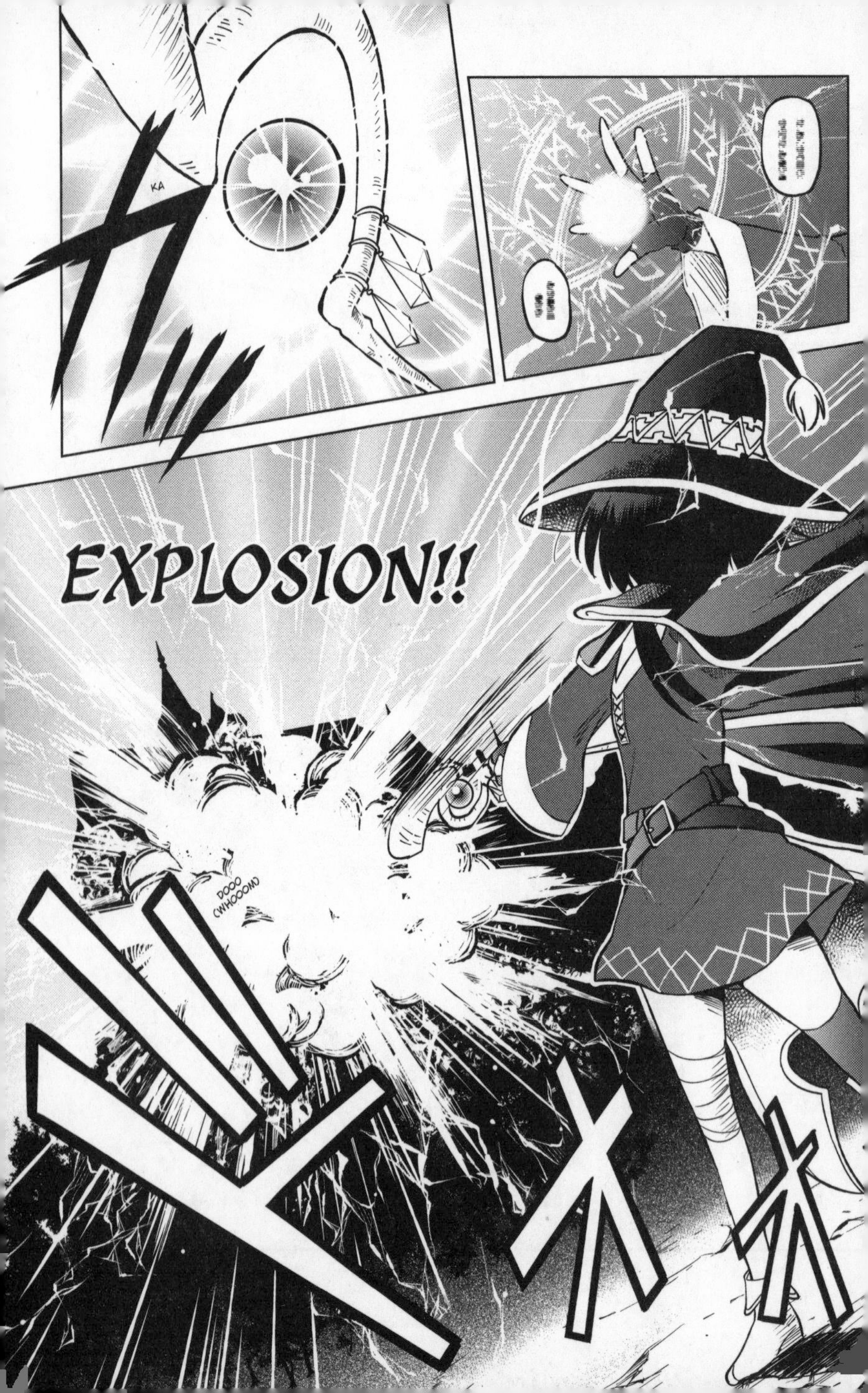
KA
EXPLOSION!!
DOOO (WHOOOM)

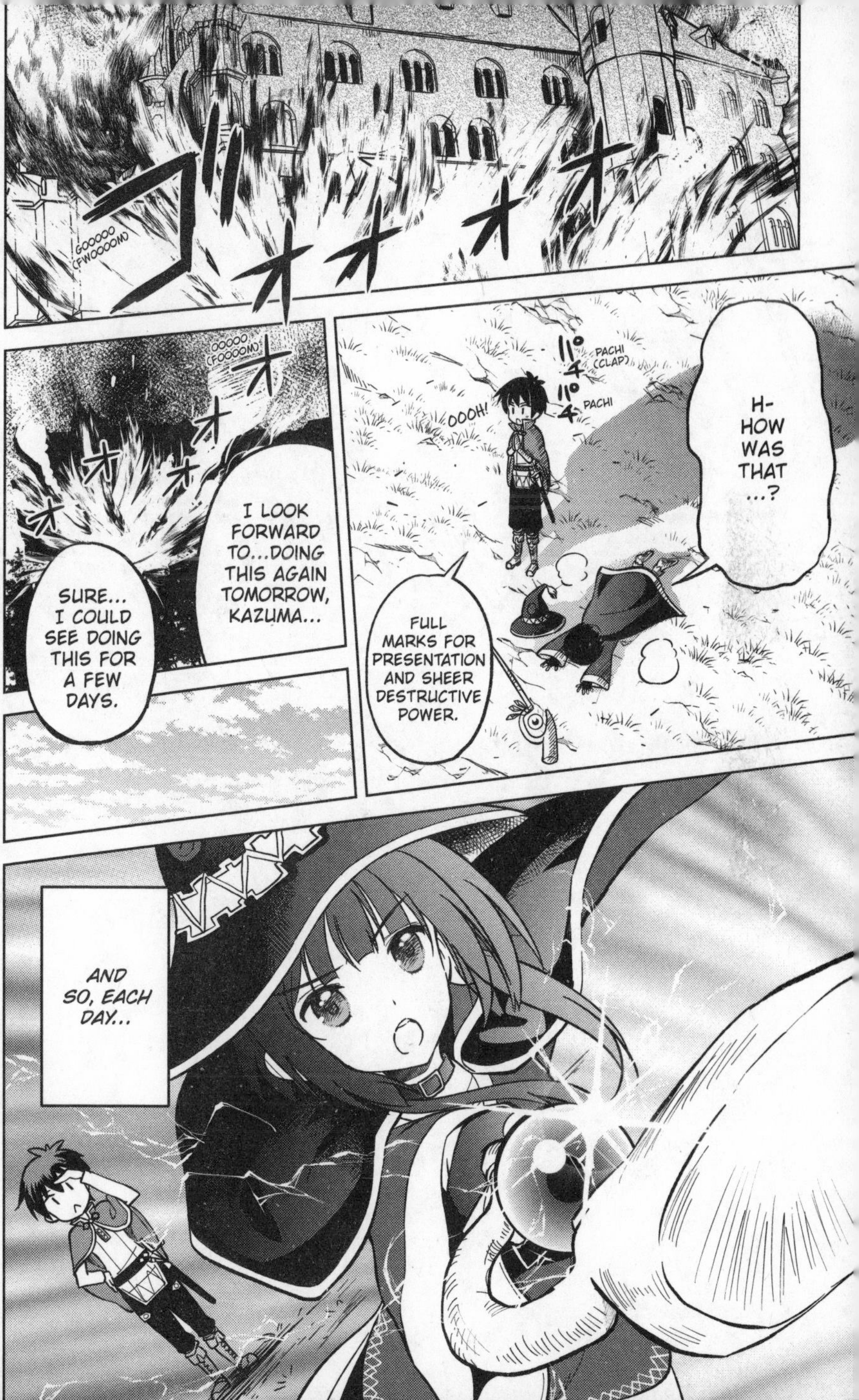
GOOOOO (FWOOOOM)
H-HOW WAS THAT...?
PACHI (CLAP)
PACHI
OOOH!
FULL MARKS FOR PRESENTATION AND SHEER DESTRUCTIVE POWER.
OOOOO (FOOOOM)
I LOOK FORWARD TO...DOING THIS AGAIN TOMORROW, KAZUMA...
SURE... I COULD SEE DOING THIS FOR A FEW DAYS.
AND SO, EACH DAY...

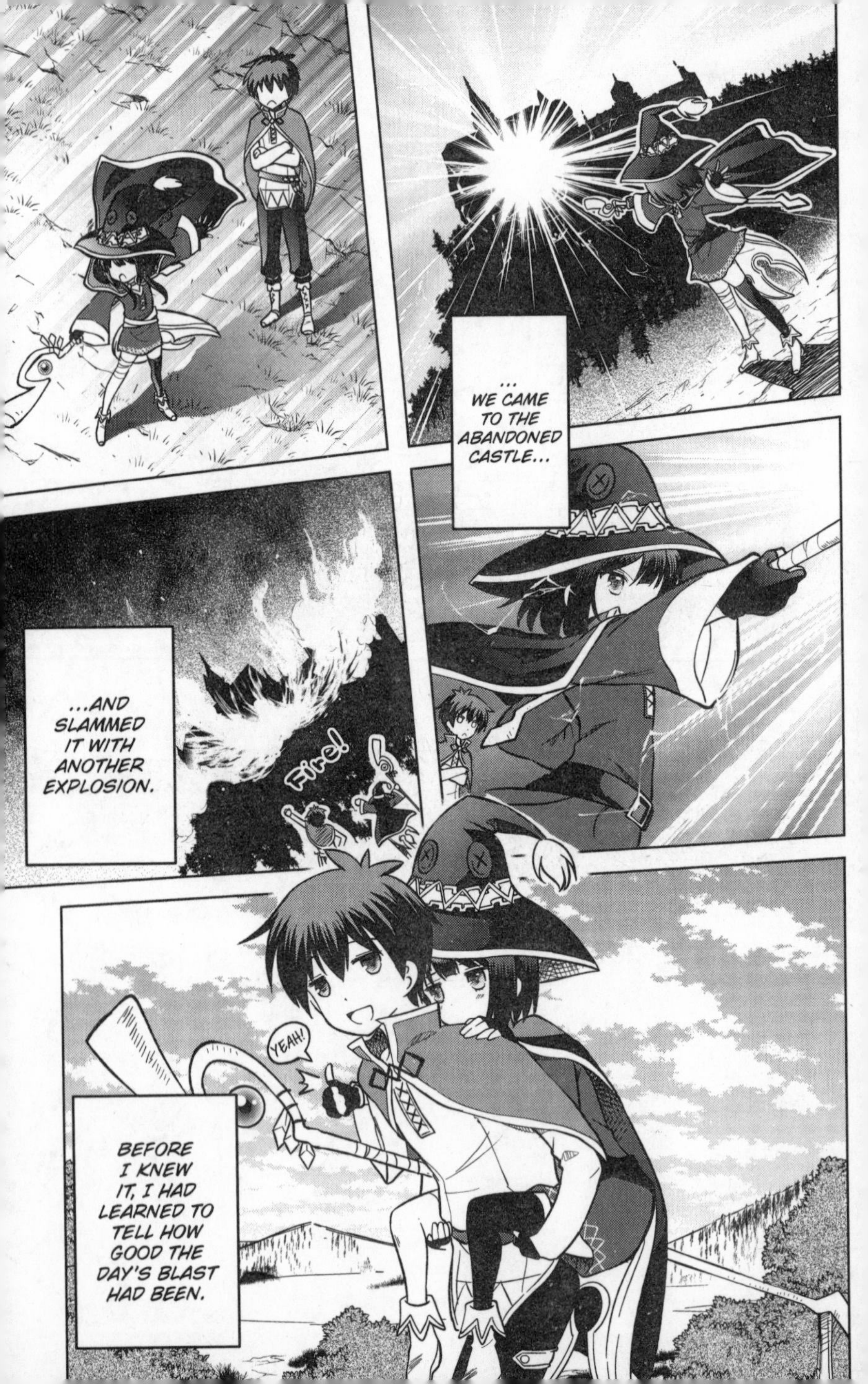
...WE CAME TO THE ABANDONED CASTLE...
Fire!
...AND SLAMMED IT WITH ANOTHER EXPLOSION.
YEAH!
BEFORE I KNEW IT, I HAD LEARNED TO TELL HOW GOOD THE DAY'S BLAST HAD BEEN.

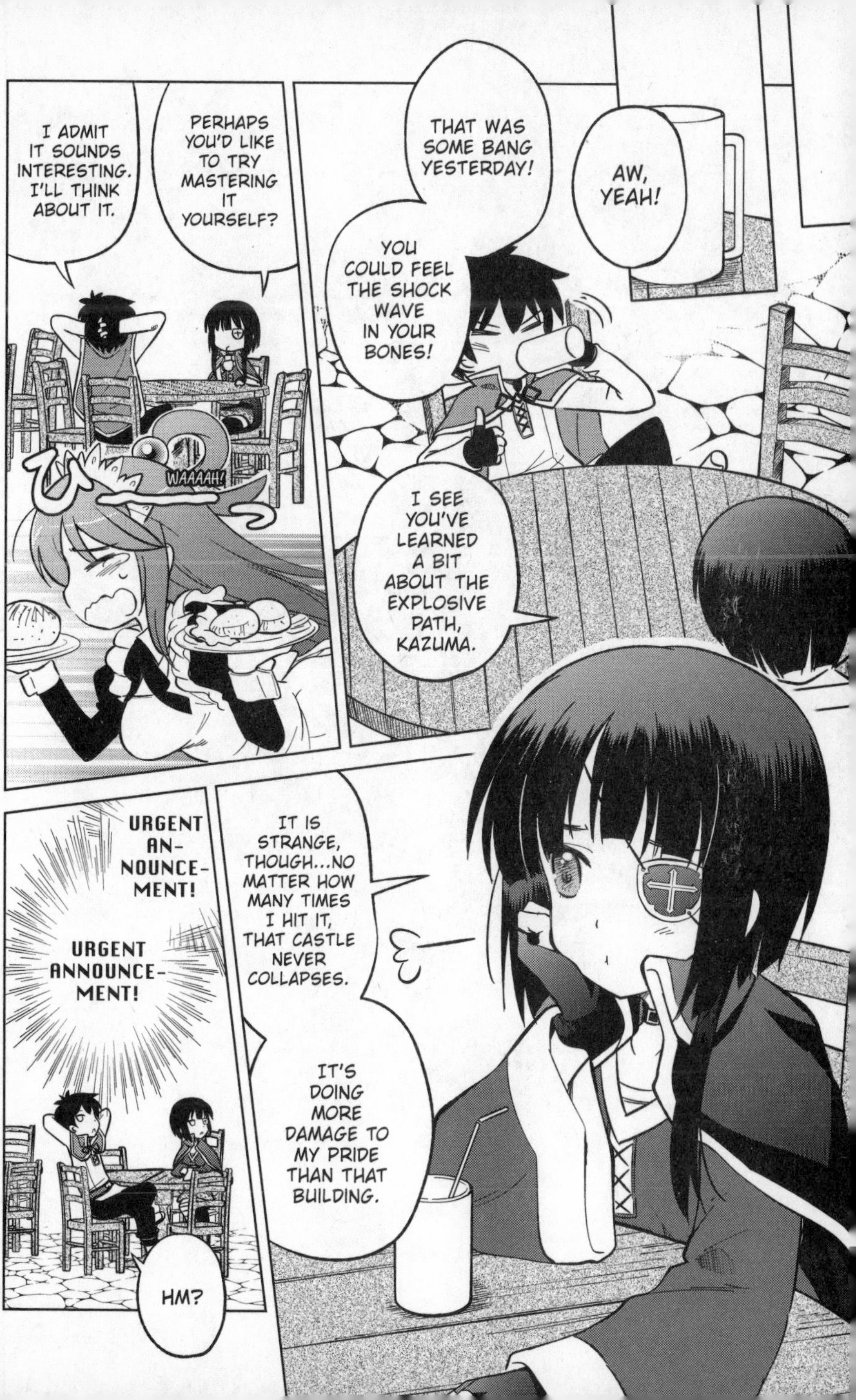
AW, YEAH!
THAT WAS SOME BANG YESTERDAY!
YOU COULD FEEL THE SHOCK WAVE IN YOUR BONES!
I SEE YOU'VE LEARNED A BIT ABOUT THE EXPLOSIVE PATH, KAZUMA.
IT IS STRANGE, THOUGH...NO MATTER HOW MANY TIMES I HIT IT, THAT CASTLE NEVER COLLAPSES.
IT'S DOING MORE DAMAGE TO MY PRIDE THAN THAT BUILDING.
PERHAPS YOU'D LIKE TO TRY MASTERING IT YOURSELF?
I ADMIT IT SOUNDS INTERESTING. I'LL THINK ABOUT IT.
WAAAAH!
URGENT AN-NOUNCE-MENT!
URGENT ANNOUNCE-MENT!
HM?

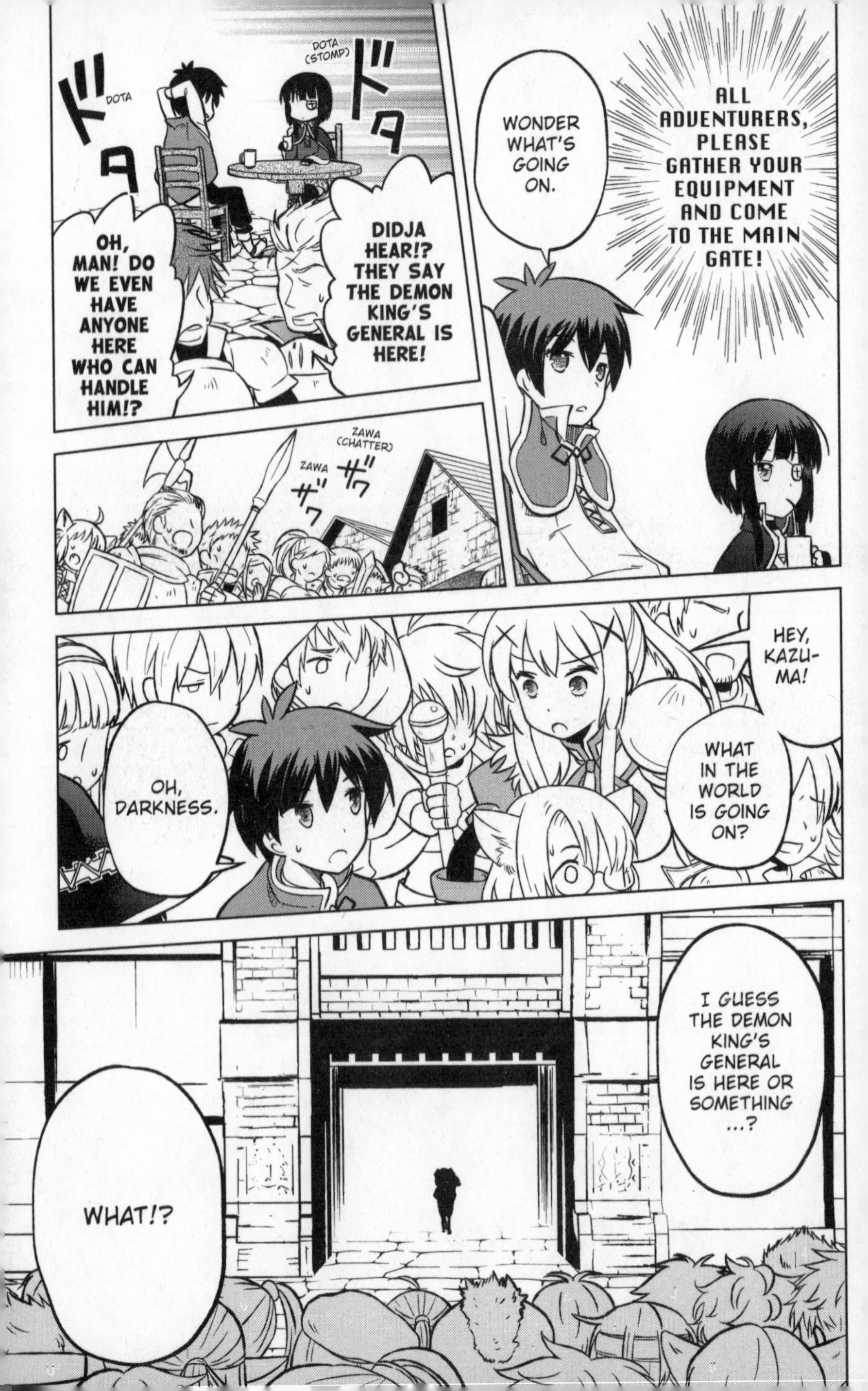
ALL ADVENTURERS, PLEASE GATHER YOUR EQUIPMENT AND COME TO THE MAIN GATE!
WONDER WHAT'S GOING ON.
ドタ
DOTA (STOMP)
ドタ
DOTA
DIDJA HEAR!? THEY SAY THE DEMON KING'S GENERAL IS HERE!
OH, MAN! DO WE EVEN HAVE ANYONE HERE WHO CAN HANDLE HIM!?
ザワ
ZAWA (CHATTER)
ザワ
ZAWA
HEY, KAZUMA!
WHAT IN THE WORLD IS GOING ON?
OH, DARKNESS.
I GUESS THE DEMON KING'S GENERAL IS HERE OR SOMETHING...?
WHAT!?

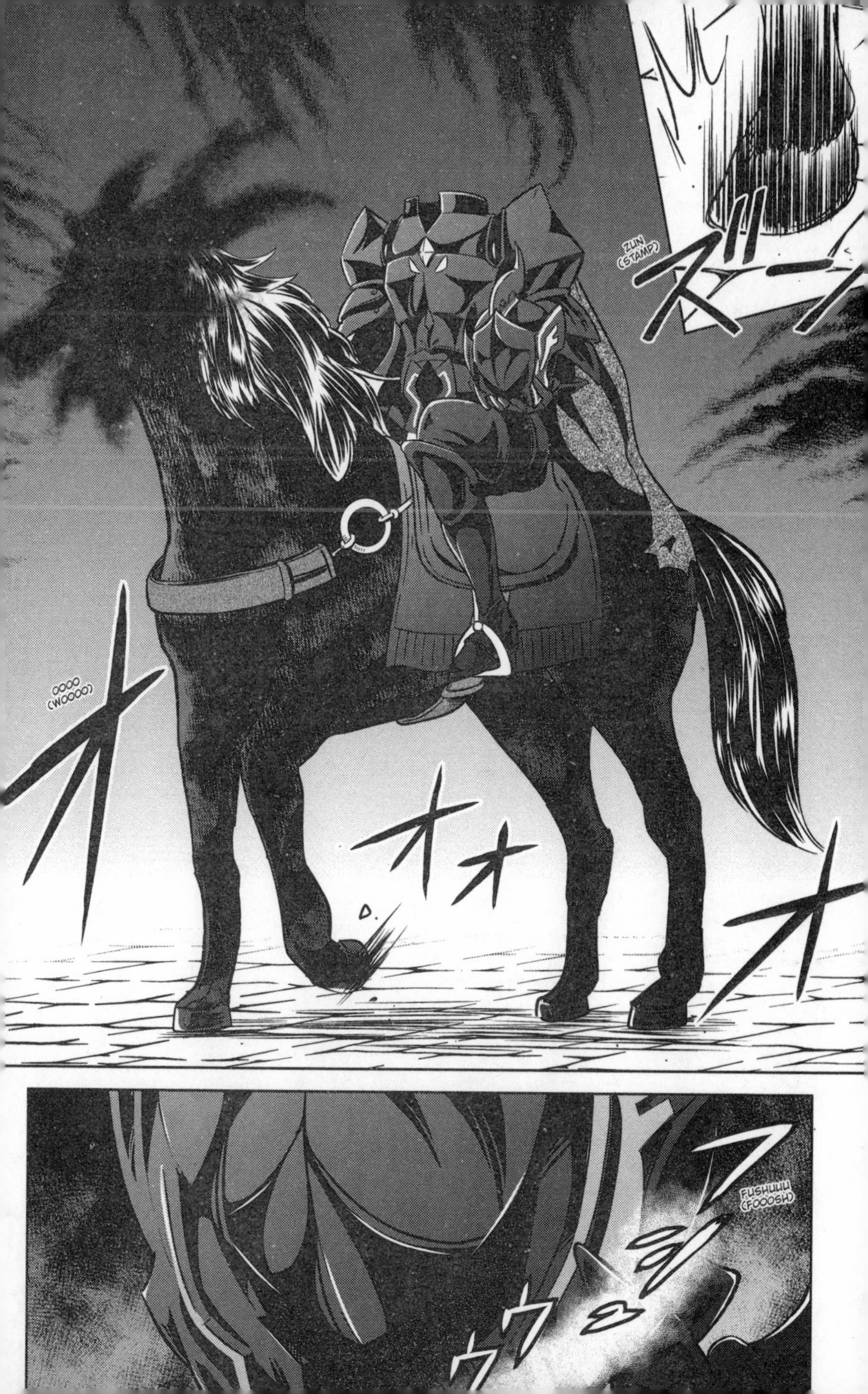
ZUN
(STAMP)
OOOO
(WOOOO)
FUSHUUU
(FOOOSH)

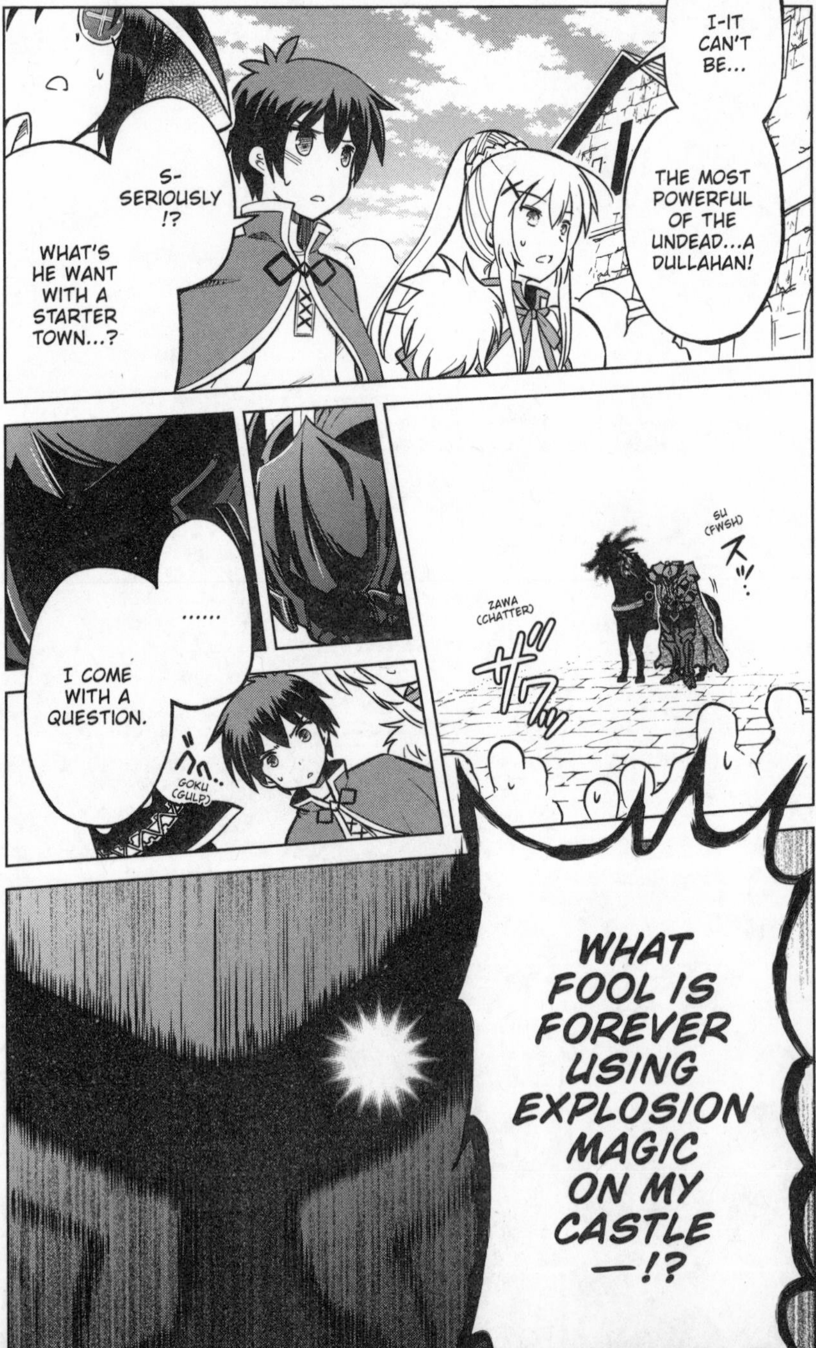
I-IT CAN'T BE...
THE MOST POWERFUL OF THE UNDEAD...A DULLAHAN!
S-SERIOUSLY!?
WHAT'S HE WANT WITH A STARTER TOWN...?
SU (FWSH)
ZAWA (CHATTER)
......
I COME WITH A QUESTION.
GOKU (GULP)
WHAT FOOL IS FOREVER USING EXPLOSION MAGIC ON MY CASTLE—!?

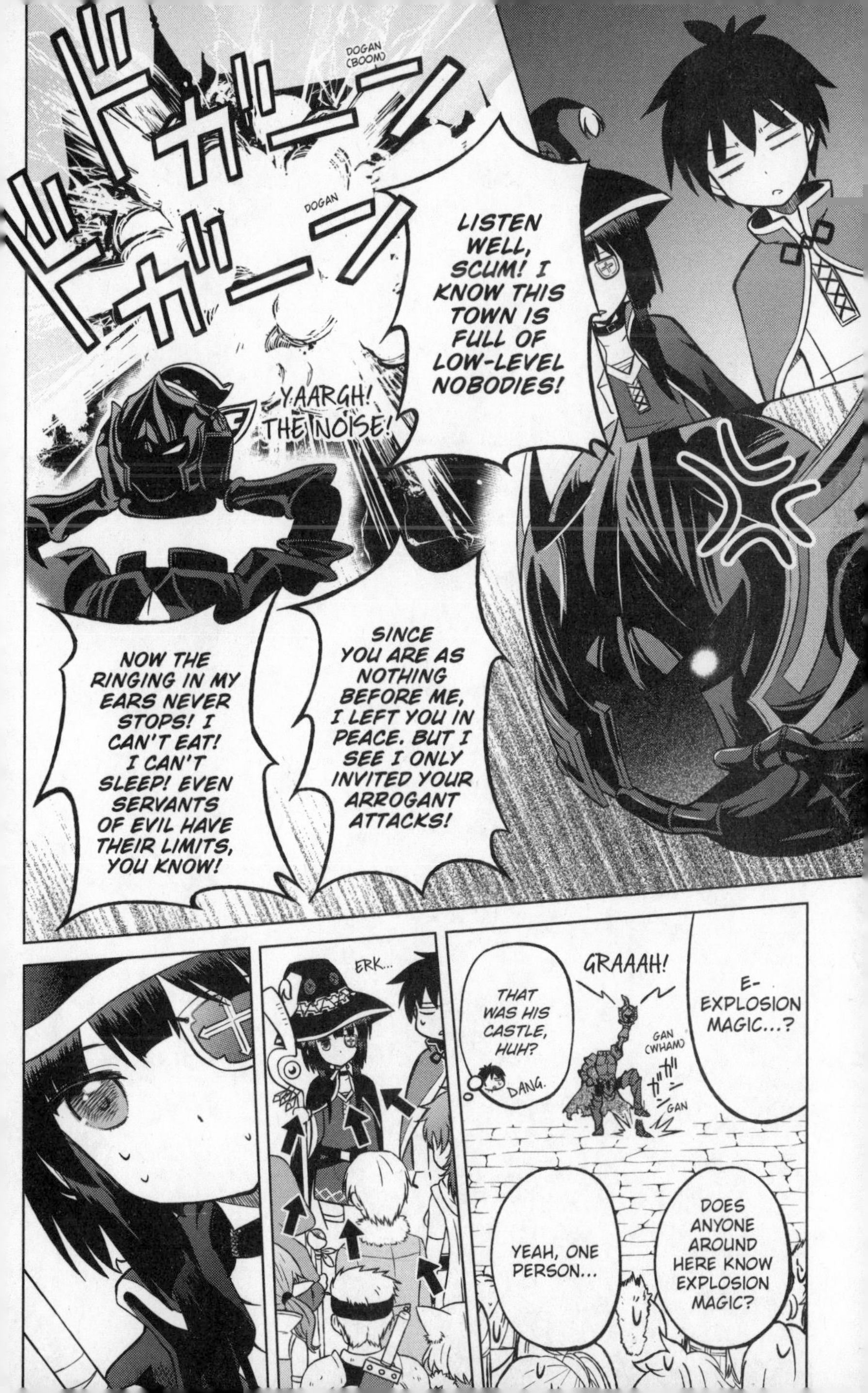
DOGAN (BOOM)
DOGAN
LISTEN WELL, SCUM! I KNOW THIS TOWN IS FULL OF LOW-LEVEL NOBODIES!
YAARGH! THE NOISE!
SINCE YOU ARE AS NOTHING BEFORE ME, I LEFT YOU IN PEACE. BUT I SEE I ONLY INVITED YOUR ARROGANT ATTACKS!
NOW THE RINGING IN MY EARS NEVER STOPS! I CAN'T EAT! I CAN'T SLEEP! EVEN SERVANTS OF EVIL HAVE THEIR LIMITS, YOU KNOW!
E-EXPLOSION MAGIC...?
GRAAAH!
GAN (WHAM)
GAN
THAT WAS HIS CASTLE, HUH?
DANG.
DOES ANYONE AROUND HERE KNOW EXPLOSION MAGIC?
YEAH, ONE PERSON...
ERK...

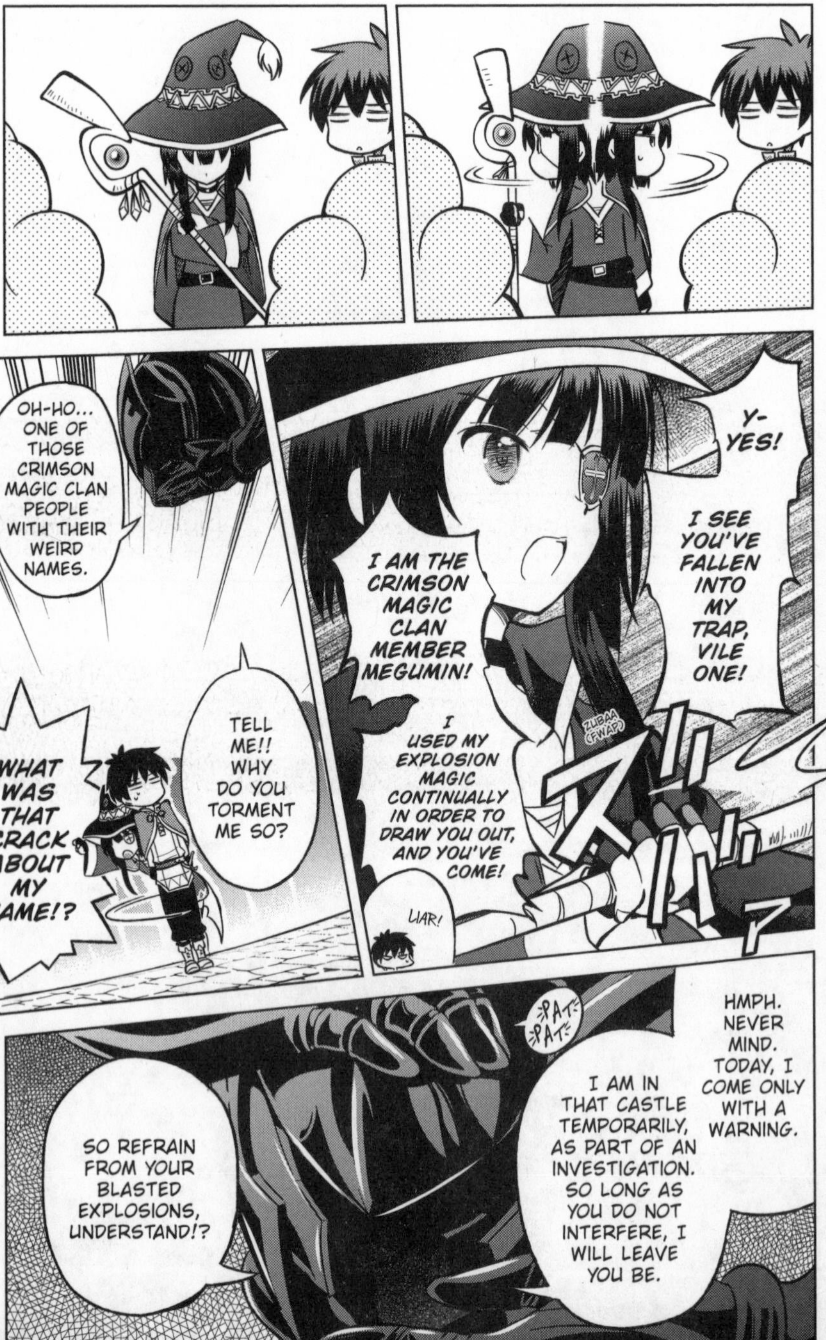
Y-YES!
I SEE YOU'VE FALLEN INTO MY TRAP, VILE ONE!
I AM THE CRIMSON MAGIC CLAN MEMBER MEGUMIN!
ZUBAA (FWAP)
I USED MY EXPLOSION MAGIC CONTINUALLY IN ORDER TO DRAW YOU OUT, AND YOU'VE COME!
LIAR!
OH-HO... ONE OF THOSE CRIMSON MAGIC CLAN PEOPLE WITH THEIR WEIRD NAMES.
TELL ME!! WHY DO YOU TORMENT ME SO?
WHAT WAS THAT CRACK ABOUT MY NAME!?
PAT PAT
HMPH. NEVER MIND. TODAY, I COME ONLY WITH A WARNING.
I AM IN THAT CASTLE TEMPORARILY, AS PART OF AN INVESTIGATION. SO LONG AS YOU DO NOT INTERFERE, I WILL LEAVE YOU BE.
SO REFRAIN FROM YOUR BLASTED EXPLOSIONS, UNDERSTAND!?

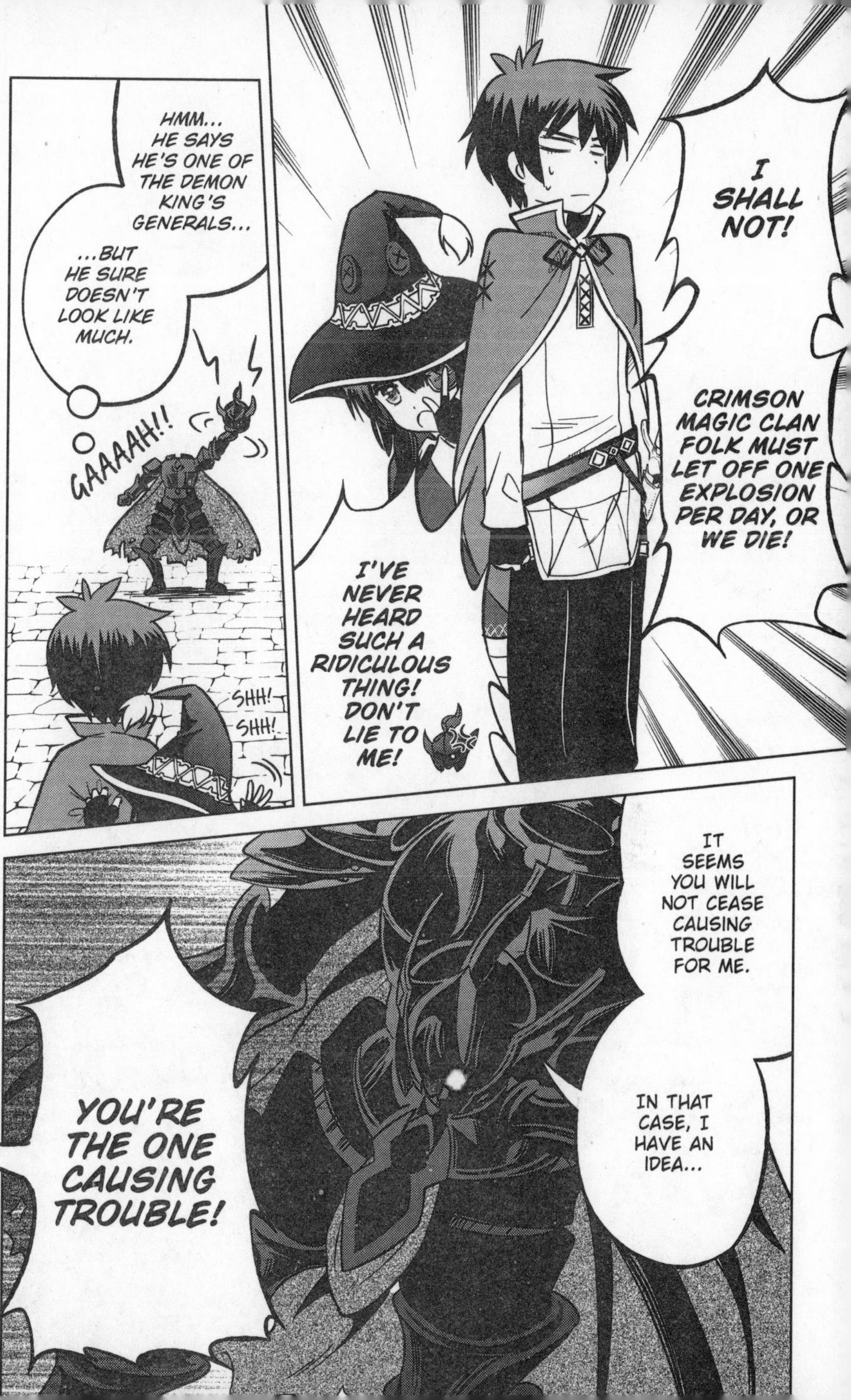
I SHALL NOT!
CRIMSON MAGIC CLAN FOLK MUST LET OFF ONE EXPLOSION PER DAY, OR WE DIE!
I'VE NEVER HEARD SUCH A RIDICULOUS THING! DON'T LIE TO ME!
HMM... HE SAYS HE'S ONE OF THE DEMON KING'S GENERALS...
...BUT HE SURE DOESN'T LOOK LIKE MUCH.
GAAAAH!!
SHH!
SHH!
IT SEEMS YOU WILL NOT CEASE CAUSING TROUBLE FOR ME.
IN THAT CASE, I HAVE AN IDEA...
YOU'RE THE ONE CAUSING TROUBLE!

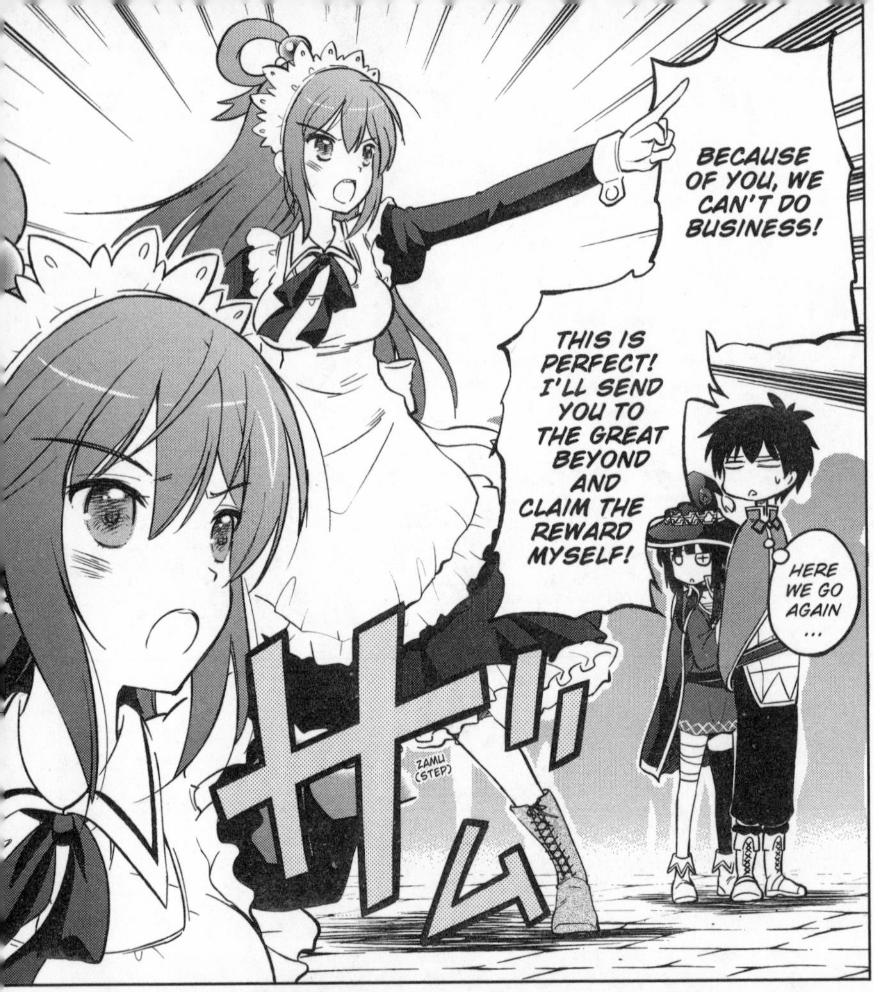
BECAUSE OF YOU, WE CAN'T DO BUSINESS!
THIS IS PERFECT! I'LL SEND YOU TO THE GREAT BEYOND AND CLAIM THE REWARD MYSELF!
HERE WE GO AGAIN ...
ZAMU (STEP)
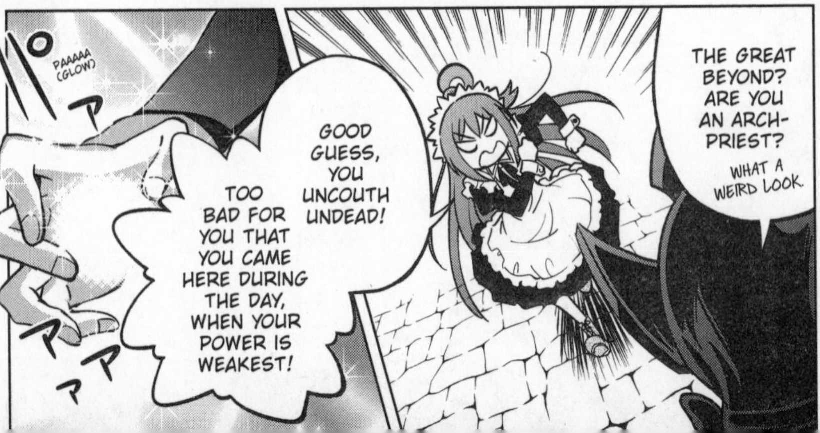
THE GREAT BEYOND? ARE YOU AN ARCH-PRIEST?
WHAT A WEIRD LOOK.
GOOD GUESS, YOU UNCOUTH UNDEAD!
TOO BAD FOR YOU THAT YOU CAME HERE DURING THE DAY, WHEN YOUR POWER IS WEAKEST!
PAAAAA (GLOW)

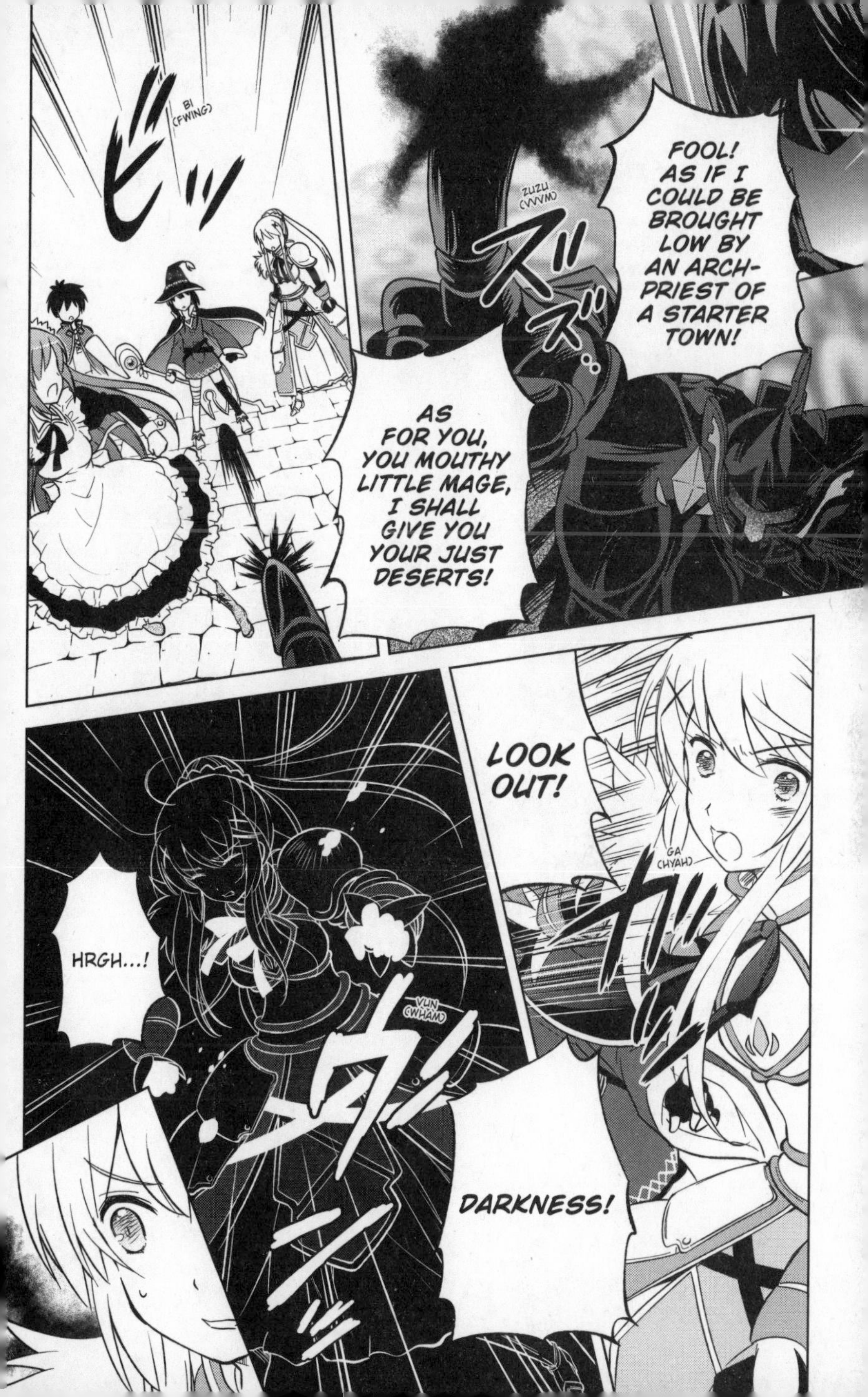
FOOL! AS IF I COULD BE BROUGHT LOW BY AN ARCH-PRIEST OF A STARTER TOWN!
ZUZU (VVVM)
AS FOR YOU, YOU MOUTHY LITTLE MAGE, I SHALL GIVE YOU YOUR JUST DESERTS!
BI (FWING)
LOOK OUT!
GA (HYAH)
HRGH...!
VUN (WHAM)
DARKNESS!

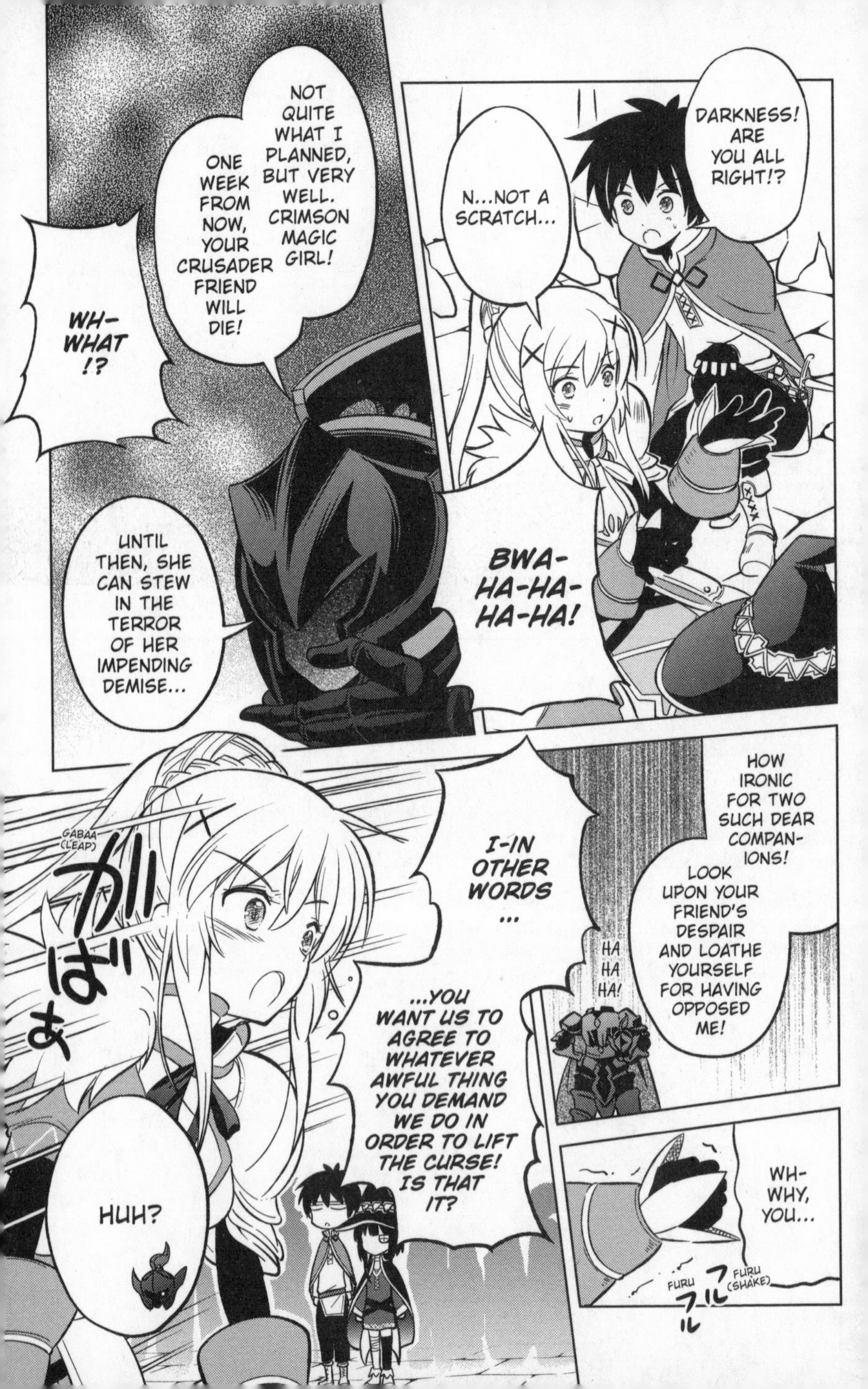
DARKNESS! ARE YOU ALL RIGHT!?
N...NOT A SCRATCH...
BWA-HA-HA-HA-HA!
NOT QUITE WHAT I PLANNED, BUT VERY WELL. CRIMSON MAGIC GIRL!
ONE WEEK FROM NOW, YOUR CRUSADER FRIEND WILL DIE!
WH-WHAT!?
UNTIL THEN, SHE CAN STEW IN THE TERROR OF HER IMPENDING DEMISE...
HOW IRONIC FOR TWO SUCH DEAR COMPANIONS!
LOOK UPON YOUR FRIEND'S DESPAIR AND LOATHE YOURSELF FOR HAVING OPPOSED ME!
HA HA HA!
WH-WHY, YOU...
FURU FURU (SHAKE)
GABAA (LEAP)
I-IN OTHER WORDS...
...YOU WANT US TO AGREE TO WHATEVER AWFUL THING YOU DEMAND WE DO IN ORDER TO LIFT THE CURSE! IS THAT IT?
HUH?

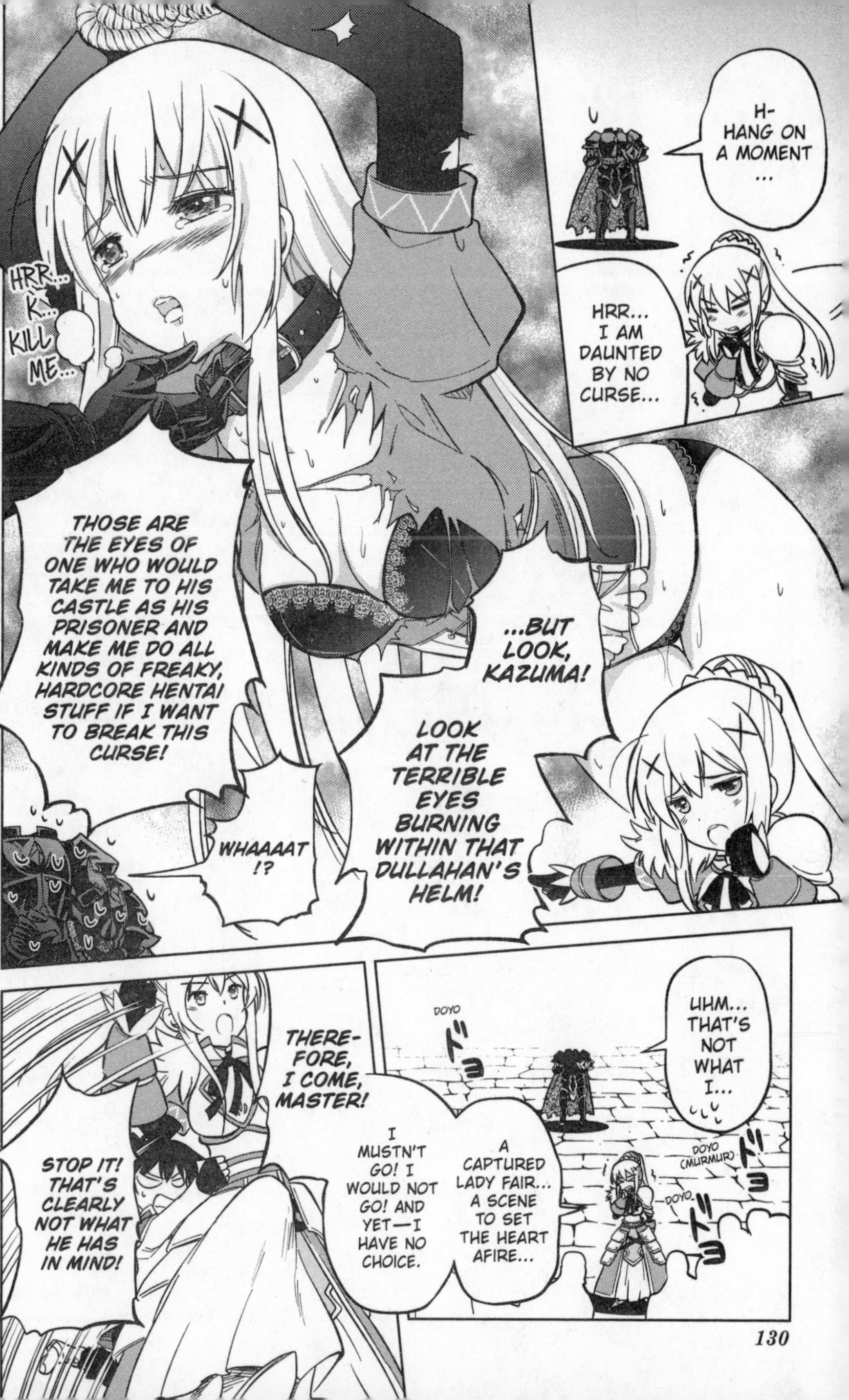
H-HANG ON A MOMENT...
HRR... I AM DAUNTED BY NO CURSE...
...BUT LOOK, KAZUMA!
LOOK AT THE TERRIBLE EYES BURNING WITHIN THAT DULLAHAN'S HELM!
THOSE ARE THE EYES OF ONE WHO WOULD TAKE ME TO HIS CASTLE AS HIS PRISONER AND MAKE ME DO ALL KINDS OF FREAKY, HARDCORE HENTAI STUFF IF I WANT TO BREAK THIS CURSE!
WHAAAAT!?
HRR... K... KILL ME...
DOYO
UHM... THAT'S NOT WHAT I...
DOYO (MURMUR)
DOYO
A CAPTURED LADY FAIR... A SCENE TO SET THE HEART AFIRE...
I MUSTN'T GO! I WOULD NOT GO! AND YET—I HAVE NO CHOICE.
THEREFORE, I COME, MASTER!
STOP IT! THAT'S CLEARLY NOT WHAT HE HAS IN MIND!

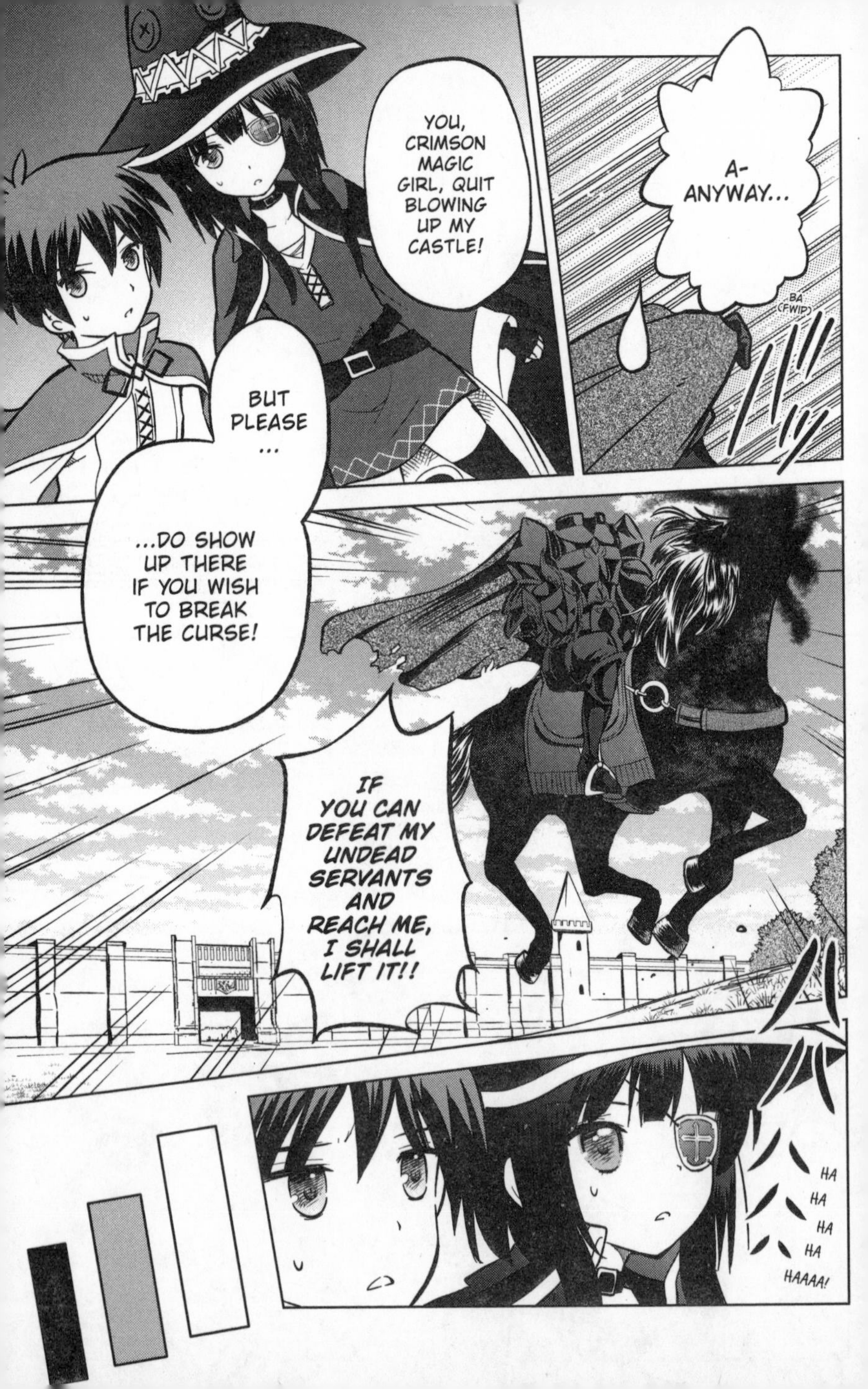
A-
ANYWAY...
BA (FWIP)
YOU, CRIMSON MAGIC GIRL, QUIT BLOWING UP MY CASTLE!
BUT PLEASE ...
...DO SHOW UP THERE IF YOU WISH TO BREAK THE CURSE!
IF YOU CAN DEFEAT MY UNDEAD SERVANTS AND REACH ME, I SHALL LIFT IT!!
HA HA HA HA HAAAA!

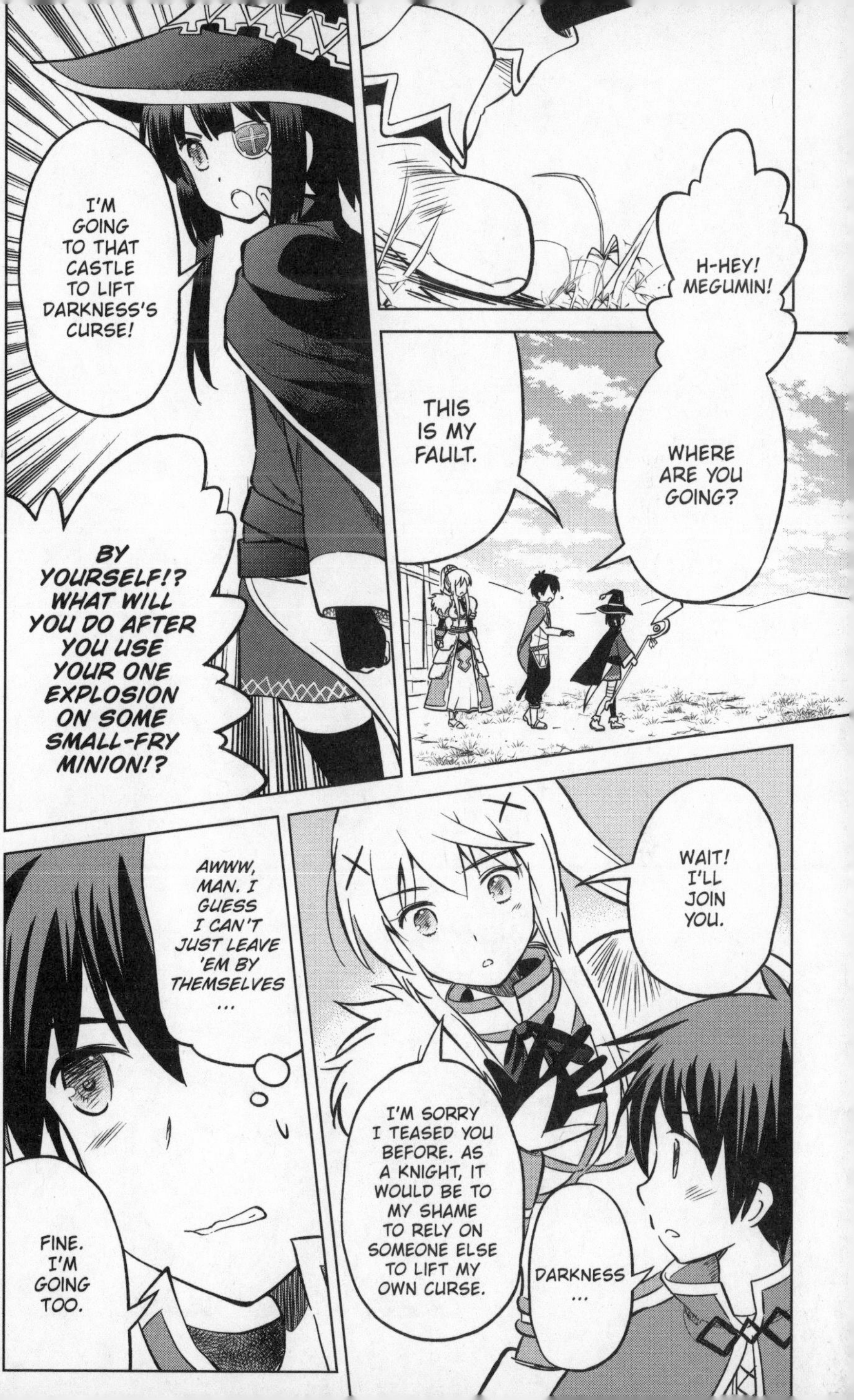
H-HEY! MEGUMIN!
WHERE ARE YOU GOING?
THIS IS MY FAULT.
I'M GOING TO THAT CASTLE TO LIFT DARKNESS'S CURSE!
BY YOURSELF!? WHAT WILL YOU DO AFTER YOU USE YOUR ONE EXPLOSION ON SOME SMALL-FRY MINION!?
WAIT! I'LL JOIN YOU.
I'M SORRY I TEASED YOU BEFORE. AS A KNIGHT, IT WOULD BE TO MY SHAME TO RELY ON SOMEONE ELSE TO LIFT MY OWN CURSE.
DARKNESS...
AWWW, MAN. I GUESS I CAN'T JUST LEAVE 'EM BY THEMSELVES...
FINE. I'M GOING TOO.

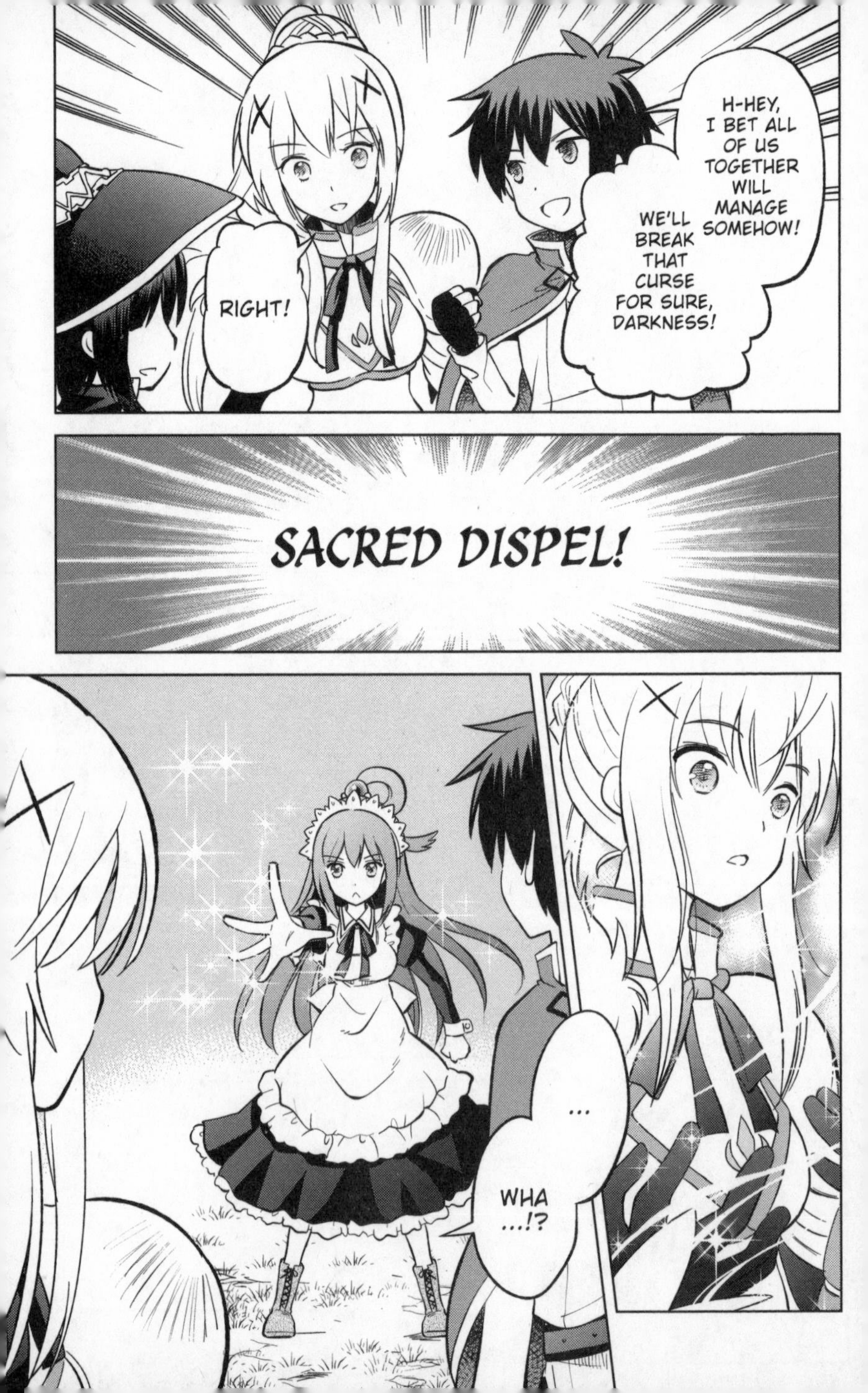
H-HEY, I BET ALL OF US TOGETHER WILL MANAGE SOMEHOW!
WE'LL BREAK THAT CURSE FOR SURE, DARKNESS!
RIGHT!
SACRED DISPEL!
...
WHA ...!?

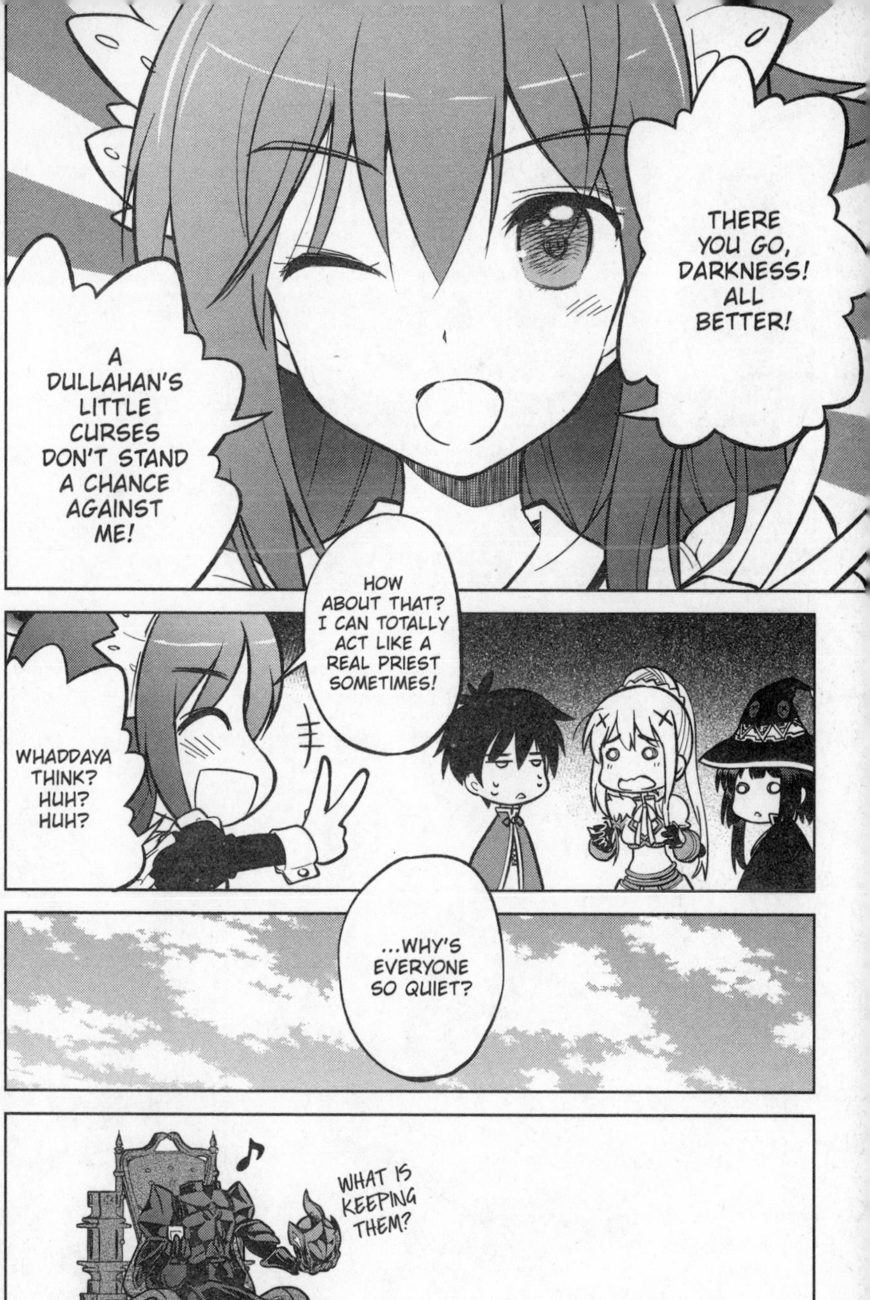
THERE YOU GO, DARKNESS! ALL BETTER!
A DULLAHAN'S LITTLE CURSES DON'T STAND A CHANCE AGAINST ME!
HOW ABOUT THAT? I CAN TOTALLY ACT LIKE A REAL PRIEST SOMETIMES!
WHADDAYA THINK? HUH? HUH?
...WHY'S EVERYONE SO QUIET?
WHAT IS KEEPING THEM?

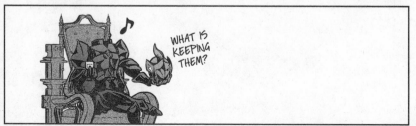

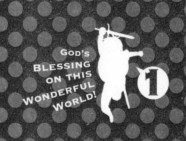

GOD'S
BLESSING
ON THIS
WONDERFUL
WORLD!

1

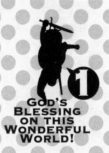

GOD'S
BLESSING
ON THIS
WONDERFUL
WORLD!

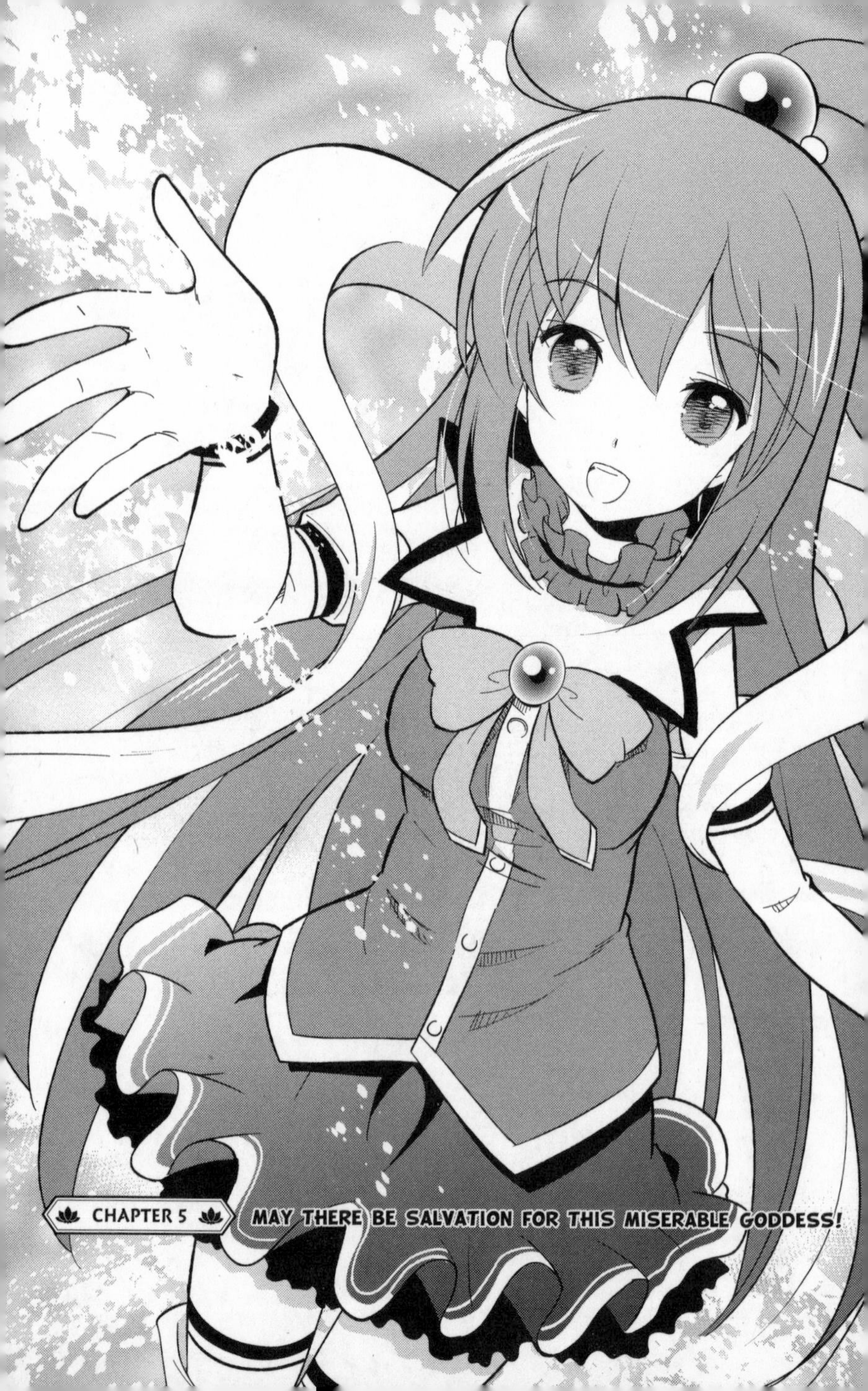
CHAPTER 5
MAY THERE BE SALVATION FOR THIS MISERABLE GODDESS!

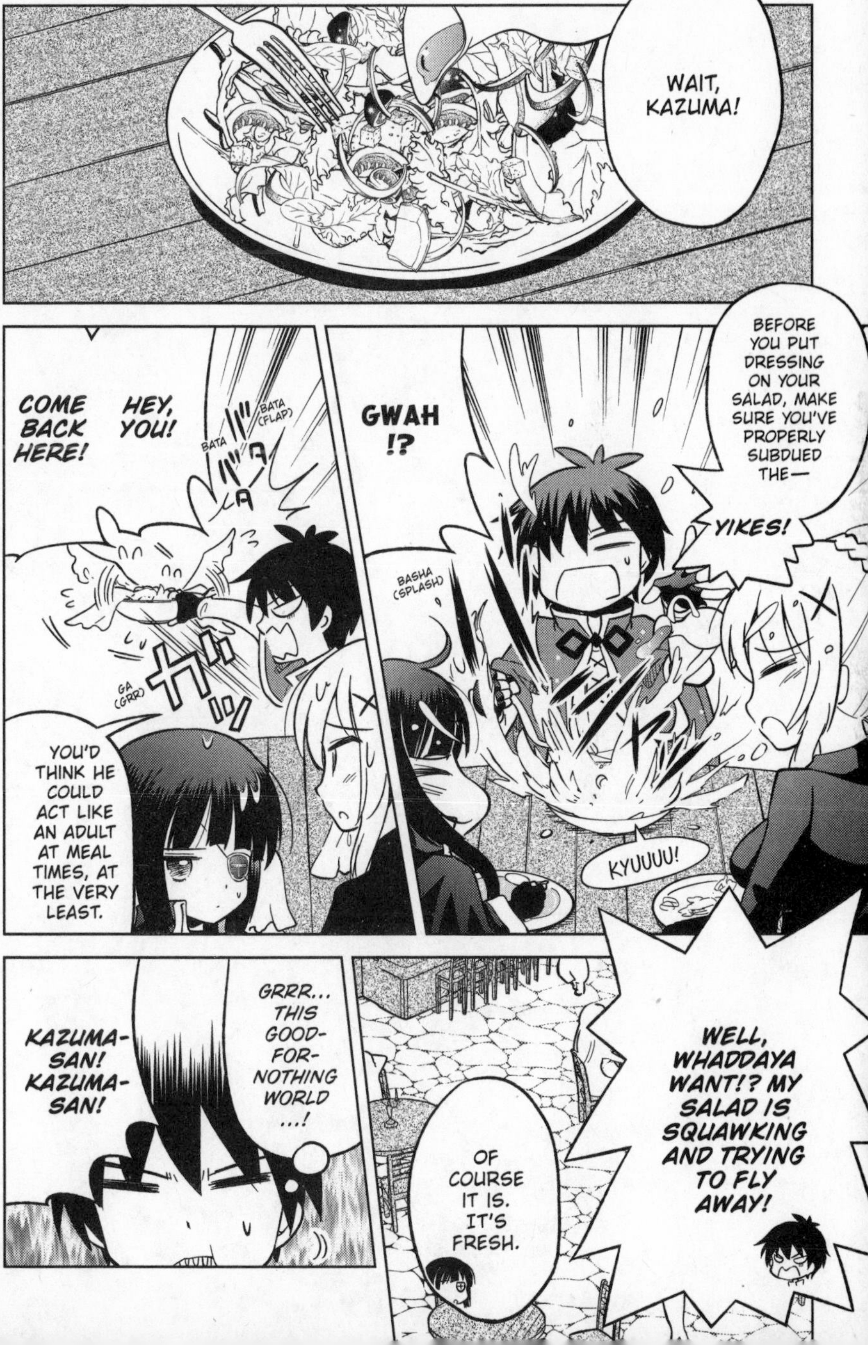
WAIT, KAZUMA!
BEFORE YOU PUT DRESSING ON YOUR SALAD, MAKE SURE YOU'VE PROPERLY SUBDUED THE—
YIKES!
GWAH !?
BASHA (SPLASH)
KYUUUU!
HEY, YOU!
COME BACK HERE!
BATA BATA (FLAP)
GA (GRR)
YOU'D THINK HE COULD ACT LIKE AN ADULT AT MEAL TIMES, AT THE VERY LEAST.
WELL, WHADDAYA WANT!? MY SALAD IS SQUAWKING AND TRYING TO FLY AWAY!
OF COURSE IT IS. IT'S FRESH.
GRRR... THIS GOOD-FOR-NOTHING WORLD ...!
KAZUMA-SAN! KAZUMA-SAN!

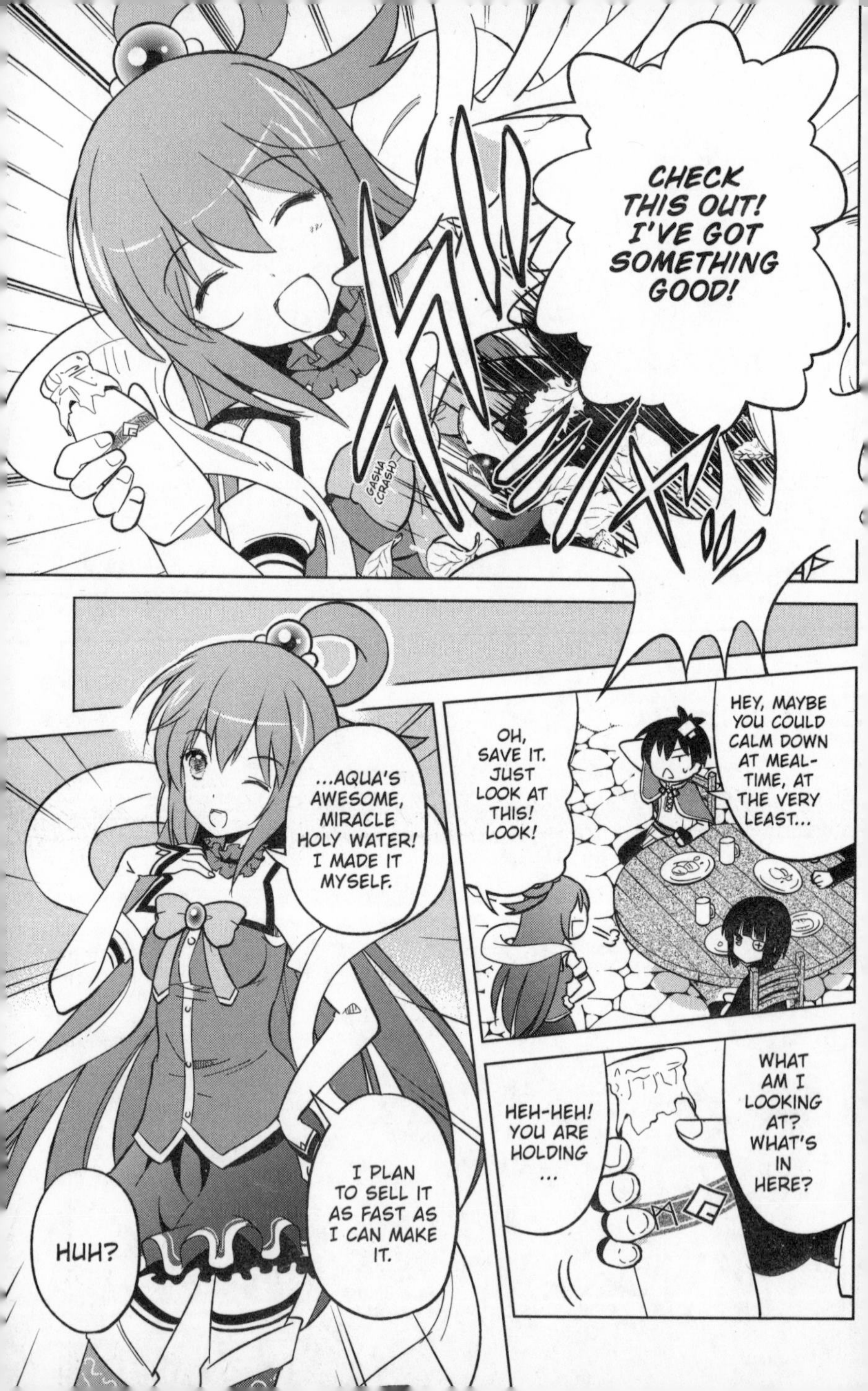
CHECK THIS OUT! I'VE GOT SOMETHING GOOD!
GASHA (CRASH)
HEY, MAYBE YOU COULD CALM DOWN AT MEAL-TIME, AT THE VERY LEAST...
OH, SAVE IT. JUST LOOK AT THIS! LOOK!
WHAT AM I LOOKING AT? WHAT'S IN HERE?
HEH-HEH! YOU ARE HOLDING ...
...AQUA'S AWESOME, MIRACLE HOLY WATER! I MADE IT MYSELF.
I PLAN TO SELL IT AS FAST AS I CAN MAKE IT.
HUH?

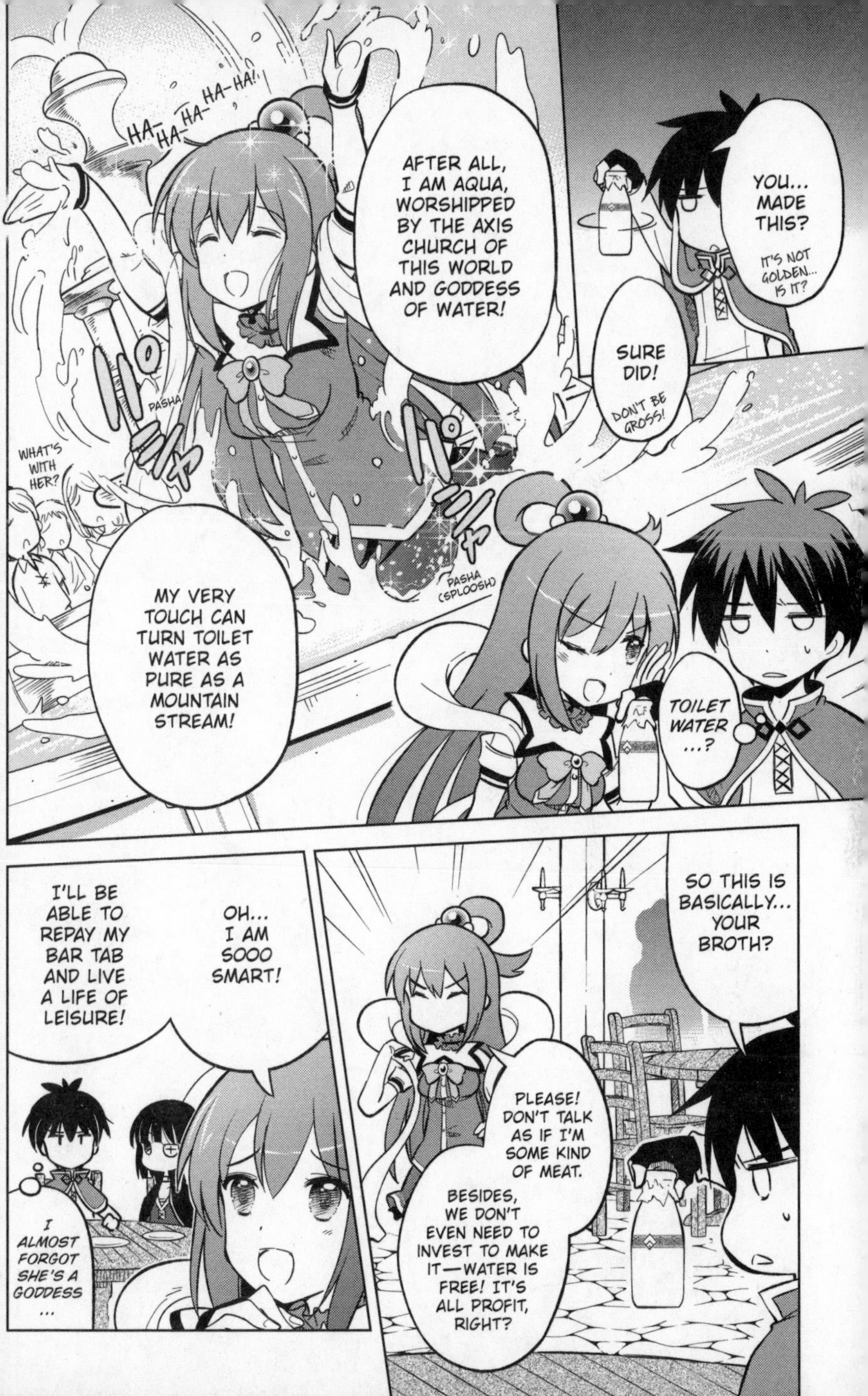
YOU... MADE THIS?
IT'S NOT GOLDEN... IS IT?
SURE DID!
DON'T BE GROSS!
HA-HA-HA-HA-HA!
AFTER ALL, I AM AQUA, WORSHIPPED BY THE AXIS CHURCH OF THIS WORLD AND GODDESS OF WATER!
PASHA
PASHA (SPLOOSH)
WHAT'S WITH HER?
MY VERY TOUCH CAN TURN TOILET WATER AS PURE AS A MOUNTAIN STREAM!
TOILET WATER ...?
SO THIS IS BASICALLY... YOUR BROTH?
PLEASE! DON'T TALK AS IF I'M SOME KIND OF MEAT.
BESIDES, WE DON'T EVEN NEED TO INVEST TO MAKE IT—WATER IS FREE! IT'S ALL PROFIT, RIGHT?
OH... I AM SOOO SMART!
I'LL BE ABLE TO REPAY MY BAR TAB AND LIVE A LIFE OF LEISURE!
I ALMOST FORGOT SHE'S A GODDESS ...

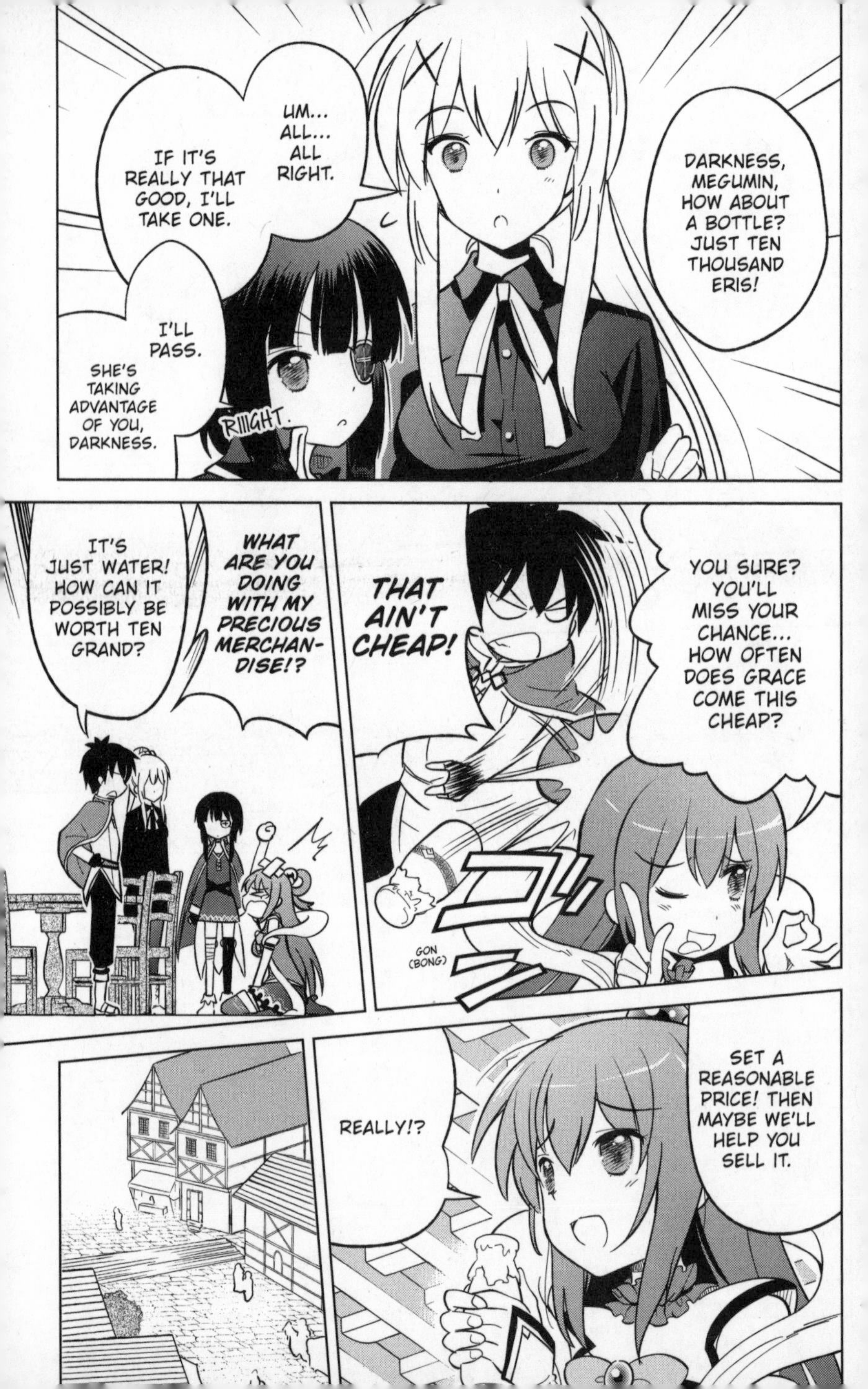
DARKNESS, MEGUMIN, HOW ABOUT A BOTTLE? JUST TEN THOUSAND ERIS!
UM... ALL... ALL RIGHT.
IF IT'S REALLY THAT GOOD, I'LL TAKE ONE.
I'LL PASS.
SHE'S TAKING ADVANTAGE OF YOU, DARKNESS.
RIIIGHT.
YOU SURE? YOU'LL MISS YOUR CHANCE... HOW OFTEN DOES GRACE COME THIS CHEAP?
THAT AIN'T CHEAP!
GON (BONG)
WHAT ARE YOU DOING WITH MY PRECIOUS MERCHANDISE!?
IT'S JUST WATER! HOW CAN IT POSSIBLY BE WORTH TEN GRAND?
SET A REASONABLE PRICE! THEN MAYBE WE'LL HELP YOU SELL IT.
REALLY!?

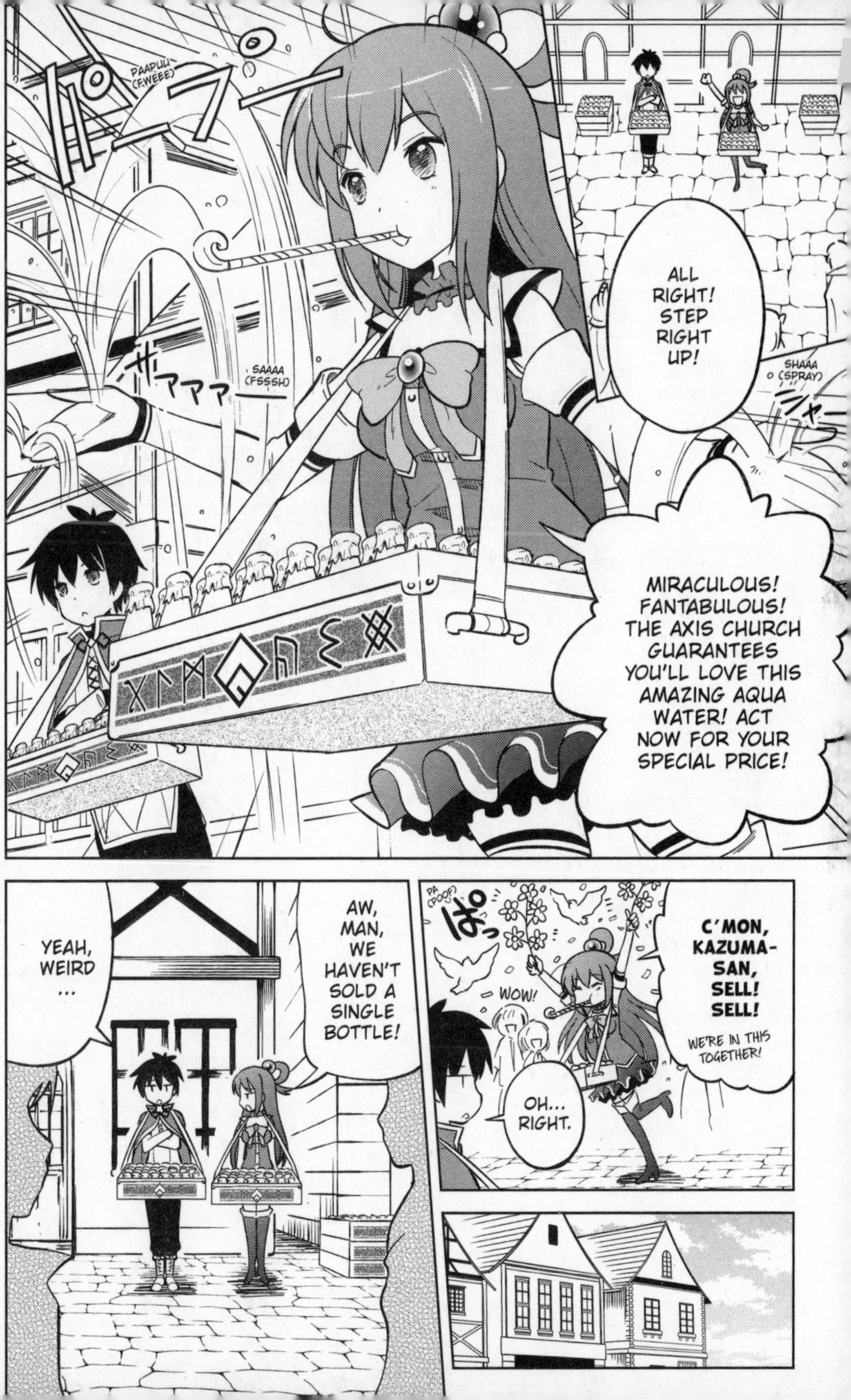
ALL RIGHT! STEP RIGHT UP!
SHAAA (SPRAY)
MIRACULOUS! FANTABULOUS! THE AXIS CHURCH GUARANTEES YOU'LL LOVE THIS AMAZING AQUA WATER! ACT NOW FOR YOUR SPECIAL PRICE!
PAAPUU (FWEEE)
SAAAA (FSSSH)
PA (POOF)
C'MON, KAZUMA-SAN, SELL! SELL!
WE'RE IN THIS TOGETHER!
WOW!
OH... RIGHT.
AW, MAN, WE HAVEN'T SOLD A SINGLE BOTTLE!
YEAH, WEIRD...

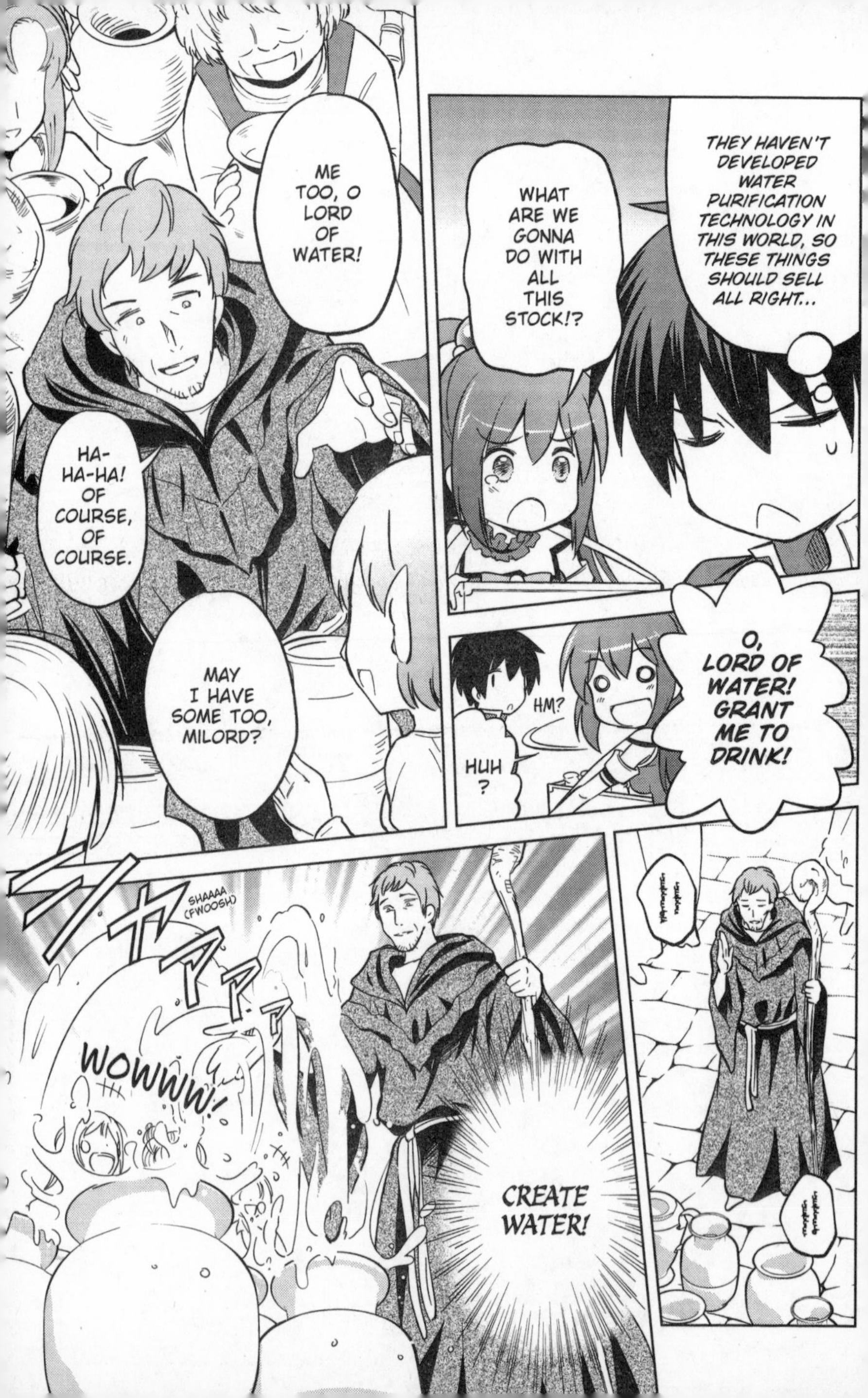
THEY HAVEN'T DEVELOPED WATER PURIFICATION TECHNOLOGY IN THIS WORLD, SO THESE THINGS SHOULD SELL ALL RIGHT...
WHAT ARE WE GONNA DO WITH ALL THIS STOCK!?
O, LORD OF WATER! GRANT ME TO DRINK!
HM?
HUH?
ME TOO, O LORD OF WATER!
HA-HA-HA! OF COURSE, OF COURSE.
MAY I HAVE SOME TOO, MILORD?
CREATE WATER!
SHAAAA (FWOOSH)
WOWWW!

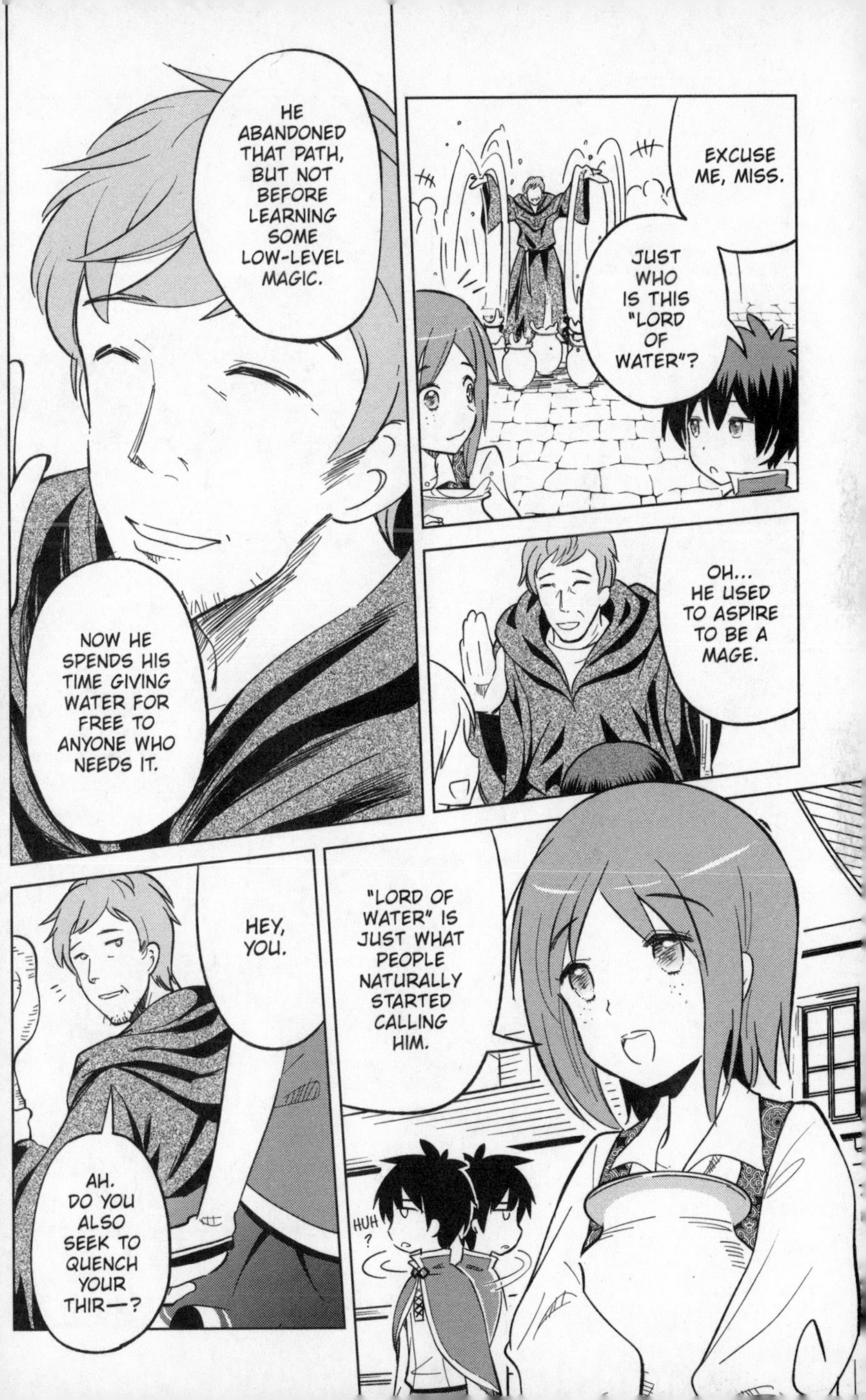
EXCUSE ME, MISS.
JUST WHO IS THIS "LORD OF WATER"?
OH... HE USED TO ASPIRE TO BE A MAGE.
HE ABANDONED THAT PATH, BUT NOT BEFORE LEARNING SOME LOW-LEVEL MAGIC.
NOW HE SPENDS HIS TIME GIVING WATER FOR FREE TO ANYONE WHO NEEDS IT.
"LORD OF WATER" IS JUST WHAT PEOPLE NATURALLY STARTED CALLING HIM.
HUH ?
HEY, YOU.
AH. DO YOU ALSO SEEK TO QUENCH YOUR THIR—?

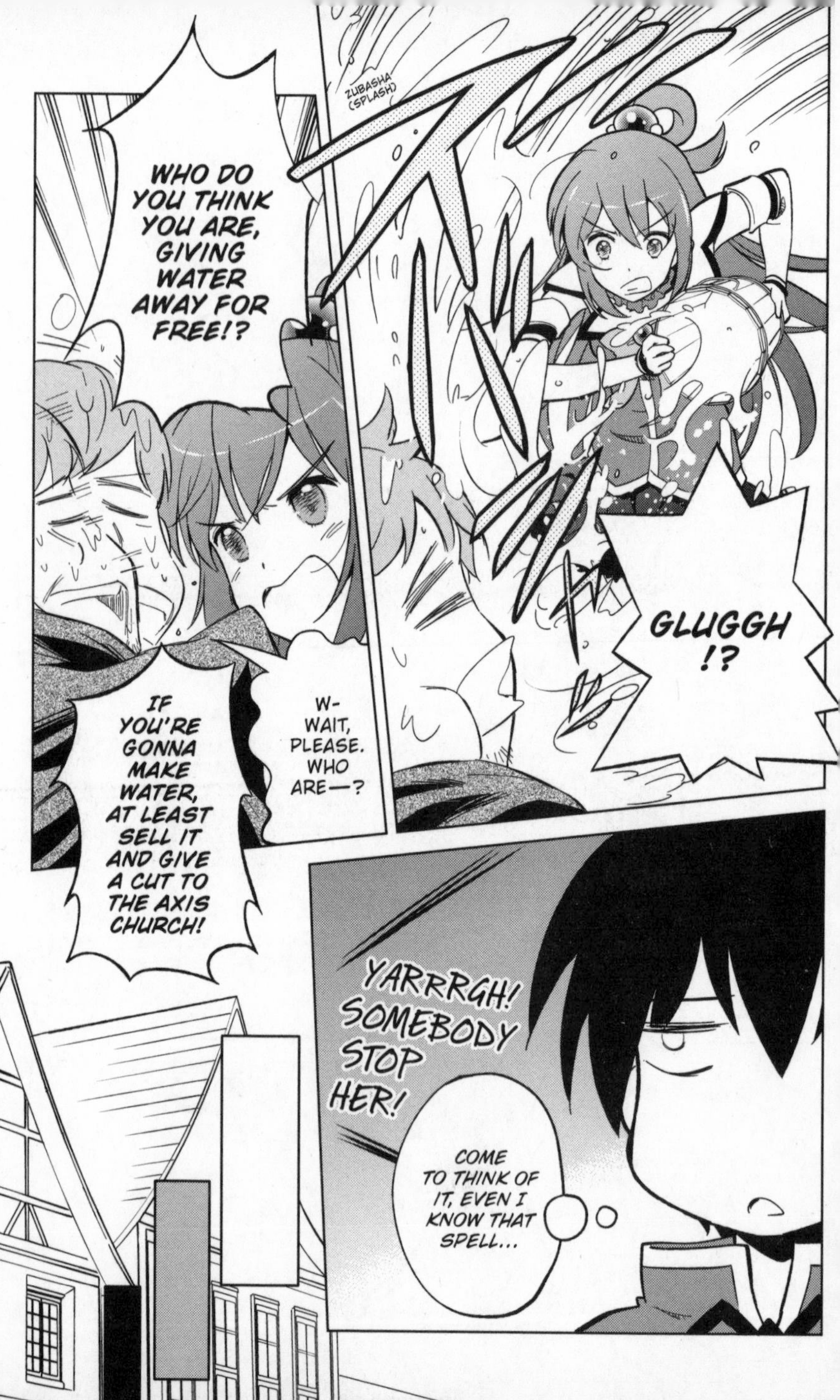
ZUBASHA (SPLASH)
GLUGGH!?
WHO DO YOU THINK YOU ARE, GIVING WATER AWAY FOR FREE!?
W-WAIT, PLEASE. WHO ARE—?
IF YOU'RE GONNA MAKE WATER, AT LEAST SELL IT AND GIVE A CUT TO THE AXIS CHURCH!
YARRRGH! SOMEBODY STOP HER!
COME TO THINK OF IT, EVEN I KNOW THAT SPELL...

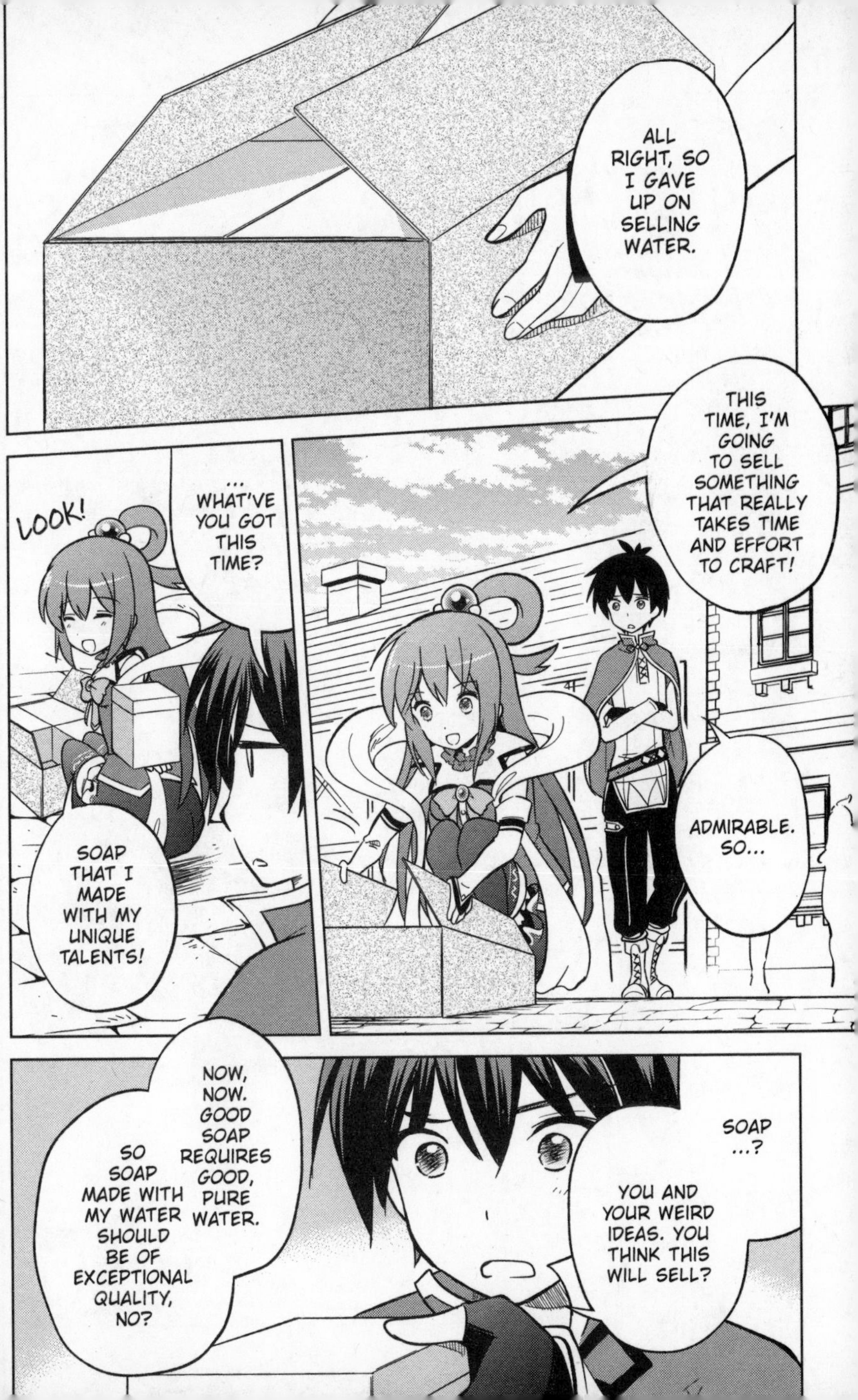
ALL RIGHT, SO I GAVE UP ON SELLING WATER.
THIS TIME, I'M GOING TO SELL SOMETHING THAT REALLY TAKES TIME AND EFFORT TO CRAFT!
ADMIRABLE. SO...
... WHAT'VE YOU GOT THIS TIME?
LOOK!
SOAP THAT I MADE WITH MY UNIQUE TALENTS!
SOAP ...?
YOU AND YOUR WEIRD IDEAS. YOU THINK THIS WILL SELL?
NOW, NOW. GOOD SOAP REQUIRES GOOD, PURE WATER.
SO SOAP MADE WITH MY WATER SHOULD BE OF EXCEPTIONAL QUALITY, NO?

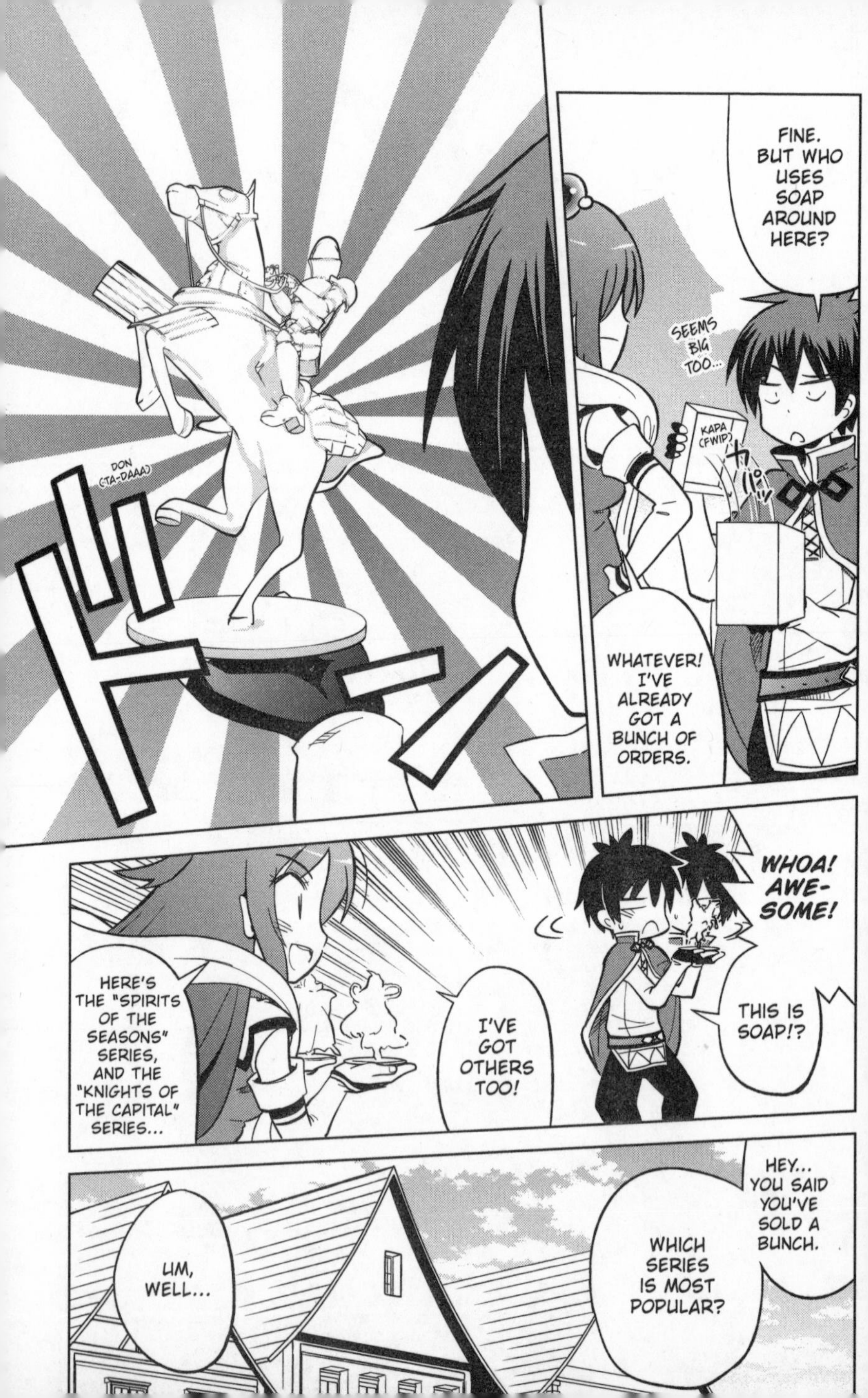
FINE. BUT WHO USES SOAP AROUND HERE?
SEEMS BIG TOO...
KAPA (FWIP)
WHATEVER! I'VE ALREADY GOT A BUNCH OF ORDERS.
DON (TA-DAAA)
WHOA! AWE-SOME!
THIS IS SOAP!?
I'VE GOT OTHERS TOO!
HERE'S THE "SPIRITS OF THE SEASONS" SERIES, AND THE "KNIGHTS OF THE CAPITAL" SERIES...
HEY... YOU SAID YOU'VE SOLD A BUNCH.
WHICH SERIES IS MOST POPULAR?
UM, WELL...

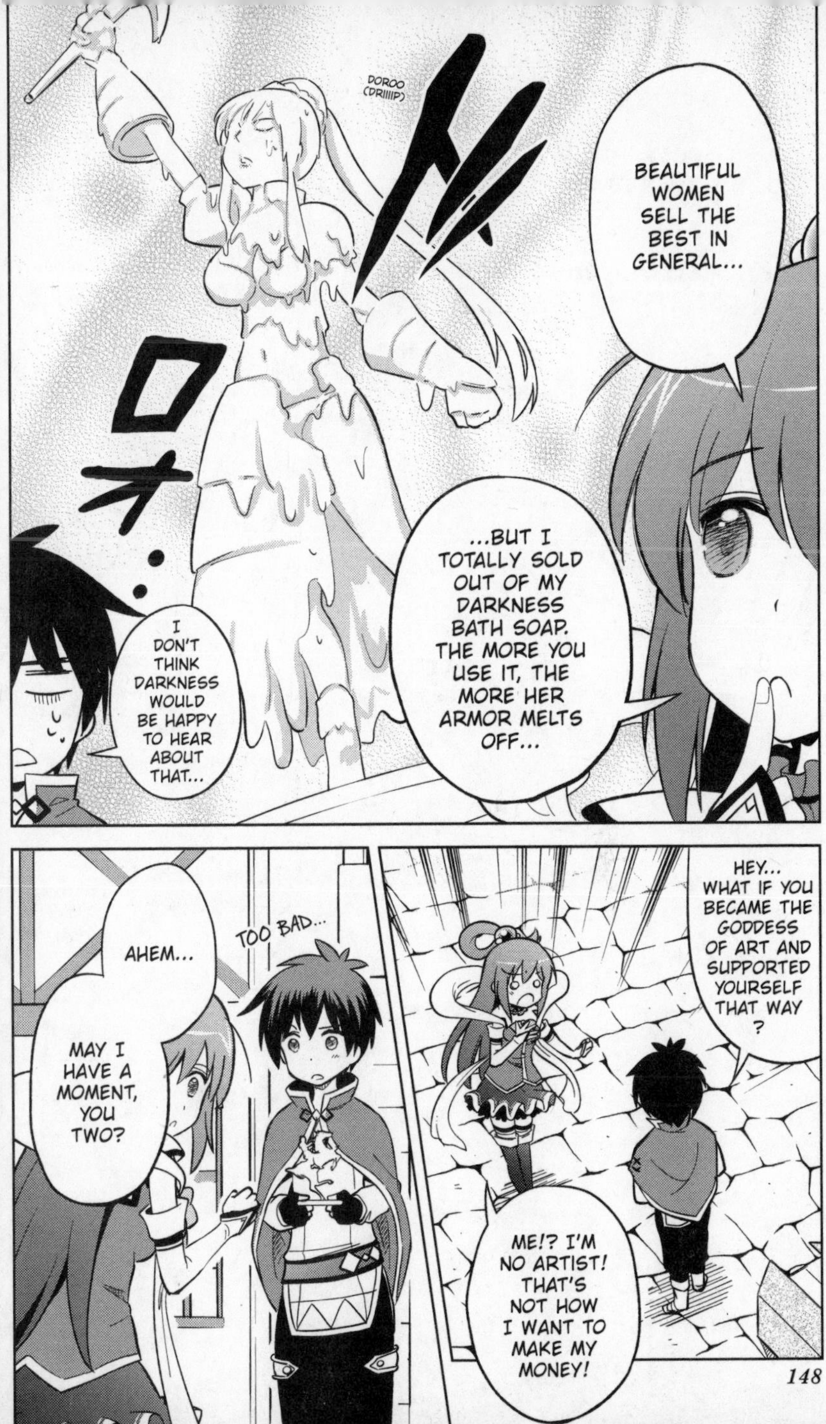
BEAUTIFUL WOMEN SELL THE BEST IN GENERAL...
DOROO (DRIIIP)
...BUT I TOTALLY SOLD OUT OF MY DARKNESS BATH SOAP. THE MORE YOU USE IT, THE MORE HER ARMOR MELTS OFF...
I DON'T THINK DARKNESS WOULD BE HAPPY TO HEAR ABOUT THAT...
HEY... WHAT IF YOU BECAME THE GODDESS OF ART AND SUPPORTED YOURSELF THAT WAY?
ME!? I'M NO ARTIST! THAT'S NOT HOW I WANT TO MAKE MY MONEY!
TOO BAD...
AHEM...
MAY I HAVE A MOMENT, YOU TWO?

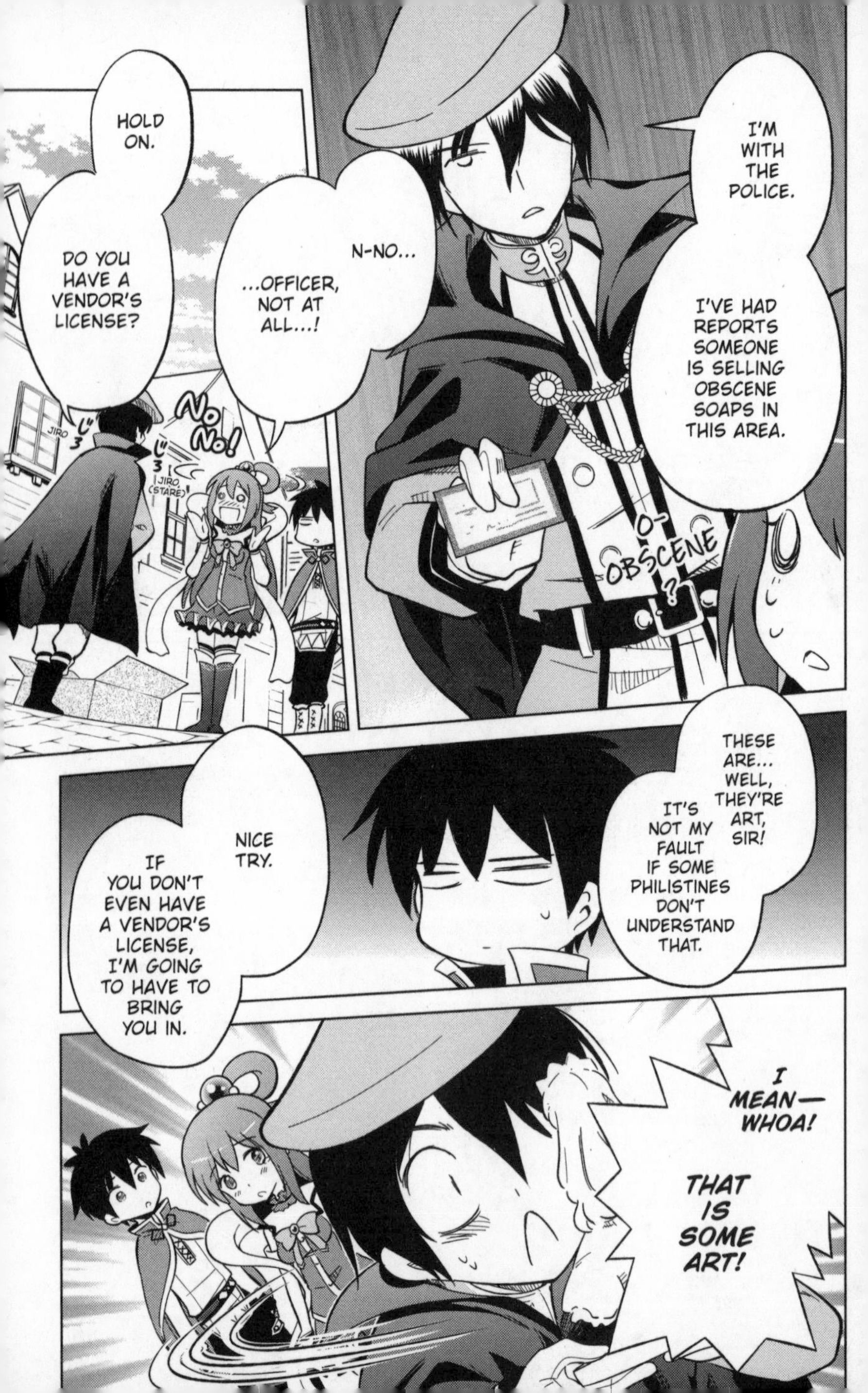
I'M WITH THE POLICE.
I'VE HAD REPORTS SOMEONE IS SELLING OBSCENE SOAPS IN THIS AREA.
O-OBSCENE?
N-NO...
...OFFICER, NOT AT ALL...!
NO NO!
HOLD ON.
DO YOU HAVE A VENDOR'S LICENSE?
JIRO
JIRO (STARE)
THESE ARE... WELL, THEY'RE ART, SIR!
IT'S NOT MY FAULT IF SOME PHILISTINES DON'T UNDERSTAND THAT.
NICE TRY.
IF YOU DON'T EVEN HAVE A VENDOR'S LICENSE, I'M GOING TO HAVE TO BRING YOU IN.
I MEAN—WHOA!
THAT IS SOME ART!

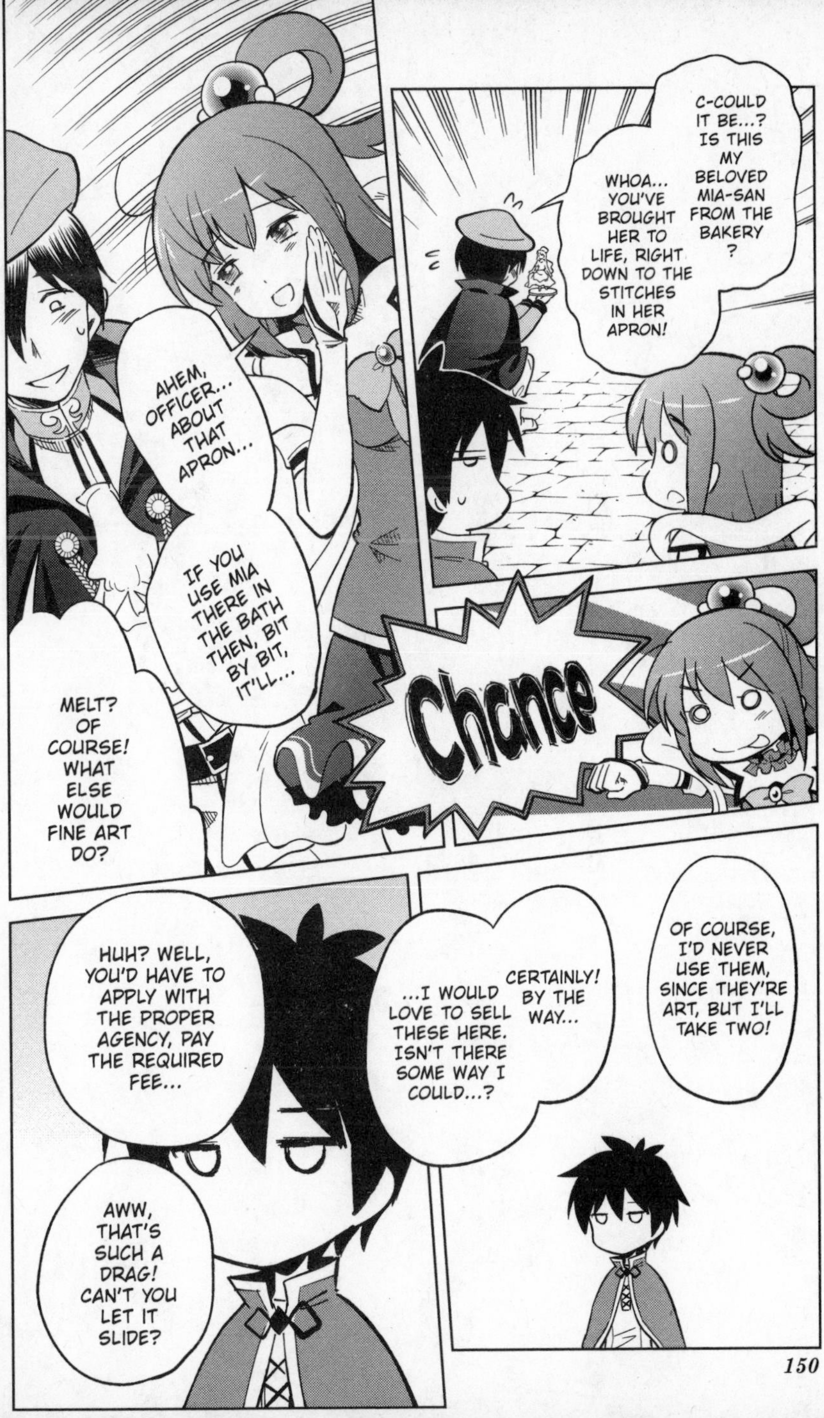
C-COULD IT BE...? IS THIS MY BELOVED MIA-SAN FROM THE BAKERY?
WHOA... YOU'VE BROUGHT HER TO LIFE, RIGHT DOWN TO THE STITCHES IN HER APRON!
Chance
AHEM, OFFICER... ABOUT THAT APRON...
IF YOU USE MIA THERE IN THE BATH THEN, BIT BY BIT, IT'LL...
MELT? OF COURSE! WHAT ELSE WOULD FINE ART DO?
OF COURSE, I'D NEVER USE THEM, SINCE THEY'RE ART, BUT I'LL TAKE TWO!
CERTAINLY! BY THE WAY...
...I WOULD LOVE TO SELL THESE HERE. ISN'T THERE SOME WAY I COULD...?
HUH? WELL, YOU'D HAVE TO APPLY WITH THE PROPER AGENCY, PAY THE REQUIRED FEE...
AWW, THAT'S SUCH A DRAG! CAN'T YOU LET IT SLIDE?

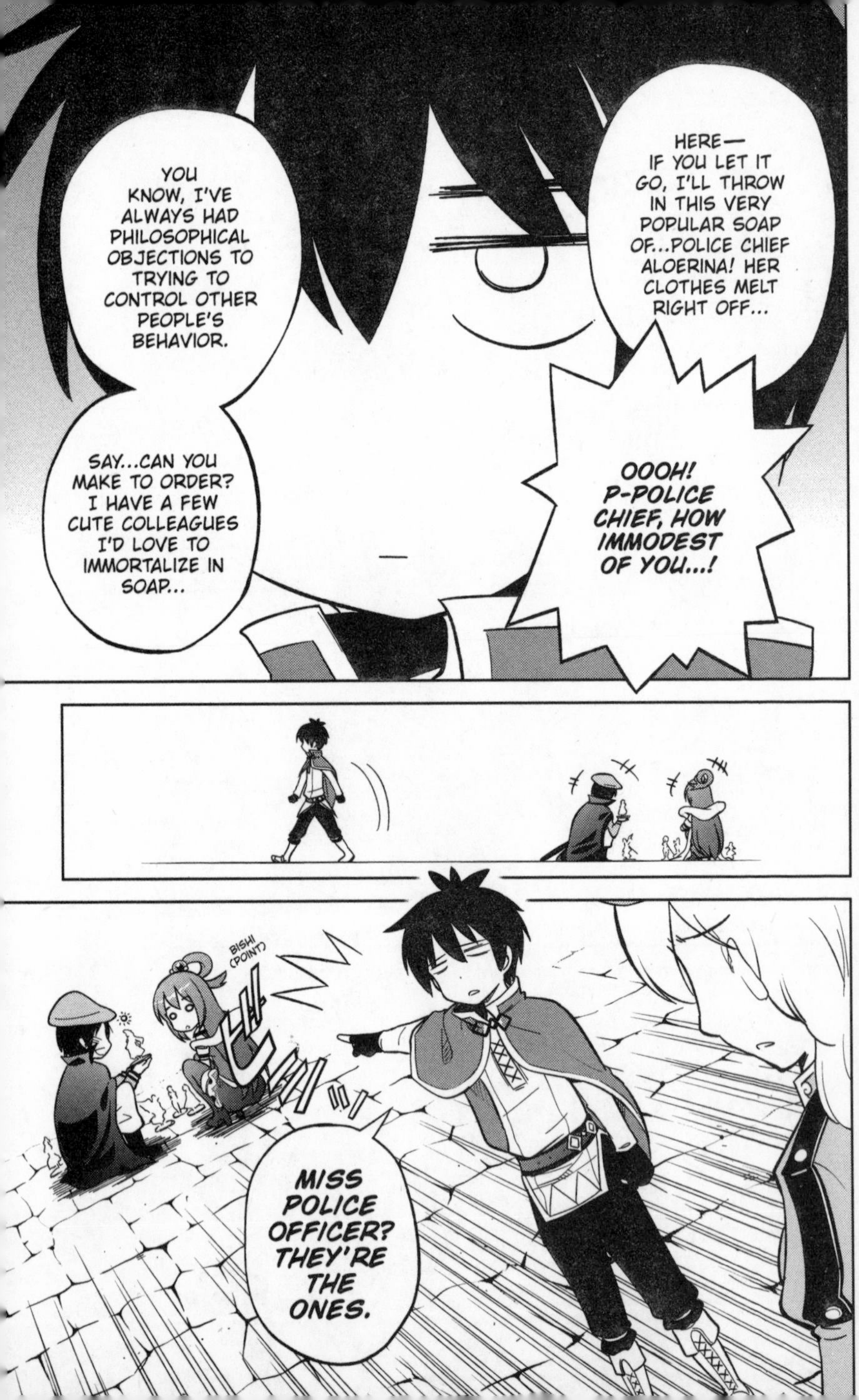
HERE— IF YOU LET IT GO, I'LL THROW IN THIS VERY POPULAR SOAP OF...POLICE CHIEF ALOERINA! HER CLOTHES MELT RIGHT OFF...
YOU KNOW, I'VE ALWAYS HAD PHILOSOPHICAL OBJECTIONS TO TRYING TO CONTROL OTHER PEOPLE'S BEHAVIOR.
OOOH! P-POLICE CHIEF, HOW IMMODEST OF YOU...!
SAY...CAN YOU MAKE TO ORDER? I HAVE A FEW CUTE COLLEAGUES I'D LOVE TO IMMORTALIZE IN SOAP...
BISHI (POINT)
MISS POLICE OFFICER? THEY'RE THE ONES.

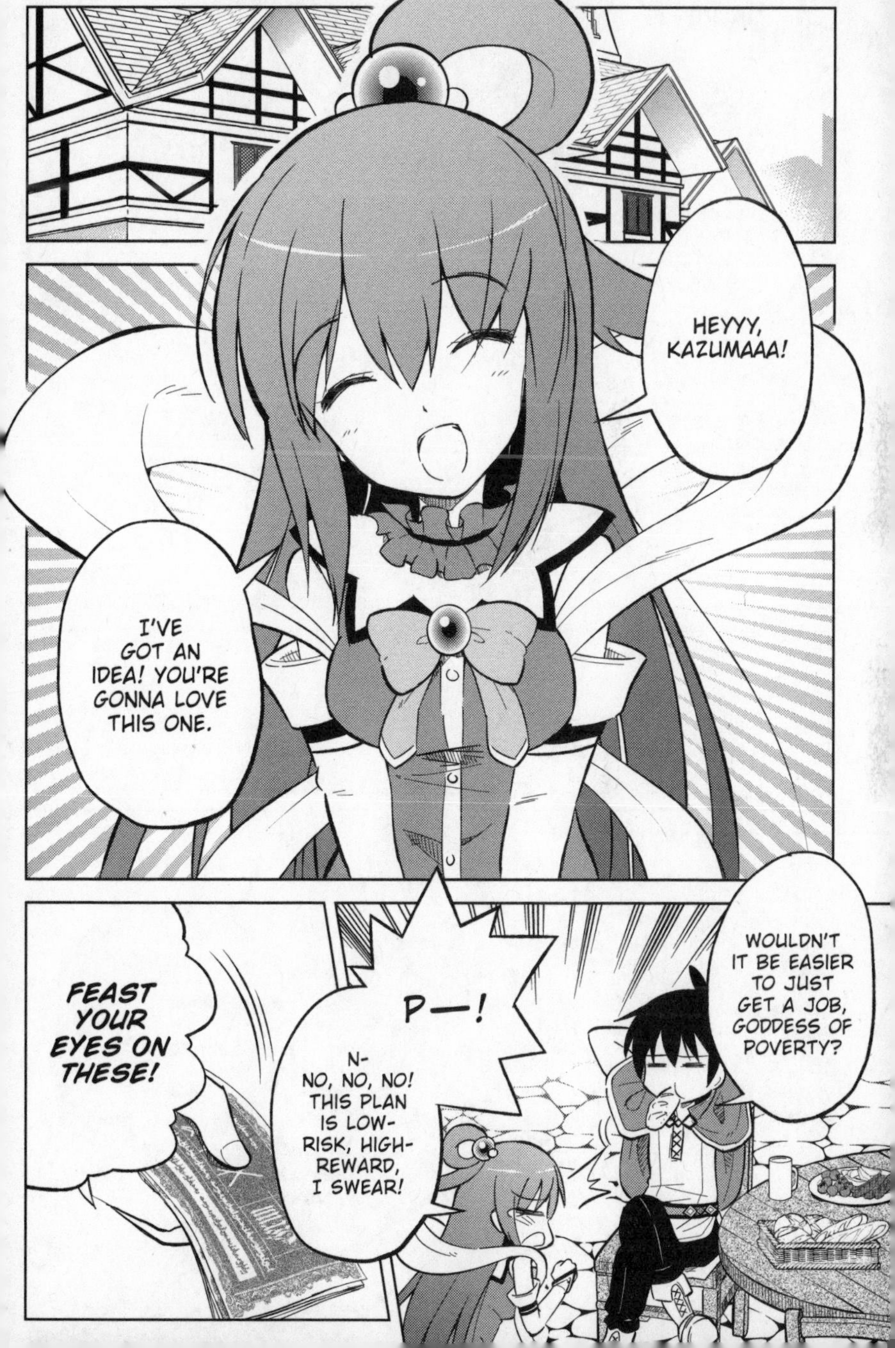
HEYYY, KAZUMAAA!
I'VE GOT AN IDEA! YOU'RE GONNA LOVE THIS ONE.
WOULDN'T IT BE EASIER TO JUST GET A JOB, GODDESS OF POVERTY?
P—!
N- NO, NO, NO! THIS PLAN IS LOW-RISK, HIGH-REWARD, I SWEAR!
FEAST YOUR EYES ON THESE!

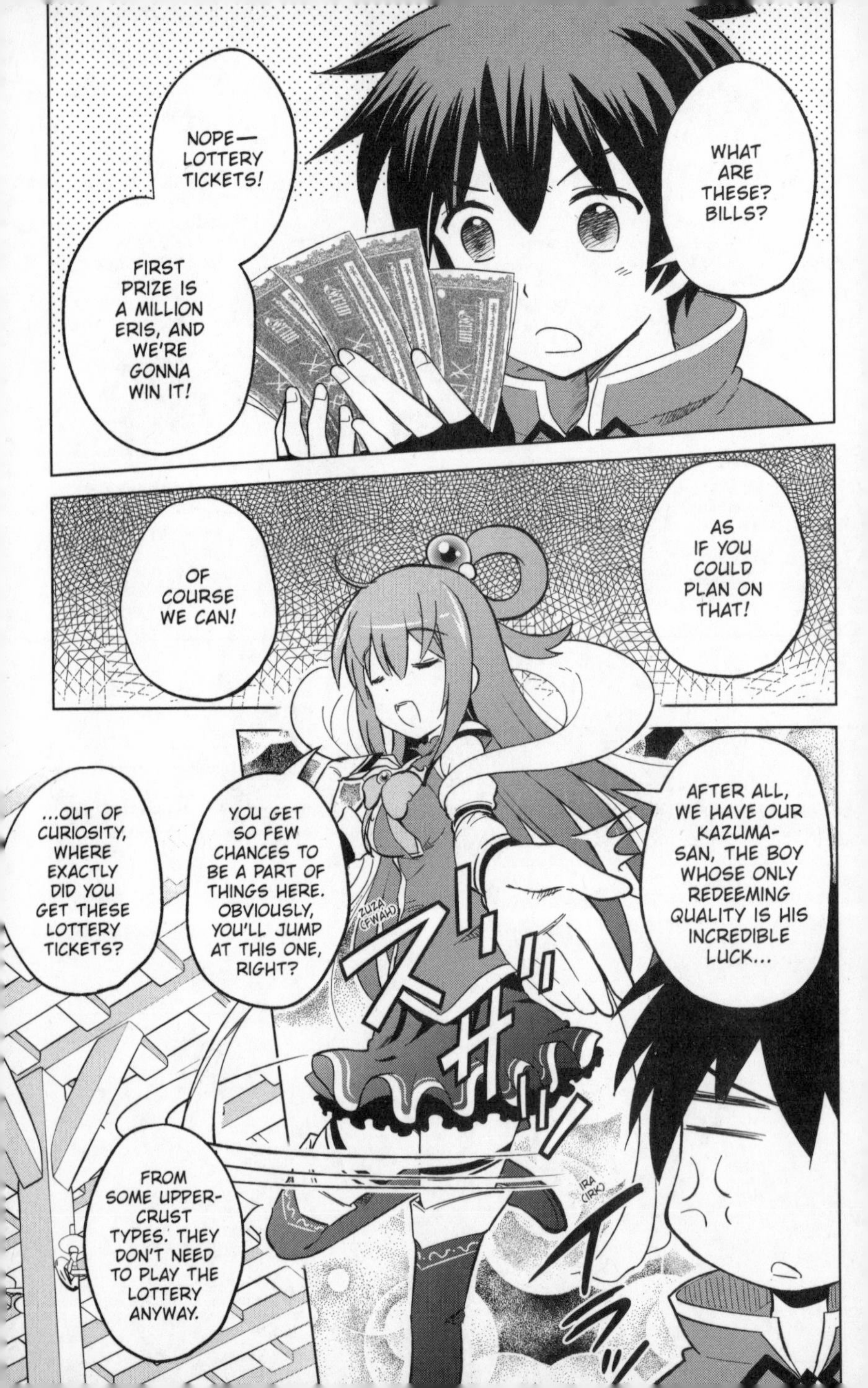
WHAT ARE THESE? BILLS?
NOPE— LOTTERY TICKETS!
FIRST PRIZE IS A MILLION ERIS, AND WE'RE GONNA WIN IT!
AS IF YOU COULD PLAN ON THAT!
OF COURSE WE CAN!
AFTER ALL, WE HAVE OUR KAZUMA-SAN, THE BOY WHOSE ONLY REDEEMING QUALITY IS HIS INCREDIBLE LUCK...
YOU GET SO FEW CHANCES TO BE A PART OF THINGS HERE. OBVIOUSLY, YOU'LL JUMP AT THIS ONE, RIGHT?
ZUZA (FWAH)
...OUT OF CURIOSITY, WHERE EXACTLY DID YOU GET THESE LOTTERY TICKETS?
IRA (IRK)
FROM SOME UPPER-CRUST TYPES. THEY DON'T NEED TO PLAY THE LOTTERY ANYWAY.

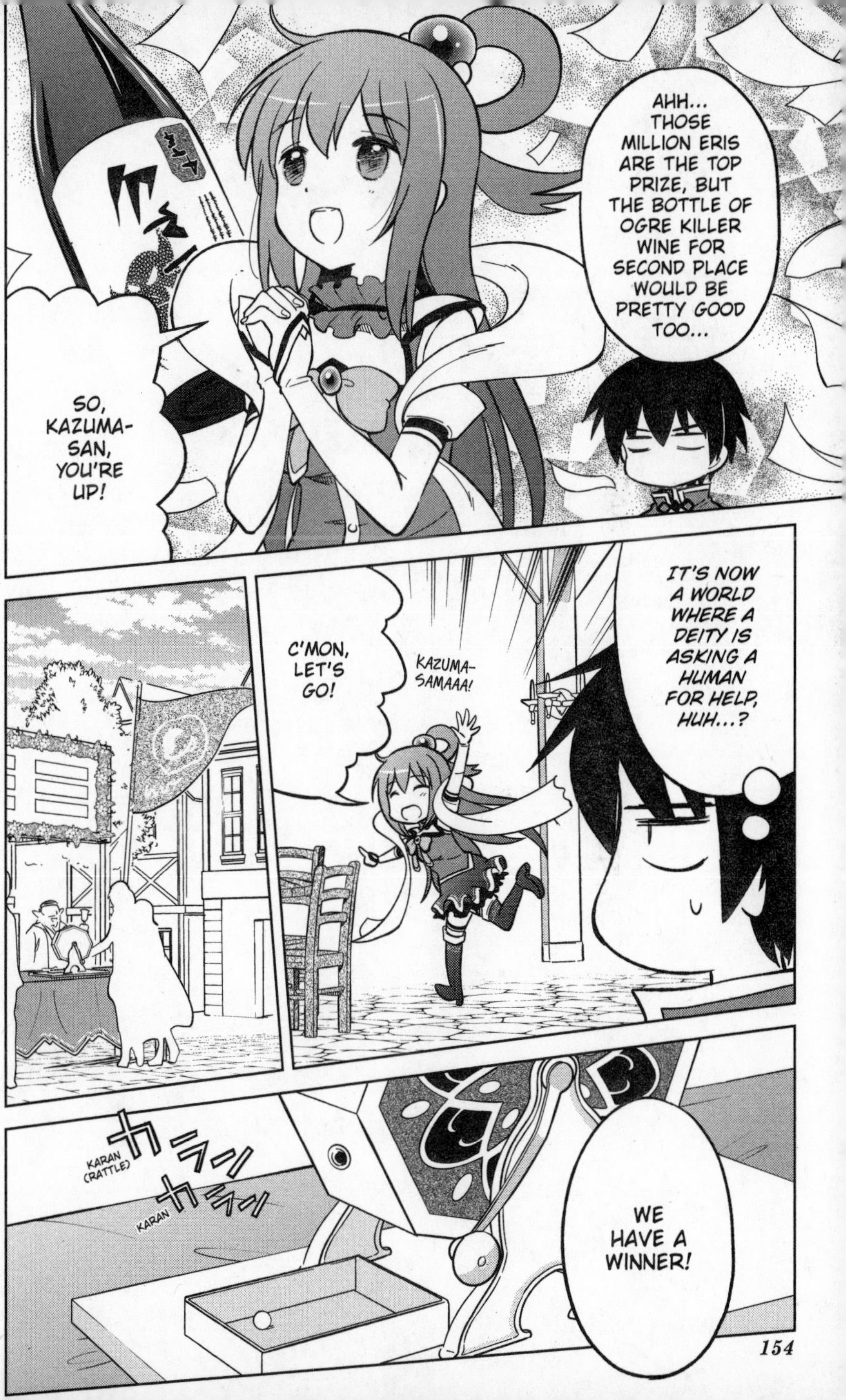
AHH... THOSE MILLION ERIS ARE THE TOP PRIZE, BUT THE BOTTLE OF OGRE KILLER WINE FOR SECOND PLACE WOULD BE PRETTY GOOD TOO...
SO, KAZUMA-SAN, YOU'RE UP!
IT'S NOW A WORLD WHERE A DEITY IS ASKING A HUMAN FOR HELP, HUH...?
KAZUMA-SAMAAA!
C'MON, LET'S GO!
WE HAVE A WINNER!
KARAN (RATTLE)
KARAN

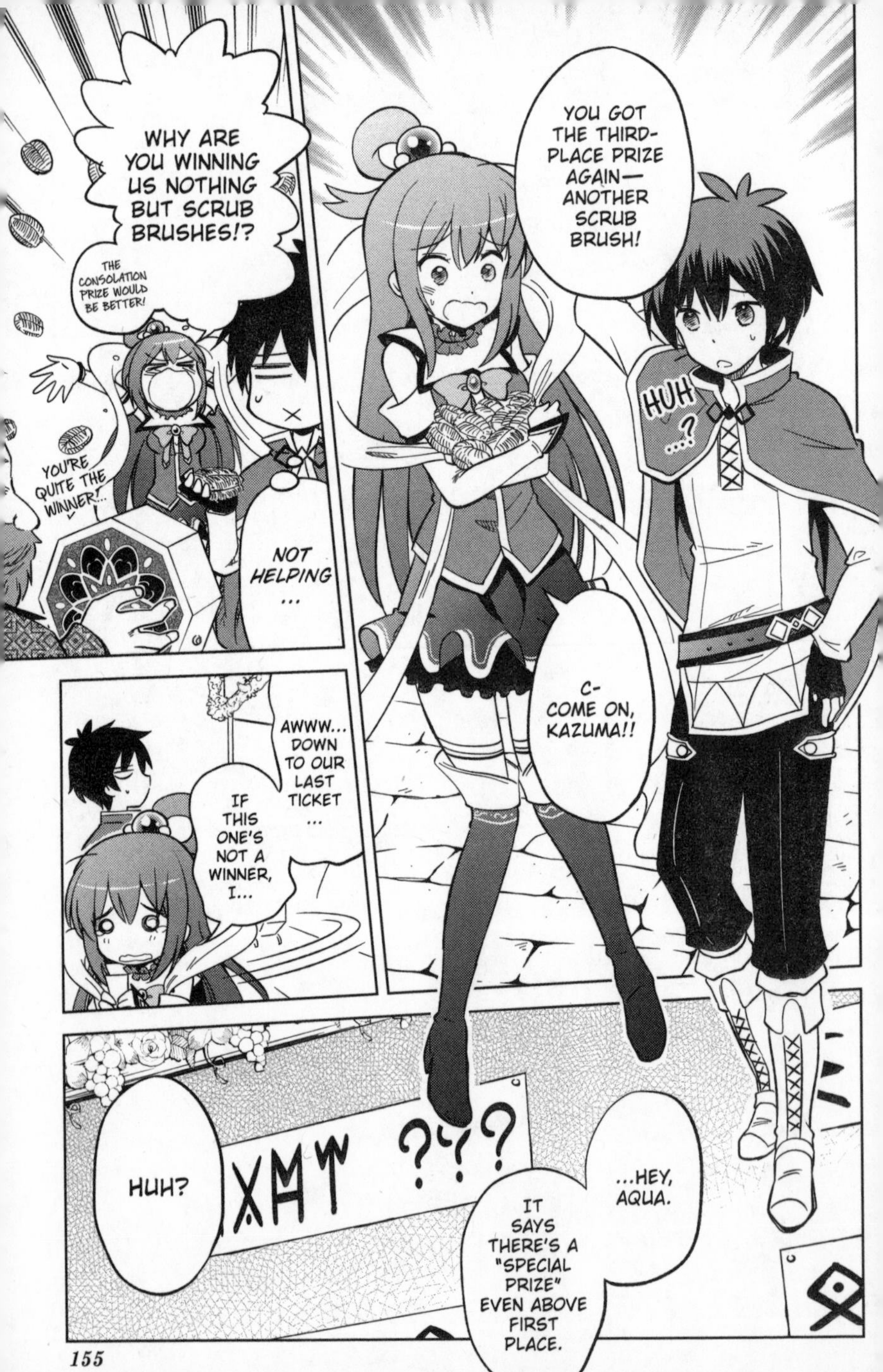
YOU GOT THE THIRD-PLACE PRIZE AGAIN—ANOTHER SCRUB BRUSH!
HUH ...?
C-COME ON, KAZUMA!!
WHY ARE YOU WINNING US NOTHING BUT SCRUB BRUSHES!?
THE CONSOLATION PRIZE WOULD BE BETTER!
YOU'RE QUITE THE WINNER!...
NOT HELPING ...
AWWW... DOWN TO OUR LAST TICKET ...
IF THIS ONE'S NOT A WINNER, I...
...HEY, AQUA.
IT SAYS THERE'S A "SPECIAL PRIZE" EVEN ABOVE FIRST PLACE.
HUH?

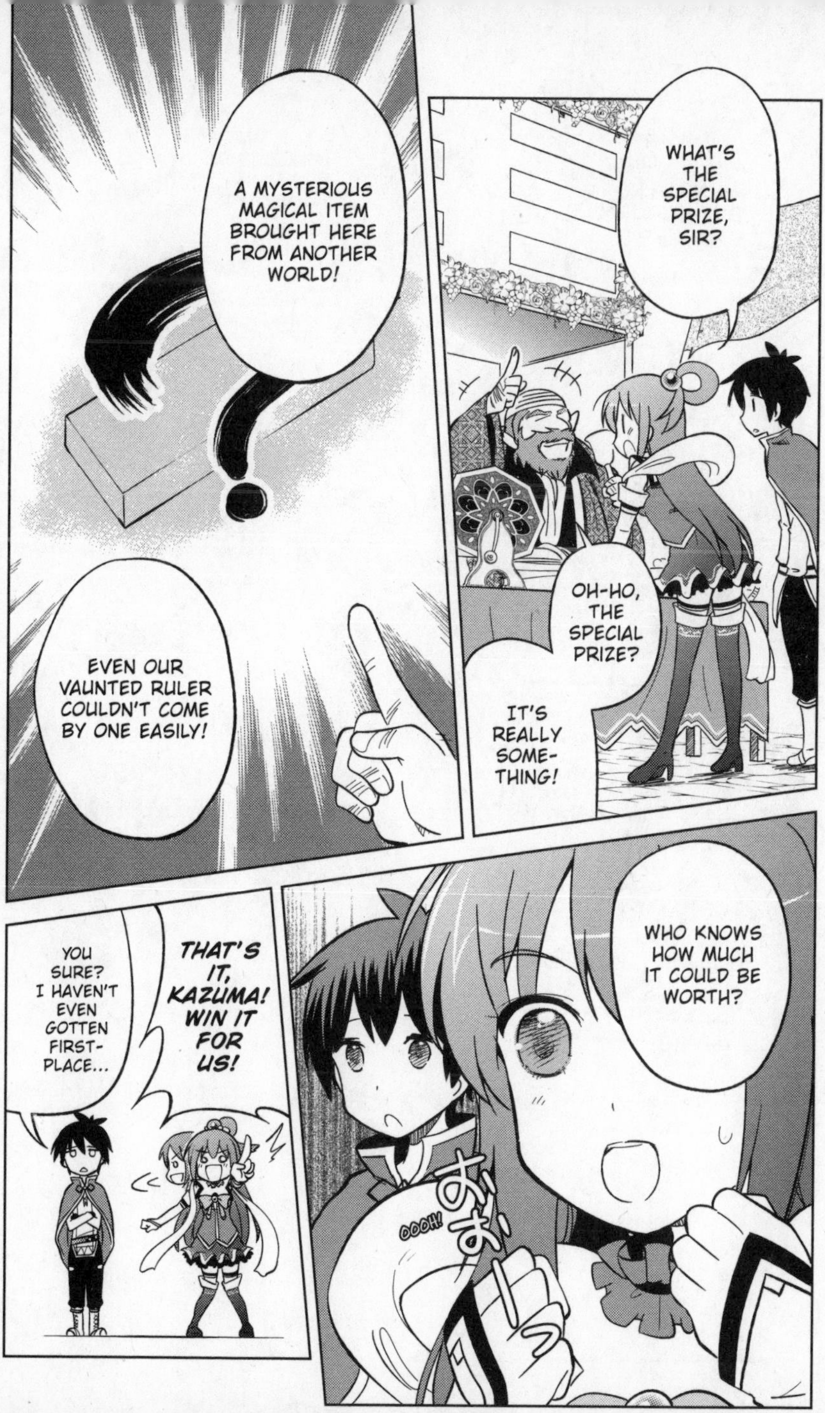
WHAT'S THE SPECIAL PRIZE, SIR?
OH-HO, THE SPECIAL PRIZE?
IT'S REALLY SOME-THING!
A MYSTERIOUS MAGICAL ITEM BROUGHT HERE FROM ANOTHER WORLD!
EVEN OUR VAUNTED RULER COULDN'T COME BY ONE EASILY!
WHO KNOWS HOW MUCH IT COULD BE WORTH?
OOOH!
THAT'S IT, KAZUMA! WIN IT FOR US!
YOU SURE? I HAVEN'T EVEN GOTTEN FIRST-PLACE...

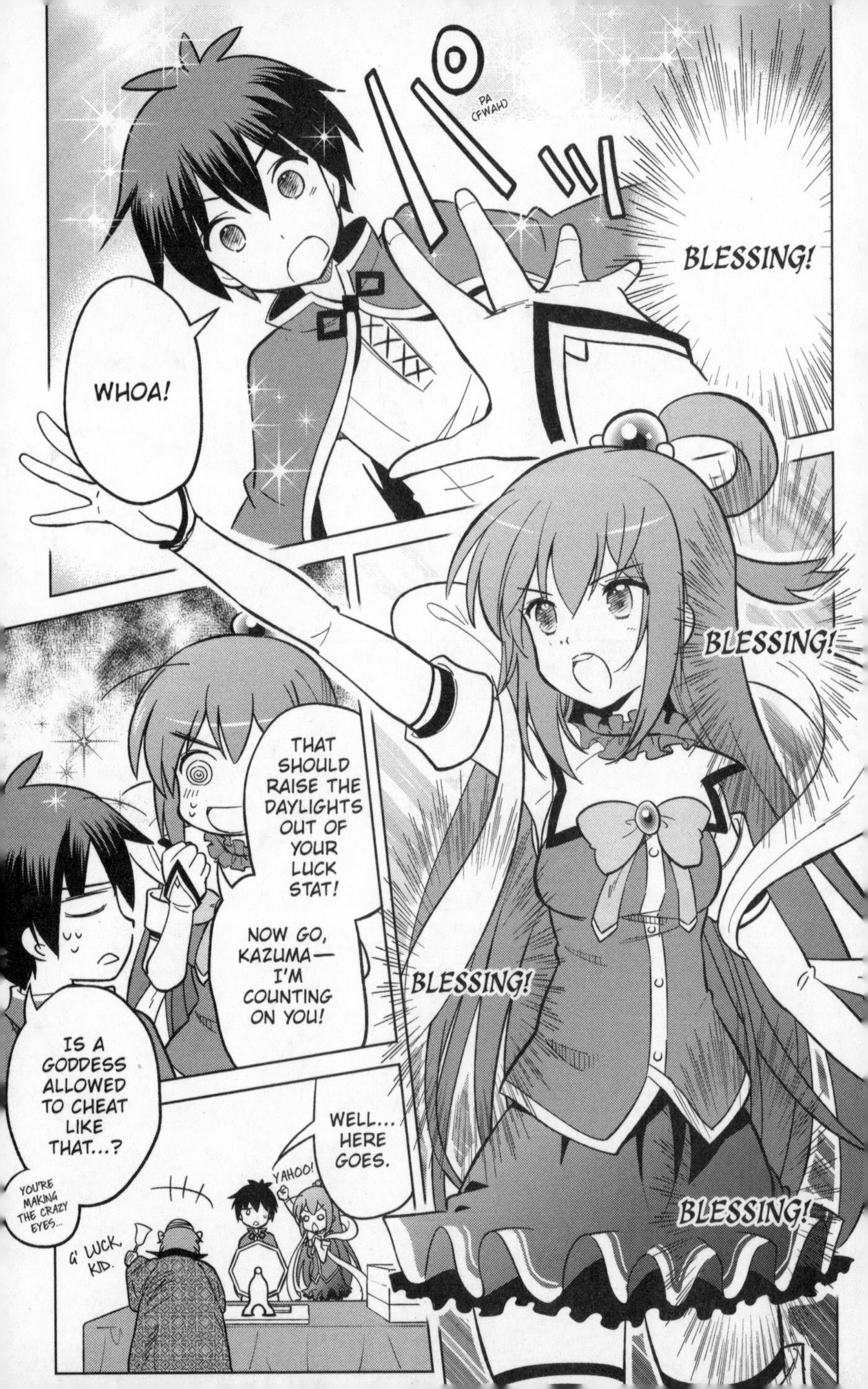
PA (FWAH)
BLESSING!
WHOA!
BLESSING!
BLESSING!
BLESSING!
THAT SHOULD RAISE THE DAYLIGHTS OUT OF YOUR LUCK STAT!
NOW GO, KAZUMA— I'M COUNTING ON YOU!
IS A GODDESS ALLOWED TO CHEAT LIKE THAT...?
WELL... HERE GOES.
YAHOO!
YOU'RE MAKING THE CRAZY EYES...
G' LUCK, KID.

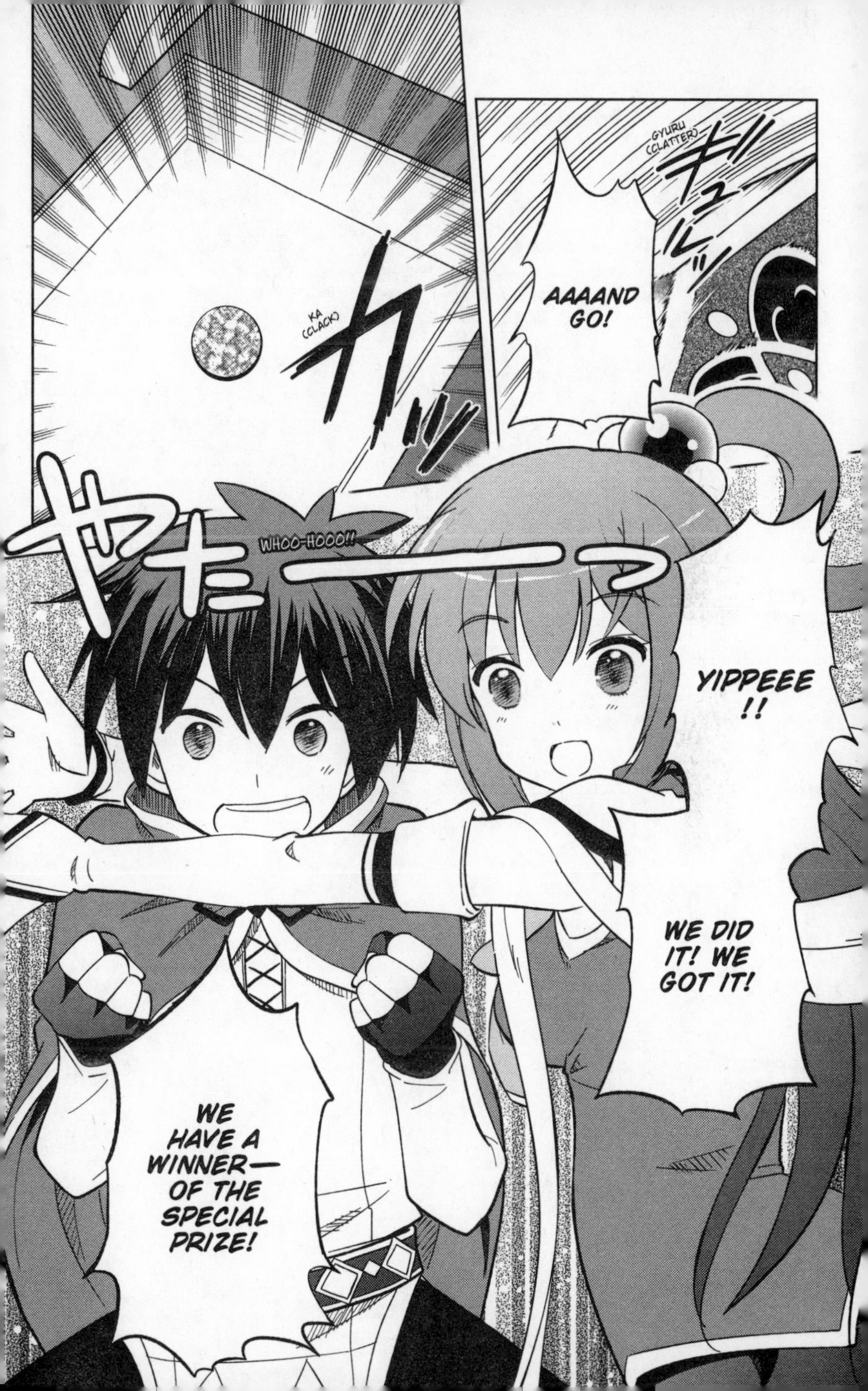
GYURU (CLATTER)
AAAAND GO!
KA (CLACK)
WHOO-HOOO!!
YIPPEEE !!
WE DID IT! WE GOT IT!
WE HAVE A WINNER— OF THE SPECIAL PRIZE!

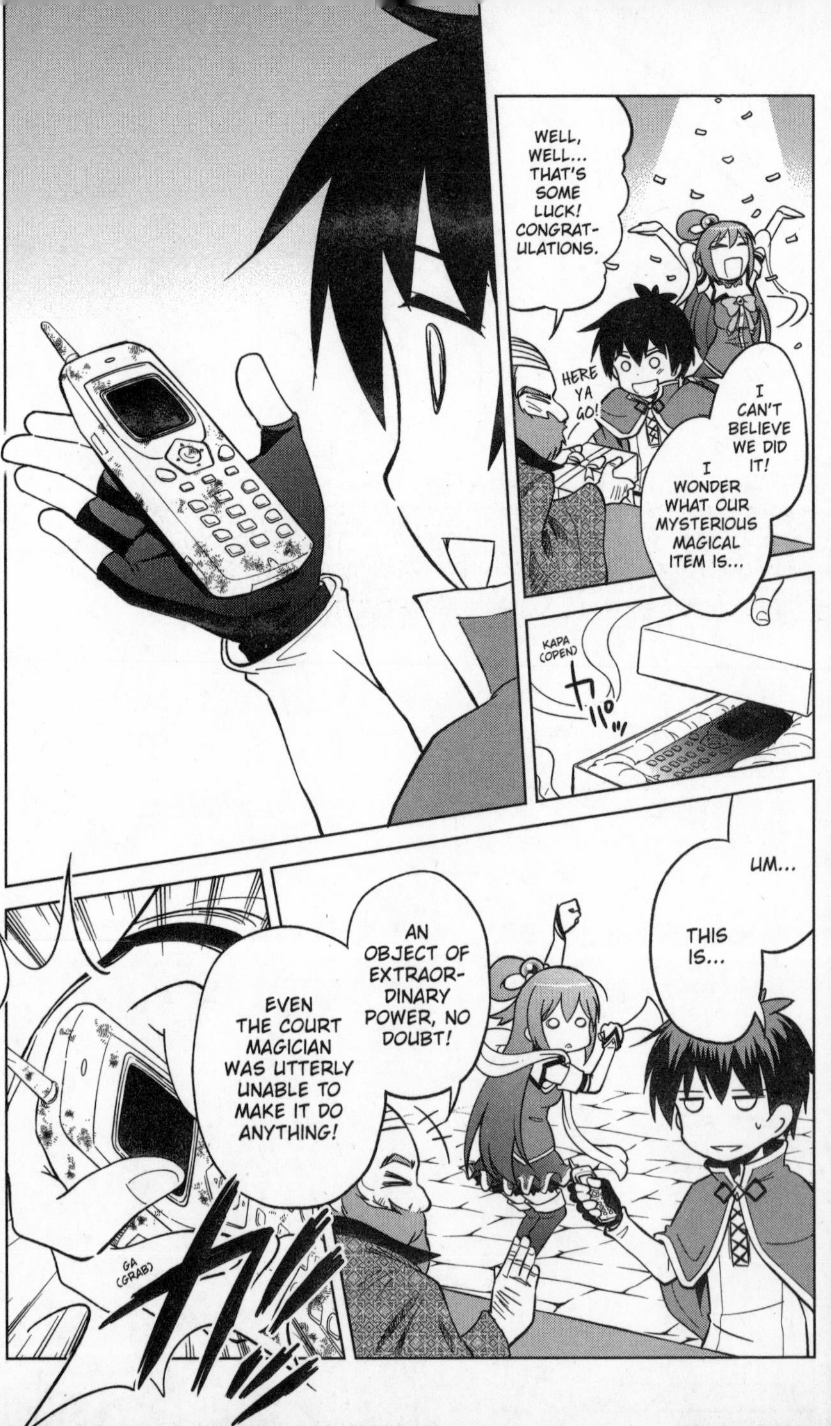
WELL, WELL... THAT'S SOME LUCK! CONGRAT-ULATIONS.
HERE YA GO!
I CAN'T BELIEVE WE DID IT!
I WONDER WHAT OUR MYSTERIOUS MAGICAL ITEM IS...
KAPA (OPEN)
UM...
THIS IS...
AN OBJECT OF EXTRAOR-DINARY POWER, NO DOUBT!
EVEN THE COURT MAGICIAN WAS UTTERLY UNABLE TO MAKE IT DO ANYTHING!
GA (GRAB)

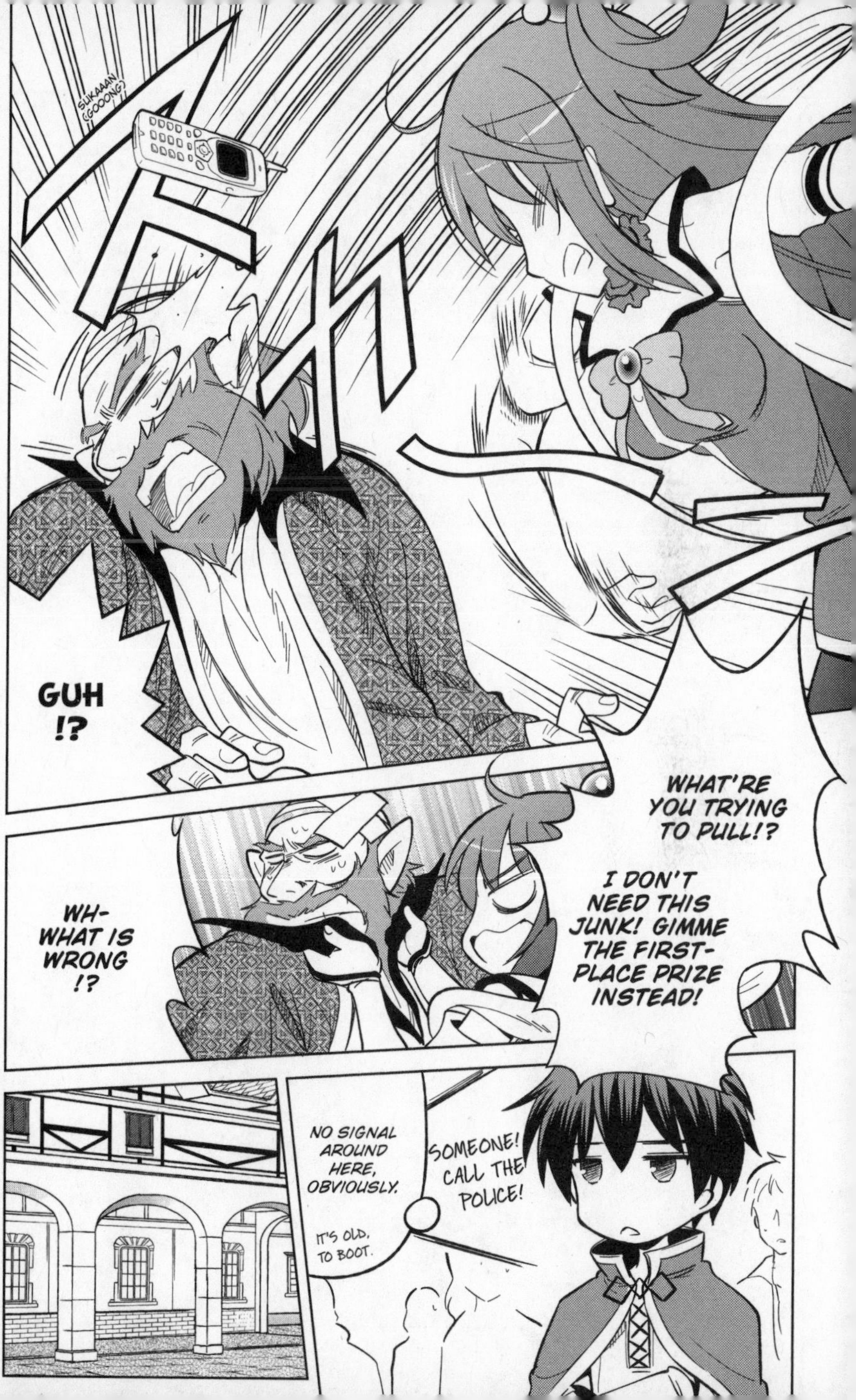
SUKAAAN (GOOONG)
GUH !?
WHAT'RE YOU TRYING TO PULL!?
I DON'T NEED THIS JUNK! GIMME THE FIRST-PLACE PRIZE INSTEAD!
WH- WHAT IS WRONG !?
SOMEONE! CALL THE POLICE!
NO SIGNAL AROUND HERE, OBVIOUSLY.
IT'S OLD, TO BOOT.

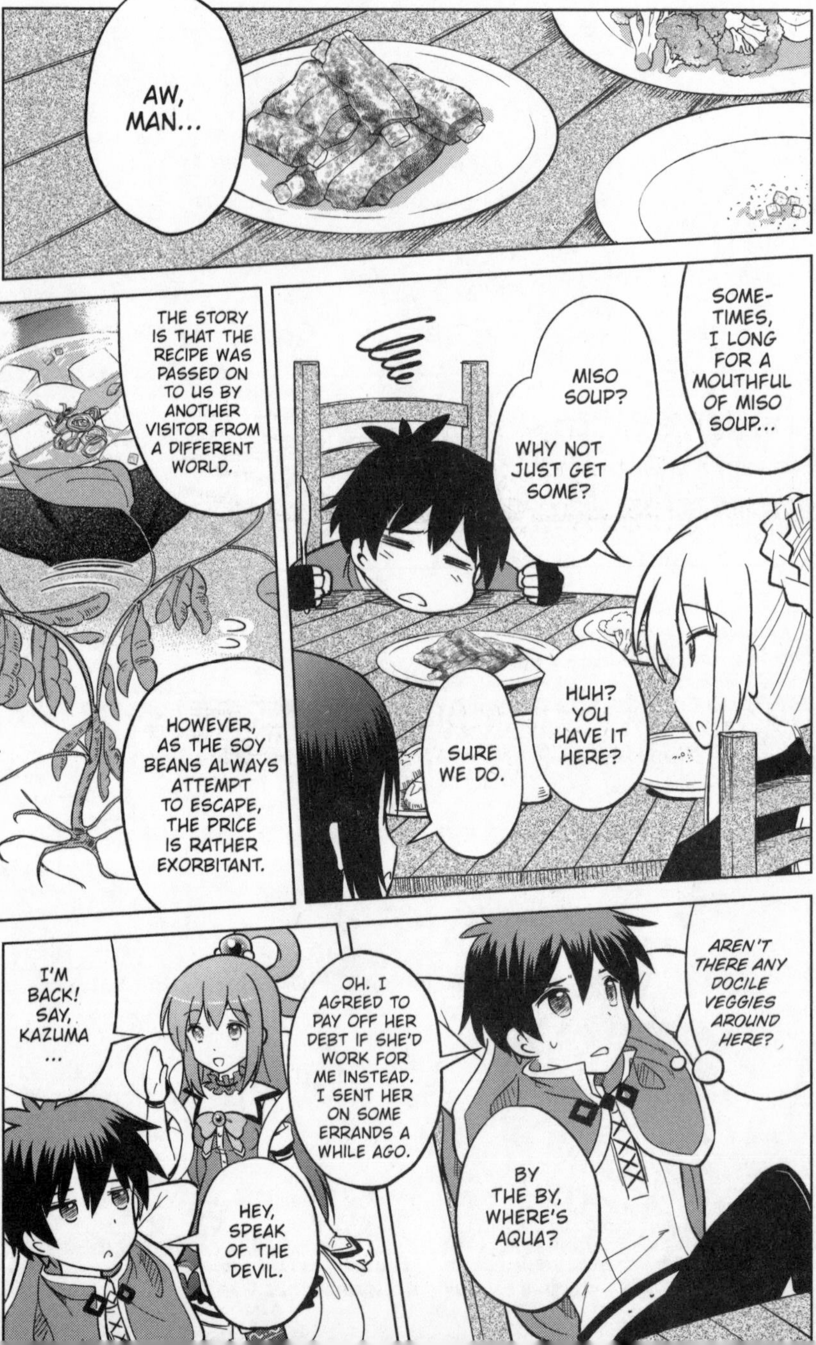
AW, MAN...
SOME-TIMES, I LONG FOR A MOUTHFUL OF MISO SOUP...
MISO SOUP?
WHY NOT JUST GET SOME?
HUH? YOU HAVE IT HERE?
SURE WE DO.
THE STORY IS THAT THE RECIPE WAS PASSED ON TO US BY ANOTHER VISITOR FROM A DIFFERENT WORLD.
HOWEVER, AS THE SOY BEANS ALWAYS ATTEMPT TO ESCAPE, THE PRICE IS RATHER EXORBITANT.
AREN'T THERE ANY DOCILE VEGGIES AROUND HERE?
BY THE BY, WHERE'S AQUA?
OH. I AGREED TO PAY OFF HER DEBT IF SHE'D WORK FOR ME INSTEAD. I SENT HER ON SOME ERRANDS A WHILE AGO.
HEY, SPEAK OF THE DEVIL.
I'M BACK! SAY, KAZUMA...

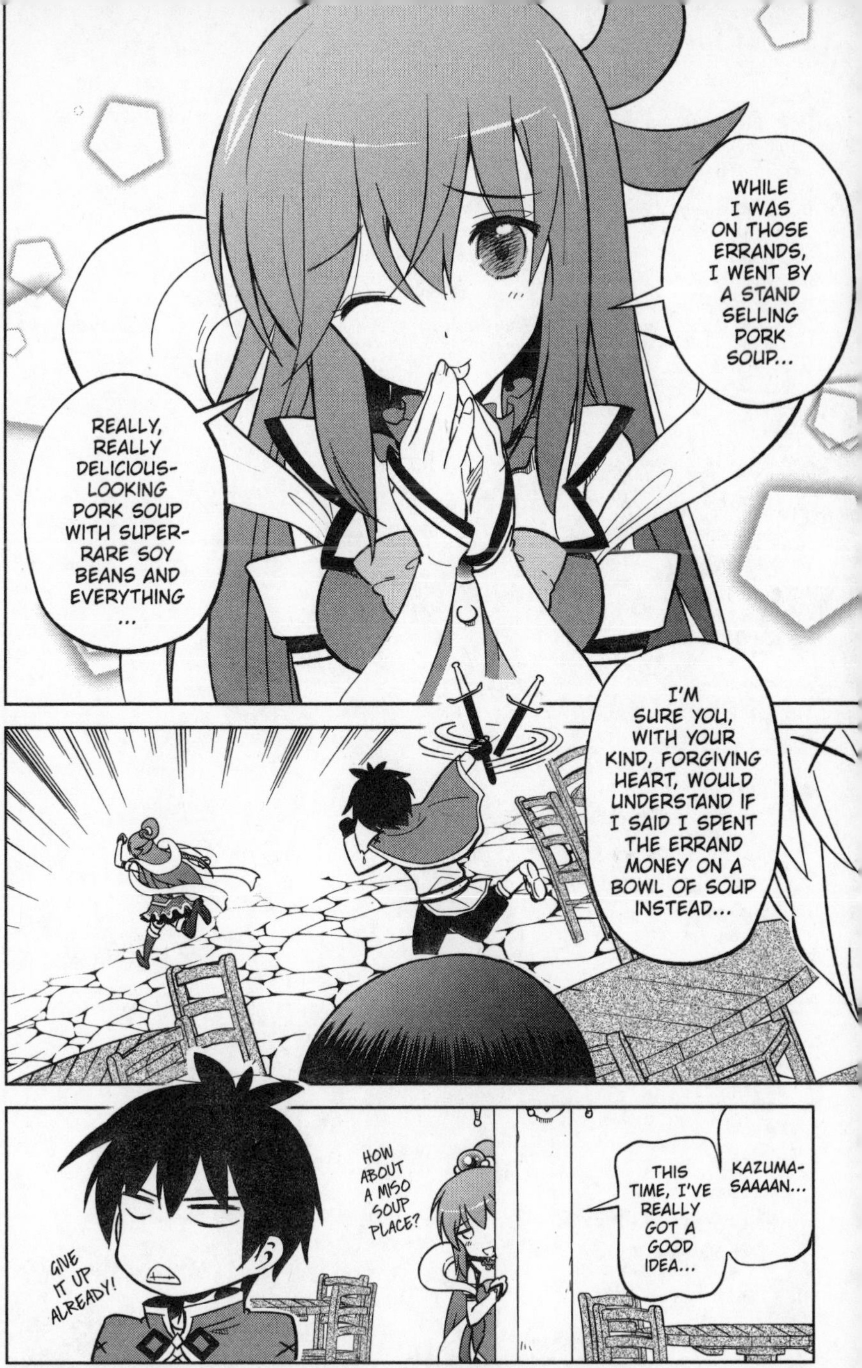
WHILE I WAS ON THOSE ERRANDS, I WENT BY A STAND SELLING PORK SOUP...
REALLY, REALLY DELICIOUS-LOOKING PORK SOUP WITH SUPER-RARE SOY BEANS AND EVERYTHING ...
I'M SURE YOU, WITH YOUR KIND, FORGIVING HEART, WOULD UNDERSTAND IF I SAID I SPENT THE ERRAND MONEY ON A BOWL OF SOUP INSTEAD...
KAZUMA-SAAAAN...
THIS TIME, I'VE REALLY GOT A GOOD IDEA...
HOW ABOUT A MISO SOUP PLACE?
GIVE IT UP ALREADY!

KONOSUBA: GOD'S BLESSING ON THIS WONDERFUL WORLD ① END

TRANSLATION NOTES

COMMON HONORIFICS

no honorific: Indicates familiarity or closeness; if used without permission or reason, addressing someone in this manner would constitute an insult.

-san: The Japanese equivalent of Mr./Mrs./Miss. If a situation calls for politeness, this is the fail-safe honorific.

-sama: Conveys great respect; may also indicate that the social status of the speaker is lower than that of the addressee.

-chan: An affectionate honorific indicating familiarity used mostly in reference to girls; also used in reference to cute persons or animals of either gender.

PAGE 3

Hikikomori refers to people who experience severe social anxiety when outside their homes or interacting with others and so, sometimes voluntarily, withdraw from society. They are often called "shut-ins" or "modern-day hermits."

PAGE 8

NEET is originally a British term but has been adopted by Japan, standing for "not in education, employment, or training." It is usually used pejoratively, to look down on people who are seen as lazy or as freeloaders who won't get a job.

PAGE 20

"you hikiNEET": To bash Kazuma, Aqua combines the terms *hikikomori* and NEET on the fly.

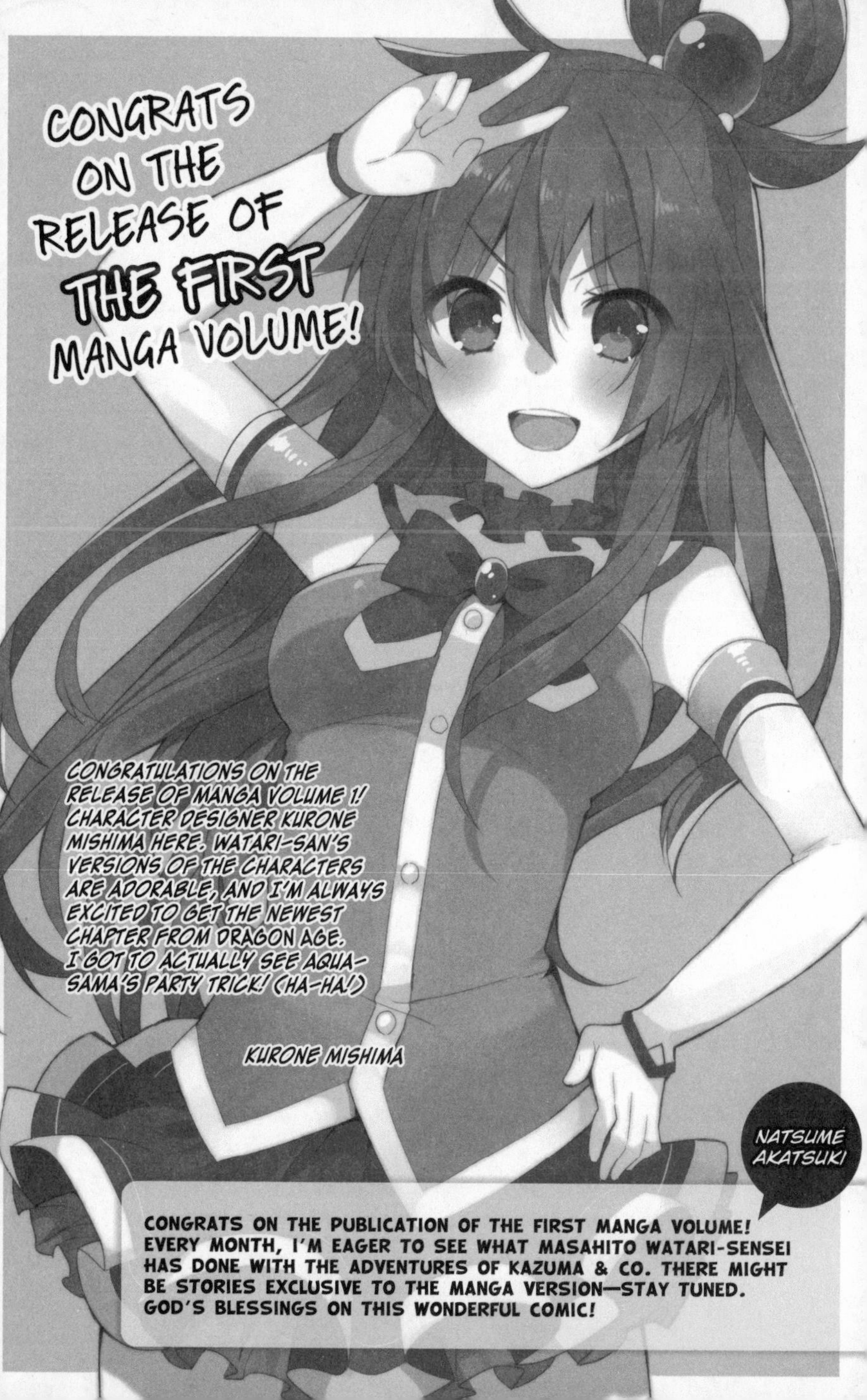
CONGRATS ON THE RELEASE OF THE FIRST MANGA VOLUME!
CONGRATULATIONS ON THE RELEASE OF MANGA VOLUME 1! CHARACTER DESIGNER KURONE MISHIMA HERE. WATARI-SAN'S VERSIONS OF THE CHARACTERS ARE ADORABLE, AND I'M ALWAYS EXCITED TO GET THE NEWEST CHAPTER FROM DRAGON AGE. I GOT TO ACTUALLY SEE AQUA-SAMA'S PARTY TRICK! (HA-HA!)
KURONE MISHIMA
NATSUME AKATSUKI
CONGRATS ON THE PUBLICATION OF THE FIRST MANGA VOLUME! EVERY MONTH, I'M EAGER TO SEE WHAT MASAHITO WATARI-SENSEI HAS DONE WITH THE ADVENTURES OF KAZUMA & CO. THERE MIGHT BE STORIES EXCLUSIVE TO THE MANGA VERSION—STAY TUNED. GOD'S BLESSINGS ON THIS WONDERFUL COMIC!

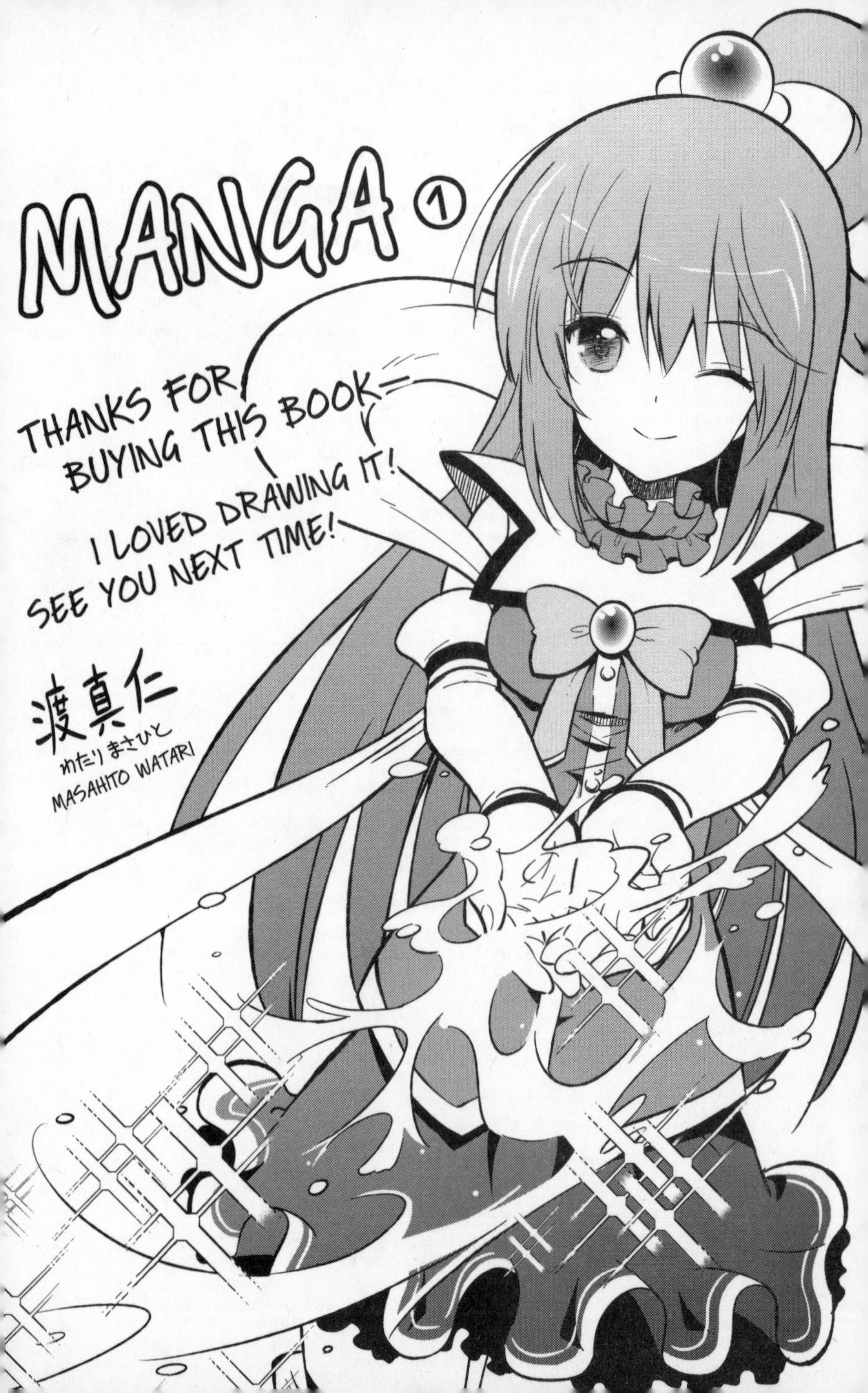
MANGA 1
THANKS FOR BUYING THIS BOOK
I LOVED DRAWING IT!
SEE YOU NEXT TIME!
渡真仁
わたりまさひと
MASAHITO WATARI

TRANSLATION: Kevin Steinbach ● LETTERING: Bianca Pistillo

This book is a work of fiction. Names, characters, places, and incidents are the product of the author's imagination or are used fictitiously. Any resemblance to actual events, locales, or persons, living or dead, is coincidental.

KONO SUBARASHII SEKAI NI SYUKUFUKU WO! Volume 1
©MASAHITO WATARI 2015
©NATSUME AKATSUKI, KURONE MISHIMA 2015
First published in Japan in 2015 by Kadokawa Corporation, Tokyo. English translation rights arranged with KADOKAWA Corporation, Tokyo through Tuttle-Mori Agency, Inc., Tokyo.

English translation © 2016 by Yen Press, LLC

Yen Press, LLC supports the right to free expression and the value of copyright. The purpose of copyright is to encourage writers and artists to produce the creative works that enrich our culture.

The scanning, uploading, and distribution of this book without permission is a theft of the author's intellectual property. If you would like permission to use material from the book (other than for review purposes), please contact the publisher. Thank you for your support of the author's rights.

Yen Press
1290 Avenue of the Americas
New York, NY 10104

Visit us at yenpress.com
facebook.com/yenpress
twitter.com/yenpress
yenpress.tumblr.com
instagram.com/yenpress

First Yen Press Edition: November 2016

Yen Press is an imprint of Yen Press, LLC.
The Yen Press name and logo are trademarks of Yen Press, LLC.

The publisher is not responsible for websites (or their content) that are not owned by the publisher.

Library of Congress Control Number: 2016946112

ISBNs: 978-0-316-55256-1 (paperback)
        978-0-316-46866-4 (ebook)

10 9 8

WOR

Printed in the United States of America